6

H

FOOD

FOOD

A 20TH-CENTURY ANTHOLOGY

EDITED BY

CLARISSA
DICKSON WRIGHT

EBURY PRESS
LONDON

DEDICATION

To my sister June and my brother Anthony, who sat
by my bed one chill winter's afternoon and taught me
to read because they were fed up with reading to me.
They gave me the greatest gift of my life.

THIS EDITION FIRST PUBLISHED 2000

1 3 5 7 9 10 8 6 4 2

COMPILATION, ESSAYS AMD INTRODUCTION COPYRIGHT © CLARISSA DICKSON WRIGHT 1999

CLARISSA DICKSON WRIGHT HAS ASSERTED HER RIGHT UNDER THE COPYRIGHT, DESIGNS
AND PATENTS ACT 1988 TO BE IDENTIFIED AS THE AUTHOR OF THIS WORK.

THE SOURCES OF TEXT AND ILLUSTRATIONS REPRODUCED IN THIS ANTHOLOGY ARE LISTED
IN FULL ON PAGES 317-19.

EBURY PRESS
RANDOM HOUSE, 20 VAUXHALL BRIDGE ROAD, LONDON SW1V 2SA

RANDOM HOUSE AUSTRALIA PTY LIMITED
20 ALFRED STREET, MILSONS POINT, SYDNEY, NEW SOUTH WALES 2061, AUSTRALIA

RANDOM HOUSE NEW ZEALAND LIMITED
18 POLAND ROAD, GLENFIELD, AUCKLAND 10, NEW ZEALAND

RANDOM HOUSE SOUTH AFRICA (PTY) LIMITED
ENDULINI, 5A JUBILEE ROAD, PARKTOWN 2193, SOUTH AFRICA

THE RANDOM HOUSE GROUP LIMITED REG. NO. 954009

WWW.RANDOMHOUSE.CO.UK

PAPERS USED BY EBURY PRESS ARE NATURAL, RECYCLABLE PRODUCTS MADE FROM WOOD
GROWN IN SUSTAINABLE FORESTS.

A CIP CATALOGUE RECORD FOR THIS BOOK IS AVAILABLE FROM THE BRITISH LIBRARY.

ISBN 0 09 187821 7

DESIGN BY DAVID FORDHAM
PICTURE RESEARCH BY NADINE BAZAR
TYPSET BY MATS, SOUTHEND-ON-SEA

PRINTED AND BOUND IN SPAIN BY GRAFICAS ESTELLA

CONTENTS

INTRODUCTION 7

ABROAD 11
ABUSE 15
ACTION 17
ADVENTURE 18
AMERICA 19
APHRODISIAC 21
APPETISERS 22
ARTICHOKES 23
ASPARAGUS 26

BALANCE 28
BEEF 31
BERG 33
BIGOTRY 35
BOUILLABAISSE 38
BREAD 40
BREAKFAST 43
BUTCHER 47

CABBAGE 48
CANNIBALISM 50
CHEFS 52
CHEMISTRY 54
CHOICES 55
CHILDHOOD 57
CORRECTNESS 58
CRABS 59
CUTTING 60

DEBUTANTE 63
DELICATESSEN 64
DISGUSTING 68
DIXIE 70
DRIPPING 73
DRUGS 76
DUCK 77

ENDIVES 78

ENTHUSIASM 80
EXCELLENCE 81
EXCESSES 83

FASCIST/FUTURISM 85
FASHION 89
FISH 89
FOOD 94
FOODIES 95
FRUSTRATION 98
FRYING PANS 100

GAME 103
GENTLEMEN 104
GLUTTONY 107
GOLDFIELDS 109
GUILT 111

HAGGIS 113
HAREMS 114
HAUTE CUISINE 116
HEALTH 117
HEROISM 122
HOPE 124
HORS D'OEUVRE 127
HOSPITALITY 128
HUNGER 131

ICE CREAM 133
IGUANA 136
ILLUSION 137
INSECTS 139
INTREPID 139
IRELAND 141

JAM 142
JELLYFISH 144
JEWISH 145
JUNK FOOD 149

KEROSENE	150	SMELL	239
KILLING	153	SNOEK	239
KING	155	SONG	242
KITCHENS	158	SOUFFLÉ	245
		SPAM	247
LETTUCE	163	STAFF	248
LIBERAL	164	STRINE	248
LIVESTOCK	165		
LUNCHEON	168	TEA	251
LUXURY	173	TEA-TIME	256
		TOAST	258
MACRONEUROTICS	176	TOMATOES	262
MAHARAJAHS	177	TRADE	263
MEAT	179	TRUFFLES	265
MEMSAHIBS	182	TURTLE	267
MENUS	185		
		UBIQUITOUS	268
NASTY	185	UNEMPLOYED	271
NAUTICAL	191	UTOPIA	272
NOSTALGIA	193		
NUTRITION	194	VEGETABLES	273
		VEGETARIAN	274
OFFAL	196	VOGUE	278
OLIVER TWIST	198		
ONE WORLD	199	WAITING	286
ONIONS	201	WAR	289
OXFORD	204	WEALTH	294
		WEDDING	297
PONG	205	WEEDS	298
POSH	206	WEIGHTY	300
POST-PRANDIAL	207	WEST INDIES	303
POVERTY	208		
		XMAS	306
QUEER	213	XQUISITE	308
QUINCE	214		
QUO VADIS	218	YARROW	309
		YOUTH	312
THE RAJ	219		
RATIONING	221	ZEALOT	314
REFORM	226		
RESTAURANTS	227		
RIDICULOUS	229		
		ACKNOWLEDGEMENTS	317
SALT PORK	232		
SEX	234		
SENTIMENT	238	INDEX OF AUTHORS	319

INTRODUCTION

I AM ALWAYS delighted to have lunch with a dishy man, so when Julian Shuckburgh invited me I accepted with alacrity. The difference with publishers, though, is that, whereas all men want something, what *they* want is hard work! So this book was born.

We are turning the century as well as the millennium, and it is a century that has seen more changes than perhaps any since the fall of the Roman Empire. What it is unique in having seen is the growth of food writing. I noticed in the research for this book that we were overwhelmed with material for the second half of the century but struggling the earlier we looked back. I have been a professional bookseller now for twelve years, and I am always amazed at the sheer volume of work produced.

The century has also seen vast changes in food, with the growth of freezing, canning and other preserving techniques, and in the availability of what were once exotic goods. Was it really only in the 1960s that Alasdair Massie sold the first avocado pear in Aberdeen? – whereas Lady Clarke was writing about the difficulty of keeping a turtle alive on Deeside in 1901.

The era began with Edwardian opulence and the housekeeping burdens of imperial and colonial wives. The horrors of two world wars changed our lifestyles and eating habits for ever. Gone were the huge households of servants, to be replaced by time-saving gadgets and pre-prepared food. Wartime rationing brought new ingenuities and the abandoning of preconceived notions. I remember the story of my mother, a woman of immense elegance and style, favouring very high heels. She attended my sister's school sports day during the war. My sister approached her to suggest she ran in the mothers' race. 'Don't be silly, darling,' chided my mother gently. 'But Mummy, the prize is a whole string of onions!' My mother's demeanour changed, she kicked off her shoes, hoisted her skirt above her knees, and with the competitive determination only an Australian can muster powered to victory. A Cartier brooch would not have had the same effect; one simply could not buy onions in 1941.

The post-war era has brought us foreign travel for the masses, and for those who escaped fish and chips in Torremolinos a new exposure to foreign food. When I was a child you could only buy olive oil in a chemist's shop, marked 'for external use only'. Today it is still hard to buy good butter, but the olive oil proliferates. On a recent visit to Andalusia I was nauseated by the smell of mass olive production.

Television and food journalism have brought us more recipes than we could ever eat in a lifetime – and some of them one wouldn't want to. When Jane Barry was writing her black comedy *Hungry*, we found the most revolting recipes for a spoof dinner party – and we didn't have to invent them, they were real. A French baker recently asked me why it is that the English produce more and more food television, and cook less and less.

I have tried to capture here all these rites of passage. Food has become the new rock 'n' roll, and is commemorated in song, humour and wit, if not on the table. When I was young people spoke of food being replaced by a pill – and so far they have got that very wrong.

FOOD

There are many people to thank: Julian, who showed a patience and trust beyond belief when nothing seemed forthcoming from me; my dear Imogen Brewer, who sat with me coaxing lists of my favourite pieces from my poor tired brain, smiling her late father's (my dearest love) smile until I wanted to weep; Mitch Goldman, the wacky American *sous-chef* who, when he finished working for me at Lennoxlove, came to help on the book. But most of all my dear friend Henrietta Palmer, without whose help and dedication this book would never have made the millennium shelves – hard-working, inspired and good-humoured in the face of my exhaustion and tantrums. I cannot thank her enough.

I hope this book will amuse you, entertain you and set you thinking of the long march of the century, and of those stalwart men and women who stood like you before their cooking stoves to provide for empire and home, or for the restaurant hordes or the hungry soldiery. It is by no means all-encompassing. There are so many pieces I would have liked to include, but space and paper prevented us. I hope you will want lovingly to revisit this book, rather than slam it shut like many anthologies I have known. Some pieces are not here because we were refused permission, for example my favourite piece from James Joyce's *Ulysses* on Leopold Bloom's love of offal, which we were refused by his grandson – so you must go and read it for yourself. A firm of solicitors who represent T. E. Lawrence's executors also refused us the Bedouin banquet from *Seven Pillars of Wisdom*, but that may be because they were inadvertently sent my introduction, which described his life as one of the great Boy's Own adventures of the 20th century, despite the fact that he was an alcoholic, a runt and a homosexual in the days when that was still illegal. He was a patient of my father's, so I was talking from an informed position.

As with many anthologies, you will miss your own favourite pieces – for perforce the choices are personal. We stand on the edge of a new millennium where much will change, at a time when the health-giving quality of food has never been more under threat. Vegetarians are now knocked down from their high moral perch by the knowledge that their soya products and mainstays have been altered by the tortures of genetic modification. I pray that Professor Pastai's rats didn't die in vain. The media have provided new and irresponsible food scares, from a former parliamentarian who now writes soft-porn blockbusters, who so damaged the egg market that it has still not recovered, to Professor Patterson's BSC scare. In our age we have turned from God, or any form of spirituality which requires self-discipline, and death – despite the advances of medicine – has become a fear born of despair. To quote Milton, 'the hungry sheep look up and are not fed' – and that goes for priests and *soi-disant* nutritionists alike.

How much we are coming to appreciate the wisdom of Lady Evelyn Balfour, who had a spiritual awakening when she made her first compost heap, and was the first female to take a degree in agricultural science at Reading University. You will find an extract from her writing herein, under the heading 'Health'. Let us take her sound common sense with us through the gates of the millennium. But I begin to preach, and remembering Dr Johnson I will desist, and leave you to your book.

Clarissa Dickson Wright, *July 1999*

ABROAD

BEFORE ELIZABETH DAVID IT WAS, in the words of Nancy Mitford, 'bloody abroad'. Whilst haute cuisine French dishes were acceptable, the Continent was the place that smelt of Gauloise, garlic and cheap wine, and where one spoke very loudly and very distinctly to be understood. Elizabeth loved abroad, more one suspects than home. She is the one that ruined the lives of thousands of tourists who have searched in vain, as I have, for the Continent of her dreams. Like the children who followed the Pied Piper, we look in vain for the blue aromatic smoke, the crackling vine shoots, the perfect soups in their deep bowls, the purple lavender fields and wine-dark seas, and find only dirt and neglect and indifference to our coughing progress. This passage on a farmhouse dinner is typical of Elizabeth's abroad, and has the sort of recipe for hare royale that few others would have the courage to recite – and even fewer of us the courage to cook. I hope Elizabeth really found her foreign paradise. One would like to think it was there for a few brief years before her genius faded and the misery set in. To my generation she was a bright star in the firmament. I remember the first time I picked up the phone to her I dropped it. When she asked me what was wrong I stammered that it was like answering the phone to God. Thereafter it was always 'God calling'!

LIÈVRE À LA ROYALE

THIS famous recipe for Lièvre à la Royale was invented by Senator Couteaux, who contributed regular articles to the Paris newspaper *Le Temps*. On the 29th November 1898, instead of his usual political column, appeared this remarkable recipe. M. Couteaux related at length how he had spent a week in Poitou hunting the right kind of hare; how, the exactly suitable animal at last in his hands, he instantly took the train to Paris, sent out his invitations and hurried off to consult his friend Spüller, who ran a well-known restaurant in the Rue Favart, to arrange the preparation and cooking of his hare for the following day. The dish takes from noon until 7 o'clock to prepare and cook, and Senator Couteaux tells how by 6 o'clock the exquisite aroma had penetrated the doors of Spüller's restaurant, floated down the street and out into the boulevard, where the passers-by sniffed the scented air; an excitable crowd gathered, and the whole *quartier* was 'mis en émoi'. If you ever feel like devoting the time (perhaps you need not after all spend a week catching your hare) and the ingredients to cooking this dish, you will see that the senator was not exaggerating.

I have translated the recipe as faithfully as possible. It is very lengthy and there are repetitions, but in those days there was plenty of space to fill up; and from the senator's precise instructions one can well imagine the delightful old gentleman bending over his 'daubière', and the pride with which he presented this beautiful creation to his gourmet friends.

'*Ingredients.*

'You require a male hare, with red fur, killed if possible in mountainous country; of fine French descent (characterised by the light nervous elegance of head and limbs), weighing from 5 to 6 pounds, that is to say older than a leveret but still adolescent. The important thing is that the hare should have been cleanly killed and so not have lost a drop of blood.

'*The fat to cook it*: 2 or 3 tablespoons of goose fat, ¼ lb. of fat bacon rashers; ¼ lb. of bacon in one piece.

'*Liquid*: 6 ozs. of good red wine vinegar. Two bottles of Macon or Médoc, whichever you please, but in any case not less than two years old.

'*Utensils*: A *daubière*, or oblong stewing pan, of well-tinned copper, 8 inches high, 15 inches long, 8 inches wide and possessed of a hermetically closing cover; a small bowl in which to preserve the blood of the hare, and later to stir it when it comes to incorporating it in the sauce; a double-handled vegetable chopper; a large shallow serving dish; a sieve; a small wooden pestle.

'*The wine to serve*: Preferably a St. Julien or Moulin à Vent.

'*Preliminary Preparations*

'Skin and clean the hare. Keep aside the heart, the liver and the lungs. Keep aside also and with great care the blood. (It is traditional to add 2 or 3 small glasses of fine old cognac to the blood; but this is not indispensable; M. Couteaux finally decided against this addition.)

'In the usual way prepare a medium-sized carrot, cut into four; 4 medium onions each stuck with a clove; 20 cloves of garlic; 40 cloves of shallot; a bouquet garni, composed of a bay leaf, a sprig of thyme and some pieces of parsley.

'Get ready some charcoal, in *large pieces*, which you will presently be needing, *burning fast*.

'First Operation (from half-past twelve until four o'clock)

'At 12.30 coat the bottom and sides of the stew pan with the goose-fat; then at the bottom of the pan arrange a bed of rashers of bacon.

'Cut off the head and neck of the hare: leaving only the back and the legs. Then place the hare at full length on the bed of bacon, on its back. Cover it with another layer of bacon. Now all your bacon rashers are used up.

'Now add the carrot; the onions; the 20 cloves of garlic; the 40 cloves of shallot; the bouquet garni.

'Pour over the hare:

(i) the 6 ozs. of red wine vinegar, and

(ii) a bottle and a half of 2-year-old Macon (or Médoc).

'Season with pepper and salt in reasonable quantity.

'At one o'clock. The *daubière* being thus arranged, put on the lid and set the fire going (either a gas stove or an ordinary range). On the top of the lid place 3 or 4 large pieces of charcoal in an incandescent state, *well alight and glowing*.

'Regulate your heat so that the hare may cook for 3 hours, over a gentle and regular fire, continuously.

'Second operation (to be carried out during the first cooking of the hare).

'First chop exceedingly finely the four following ingredients, chopping each one separately:

(i) ¼ lb. of bacon,

(iii) 10 cloves of garlic,

(ii) the heart, liver and lungs of the hare,

(iv) 20 cloves of shallot.

'The chopping of the garlic and the shallots must be so fine that each of them attain as nearly as possible a molecular state.

'This is one of the first conditions of success of this marvellous dish, in which the multiple and diverse perfumes and aromas melt into a whole so harmonious that neither one dominates, nor discloses its particular origin, and so arouse some preconceived prejudice, however regrettable.

'The bacon, the insides of the hare, the garlic and shallots being chopped very fine, and separately, blend them all together thoroughly, so as to obtain an absolutely perfect mixture. Keep this mixture aside.

'Third Operation (from four o'clock until a quarter to seven).

'At four o'clock. Remove the stew pan from the fire. Take the hare out very delicately; put it on a dish. Then remove all the débris of the bacon, carrot, onions, garlic, shallot, which may be clinging to it; return these débris to the pan.

'The Sauce. Now take a large deep dish and a sieve. Empty the contents of the pan into the sieve, which you have placed over the dish; with a small wooden pestle pound the contents of the sieve, extracting all the juice, which forms a *coulis* in the dish.

'Mixing the coulis and the hachis (the chopped mixture). Now comes the moment to make use of the mixture which was the subject of the second operation. Incorporate this into the *coulis*.

13

FOOD

'Heat the half bottle of wine left over from the first operation. Pour this hot wine into the mixture of *coulis* and *hachis* and stir the whole well together.

'*At half-past four.* Return to the stew-pan:

(i) the mixture of *coulis* and *hachis*,

(ii) the hare, together with any of the bones which may have become detached during the cooking.

'Return the pan to the stove, with the same gentle and regular fire underneath and on the top, for another 1½ hours' cooking.

'*At six o'clock.* As the excess of fat, issuing from the necessary quantity of bacon, will prevent you from judging the state of the sauce, you must now proceed to operate a *first removal of the fat.* Your work will not actually be completed until the sauce has become sufficiently amalgamated to attain a consistence approximating to that of a purée of potatoes; not quite, however, for if you tried to make it too thick, you would end by so reducing it that there would not be sufficient to moisten the flesh (by nature dry) of the hare.

'Your hare having therefore has the fat removed, can continue to cook, *still on a very slow fire*, until the moment comes for you to add the blood which you have reserved with the utmost care as has already been instructed.

'*Fourth Operation (quarter of an hour before serving).*

'*At quarter to seven.* The amalgamation of the sauce proceeding successfully, a fourth and last operation will finally and rapidly bring it to completion.

'*Addition of the blood to the hare.* With the addition of the blood, not only will you hasten the amalgamation of the sauce but also give it a fine brown colour; the darker it is the more appetising. This addition of the blood should not be made more than 30 minutes before serving; it must also be preceded by a *second removal of the fat.*

'Therefore, effectively remove the fat; after which, without losing a minute, turn to the operation of adding the blood.

'(i) Whip the blood with a fork, until, if any of it has become curdled, it is smooth again. (Note: the optional addition of the brandy mentioned at the beginning helps to prevent the curdling of the blood.)

'(ii) Pour the blood into the sauce, taking care to stir the contents of the pan from top to bottom and from right to left, so that the blood will penetrate into every corner of the pan.

'Now taste; add pepper and salt *if necessary.* A little later (45 minutes at a maximum) get ready to serve.

'*Arrangements for serving.*

'*At seven o'clock.* Remove from the pan your hare, whose volume by this time has naturally somewhat shrunk.

'At any rate, at the centre of the serving dish, place all that still has the consistency of meat, the bones, entirely denuded, and now useless, being thrown away, and now finally around this hare *en compote* pour the admirable sauce which has been so carefully created.'

Needless to say (concludes the senator) that to use a knife to serve the hare would be a sacrilege. A spoon alone is amply sufficient.

Elizabeth David, *A Book of Mediterranean Food*

Abuse

THOSE WHO HAVE NEVER WORKED in a commercial or professional kitchen may find it hard to believe in the sheer hard physical labour involved. Every profession carries its scars, and cooking is no exception. When I am interviewing I always look at the interviewer's hands and forearms to see the nicks, burns and calluses which mark the employed cook. My feet have felt the toil of years on hard kitchen floors, and when one meets another cook one exchanges more footbalm panaceas than recipes. I expect that, were I to travel back in time to any era, I would find a ready source of conversation with any chef over the knife scars and fire burns, whether it be from a spit or a closed oven. Gordon Ramsey has shown on television the abuse a commis-chef continues to receive in badly-run kitchens, but most of the injuries go with the job.

This piece from Nicholas Freeling, better known for his Amsterdam-based detective stories, describes his hands as a chef as well as I can.

COOK's hands . . . Mine are both awkward and nervous. Though he is scarcely ever without a knife in his hand the cook is trained not to cut himself: a burn is more common than a cut in the kitchen. But I was always a clumsy fellow, and my kitchen years are written on my hands. I should have liked to use my handprints as endpapers for this book, but alas, Osbert Sitwell thought of it first.

The thumb, there – early days, that one; breaking up lobster claws with a steak bat I did not know how to use. The middle knuckle of my forefinger – boning a turkey in a bad light, hurriedly; we were badly understaffed. I wound the hand in a rag; it became infected and I was out of work for six weeks, got the sack, and nearly lost the finger. Now how can that be? asks the union-minded reader – getting the sack for an industrial injury, received too under dangerous working conditions? For we were overcrowded as well; I had had to take my turkeys (five or six, for a party) into an ill-lit vegetable cellar. But cooks had no union – still have none, for all I know; cooks are a cranky, non-conformist crowd, more so even than waiters, though both are unstable, irresponsible, and often downright infamous. A cook then could get sacked for anything, such as having the cheek to ask for pay while still unable to work. No wonder that in England so many 'catering managers' are unsuccessful army officers, with a hankering for the orderly-room and a wish to put insubordinate cooks on a charge.

A deep cut – I sliced the tip off a finger and half the nail with it: I was shredding mushrooms with another cook's knife. Most cuts are had that way; under the pressure of orders against time you may suddenly be called to help another cook, you need a knife and snatch one of his, a thing not to be recommended. A knife only obeys its owner and with your own knife, a thing so integrally part of your hand that it seems to breathe with you, things can be done that cannot be risked with another's.

Even without cuts a cook's hands are unmistakable. The fingertips are flattened and ironed by the touch of hot silver dishes and copper serving-pans; for a pot you automatically take your ovencloth. The side of the forefinger becomes corrugated by the peeler, and the ball of one's thumb ploughed by a mass of tiny cuts that have not severed the toughened skin. Turning cuts these – to 'turn' or shape a piece of carrot into a small regular cylinder you hold it with thumb and forefinger, thumb down. The other hand holds a little knife by the blade, and makes six tiny shaving movements (the holding hand revolves the carrot or whatever in six regular turns). It is done fast – it must be – the eye can hardly follow – toctoctoc, toctoctoc and splash, into a bowl of water, a hundred, two hundred, five hundred times. Cooks' knitting, it was called, and the blade nicked down, each time, into the ball of the thumb. It is no longer done; cooks were cheaper then.

Last mark, but characteristic, of a cook's hands was the chopping mark. He holds the heavy chopping knife in a kind of golfer's grip, thumb and forefinger forked over the join between the knife's blade and its base: as with the golfer this gives precision of force and direction. At each blow the knife, flattened and squared at this point, jumps against the hand and the cook acquires a heavy callus at the base of his forefinger which would have puzzled Sherlock Holmes, who knew no cooks.

Why the emphasis on hands? Because the cook is a hand-craftsman, very much like a smith or a potter. The tools of cooking have not altered in essence since Louis XV and the invention of the fork, any more than those of the cabinet-maker.

A few details, such as the invention of stainless steel, itself unused for long by cook or carpenter because it did not hold a sharp edge.

Cooking is not an art, the snobs to the contrary. Art implies a noble end. That is not to say cooking is ignoble, but it is both impermanent and frivolous; scarcely ever will the cook be called upon to work for someone who is not already overfed. If handed a bowl of raw rice, and told that there was a hungry Indian waiting, he could permit himself, perhaps, to speak of his art.

A hand craft – machines are constantly tried out in the kitchen and quickly discarded. The only contrivances which during my time found acceptance were thermostatic controls for electric fryers, which at least stopped the overheating of the classic and odious fat-pot of my apprenticeships, and the electric mixer, which allowed the pastry-cook to get on with other, less demanding chores. Neither helped to cook any better: the one, since oil heated more evenly, was an economy in material; the other an economy of effort. But innumerable gadgets were thrown out after a day's trial; this was not obstinate conservatism. The old method served better, simply. Of all the jobs a cook does daily, none is repeated more than chopping onions, a fairly complex chore needing practice, a really sharp knife, and three consecutive movements or processes before the shiny globe crumbles into a pile of tiny grey dice. Every newcomer complains at this minuscular labour but no machine can be made to do it: the onion is a sensitive object and must not be bruised, or it goes an unappetising black and loses its juice.

Nicholas Freeling, *Kitchen Book*

ACTION

THERE IS A LONG-STANDING TRADITION of cookery books written by people other than cooks. In the last century a number of artists and musicians wrote recipes, and in this such unlikely candidates as Margaret, Duchess of Argyll and Barbara Cartland have followed suit. Perhaps the most unlikely, however, is the thriller writer Len Deighton, who has two fine books, *The Action Cookbook* and *Où est le Garlic*, to his credit. The great difference about the *Action Cookbook* is that it is written as a strip cartoon, not of characters but of cooking – foolproof, and easy to follow even for the feeblest cook. The 20th century has been almost boundless in its imaginative cookbooks.

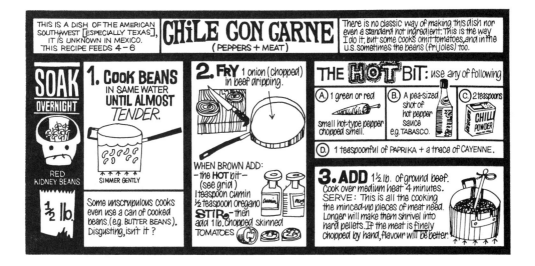

CHILE CON CARNE

THIS is not a Mexican dish, though nowadays there are plenty of Mexican roads littered with Chile signs. That's to attract American tourists, for Chile con carne is an American dish – specifically a dish from the U.S. south-west. Like chop suey, spaghetti and pizza, it has become a part of the American diet, and a housewife who would balk at steak and kidney pudding will take these dishes in her stride.

There is certainly an enormous selection of beans available: all kinds of yellow, red, brown spotted ones, and black-eyed ones too. Everyone has his own method for dried beans (fresh beans make it even better, if you get some). Don't cook the beans to a mush. If you use any sort of powder for the hot bit, cook it gently for at least three minutes. Tiny hot peppers are the best, but chop them very small, and don't wipe your eyes with the hand that's touched them – it will hurt. Lastly, don't overcook the meat. The moisture should still be in it when it's served. Exactly the same advice goes for the meat in a spaghetti sauce. Such tiny pieces of meat cook almost immediately upon entering the saucepan.

FOOD

Bachelor cooks should use tabasco sauce (needs no cooking or chopping), canned beans (baked beans will do at a pinch) and tinned tomatoes; proceed as number three. A five-minute meal.

Len Deighton, *Action Cookbook*

ADVENTURE

WHEN I HAD THE PLEASURE of meeting Lesley Blanche she was in her 80s, but still showing the energy and enthusiasm that imbues her writing and led her on her adventures. True travellers are born not made, and are as far removed from tourists as the Sahara from the Arctic. However, at the end of the day the true joy of travelling is to come home, and this nostalgic piece shows it was so of the intrepid Lesley as it is of me.

IN THE England of my youth which, I hasten to add, was not Victorian, nor even Edwardian, I used to stay in country houses where breakfasts would have been indeed worth getting up for, were it not for the numbers of rather hearty guests assembled in the dining room. These country house-party breakfasts were in the nature of gargantuan feasts, for exercise, in one form or another, hunting, shooting or fishing, or the walks undertaken constantly by all but myself required a good, solid send-off. And that they certainly were.

Let me recall some of those spreads. A central table was laid ceremoniously; a large fire blazed – for I do not recall ever having been to such house-parties in summer – and a butler hovered beside the long sideboards – two, certainly, dominated by impressive silver or silver-gilt tea and coffee urns. Around them, in silver chafing dishes, were a variety of hot foods which were instantly replenished if they showed signs of cooling. Bacon and eggs; eggs scrambled, eggs poached, and a whole legion of soft-boiled eggs under little cosies; omelettes; smoked haddock; kedgeree; grilled kidneys and tomatoes; devilled kidneys; mushrooms; sausages; fish cakes; kippers; and cold temptations such as York ham, tongue, or cold game pie. Then there were all the breads, toasts, scones, and 'Oxford' marmalade. . . . I don't remember ever seeing fruit at these feasts. But I must not omit porridge, which was the corner-stone. Porridge can be a most repulsive substance unless cooked and eaten correctly, in the Scots manner, which it always was in those far-off days, being made with a pinch of salt, and thick cream added to your fancy.

Apropos of both kedgeree and porridge, I recall a chilling anecdote which included both these dishes. In India, while an English family were enjoying their breakfast kedgeree, the youngest child wandered away into the garden with his porridge bowl. He had taken to doing this lately, and curious, his parents followed him quietly. They found him seated on a stone, beside him a king cobra, reared-up and swaying, the child feeding it spoonfuls of porridge – one for himself, one for the snake, in alternate mouthfuls. If the cobra tried for its mouthful out of turn, the child said 'Naughty!' and whacked it with the spoon, at which it drew back, obediently. . . . That's a true story I sometimes think of to lighten the monotony of stirring the porridge.

Lesley Blanch, *The Wilder Shores of Love*

AMERICA

AT THIS END OF THE CENTURY it seems strange to remember that at its beginning America was regarded as a rough, remote and uncivilised place. Oscar Wilde reading his plays to the applause of Yukon miners must have rather summed up the British idea of the divide. As late as 1935 we find Countess Morphy writing, in *Recipes of All Nations,* in a way that is amazing to us only 60 years later. Sadly, at this end of the century most of what we have taken from the American culinary adventure is not the strange breakfast breads but the horrors of junk food. (See Junk Food, page 149.)

AMERICAN cookery is somewhat like the American version of the English language – a version essentially American, with its own characteristic accent and pronunciation, its own idioms, its own colourful and expressive slang, often apt, humorous and original. But just as their slang is sometimes offensive to our ears, so some American dishes might be offensive to our palate, since the breaking away from tradition in food is a process not easily accomplished. The inborn conservatism of the older civilisations of Europe with regard to their national cookery makes it almost impossible to accept or understand some of America's gastronomic innovations and novelties. But if the characteristically American thirst for novelty and sensationalism sometimes leads to mixtures which are not always happy – to a somewhat drastic blending of elements which, according to our standards, are considered discordant – it has also led to the invention of the famous American salads, now adopted by European chefs, and which no mind but an American mind could have conceived. There is a boldness about them which almost amounts to 'cheek,' and some must be tasted to be 'believed.'

Originally based on English cookery, American cookery has developed on altogether different lines, and although traditional English dishes figure on the American menu, they are 'spoken with a different accent,' and are consequently distinctive and typical. Their liking for puddings and pies they hold from their English forebears. Their cooking is, generally speaking, 'plain,' and one of their favourite methods of cooking meat or poultry is broiling – or grilling, as we usually call it in England. They excel in the making of all manner of breakfast 'trimmings,' such as griddle cakes, buckwheat cakes, waffles, corn breads, with which the American breakfast table is laden. Their ices and iced drinks are excellent and their fruit cocktails are novel and pleasing. But salads may be considered the fireworks of American gastronomy. A veritable cornucopia, filled with an abundance of the most varied ingredients, is emptied into the salad basin, and we find tangerines and truffles, and pimientos and asparagus meeting on the most friendly terms, with a salad dressing to which a welcome dash of brandy has been added; or again, the novel blend of avocado pears, apples, grape-fruit, celery, pimientos, chestnuts, pineapple, with a mayonnaise dressing mixed with pieces of mango.

American cookery has been much influenced by climatic conditions, the cooking of the Northern States being different from that of the Southern States, while New England boasts of its own typical dishes. America is blessed with a wealth of vegetables and fruit unknown in this country in their fresh condition. There are various kinds of pumpkins or 'squash,' there is the egg-plant, or

aubergine, sweet corn, which is extremely wholesome and nutritious when fresh, okra, sweet peppers or pimientos, and all manner of delicious fruit, including the avocado pear, or alligator pear, which is largely imported from Cuba, and is one of the most delicious things which nature has produced. In the South they are blessed with the sweet potato, with the sugar cane, with various tropical fruit, such as the persimmon, the mango, oranges, bananas and many other good things, of which extensive use is made. Little wonder that with such a wide range of fruit and vegetables the Americans should be noted for their ingenious fruit-cocktails and their salads.

Countess Morphy, *Recipes of All Nations*

APHRODISIAC

NORMAN DOUGLAS was not only an epicure, but a wit, and a great friend of and influence over Elizabeth David (with whom he is reputed to have had an affair). He produced a book of aphrodisia with the delightful title *Venus in the Kitchen.*

STEWED CRABS
BOIL a dozen fine large crabs about five minutes in order to kill them. Take them off the fire and when sufficiently cooled cut off the claws and crack, separating the joints. Remove the 'apron' or *tablier* of the crab and the 'dead man's fingers', and take off the spongy substance. These are the portions that are uneatable. Remove the shell, cut the body of the crab into four parts, cutting down the centre across.

Chop a large onion very fine and brown with butter or lard, using a tablespoonful of either. Add a dozen large fresh tomatoes, chopped fine, in their liquor, and brown nicely; stir in chopped celery, thyme, parsley, one bay-leaf chopped fine; pepper and salt to taste, and a dash of Cayenne pepper. Add one clove of garlic, chopped fine. Taste and add more seasoning if necessary. Let the mixture cook ten minutes, then add the crabs and let them cook ten minutes longer.

Crab is recommended as an aphrodisiac by several poets (and so, by the way, are crab apples).

SKINK
(a reptile aphrodisiac)
THE skink is lauded as a stimulant by many ancients. The difficulty will be to find it. But if someone chances to be in Africa or Arabia he will be able to do so. One way of cooking skink is the following:

Fillet them (along the backbone), soak them in beaten eggs, season, and fry in olive oil. Mesue preferred the tails of skink. Tristram speaks well of roasted skink.

Arabs still make use of it; the ancient Greeks did likewise, and Pliny the Elder has left us a Roman recipe which differs from the one here given.

Norman Douglas, *Venus in the Kitchen*

APPETISERS

I HAVE BEEN fascinated by street food ever since my childhood visits to a pre-sanitised Singapore, and I love this piece of Diana Kennedy's on Mexican street food. She is the doyenne of Mexican cooking, and rescued it in my mind from the horrors of Tex Mex. Read this and get on the next plane.

WITHOUT doubt the Mexicans are the most persistent noshers in the world; who wouldn't be, with such an endless variety of things to nibble on along the streets and in the marketplaces? A whole book could be devoted to that alone. Even if you think you are not hungry you will be enticed, by the smell, the artistry with which the food is displayed, or just because it is something new to try, for Mexican cooks are among the most creative anywhere. Next time you wander around the streets of any Mexican city or small town, pause a little at the *taqueria* on the corner and see if your mouth doesn't start to water as the floppy, hot tortillas are crammed with shredded meat or *carnitas* and doused in a robust green tomato sauce from an enormous black *molcajete*, or as the *quesadillas* are patted out and stuffed with squash flowers and browned on a comal. Any hour of the day and well into the night there will always be groups of people standing and eating with great concentration – for this is no time to talk.

I often think of what is perhaps my favorite of all *taquerías*, one I was introduced to only last summer in the Bajio. The whole town knows that promptly at five in the afternoon the pig that Pasquelitos has killed and cooked will be coming out of the oven, and long before that the line starts to form. Everything goes by the board so people can get there on time, for even a 120-pound porker doesn't last forever, especially when the flesh is so succulent. The tortillas are straight off the comal and the *guacamole* is simple and delicious, made of the little black avocados of the region that have that subtle flavor of anise and hazelnuts.

In Ensenada it is the pismo clam that is the favorite of the sidewalk carts; in the La Paz market the *tacos* are made of shredded fish, and in Morelia they are made of brains sprinkled with chopped coriander. As you wander around the markets of central Mexico you will be offered completely pre-Hispanic food, small fish wrapped in corn husks and cooked over charcoal, or *tlacoyos*, oval pieces of rather thick dough filled with a paste of beans; at the back of the Oaxaca market you can snack on toasted grasshoppers and the perennial favorite everywhere, ears of corn hot from the steamer or roasted to a dark brown over charcoal . . .

As I travel alone around the country, I have plenty of time in the evenings to wander around the streets, and one thing that n ever ceases to fascinate me is the ingenuity of the cooking arrangements on the small carts that are set up on street corners. An oil lamp will be slung from the awning overhead, somewhere a gas tank will be wired to a small stove; a large wooden chopping block and a cleaver are a must, as are little dishes of *chiles en escabeche*, shredded lettuce, sliced tomatoes, various fiery sauces, and piles of chopped onion – something for everybody's taste. If the carts' owners don't cook on the spot, there will be an arrangement like an ice-cream stand, and the *barbacoa* and tortillas will come steaming from their deep wells . . .

Food vendors will push their little barrows for miles to post themselves outside some big institution or government office, hospital, school, or prison to offer sustenance to the constant flow of people coming and going. Whenever a crowd gathers to watch the police or firemen at work, out of nowhere appears a little man pushing his cart of goodies to sustain the excited onlookers. And so Sr. Sanchez once more reminds me both of the scenes that I took for granted during my years in Mexico and the brilliant cartoons of Abel Quezada in *Excelsior*, whose devastatingly witty pen comments on the foibles of his fellow countrymen. He concludes: 'Any of the dozens of varieties make ideal snacks to appease the appetite while waiting for dinner or to bolster the stomach against the effect of cocktails when entertaining guests, or simply to justify their very name *antojito* – a little whim.'

Diana Kennedy, *The Cuisine of Mexico*

ARTICHOKES

IN THE 1980S NEW WAVE AMERICAN was born. This culinary revolution, which smashed all the preconceived established mathematical equations of food, is now an accepted entity – so much so that it is now hard to remember back to how exciting it was. Among the forerunners in its development was Alice Waters, who carried it a stage further. Her Restaurant Chez Panisse began by growing its own herbs and vegetables, and then started to commission local farmers to grow for them. She has been a major influence on the increase in farmers' markets and organically grown food in the face of an America polluted by genetically modified vegetables and chemical farming. Here she writes about artichokes.

ARTICHOKES are the edible, immature flowers of a cultivated thistle that was introduced to America by Italian immigrants who settled near Half Moon Bay in California around the turn of the century. Italians have been practicing artichoke cultivation for at least two thousand years, and to this day they have a more highly developed expertise in its use than most Americans. For example, in Venice, in the spring, it is routine for fresh artichokes to be sold in the market already pared down to their hearts, or bottoms – large globe artichokes expertly turned by hand, as on a lathe, all the leaves cut off, leaving just the thick disk of the flower base and the immature fuzzy flowerets which form what is known as the choke. Experienced market folk turn out these hearts in seconds flat; the leaves get discarded, and the raw white artichoke bottoms are tossed in buckets of water acidulated with lemon juice.

There are artichokes shaped like truncated cones; artichokes that are almost perfectly round; and artichokes with nasty thorns. There are green artichokes, green and violet artichokes, and purple artichokes. They are prepared at Chez Panisse in a great many ways, both raw and cooked, depending on their size and relative maturity. Larger ones are steamed whole and served with aioli (with the leaf tips snipped off if they are very thorny); quartered, stewed, and served in salads; or

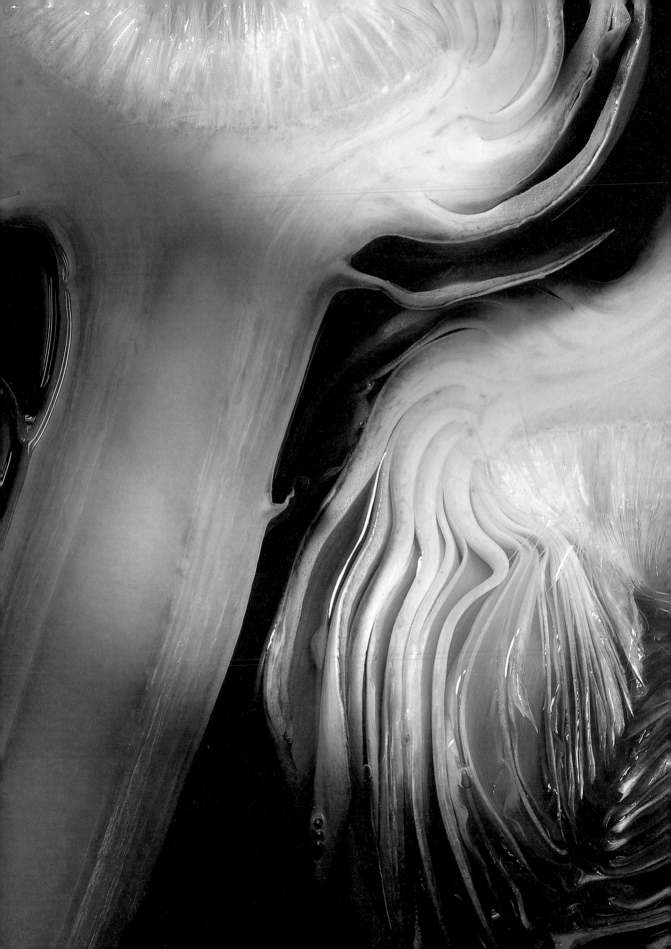

cut into wedges, browned with tiny new potatoes and small, round spring onions, and finished with a persillade. Artichoke hearts are sliced very thin and baked in a gratin with thyme, cream, and Parmesan. Artichokes are trimmed and stuffed à la Provençal – with bread crumbs, parsley, garlic, and anchovies – or with onion, sausage, and mushrooms.

Especially delicious are the tender young buds of artichokes picked before their prickly chokes have developed: simmered at a low temperature in olive oil until soft, then fried at a higher heat so that the leaves open out, flowerlike, and sprinkled with persillade and lemon juice; cooked rapidly in olive oil with white wine, a few thyme sprigs, and garlic slivers until quite soft, a few drops of lemon juice and Parmesan shaved over; or sliced very, very thin and tossed, raw, with olive oil, shavings of Parmesan, and shavings of white truffle. Young artichokes can also be simmered in oil and spices, including a little hot pepper, and preserved in the same oil for an antipasto. Risotti with young artichokes, accompanied by young peas or fava beans, whole or puréed, with Parmesan grated over, breathe springtime. So does a ragout made with the same ingredients.

Artichokes produce two crops a year. After the first harvest in the spring, a second crop is ready in the early fall. The artichoke's quality varies dramatically over its life cycle. Immature flower heads are crisp and dense, but late in the season they become chokey, and start to open, a sign of overripeness. An artichoke should be harvested and eaten only in the bloom of its youth, never in its maturity. Therefore look for artichokes in the market that are unblemished, tightly closed, entirely unopened, and vibrant in color whether lime-green or bright green and purple. Look at the stem end. The scar should tell you something about how recently it was cut. Buy artichokes as fresh as you can, and don't keep them long before cooking them. Experiment with unusual varieties if you see them in your market; different varieties have distinctly different flavors.

To prepare large artichoke hearts, tear off any small leaves attached to the stem or base, and cut crosswise through the leaves where they begin to taper in toward the top, about an inch and a half above the base; younger artichokes can be cut higher up to preserve more of the tender leaves in the center. Put the artichoke cut side down and carefully trim the leaves (actually scales or bracts) away, leaving just their pale green centers. Pare away the deep green part of the head and stem. You will have only the heart left, with a length of stem still attached. Cut off all but an inch or so of the stem. With a soup spoon or a teaspoon scrape and scoop out the choke from the heart. Fresh artichokes are crisp enough so that this is an easy and simple task, and with a little practice can be done in one motion. Have ready a bowl of acidulated water into which you can immediately drop the artichokes as they are trimmed, to reduce browning from oxidation. Or lightly rub the artichoke hearts with some olive oil. The hearts are now ready for however they are to be cooked – sliced, sautéed, boiled, stuffed and braised, and so on.

Whole young artichokes are handled in a similar way. Any small leaves on the stem are torn off, and the very tops of the bracts are cut off. Break and peel off the outer layers of leaves until the tender, pale green inner leaves show. If you wish, you can pare the slightly ragged edges of the base where the outer leaves were torn off, although this is unnecessary, but do trim the end of the stem. Drop the little artichokes into acidulated water; or, if they are to be deep-fried, rub them with a cut lemon or olive oil (soaking them in water complicates their frying in hot oil).

FOOD

Artichoke plants have a productive life of three to four years. They flourish in California's cool-summer coastal climate, and grow easily here in people's gardens. Like cardoons, if allowed to bloom artichokes make a striking display of purplish blue thistle flowers. The new plants are usually started from cuttings of a healthy plant; planting from seed is possible, though much more difficult. Plant artichokes away from other vegetables and flowers, three to four feet apart in good, fertile soil. Although artichokes are tolerant of drought, seedlings require deep-watering once a week. Artichokes flourish in nitrogen-rich soil.

Plant artichokes in the fall, and if they go in early enough, they will produce the next year. Several stalks are sent up by each plant, and each stalk will produce a large, central head with several smaller ancillary heads surrounding it. Harvest the central head when it stops increasing in size and its bracts are still tightly closed, cutting it so that at least one inch of stem is left on the butt. After the central head is cut, the secondary heads will continue to grow, but without ever achieving the grand size of the main head. After the first crop cut the plants back to the ground, and they will rebound to produce a nice fall crop.

Alice Waters, *Chez Panisse Vegetables*

ASPARAGUS

MY MOTHER ALWAYS TOLD ME you could assess someone's sexual abilities by the way they ate asparagus; and you can certainly assess their class bracket in this country. I remember being deeply anxious when a friend brought their latest flame to dinner and he ate his asparagus precisely with a knife and fork, leaving the tips! After much experimentation I have found my mother to be totally accurate, although I can only speak for the men on the first count. There is, I should say, one man who makes me go weak at the knees just watching him eat this vegetable. Like Nigel Slater, I find asparagus deeply sexy, and after all no one would ever describe me as a prude. I now only eat local asparagus, as I have found that it doesn't travel more than a few miles and should have been picked within eight hours of eating. This cuts down on my consumption but greatly heightens my enjoyment. Nigel is a dear friend, a great writer and a splendid and voluptuous cook.

TENDER, PURPLE AND PROUD
ONLY a prude can ignore the sexual overtones of *Asparagus officinalis*. Sitting opposite someone devouring a plate of warm asparagus spears eaten in the traditional way – with fingers instead of forks – my imagination has wandered more than once. This tender vegetable is known as the king of vegetables, as much for its flavour as its price. Its root is known as a crown. From May till July, tied in fat bundles, the pointed stalks sit on market stalls like coronets among the cabbages.

My cat and I often share a plate of asparagus come early June, when the supplies of English-grown spears approach a glut and the price falls to an affordable sum. Just the two of us with no one

to tut at such apparent decadence. Bliss for around a pound. There is something serene about a dozen fat green and mauve spears on a large white plate. A simple and sensuous plateful to be eaten with respect rather than wolfed like a portion of hot, salty chips.

Nothing can spoil the joy of finding the first, expensive local asparagus in early May, no matter how much is flown in year round from Chile and Spain. As the pace of the season quickens, and spears shoot up along the rows of neatly tilled fields in Norfolk, Suffolk and Worcestershire, the prospect of such a luxurious plateful becomes a possibility for all.

I long to taste the thin spears of climbing wild asparagus that sprout from derelict walls come spring in Southern Italy. They have both enchanted Patience Gray and evaded Elizabeth David, who found she was actually eating hop shoots. The nearest we get to such *Asparagus acutifolius* here is the fine, quivering sprue sold in the markets for a song. I am happy to sing its praises. Recommended and sold for soup, its flavour is underrated. Trimmed of its tough ends and curled round like spaghetti, it will cook in two minutes.

When prices fall dramatically as the season ends, there is still a touch of luxury about such a supper – and for less gold than the same weight of peas. By July, the English season all but spent, smooth green soups will be chilling, mild-flavoured purées may sit alongside poached salmon, and fat, steamed asparagus tips will have been stirred into creamy scrambled eggs. We will have had our fill till next year.

Nigel Slater, *Real Cooking*

BALANCE

BANTING, DIETING OR (as Lady Jekyll puts it) starving for shape is a phenomenon of this century. The Edwardian matron put on her dignity with her mono-bust and her Junoesque figure, buxom was a complimentary term, and Worth the greatest designer of women's clothes – one who actually liked women, and adorned them to suit. Then came the mitigating of the divorce laws, fashion designed by men who only liked boys and androgenes – and of course the dreaded Wallis Simpson with her 'one can never be too rich or too thin'.

I suppose the ending of the century with its 'Heroine Chic' says it all. These two pieces, the first from Lady Jekyll in 1922 pragmatically talking about figures, and the second from Reay Tannahill fifty years later in 1973, on the insanities of the dietary industry and world starvation, show how out of kilter the balance has become.

FOR THE TOO THIN

MANY women of the present day are below their proper weight in relation to their age and height. With some this is the result of what our fashionable American friends call 'Starving for Shape'; others object to eating many of the ordinary foods on grounds of principle or humanitarianism, so that, without pressing for specially cooked dishes, (an egotism many shrink from), they frequently go without adequate nourishment. Both sexes often restrain their natural appetite for athletic reasons, wanting to ride, run, and dance light, and to excel in games and sports where weight is a handicap. Numbers of influenza convalescents, too, get reduced by illness, and their doctors will urge them 'to feed up,' 'to put on weight,' knowing by experience how excessive thinness induces nervous disorders with resultant neurasthenia.

The fattening properties of milk, farinaceous puddings, and sweets with Devonshire cream, of plenty of fresh butter with bread and potatoes, and of oatmeal, pulses, and cereals, of root vegetables and some fruits – these are too well known to require stressing. But inclination often fails, and fashion cries 'Beware.' A few attractive dishes are therefore suggested, hoping to make the observance of doctor's orders something of a pleasure as well as a duty, their niceness being, as it were, the smile on the face of the stern lawgiver.

FOR THE TOO FAT

WE are reminded in Scripture that 'all flesh is grass,' but, as a great artist once added reassuringly, 'We cannot be sufficiently thankful that all grass is not flesh.' No one likes to be fat; it is unbecoming, fatiguing, and impairs efficiency. And although the condition is oftener the result of defective metabolism than of undue or indiscriminate appetite, still the experience of the war years, with their scarcity of the flesh-making foods, shows that weight can be reduced by a diminished consumption of dairy produce, sugar, and starchy foods. Unfortunately, all the nicer things are on a weights and measures black list, and the annual advice of an eminent financial authority to 'spend less' must be paraphrased into a diminished consumption of all nourishment for those who would grow thinner. The important drinking of sufficient fluid, moreover, should be transferred from meal times to a previous or subsequent hour. Such inconvenient advice is only acted on when it is given in return for payment by a medical expert, but there may possibly be some chance for a few gratuitous suggestions towards making an austere diet more varied and pleasurable than it often is.

Lady Jekyll, *Kitchen Essays*

THE WORLD OF THE UNDERFED

IN November 1974 a World Food Conference was held in Rome under the auspices of the United Nations. Its eleven days were distinguished by the expression of many high-flown sentiments, an unedifying search for compromises, some blatant jockeying for position by the United States and the oil-producing nations, and a number of final recommendations amounting to little more than a statement of virtuous intentions. The conference's pledge that 'within a decade no child will go to bed hungry, that no family will fear for its daily bread' had a hollow ring even at the time.

Three-quarters of the way through that decade, no fewer than eighteen African nations were facing serious food shortages, while in Bangladesh the United States alone distributed food aid to 7 million starving people. At the very end of the decade, another 7 million in Ethiopia were in even more desperate need.

In October 1985 pop singer Bob Geldof said to the European Parliament in Strasbourg what half the world was thinking. 'It makes no political sense, little emotional sense and nil moral sense that Europe should wallow in food while millions of people in Africa are dying of starvation.'

The world had rarely seemed a more paradoxical place, with vast quantities of unwanted food stockpiled in the warehouses of the developed countries while a famine of appalling proportions raged in Africa. Especially when, just a year before, a meeting of the United Nations World Food Council – held in Ethiopia itself – had discussed the proposition that 'the potential for mass famine has been largely eliminated.'

This thesis was, in fact, less unsound than it appeared. There was no world shortage of food, and experts were by this time able to identify the symptoms of a forthcoming famine well in advance of the actuality. In theory, it should have been perfectly possible to forestall the kind of disaster that occurred in Ethiopia and, soon after, Sudan and Mozambique.

But theory only too often falls foul of human frailty. If no one is there to observe the symptoms; if for political reasons a government chooses to suppress them; if the life-saving food therefore arrives too late and its distribution is wilfully hindered then people die. For hunger to be conquered it needs more than grain and goodwill. It needs agricultural education in the danger areas, technology of a kind manageable by the poorest peasant, instruction in the art of self-sufficiency and – hardest of all to achieve – enough democracy for the first warnings of shortage to be not only reported by the peasants, but heeded by those who govern them.

There had been warnings enough, from Western observers, of the growing famine in Ethiopia. But it took a television news programme to activate the strength of public feeling that in turn activates governments.

In the few months covering late 1984 and early 1985 Western nations pledged something like £400 million in food for Ethiopia. On paper, there was more than enough to feed the 8 million of the starving for over half a year. But by April 1985 neither food nor medicine had reached two-thirds of them, and the Ethiopian government was refusing to allow relief aid into the rural areas of the province of Tigre, where there were 2 million of the most desperately afflicted. In February 1988, with a new Ethiopian famine clearly foreseen for more than six months, only 300,000 tonnes of the 700,000 tonnes pledged by donor nations and organizations had actually arrived.

One heart-warming lesson of the Ethiopian famines was that ordinary people in the spoilt and selfish West were still, despite everything, possessed of an enormous fund of private kindliness and generosity. The other, harsher lesson was that, whatever the availability of grain and money, famine relief can still be sabotaged by inefficiency on the part of the donors as well as by lack of the shipping tonnage, rail transport, packing and, above all, local cooperation and distribution that are needed to ensure that the last handful of food actually reaches the mouth of the last starving child, instead of being wasted, lost or stolen along the way.

THE WORLD OF THE OVERFED

ALTHOUGH hunger in a world of plenty is a tale as old as time, the contrast has seldom been demonstrated more graphically than it was in 1985. While the American administration sent $500 million to help save the lives of the wasted skeletons of Ethiopia, Americans themselves spent $5,000 million on trying to lose weight.

Diet guides, diet drugs, low-calorie foods, health clubs and health farms – all these profited in all Western countries (with the honourable exception of France) from the obsession with image and self. Said one failed dieter, 'To most people, being overweight is a judgement. It says you're weak, self-destructive.' But a nutritionist put it less emotively. 'If you're overweight, all it says is that you eat too much.'

Curiously – or perhaps not so curiously, human nature being what it is – in the health-mad mid-80s even the hautest of American haute cuisine was noticeably more fattening than the European. Despite an occasional flirtation with the new, abstemious French styles, the kind of New York restaurant that boasted a four-week wait for reservations in 1986 was more likely to specialize in duck and lamb dishes, corn cakes with caviar and crème fraiche, apple desserts with caramel sauce, and chocolate bread pudding. In California it was pizza with wild mushrooms, red pepper fettucine, fried oysters with smoked ham, spicy sausages with fennel and whisky, ham hock and lentil salad, and – of course – chocolate cake.

Massachusetts tried to decide whether the Official State Muffin should be cranberry or apple filled. Gourmet popcorn was introduced. The search for the better bagel continued. The chocolate-covered potato crisp was invented.

Yuppy influence, however, ensured that beer and spirits were out. To get fit, get successful and get rich it was necessary to feel in control of the situation. Since alcohol addles the brain, the liquor manufacturers found themselves facing their toughest time since Prohibition. Not so the producers of tonic water. The whole American continent broke out in a rash of little green bottles. 'Coolers' were in, too, flavoured white-wine-and-soda spritzers like the Wineberry Sausalito Sling, which had a taste 'suggestive of ginger ale and bubble gum'. The ideal accompaniment, no doubt, to the smoked duck garnished with pecans and braised red cabbage.

In Europe, despite the growing number of specialist magazines and television programmes, the most-to-be-dreaded words in the American language ('My husband is a gourmet cook') raised a mercifully faint echo. Things were different in other ways, too. *Cuisine minceur* and *nouvelle cuisine* ensured that, in the most fashionable restaurants, diners lost rather than gained weight. So also did their credit cards, since the overheads of such establishments were high. A typical dish consisting of three slices of breast of pheasant, mirrored in a pool of raspberry sauce and flanked by three black olives, five criss-crossed French beans and a single frond of some out-of-season herb required the services of one master chef, three sous-chefs, a full kitchen brigade and a fourth sous-chef with a background in the art of ikebana.

These demanding cuisines were to find no real place in the domestic kitchen, but inferior restaurants became adept at imitating their tricks of presentation and pricing while ignoring their finesse, and it became necessary for the more highly-exposed chefs (and diners) to change direction.

The most favoured new cooking style became *cuisine naturelle*, the most favoured new art style, Dutch still life.

Nouvelle cuisine, at its peak, had been revolutionary in more than the obvious sense. A style for people with expense accounts, it completely reversed the historical tradition that a laden table and a stout figure are evidence of riches and success.

Reay Tannahill, *Food in History*

BEEF

Scotland has the best beef in the world, and my friend Claire Macdonald in the haven of peace that is Kinloch Lodge Hotel on the Isle of Skye cooks some of the best of that beef. She is a spokesman for 'Squabbler', the Scottish Beef and Lamb Agency, and is full of enthusiasm and common sense on the subject. In the days of the horrors of BSE and the idiocy of government, hers was a clarion call to sanity.

THERE are five breeds of beef cattle in Scotland, which give, in my opinion, the best beef in the world. They are Longhorn, Shorthorn, Galloway and the last two are the best known, Highland and Aberdeen Angus – the last being the best known of the lot. These cattle mature slowly, unlike cattle raised for the lower end of the food market, are killed at about 24 months (unlike their counterparts which are destined for altogether cheaper meat, which are slaughtered at around 11 months), and are well hung. Cattle which are raised for cheaper meat are fed a high grain diet, whereas the best beef cattle are fed a very low grain diet – their feed consists mostly of grass. Cheaper beef is hung for the minimal amount of time, and you can see the difference between the two extremes of beef at a glance, before you even notice the price tag – the less expensive meat has a bright pinkish red colour, isn't marbled with fat, and the fat that surrounds it is white. Whereas with best quality beef the meat is dark plummy red, marbled and surrounded with a creamy-yellow coloured fat, which tells you that the animal has been grass-fed.

Hanging is all-important, but every day that the meat hangs results in some shrinkage, so it means the beef must cost more. The ideal hanging time is 14 to 17 days, but cheaper meat is hung for as little as three days. I would far rather eat beef less often and pay more for the beef when I do choose to indulge.

When the word 'beef' is spoken in Scotland there are two cuts which spring to mind – the rib roast and the fillet. As I write there is still the ridiculous ban on buying beef on the bone in domestic and catering establishments. Rarely has there been such idiocy in food laws. Also precluded is the best part of the animal, as far as I am concerned, for cooking into the most rich and satisfying casserole of all, oxtail. This ban, when it comes to oxtail, is, if possible, even more ridiculous because the spinal cord ends at the vertebra before the tail begins. So the whole thing is a nonsense. Oxtail stew, or casserole, needs the lengthiest cooking time – no time is too long – at a low temperature.

The meat should be falling from the bones. But there is one warning about oxtail, it is the only part of the animal which doesn't freeze raw. It is always possible to tell, at the first mouthful, if the stew has been made with an oxtail which has been frozen, it is very inferior in both taste and texture. Once cooked, the dish freezes as well as does any other type of beef when casseroled. Minced raw beef is endlessly useful in a number of dishes. So, too, is silverside, although it is rather too lean a cut for my liking. And brisket, when first browned all over then slowly pot-roasted with an assortment of root vegetables, makes a most delicious dish.

One of the most British of all recipes is the steak and kidney combination. It goes without saying that the kidney must be ox kidney, which needs lengthy cooking. Whether the steak and kidney is covered with rich puff pastry, or whether it is enclosed and steamed within a suet crust and is therefore a steak and kidney pudding, it is one of the best, most comforting of all winter eating. How long you roast beef depends entirely on how rare or better-cooked you like to eat your meat. For a very rare result, 10 minutes per pound weight, with 10 minutes over, gives a good result in a very hot oven – 420°F, 220°C, gas mark 7. Or the top oven in an Aga or Raeburn. Just increase the cooking time per pound if you like it less bloody. And, oh joy, it is still possible to buy a rib roast on the bone because, thankfully, there are still butchers brave enough to take no notice of the ban. If you can find such a source, buy from it. There really is no contest for flavour between meat cooked on the bone and the inferior boned beef.

Claire Macdonald

BERG

THE FINE Scottish food writer Sue Lawrence is a great friend, and full of adventure. There are few places she will not intrepidly go in search of the finest food, as you can see.

I SAT over a hole in the ice, dangling a line in the vain hope of catching a fish, and heading for a severe sense-of-humour failure. The temperature was minus 30C, made chillier by a sharp Arctic wind whistling over the frozen lake. My fingers were about to drop off. My nose had passed the Rudolf-red phase and was now, in keeping with my other bodily extremities, a hypothermal white. My irritatingly jovial fishing companions, who were teasing fish out from under the metre-thick ice with infuriating ease, suggested I warm my hands by thrusting them into the icy water, which admittedly, was warmer than the temperature of the air.

By this time I was having difficulty speaking, so numb were my purple lips, and could only attempt a nod in the general direction of the car. Shod with its heavy-duty winter tyres, the car had transported us right into the middle of the frozen lake some two hours earlier and had been looking temptingly snug for some time. Until then I had felt I should soldier on stoically and attempt a semblance of enjoyment, if only for the sake of my hosts. But, as the last of the warm blood strove to course through my veins, I realised that if I did not make a move I would have to be carried off, frozen stiff, yet still nobly attached to my fishing line.

FOOD

As I slithered towards the car, I began hallucinating about switching on the heating: I even began to imagine the excruciating pleasure of the blood flowing painfully back into my fingertips. Then, as I opened the car door and shuffled onto the seat, I saw a wondrous sight. It was a thermos flask, sitting bright and shiny on the passenger seat. Never has such a mundane object evoked such inner joy.

Slowly, painfully, I struggled to take off the layers of gloves, scarves and hats, then began tackling the flask. And just as I was beginning to unscrew it, I suddenly remembered it was Thursday, which meant only one thing: pea soup – thick, hearty, pork-studded, mustard-flavoured and piping hot. All over Finland and Sweden, Thursday is the day for pea soup and pancakes. This is a relic from medieval times when people ate substantial pork-based soup and batter pudding to tide them over the traditional Friday fast and abstinence.

The pancake is usually cooked in the oven. Called panukakku in Finnish, it is a sweet Yorkshire pudding-like dish that is served hot, straight from the oven, with a dollop of lingonberry jam. A filling of sliced apples, lingonberries or blueberries can also be added to the base of the dish before adding the batter and baking.

And so as I sat in the car, hands clasped around a mug of steaming pea soup, I began to dream of returning home to the sight of a huge pancake billowing out from the oven. I looked at the mad Finns dangling their lines through 3ft of ice and even managed to smile as they whooped for joy when a fish was landed. I looked at the clear blue sky and forbidding icy terrain and thought how stunningly beautiful it all was. And as I poured out another mug of warming pea soup, I also thought, thank God it's Thursday.

PEA SOUP WITH MUSTARD

Recipe serves 6

Instead of bacon, you can use a smoked gammon hock. Cut off chunks of the meat and add to the soup. You can also stir in some grainy mustard just before serving.

    400g dried green split peas
    25g butter
    250g smoked bacon, chopped
    1 onion, peeled, chopped
    1 litre hot ham (or chicken) stock
    2 tbsp Dijon mustard

Soak the peas overnight, then rinse well.

Heat the butter in a large saucepan, add the bacon and onion, gently fry for about 10 minutes, then add the peas, hot stock, mustard, salt and pepper.

Bring to the boil, remove any scum with a slotted spoon, then cover and simmer for 45 minutes, or until the peas are cooked. Whiz with a handheld blender (or liquidise in a blender) and check seasoning. Add another 100ml of boiling water if it is too thick. Serve piping hot, with extra mustard to stir in, if you like. Sue Lawrence, 'Chill Out', *Sunday Times*, 8 November 1995

BIGOTRY

REAY TANNAHILL'S WORDS ON FOOD FASCISTS exactly mirror my feelings. These unhappy bigots don't want a world where we all enjoy the best the land has to offer, but rather to turn food into a hair shirt and a whip for self-chastisement. I used to look at them and think, soon the barbarian will come over the wall and the simplicity of survival will bring common-sense; but now I realise the Visigoth has come, this time, by stealth from the West bringing junk food instead of pestilence, dieting instead of starvation, and hormones and GM food instead of simple death.

CONFUSED NEW WORLD

IF SOME ill-directed time machine had decanted Brillat-Savarin into the 1960s, he might have thought twice before he said, 'Tell me what you eat: I will tell you what you are.' Certainly, he would have qualified it, for no sane analyst of gastronomic history could have deduced a Liverpool pop singer from yoghurt and unpolished rice, or a Manhattan millionaire from black-eyed peas and chitterlings; identified a Frenchman from Scotch whisky, or a Japanese from French bread.

These wild deviations from the logic of the table had very little to do with food. They were political or social gestures, and those who made the gestures knew exactly what they were doing.

But other attitudes towards food were born in the 1960s that over the next twenty years were to introduce genuine confusion not only into the logic of the table but also the minds of the people who sat at it.

The first, conceived and nurtured in America (like so many twentieth-century obsessions), was concerned with appearances. The slim, leggy teenage look was in and, with the ardent encourage-ment of a new breed of experts and advisers, every woman who was not a slim, leggy teenager either embarked on, or contemplated embarking on, a craze for dieting that has scarcely faltered since. It was to change in only one important respect over the years. When men joined in, vanity became inadmissible as a motive for so much concentrated effort, and dieting for health became the motto.

The second 1960s strand in today's food stemmed from the flower children's deliberate adoption of poverty, reflected in and symbolized by lentils and brown rice, foods endowed with an aura of spirituality through association with the Asian gurus – many of them Buddhist – to whom so many of the sixties generation attributed great and disinterested wisdom. Even when, later, most of the flower children rejoined the sinful human race and gave up their communes for houses and their freedom for wages, they continued to eat 'health foods' as if to reassure themselves that, despite appearances, they had not abandoned their ideals.

The third strand was very different and far less obvious. Before the 1960s there were many among the silent majority in the Western world who canalized their ordinary human need to feel superior into what had for centuries been a socially acceptable (if less than admirable) intolerance of homosexuals, Jews, people who ate garlic or dyed their hair, Catholics, blacks, old clothes, four-

letter words, promiscuity, pacifism . . . and so on. Then, at one blow, all these faithful old prejudices became unrespectable, and those who had held them were deprived of an outlet for their need to disapprove.

The next generation, however, with the same need and no traditional focus for it, was saved by the American evangelical tradition and the new obsession with diet and health. Those who might easily have been reborn on the side of the angels. Sometimes, proclaiming the anti-fat, anti-sugar, anti-meat, anti-salt gospel, the new evangelists sound very much like Mrs Horace Mann in *Christianity in the Kitchen*. 'There is no more prolific cause of bad morals than abuses of diet . . .'

Reay Tannahill, *Food in History*

BOUILLABAISSE

IN THE 20TH CENTURY the French managed to get a death grip on the myth that they produce the world's best food. The hype has been carefully orchestrated, and despite the fact that the most popular food in the last quarter has undoubtedly been Italian the French have managed to maintain that mental grip. Don't get me wrong: there are some very fine French chefs. But the French domination is a chimera. However there is no doubt that French rustic cookery has outlasted our own traditions, and this piece by Raymond Oliver, translated for the Wine and Food Society, conveys the passion the French undoubtedly feel for their food.

I THINK there is no longer any doubt that cookery is one of the humanities whose entire philosophy is in step with the progress of civilization throughout the centuries, reflecting the development of man as surely through a recipe as through the Capitularies of Charlemagne or the *Code Napoléon*. The evolution of cookery follows an ethical progression geared to an unceasing search for greater comfort.

To choose *bouillabaisse* as a theme is to select the most vibrant and passionate example (whether of loathing or love) of a dish which in itself represents a whole region and its deepest motivations and symbols.

Among Mediterranean traditions, *bouillabaisse* is as non-Marseillais as possible. Let us understand each other: I begrudge the Marseillais nothing, neither *bouillabaisse*, nor *aïoli*, but I want to be as objective as possible in retracing the former's origins and history to date. We must analyse the dish itself and assemble the pieces of the jigsaw puzzle: first the recipe itself and all the phases of its development, and then its etymology with its specifically Provençal character.

FOOD

Apparently, the Phoenicians taught the method to Ulysses, Achilles and Agamemnon. Pythagoras left a recipe which was taken up by Pliny the Elder 500 years later. I am convinced that in Antiquity the best scorpion-fish soup was made at Syracuse, and that Archimedes, a sound gastronome, knew it. By the way, two ancient gastronomes paid dearly for their status: Archimedes, who, fleeing the Roman soldiery, refused to hide in a bean field because he disliked beans, and Pliny the Elder who was barbecued on Vesuvius. Predestination?

From Pliny onwards, we have a written tradition concerning a soup which contains *rascasse*. The classical *bouillabaisse* so fiercely defended by the Marseillais must contain *rascasse*. The reason for this is curious though ill-defined. *Rascasse*, or scorpion-fish, owes its name to a poison it secretes between its skin and flesh which earned it the name of sea-scorpion. It is a less violent poison, and more difficult to inject into a victim than the venom of the sting-fish, and rapidly loses its strength when exposed to air. Its main property, apart from being poisonous, is that of a fixative. In cookery, as in scent-making, the lighter and more delicate the aroma, the more difficult it is to preserve. Though modern cookery has abandoned certain fixing methods of the past, such as the use of musk or ambergris, it has unconsciously retained certain empirical processes: the inclusion of whole live *rascasses* or the red part of carrots is a survival of these methods. The fat used in the distillation of perfume (extract of rose or jasmine) is widely used in cookery and preserves certain delicate nuances in sauces and consommés which are otherwise difficult to keep. Oil has the same properties as fat.

Although *bouillabaisse* is a soup in the full sense of the word, with slices of bread and with broth, the juice must not be too liquid. It must be smooth, an effect obtained by emulsifying the ingredients. The whole thing must be very light which is one of the reasons why fish from rocks are used exclusively, whereas in *bourride*, for instance, fatty fish are acceptable. Originally *bourride* was a soup of sardines bound with *aïoli*, and one knows that sardines are fatty fish. *Bourride* and *bouillabaisse* have had parallel careers although *bourride* has excited no passions.

To start with, *bouillabaisse* was a fish soup, consisting mainly of *rascasse* with olive oil, garlic, leek, onion, and sea water. Later, in Greco-Roman times, herbs and spices were added; then after Arab supremacy, saffron; and after the discovery of America, tomatoes and potatoes. The great vogue for *bouillabaisse* is contemporary with the apogee of French cookery at the beginning of the twentieth century. Its status was slow to be established, step by step, until it became a classic with its own strict rules. These were, first of all and without question, that it should contain fish from the rocks, *rascasse*, leek, saffron, oil, tomato and fennel. Not until the end of the eighteenth century did it assume the name of *bouille abaisse* in two words, then later in three words and finally in one.

Raymond Oliver, *The French at Table*

BREAD

THE LAWYER A.P. HERBERT WAS A PRODUCT OF HIS ERA but I feel this type of quirky, funny, eclectic Englishman is found in every century. Just thinking of his White Swan makes my eyes fill with tears, and however glum I am feeling his legal stories make me chuckle. His eclecticism even turns to food.

WHEAT, I see, is giving trouble. But wheat is always giving trouble. Either the people are not getting enough wheat or the wheat-grower is not getting enough for his wheat. Sometimes both. Good statesmen are always worrying about wheat. And at the back of their minds there is always, I believe, a gigantic error – the belief that *bread is a good thing, and that above all things the people need bread.*

The people do not need bread.

I am not going to say (as Dr. Hay does) that bread is wholly redundant; but to say, as my encyclopaedia says, that 'bread is the chief food of civilized peoples', is to say that which is clearly wrong.

Every class is agreed about this, though I am the first person who has the courage to express the truth. Begin at the nursery. The pampered child of the rich does not want bread; he wants jam and cake. And when he is ordered to eat two slices of bread before passing to cake he does so with reluctance – and rightly.

Nor does the child of the poor want bread. Invite some slum-child into your house, offer him a nice hunk of bread, and see what he says.

Nor does the indigent adult want bread. He wants fried fish and sausages and a steak and vegetables and beer. Offer the next poor tramp who calls at your door a nice half-loaf and see what *he* says. No doubt, if he is really starving and you have nothing more to offer, he will wolf the bread. But in those circumstances he would wolf Brazil-nuts and potato-skins. We should not on that account say that Brazil-nuts or potato-skins were the chief food of civilized peoples. It is an obvious blunder to assess the value of a foodstuff to the civilized world by reference to the willingness of a starving man to eat it. We must assume that in the civilized world the great majority of the people are not starving, which happily is still the case.

For a fair test go to any public eating-place and see the proportionate part that bread plays in any given meal. It is amazingly small. Bread, you will find, is the only food left behind on the tables and plates (except some little heaps of mustard and salt). Indeed, I should describe bread not as 'the staple food' of Man but as the Principal Condiment of Man. It is an effective adjunct to almost every food. It is (in the form of toast) the perfect platform for an egg, a mushroom or a kidney. It is excellent (crumbled) as the decent covering of a sole or as companion to a grouse. For such purposes as the mopping-up of delicious gravy its value is undeniable. It is a useful ingredient in a sauce or a fishcake. It serves as the machinery of a sandwich or the basis of a primitive poultice. But a platform, an ingredient, a gravy-mop, a poultice – how can such an article be described as our chief food?

FOOD

Note at the end of your next picnic what food it is you throw away or give to the birds. The bread. You do not throw the cold tongue and ham, the potato-salad or gelatine to the birds. You pack them up carefully and take them home.

Cast your bread upon the waters and after many days it will return to you. Nobody wants it. But cast a case of kippers or a barrel of beer on the waters and see how soon they return to you.

What is the traditional thing that (besides the shilling) the angry father cuts off his erring child with when he turns her out of the home? A crust of bread – the most contemptuous form of nourishment that he can think of.

Bread, in short, has no independent existence of its own. By itself it is just the dullest thing you can eat. You cannot persuade the rich to eat it at all unless it is done up or disguised in some fancy fashion as French rolls, or toast, or bread-crumbs, or soup-billets, or prepared in some patent way that is alleged to do them good. And the poor won't eat it if they can get anything better . . .

In the case of bread the cause of all this loose thinking is the longevity and power of words. Things change, but expressions remain – old phrases about 'our daily bread', 'the bread-winner', and so on. They date from times and stages of civilization when bread was really important because most people could get very little else. I have no doubt that among certain remote and backward tribes bread is still 'the staple food'. I gather that it is in Russia. But in the civilized world bread is only one of many foods equally important. A man who won nothing but bread for his family to-day would be locked up for neglecting them. We ought, in short, to speak of the eggs-and-bacon-tea-milk-and-sugar-sausage-and-mash-kipper-meat-and-two-veg.-fish-and-chip-beer-butter-and-bread-winner. That shows bread in its right proportion and at once illuminates the whole wheat problem. The people have grown out of bread, but the poor farmer away out in the Middle West has not yet discovered it. The only solution, therefore, if we want to keep the wheat-farmer going, is to force the people to eat more bread. Among ourselves we can do a certain amount in a voluntary way. If every householder bought an extra half-loaf every day and gave it to the birds it might ease the wheat-problem. Probably there would be a sad outbreak of mortality among the birds if they ate all the bread, but I have noticed that even the birds soon tire of this food (yes, even swans); so perhaps they would survive. But then, the doctors and nutrition-experts inform us now that we eat too much bread. It is *not* a good thing. The staff of life is dangerous. Read this:

'It is not the staff of life, and in its refined form it is verily the staff of death, for its use in this form, white, denatured, emasculated thoroughly, is one of the surest and the quickest roads to acidosis, the fatal alkalin deficiency that is the great cause of disease.

'Whole grain can be used, even to some advantage, by the labourer, if taken in such combinations as will allow it to digest without the usual fermentation, but it is *never necessary* even to the labourer, and to the desk worker it is a continual and immediate source of danger.' (*Health via Food*, Dr. W. H. Hay.)

So, you see, I am right. It is all very difficult.

A. P. Herbert, *Mild and Bitter*

BREAKFAST

I LOVE THIS PIECE from the great American novelist Steinbeck.

THIS thing fills me with pleasure. I don't know why, I can see it in the smallest detail. I find myself recalling it again and again, each time bringing more detail out of a sunken memory, remembering brings the curious warm pleasure.

It was very early in the morning. The eastern mountains were black-blue, but behind them the light stood up faintly colored at the mountain rims with a washed red, growing colder, grayer and darker as it went up and overhead until, at a place near the west, it merged with pure night.

And it was cold, not painfully so, but cold enough so that I rubbed my hands and shoved them deep into my pockets, and I hunched my shoulders up and scuffled my feet on the ground. Down in the valley where I was, the earth was that lavender gray of dawn. I walked along a country road and ahead of me I saw a tent that was only a lighter gray than the ground. Beside the tent there was a flash of orange fire seeping out of the cracks of an old rusty iron stove. Gray smoke spurted up out of the stubby stovepipe, spurted up a long way before it spread out and dissipated.

I saw a young woman beside the stove, really a girl. She was dressed in a faded cotton skirt and vest. As I came close I saw that she carried a baby in a crooked arm and the baby was nursing, its head under her waist out of the cold. The mother moved about, poking the fire, shifting the rusty lids of the stove to make a greater draft, opening the oven door; and all the time the baby was nursing, but that didn't interfere with the mother's work, nor with the light quick gracefulness of her movements. There was something very precise and practiced in her movements. The orange fire flicked out of the cracks in the stove and threw dancing reflections on the tent.

I was close now and I could smell frying bacon and baking bread, the warmest, pleasantest odors I know. From the east light grew swiftly. I came near to the stove and stretched my hands out to it and shivered all over when the warmth struck me. Then the tent flap jerked up and a young man came out and an older man followed him. They were dressed in new blue dungarees and in new dungaree coats with the brass buttons shining. They were sharp-faced men, and they looked much alike.

The younger had a dark stubble beard and the older had a gray stubble beard. Their heads and faces were wet, their hair dripped with water, and water stood out on their stiff beards and their cheeks shone with water. Together they stood looking quietly at the lightening east; they yawned together and looked at the light on the hill rims. They turned and saw me.

'Morning,' said the older man. His face was neither friendly nor unfriendly.

'Morning, sir,' I said.

'Morning,' said the young man.

The water was slowly drying on their faces. They came to the stove and warmed their hands on it.

The girl kept to her work, her face averted and her eyes on what she was doing. Her hair was tied back out of her eyes with a string and it hung down her back and swayed as she worked. She set tin cups on a big packing box, set the plates and knives and forks out too. Then she scooped fried bacon out of the deep grease and laid it on a big tin platter, and the bacon cricked and rustled as it grew crisp. She opened the rusty oven door and took out a square pan full of high big biscuits.

When the smell of that hot bread came out, both of the men inhaled deeply. The young man said softly, 'Kee-rist!'

The elder man turned to me, 'Had your breakfast?'

'No.'

'Well, sit down with us, then.'

That was the signal. We went to the packing case and squatted on the ground about it. The young man asked, 'Picking cotton?'

'No.'

'We had twelve days' work so far,' the young man said.

The girl spoke from the stove. 'They even got new clothes.'

The two men looked down at their new dungarees and they both smiled a little.

The girl set out the platter of bacon, the brown high biscuits, a bowl of bacon gravy and a pot of coffee, and then she squatted down by the box too. The baby was still nursing, its head up under her waist out of the cold. I could hear the sucking noises it made.

We filled our plates, poured bacon gravy over our biscuits and sugared our coffee. The older man filled his mouth full and he chewed and chewed and swallowed. Then he said, 'God Almighty, it's good,' and he filled his mouth again.

The young man said, 'We been eating good food for twelve days.'

We all ate quickly, frantically, and refilled our plates and ate quickly again until we were full and warm. The hot bitter coffee scalded our throats. We threw the last little bit with the grounds in it on the earth and refilled our cups.

There was dolor in the light now, a reddish gleam that made the air seem colder. The two men faced the east and their faces were lighted by the dawn, and I looked up for a moment and saw the image of the mountain and the light coming over it reflected in the older man's eyes.

Then the two men threw the grounds from their cups on the earth and they stood up together. 'Got to get going,' the older man said.

The younger turned to me. 'F'you want to pick cotton, we could maybe get you on.'

'No. I got to go along. Thanks for breakfast.'

The older man waved his hand in a negative. 'O.K. Glad to have you.' They walked away together. The air was blazing with light at the eastern skyline. And I walked away down the country road.

That's all. I know, of course, some of the reasons why it was pleasant. But there was some element of great beauty there that makes the rush of warmth when I think of it.

John Steinbeck, *The Breakfast*

FOOD

I SOMETIMES PINE FOR THE GRANDEUR of the grand hotel in the stylish days before the Second World War, where even breakfast was as complicated and lavish as these menus from the Epicurian. Now so-called luxury hotels merely offer a second-rate service or, worse, a self-service buffet. Only the Dorchester of the great London hotels keeps up the standard.

BILLS OF FARE
February – Breakfast

Caviare canapés
Bonvalet omelet
Codfish tongues with chopped sauce
Truffled pigs' feet
Kernel of veal with thickened gravy
German salad with croûtons
Broiled ptarmigan
Dessert

Matelote à la marinière, St. Mandé
Scrambled eggs with fine herbs
Lambs' trotters, Chantilly
Hashed chicken, Ancient style
Sarah potatoes
Broiled teal duck
Corn salad
Souffléd fritters with lemon peel

Bouillabaisse Parisian
Eggs on a dish, Bienvenue
Pork cutlets with mashed potatoes
Poulpetonnière pigeons
Broiled bear steak
Pont-Neuf potatoes
Stewed or compoted fruits
Coffee

Chiffonade potatoes
Hard-boiled eggs, New York style
Frost fish or whiting baked
Lamb hash with bananas
Potatoes à la Parmentier
Rump steak à la Villageoise
Apple tartlets
Coffee

Oysters and lemons
Eggs miroir à la Provençal
Chicken halibut baked with Parmesan
Blanquette of breast of veal à la Jacquart
Sauerkraut garnished
Beefsteak with fine herbs
Celery salad
Preserved large white currants

Quenelles of fish, Montglas
Turkey giblets, salamander
Beef hash, Sam Ward
Green peas, English style
Veal kidneys à l'Anderson
Broiled ptarmigan
Rum omelet
Fruits

Westphalian ham
Bertini omelet
Salt herring with mashed potatoes
Lamb carbonade à la Rambuteau
Broiled pullet, tartar sauce
Cream of biscuits with kirsch
Cheese
Dessert

Scrambled eggs with tomatoes
Minced leg of mutton à la Lyonnaise
Marchioness potatoes
Veal kidneys à la Roederer
Pigs' feet à la St. Menehould
Mushrooms à la Raynal
Apples with butter
Dessert

Charles Ranhofer, *The Epicurean*

BUTCHER

I DON'T KNOW THAT I RECOMMEND THIS, but we may all be driven to it by the fluffy bunny brigade and the supermarkets.

BECOME YOUR OWN BEST BUTCHER

THIS little section is not for the faint-hearted. If you like chewing on delicately charred morsels of succulent flesh but refuse to pay the butcher's exorbitant prices, strike out and become your own best butcher. Buy a little hat and a stripey apron and lots of sharp tools.

When any unwary animal nonchalantly waltzes past, start thinking 'how can I best divide this creature into simple-to-sever segments?' Practise a little. Take long walks mentally dissecting any animals you happen to see.

DON'T be squeamish. Cooking is a brutal art. You never consider the silent screams of tender turnips untimely nipped from tearful taproots, so don't fool around with baby animals. Earplugs in and cleavers out. Leave hypocrisy at home.

DON'T be afraid to strike up a casual but affectionate relationship with your prospective Sunday Joint. Take pride in following it from gambolling quadruped to swinging carcass. Imagine a poignant moment at a dinner party when you turn to your neighbour and announce, 'I knew this chop'.

LAMBS: They are so skittish that there is nothing for it but to rush in waving your trusty cleaver and cut them up there and then. Try telling sheep to keep young and beautiful if they want to be scoffed. Unfortunately many do not listen. They lose their looks and taste and then no one wants to eat them. So grab the mutton, tenderise it brutally and using a very, very sharp chopper slice it into a stewing pot.

CALVES AND OTHER BOVINETTES

These creatures are often so stupid you can cut them up as they stand chewing the cud. Perhaps they are resigned to their destiny. Perhaps they are taught to accept their fate from an early age, who can tell?

RABBIT AND OTHER FLUFFY GAME FOUND IN HOLES

Choose your bunny. Take him/her on one side, away from his/her friends and loved ones and ask gently, 'Have you ever considered a career in catering supply, Bunny?' While Bunny considers a clever reply stuff him/her in the toaster/oven.

George Moule and Steven Appleby, *No, honestly it was simply delicious but I couldn't eat another mouthful*

CABBAGE

I THINK CABBAGE THE MOST DELICIOUS VEGETABLE, and one which should never be cooked in water. I come from a scientifically oriented family – my great-uncle Almroth boasted that he left lying about the saucer of aspic on which Fleming found his penicillin (he was both notoriously untidy and Alex Fleming's boss). This quaint little piece of scientific error from Florence White's *Good Things in England* proves to me yet again that scientists should stick to the laboratory and leave the kitchen to cooks.

THE RIGHT WAY TO COOK CABBAGE

THERE is no doubt about the correct way to cook cabbage, because this is a culinary operation that has been dealt with scientifically by Dr. Ellen Marion Delf (Mrs. Percy Smith, D.Sc.) whose name is known all the world over in connection with the scientific tests she made for several years with various fruits and vegetables (particularly with orange and swede juice, cabbage and tomatoes) to discover their vitamin value and the best method of preserving it when they were cooked. She worked for five years at the Lister Institute, and later with the Medical Research Council, and has been now for some time Lecturer on Botany in the University of London. What she taught me is embodied in the following:

1. After washing the cabbage, cut it into quarters, remove any old leaves and cut out any tough stems.

2. Throw it into a saucepan of rapidly boiling slightly salted water.

3. *On no account must any soda, bicarbonate or kitchen soda of any kind be added*: it destroys all the vitamin value of the cabbage.

4. Boil rapidly with the lid off for 10 to 15 minutes; not a minute longer. Ten minutes is the best time. Lift out and drain; and press lightly. If the cabbage is properly boiled it will not be saturated with water but will be crisp yet tender, and light pressing will be sufficient to remove the superfluous water. When it is saturated it means it has boiled too long and is permeated with water. It then begins to sink and lose its colour. Old cabbage should never be cooked at all: it is worthless.

5. It is delicious served simply in this way with hot roast meat or any dish that has a good brown gravy, but if required as a vegetable with cold meat, or as a separate course, it may be chopped up finely [put through a mincer to-day] and blended with a good white melted butter sauce without being recooked or even reheated. The piping-hot sauce into which it is stirred will be sufficient to heat it through, and the saucepan can be stood in a pan of boiling water to preserve its heat until

it is sent to table. But cabbage should not be kept waiting; it should be cooked and served immediately.

6. It has been proved conclusively and scientifically that rapid brief cooking at a comparatively high temperature preserves the value of the fugitive delicate vitamin C contained in any vegetable far better than slower cooking at a lower heat.

7. The water in which cabbage has been boiled in this manner should never be thrown away; it makes a delicate and delicious foundation for soups, sauces, and gravies.

Florence White, *Good Things in England*

CANNIBALISM

THIS PIECE IS HERE simply to celebrate the wit and humour of the late, great Evelyn Waugh.

BASIL nodded and in the circle of fuzzy heads rose to declaim Seth's funeral oration. It was no more candid than most royal obituary. It was what was required. 'Chiefs and tribesmen of the Wand,' he said, speaking with confident fluency in the Wanda tongue of which he had acquired a fair knowledge during his stay in Azania. 'Peace be among you. I bring the body of the Great Chief, who has gone to rejoin Amurath and the spirits of his glorious ancestors. It is right for us to remember Seth. He was a great Emperor and all the peoples of the world vied with each other to do him homage. In his own island, among the people of Sakuyu and the Arabs, across the great waters to the mainland, far beyond in the cold lands of the North, Seth's name was a name of terror. Seyid rose against him and is no more. Achon also. They are gone before him to prepare suitable lodging among the fields of his ancestors. Thousands fell by his right hand. The words of his mouth were like thunder in the hills. Weep, women of Azania, for your royal lover is torn from your arms. His virility was inexhaustible, his progeny numerous beyond human computation. His staff was a grown palm tree. Weep, warriors of Azania. When he led you to battle there was no retreating. In council the most guileful, in justice the most terrible, Seth the magnificent is dead.'

The bards caught phrases from the lament and sang them. The wise men ran whooping among the spectators carrying torches. Soon the pyre was enveloped in towering flames. The people took up the song and swayed on their haunches, chanting. The bundle on the crest bubbled and spluttered like fresh pine until the skin cerements burst open and revealed briefly in the heart of the furnace the incandescent corpse of the Emperor. Then there was a subsidence among the timbers and it disappeared from view.

Soon after sunset the flames declined and it was necessary to refuel them. Many of the tribesmen had joined the dance of the witches. With hands on each other's hips they made a chain round the pyre, shuffling their feet and heaving their shoulders, spasmodically throwing back their heads and baying like wild beasts.

The chiefs gave the sign for the feast to begin.

The company split up into groups, each round a cookpot. Basil and Joab sat with the chiefs. They ate flat bread and meat, stewed to pulp among peppers and aromatic roots. Each dipped into the pot in rotation, plunging with his hands for the best scraps. A bowl of toddy circulated from lap to lap and great drops of sweat broke out on the brows of the mourners.

Dancing was resumed, faster this time and more clearly oblivious of fatigue. In emulation of the witch doctors, the tribesmen began slashing themselves on chest and arms with their hunting knives; blood and sweat mingled in shining rivulets over their dark skins. Now and then one of them would pitch forward on to his face and lie panting or roll stiff in a nervous seizure. Women joined in the dance, making another chain, circling in the reverse way to the men. They were dazed with drink, stamping themselves into ecstasy. The two chains jostled and combined. They shuffled together interlocked.

Basil drew back a little from the heat of the fire, his senses dazed by the crude spirit and the insistence of the music. In the shadows, in the extremities of the market-place, black figures sprawled and grunted, alone and in couples. Near him an elderly woman stamped and shuffled; suddenly she threw up her arms and fell to the ground in ecstasy. The hand-drums throbbed and pulsed; the flames leapt and showered the night with sparks.

The headman of Moshu sat where they had dined, nursing the bowl of toddy. He wore an Azanian white robe, splashed with gravy and spirit. His scalp was closely shaven; he nodded down to the lip of the bowl and drank. Then he clumsily offered it to Basil. Basil refused; he gaped and offered it again. Then took another draught himself. Then he nodded again and drew something from his bosom and put it on his head. 'Look,' he said. 'Pretty.'

It was a beret of pillar-box red. Through the stupor that was slowly mounting and encompassing his mind Basil recognized it. Prudence had worn it jauntily on the side of her head, running across the Legation lawn with the *Panorama of Life* under her arm. He shook the old fellow roughly by the shoulder.

'Where did you get that?'

'Pretty.'

'Where did you get it?'

'Pretty hat. It came in the great bird. The white woman wore it. On her head like this.' He giggled weakly and pulled it askew over his glistening pate.

'But the white woman. Where is she?'

But the headman was lapsing into coma. He said 'Pretty' again and turned up sightless eyes.

Basil shook him violently. 'Speak, you old fool. Where is the white woman?'

The headman grunted and stirred; then a flicker of consciousness revived in him. He raised his head. 'The white woman? Why, here,' he patted his distended paunch. 'You and I and the big chiefs – we have just eaten her.'

Then he fell forward into a sound sleep.

Evelyn Waugh, *Black Mischief*

CHEFS

THE CHEF AS A CELEBRITY is a 20th-century creation. Until this century there have been chefs who have been remembered because they were truly great, such as Chiquart, Taillevent, Robert May, Patrick Lamb, or Carême. You will notice that is about one in every hundred years. In the first half of this century only the name Auguste Escoffier is really remembered. In 1978 Quentin Crewe produced a remarkable book, *Great Chefs of France*, with innovative and powerful black and white photographs by Anthony Blake. This, to my mind, is where it all began. The personification and glorification of chefs has grown out of all proportion, greatly encouraged by television. In Europe a cook may not even call himself a chef until he has spent ten years in a professional brigade kitchen. In Britain, and to a lesser extent in America, the cult of the celebrity chef raises some who I wouldn't trust to cook my egg and bacon. At least Quentin's collection were the real thing.

It is puzzling that Paul Haeberlin does not seem to fit in with any of the assumptions which one might make about great chefs from the study of the others in this book. Each, by the very fact of being human, has a distinct personality of his own, but they all share to a greater or lesser degree some characteristics which one could suppose syllogistically to be an essential part of the make-up of a great chef. They are all spurred by a need to express themselves in generosity, but not Paul Haeberlin. This is not to say that he is mean. Far from it. But for him the act of giving is no part of his motive in cooking. They all have about them a certain shrewdness, but not Paul Haeberlin. He is rather a simple character, who leaves anything to do with money to the rest of the family. When he was younger and actively resisting the pressure to run the family holdings, he could not bear to get rid of the family horses, but kept them well-fed without ever working them, so that for the villagers of Illhaeusern the illustration of a life of ease was a Haeberlin horse. The other chefs need encouragement, praise and recognition; Paul seems indifferent or, at any rate, satisfied merely with achievement for its own sake. Perhaps the only quality he has in common with the others is immense endurance.

Paul Haeberlin's kitchen provides part of the solution to the puzzle. It is not like Bocuse's or Pic's or Troisgros' or Chapel's, the carefully planned workshop of a master craftsman. Instead, it resembles an overgrown, everyday kitchen of an ordinary housewife. A large Bertrand mixer, looking like a machine-gun, lies casually on one shelf dripping a bit of ice-cream on the floor. Paul calls out the orders in his high-pitched voice, but no-one bothers to answer with eager cries of *'oui'*; they just get on with it. There is a fair amount of chatter. There seems to be no insistence on discipline, but more an air of informality and simplicity, so that you begin to wonder whether Paul was joking when he said, 'Before we ask new employees if they can cook, we ask if they can play football, because we are proud of our team.' There is a man wearing clogs, the washers-up are girls in ordinary clothes. Old Mrs Haeberlin makes the coffee. There is a tin-opener screwed to one bench, where a boy opens a tin of duck livers for the *gratin de nouilles au foie de canard*. Paul has in some ways an easy-going air. It will be all right, he says to his son who fears that they haven't cooked enough chickens. Later it appears that it isn't. 'See how many we have sold,' says the young Marc reproachfully. Yet somehow, in the end, it is all right. Yes, this is a kitchen run on homely lines.

From this kitchen comes much that is traditional. Alsace is famous for its game, because after the Franco-Prussian war of 1870, when Alsace was yielded to France, the old German hunting laws were retained. Ten-year game-leases are the minimum permitted, so that it is worth the lessee's while to preserve the game. The arrangements are controlled by the mayor to protect the farmer against damage. Game, then, was a natural part of the menu of the old L'Arbre Vert and it still is of L'Auberge de l'Ill. As Paul points out, many of the dishes might have been on a menu two hundred years ago. Indeed his preference is for the produce of the region; he likes to cook game and is still fascinated by fish, although this now has to be imported since the local rivers became polluted.

Paul has no feelings about *nouvelle cuisine*. 'Weber gave me his handwritten recipe book, with many things in it in Russian. Among them was *salade Catherine la Grande*, a salad of *foie gras* and

haricots verts, which people talk about now as if it were a new idea.' All that is happening, he maintains, is that chefs are simplifying things, because people cannot eat so much nowadays. 'But if you want a good sauce, you have to use cream and butter.' However much lighter the food is, the traditional basis remains.

Against all of this we have to set one plain fact. Paul Haeberlin is a genius and, like all geniuses, he is unique. Although all that he has done, in one sense, is to plod logically and methodically on, just like his mother, grandmother and great-grandmother, producing the best food he can from his home kitchen, the fact is that everything he touches is tinged with magic. His very method of creation is prosaic. For him creation is not a cerebral affair; he is inspired only in his kitchen, at the moment of working. 'When I am working with some scallops and oysters, I think why not try them with some basil. Ah, there's an idea.' Just like a housewife, you may think, until you come to eat them and realize that this is a perfect dish no housewife could have dreamed of, in the same way that she would never have combined a peach in champagne sabayon with a pistachio ice-cream.

Quentin Crewe and Anthony Blake, *Great Chefs of France*

CHEMISTRY

MUCH OF WHAT COOKS HAVE BEEN DOING for centuries has a scientific explanation. The magic of mayonnaise or bread is all logical really. Thank God we didn't hang around for the scientists! Harold McGee's great book is compulsive reading, and here he is on emulsified sauces. Don't, however, fall into the trap of thinking that understanding it makes it easier.

THE NATURE OF EMULSIONS

AN emulsion is a colloidal system in which one liquid is dispersed in the form of fine droplets throughout another liquid with which it cannot evenly mix. (The molecules of water and alcohol, for example, mix freely together and so cannot form an emulsion.) The most common, indeed ubiquitous, emulsions in everyday life are made up of water and oil. Mayonnaise, cream, and milk are all emulsions of fat dispersed in water (with about 70, 38 and 4% fat contents by weight respectively), and butter is a water-in-oil emulsion with water accounting for about 20% of the weight. (Because some culinary oils have relatively high melting points one phase of these emulsions may frequently be solid rather than liquid but they are all formed when both phases are liquid.) Cosmetic creams, floor and furniture waxes, some paints, asphalt, and even crude oil are all emulsions of water and oil.

An emulsion consists of two phases, one continuous and the other discontinuous, or dispersed. In the usual shorthand, an 'oil-in-water' emulsion is one in which oil is dispersed in a continuous water phase; 'water-in-oil' names the reverse situation. The dispersed liquid generally takes the form of tiny spheres, between 0.1 and 1.0 micron in diameter (a few millionths of an inch), separated from each other by the continuous phase. The droplets, like intact starch granules, are large enough to deflect light rays from their normal path through the surrounding liquid, and give emulsions their characteristically opaque, milky appearance and thereby their name. The more of these droplets there are concentrated in the continuous phase, the more they squeeze the continuous phase into a very thin film between them, and the more viscous the emulsion will be. If you introduce more of the continuous phase, on the other hand, you dilute the droplets, and the emulsion will thin out. Clearly, it is important to know which phase is which when working with emulsified sauces.

FIGHTING SURFACE TENSION

PERHAPS the most important characteristic of emulsions is that they require energy, and sometimes ingenuity, for their formation. Those who make mayonnaise or hollandaise by hand may find that a sore arm the next day is part of the price: shaking a bottle of oil and vinegar is a less extreme example We all know from experience that when water and oil are poured into the same bowl, they separate into two layers: one does not spontaneously form tiny droplets and invade the other. This behavior can be described by saying that when liquids cannot mix for chemical reasons, they tend to arrange themselves in the way that exposes the least possible surface area to each other. The way they do this is to form a single large mass, which exposes less of itself to the other liquid than does the same total mass broken into pieces. As one relevant example, a cube of material measuring an inch along each edge, and thus a total surface area of 6 square inches, would have a surface area of several acres if divided into particles of colloidal size. This tendency of liquids to minimize their surface area is an expression of the force called *surface tension*, which arises from the attractive forces that hold the molecules of a liquid together. The surface of a liquid is the interface between that liquid and the air, or another liquid with which it cannot mix. At the surface, a molecule of the liquid feels the attractive force of molecules below the surface, but this force is not balanced by similar forces from the other direction. Surface molecules, then, are pulled continuously into the liquid, away from the air or the foreign liquid. If you isolate a small amount of the liquid and surround it by some other substance, all the surface molecules feel the same inward force, and a sphere – whether dewdrop or oil drop – is formed. If the liquid touches a solid or if there is enough of it to be distorted by its own weight, its shape may depart from the spherical, but the force of inward attraction will always work toward minimizing the surface area and maintaining a monolithic shape.

Harold McGee, *On Food and Cooking*

CHOICES

WITH THE CENTURY came the growth of intensive and chemically assisted farming, and it has now become obvious that the dangers inherent in these developments have damaged the health of the nation and the quality of produce available to us. Since the mid 1980s Henrietta Green has stood (initially a lone voice in the wilderness) for the rights and strengths of the small producer, and the importance for the consumer to make the choice for excellence. She writes with intense passion on her subject. In her introduction to *Food Lovers' Guide* she outlines her philosophy, which is illustrated by the selected piece on a cheese producer.

FOR good food you must have good ingredients – it makes cooking so much easier and eating far more enjoyable. Years ago I heard the late great Jane Grigson on the radio talking about the essence of her cooking. She said that it was about buying the best produce and cooking it as simply as possible to emphasize its inherent flavour, and I have never forgotten that.

But where do you buy such produce? You can try the supermarkets, but so often they disappoint with their mass-produced food. Far more satisfying is to seek out the smaller speciality producers – the craftspeople of the food world. They include the farmers and growers who raise old-fashioned breeds of animals known for their richness and depth of flavour or choose vegetables and fruit varieties for taste rather than appearance and yield; or the cheese-makers who still make by hand in the time-honoured way; or the preserve-makers who boil up whole fruit in small batches.

To discover them all and many more, my dog Violet and I have travelled the length and breadth of Britain. This has meant years of work and most of it has been pleasurable. If anyone tries to tell you that Britain suffers from a dearth of quality producers of either raw or processed foods, just don't believe them – there are hundreds. However, trying to define 'quality' is never easy; it is more than a pretty label or old-fashioned image. For me it means food produced with a commitment to taste and texture, made with the proper ingredients in the proper way with no short cuts; for example a true shortbread is made with flour, the right fats, sugar and nothing else, and for the traditional texture it must be carefully mixed and rolled out.

SLEIGHT FARM

Sleight Farm, Timsbury, Bath, Avon BA3 1HN
TEL *01761 470620* CONTACT *Mary Holbrook – telephone ahead*

MARY HOLBROOK makes some of the best goats'- and ewes'-milk cheeses in England. You do not just have to take my word for it; the numerous prizes she has won at Nantwich and The Specialist Cheesemakers' Association Shows testify to it. The farm, in the rolling Mendip Hills, offers excellent pasture for her goats and sheep and they graze extensively with the minimum use of fertilizers.

Her cheeses, made in the dairy by the farmyard, are all unpasteurized and offer such depth of flavour and smoothness of texture that they knock spots off several French equivalents. (Without wishing to appear too chauvinistic, I take great pleasure in serving them to my French friends. They can't believe they're made here – and by an Englishwoman!) They can be bought from Neal's Yard Dairy in Covent Garden, London, and several other specialist cheese shops throughout the country.

Dealing with the goats' cheeses first: Mary makes Sleight, a lightly salted young creamy and moist cheese with a mild but pronounced flavour, in 115 g (4 oz) rounds. This is either plain or coated in coarsely ground black pepper, rosemary or crushed garlic and herbs. Ash Pyramid is a more compact, creamier cheese with a flavour described by cheese specialist Juliet Harbutt as 'fermenting fruit'; moulded into 200 g (7 oz) pyramids, it is coated with charcoal. Tymsboro' is a semi-soft, mould-induced pyramid with a hint of sweetness; and Mendip, a hard cheese with a pliant texture and a taste of fresh pastures, can be eaten when young and mild at 3 months or when harder at 6 months.

Her ewes'-milk cheeses include a soft, crumbly but mild Feta that is matured for up to 6 months; mould-ripened Emlett with a smooth creamy interior that softens and mellows with age; Little Rydings, a 200 g (7 oz) mould-ripened Coulommiers shape that has a nutty sweet fullness; and Tyning, a superb hard cheese that is matured for 6-12 months; reminiscent of Pecorino it has a deeply satisfying sheep's tang. Eat it cut in slivers with fresh pears; or grate it over pasta.

One cautionary note: as I write, Mary Holbrook's future is uncertain due to the current food legislation issued both from here and the EC. Mary's hygiene is exemplary but, even so, it may not be good enough for the 'powers that be'. Currently she matures her hard cheeses in a special barn off the farmyard. Obviously they have to be transported there from the dairy, and the only way is to cover and carry them through the open air. However, the Authorities do not like this as they claim that, even though it takes a few seconds, it is not good practice. It seems ridiculous that cheeses as good as Mary's may be under threat.

Henrietta Green, *Food Lovers' Guide to Britain*

CHILDHOOD

A MEMORY FROM MY EARLIEST CHILDHOOD, this piece. Perhaps I was born a foodie, as Hare's action stayed with me far beyond Little Grey Squirrel's heroism.

'FIRE! FIRE!' shouted Moldy Warp and bang went his old blunderbuss among them! A shower of little arrows and a hail of stones fell among the scrambling Weasels. Then Fuzzypeg and Tim and Bill Hedgehog threw the old laid eggs. Every egg hit a Weasel and knocked over a dozen others. Pouf! What a smell there was!

Hare put on his gas-mask and fired his sandwiches from his catapult by mistake. It wasn't till his haversack was empty that he discovered his mistake.

'Just my luck,' he murmured. 'Excellent egg-and-cress sandwiches all gone! And I've got stones to eat.'

The Weasels struggled and fought and rolled about in the pit.

'A trap!' they cried, and they climbed on each other's backs and scrambled out . . .

Mrs. Hedgehog carried bowls of hot pea-soup to the tired little animals, and Old Hedgehog came hurrying up with a can of warm milk.

'I rolled like a ball all the way to the meadow where our Daisy was feeding. So I borrowed a pail from the dairymaid and milked the cow, and here's a sup for some of you,' said he.

'Oh, it was lovely in Moldy Warp's dug-out,' they called, waving their toys. 'We didn't want to come away.'

'You shall all come to the feast of victory,' promised Mole. 'You have been as brave as anybody. Now the war is over and the Weasels have been defeated we needn't fear them any more.'

'A feast?' cried Hare. 'Ah! That's better! That's worth fighting for!'

'Hurrah for Moldy Warp the leader!' cried the little army, and they waved their caps and mufflers and scarves.

'Hurrah for little Fuzzypeg the bomber! Hurrah for Grey Rabbit the Red Cross nurse, and Squirrel the knitter and Hare the Home Guard!'

'Courage! Fight for freedom,' they all sang, and Grey Rabbit wrote the words on the great oak tree which grew by the Roman road, so that they would always remember.

Alison Uttley, *Hare Joins the Home Guard*

BACK TO CHILDHOOD AGAIN. How many of us have been delighted by Ratty and Mole's picnic from the *Wind in the Willows*, the epitome of every child's fantasy picnic? Nowadays I suppose there aren't enough high-profile named brands or additives.

57

FOOD

THE Mole waggled his toes from sheer happiness, spread his chest with a sigh of full contentment, and leaned back blissfully into the soft cushions. '*What* a day I'm having!' he said. 'Let us start at once!'

'Hold hard a minute, then!' said the Rat. He looped the painter through a ring in his landing-stage, climbed up into his hole above, and after a short interval reappeared staggering under a fat, wicker luncheon-basket.

'Shove that under your feet,' he observed to the Mole, as he passed it down into the boat. Then he untied the painter and took the sculls again.

'What's inside it?' asked the Mole, wriggling with curiosity.

'There's cold chicken inside it,' replied the Rat briefly; 'coldtonguecoldhamcoldbeefpickled-gherkinssaladfrenchrollscresssandwidgespottedmeatgingerbeerlemonadesodawater -'

'O stop, stop,' cried the Mole in ecstasies: 'This is too much!'

'Do you really think so?' inquired the Rat seriously. 'It's only what I always take on these little excursions; and the other animals are always telling me that I'm a mean beast and cut it very fine!'

Kenneth Grahame, *The Wind in the Willows*

CORRECTNESS

ENGLAND HAS ALWAYS SPECIALISED IN producing formidable women, and I feel that Mrs Martineau, who wrote books with such splendid titles as *Caviar to Candy* and *Cabbage and Canteloupe*, was one such. She is a fine epitome of the 1930s, and here she is on cooking vegetables.

IT TAKES double the time to steam than to boil and the colour is not so good. Not that this matters if sauce is eaten with the vegetable. The water below must be kept on the boil all the time and replenished if necessary. There is an intermediate school of thought which says that vegetables need only just sufficient water to cover them, and it is well known that spinach requires no water at all, for it cooks itself. The French cook will wash her French beans, for instance, in cold water and pour them into a strainer. A small quantity of hot water and a tablespoon of salt are put into a saucepan and when boiling the beans are thrown into the water which should just cover them, then cooked till tender, adding hot water if necessary so that they do not burn. Strained in a colander, and finished off in a frying-pan with a melted lump of butter and sprinkled with home-ground white pepper. This method is used for most vegetables in France. It is the retaining of the flavour by using very little water, and the finishing of them off with butter, that makes them so delicious. The average cook gets fearfully alarmed if the word French cooking is mentioned, but most French dishes are perfectly simple once the primary rules of cooking are learned. Butter or good gravy is a necessity for this form of cooking, but then the dish is often eaten separately and not as an accompaniment to meat or poultry, and therefore not so expensive an item of the dinner.

FOOD

FOOD

Really exquisite clear soup can be made from vegetables alone. At a recent dinner the soup was so good that I complimented the hostess afterwards on it. She kindly gave me the recipe (Clear Soup for Dinner Parties), and it will be seen that no meat is used. It was quite clear, golden brown in colour, and of a flavour that one only gets when a Cordon Bleu is employed.

PEAS, GREEN, CHARTREUSE OF

LINE a charlotte mould with thin pastry well pressed to the sides. Fill with uncooked rice and bake in the oven. Take out the rice, which will have preserved the shape of the pastry, and when cold well mask the inside with a cream purée of green peas or French beans. Make a thick cream sauce and mix together with it some cut-up macaroni and button mushrooms and a little grated Parmesan cheese, and fill up the centre of the mould. Put a layer of the purée on the top and bake slowly.

PEAS, GREEN, TO COOK

SHELL into two basins, putting the larger peas into one. Have some fast boiling water slightly salted and with a speck of carbonate of soda in it and a sprig of mint. Throw the larger peas into it and cook for three or four minutes before adding the smaller peas. Then boil all till tender. This should take about fifteen minutes or longer.

PEAS, GREEN (TO COOK WHEN ELDERLY)

ALAS that peas should ever grow up! But they do, and even when home-grown one must realise that the time has come to have the face lifted! The French have achieved success in this by cooking them with lettuce and onion. You must add one or two lettuces according to size, broken in pieces, to your shelled peas, several young onions, a spoon of white sugar, some salt and ground pepper. Put a good lump of butter in the saucepan, add the rest of the ingredients when the butter has melted, and sufficient water or milk and water to cover the peas. Put the lid on and cook very slowly till the peas are tender. Mix in a tablespoon of cream at the last just before serving. If onions are not liked (after trying this dish) leave them out and use a sprig of mint instead, but this is strictly against all French ideas!

Mrs Martineau, *Cabbage and Canteloupe*

CRABS

I AM A TRUE SINOPHILE, my comfort food is Chinese, the only other language I have ever had any desire to learn is Chinese, and even in the most xenophobic days of my youth I always felt drawn to the Chinese. I don't know whether it is because my grandfather spoke ten dialects, or because of my grandmother's Chinese friends, or the fact that I used chopsticks instead of a spoon and pusher. My mother's great friend was a very elegant and educated man called Kong Tan, whose Davis Cup partner was the writer Kenneth Lo. This piece on crabs is the first piece of writing on Chinese food I remember reading.

WINTER IS, OF COURSE, the greatest eating season. When winter started to slip away and there was a feeling that spring was just around the corner, it was time for 'spring rolls'. These are pancake rolls, which the diners themselves roll at the table. Into them are added a wide variety of stuffings, mainly vegetables and shredded meats: either savoury and hot fillings which have just come out of the pan, or raw or lightly-cooked vegetables which are crunchy and thus add a new dimension to the general texture. The meat most often used is lamb (shredded), and the vegetable, 'Chiu T'sai', which has a taste somewhere between bean sprouts and chives. These were often joined by shredded cucumber, radishes and spring onion, all heavily brushed with plum sauce and various types of sweetened bean pastes to give that added piquancy.

When summer was with us there was a great harvest of fruits and vegetables. There were plentiful peaches, apples and grapes in North China. Peking even had strawberries. The dominating vegetable in the summer seemed to be tomatoes, which in season crept into many dishes. They were sometimes served stuffed in a variety of ways.

In the summer fresh-water crabs became nearly as plentiful as prawns in winter. There were restaurants which specialised in crabs, where they were simply steamed; their meat was dipped before eating in a mixture of vinegar and ginger, and the feet and claws were chewed and sucked – these were hammered last, and their meat extracted. You ate until you had built up a mountain of shells on the table.

Throughout the year, of course, you could have all the pork, lamb, beef, duck and chicken dishes. Often in some areas of the city, or immediately outside, the ponds or artificial lakes were drained, and then you suddenly had an over-supply of fresh fish in the vicinity; otherwise the Yellow River Carp which had always been so much extolled was, in the opinion of all the southerners I knew, very much over-rated. The fascination of Peking has many aspects.

Kenneth Lo, *Chinese Food*

CUTTING

EASILY THE MOST SUCCESSFUL, and the *grande dame* of American cookery, is Julia Child, whose television shows so beloved by the Yanks are rumbustious to say the least. Legend has it that when broadcasting live she once dropped the salmon, and then calmly gave the recipe for kedgeree!

CHOPPING, SLICING, AND DICING

FRENCH cooking requires a good deal of chopping, slicing, dicing, and fancy cutting, and if you have not learned to wield a knife rapidly a recipe calling for eight ounces of finely diced vegetables and 2 pounds of sliced mushroom caps is often too discouraging to attempt. It takes several weeks of off-and-on practice to master the various knife techniques, but once learned they are never forgotten. You can save a tremendous amount of time, and also derive a modest pride, in learning how to use a knife professionally.

The Knife Grip

For cutting and slicing, hold the knife with your thumb and index finger gripping the top of the blade, and wrap your other fingers around the handle.

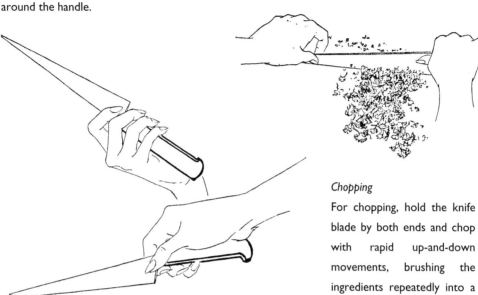

Chopping

For chopping, hold the knife blade by both ends and chop with rapid up-and-down movements, brushing the ingredients repeatedly into a heap again with the knife.

Slicing Round Objects (a)

To slice potatoes or other round or oval objects, cut the potato in half and lay it cut-side down on the chopping board. Use the thumb of your left hand as a pusher, and grip the sides of the potato with your fingers, pointing your fingernails back toward your thumb so that you will not cut them.

Slicing Round Objects (b)

Cut straight down, at a right angle

of the knife blade, pushing the potato slice away from the potato as you hit the board. The knuckles of your left hand act as a guide for the next slice. This goes slowly at first, but after a bit of practice, 2 pounds of potatoes can be sliced in less than 5 minutes.

Slicing Long Objects like Carrots

To slice long objects like carrots, cut a thin strip off one side so that the carrot will lie flat on the board. Then cut crosswise slices as for the potatoes in the preceding paragraph.

FOOD

Julienne (a)

To cut vegetables such as carrots or potatoes into julienne matchsticks, remove a thin strip off one side of the carrot and lay the carrot on the board. Then cut it into lengthwise slices ⅛ inch thick.

Julienne (b)

Two at a time, cut the slices into strips ⅛ inch across, and the strips into whatever lengths you wish.

Dicing Solid Vegetables

Proceed as for the julienne, but cut the strips, a handful at a time, crosswise into dice.

Dicing Onions and Shallots (a)

Once mastered, this method of dicing onions or shallots goes like lightning. Cut the onion in half through the root. Lay one half cut-side down, its root-end to your left. Cut vertical slices from one side to the other, coming just to the root but leaving the slices attached to it, thus the onion will not fall apart.

ROOT END

FOOD

Dicing Onions and Shallots (b)
Then make horizontal slices from bottom to top, still leaving them attached to the root of the onion.

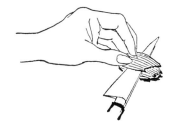

Dicing Onions and Shallots (c)
Finally, make downward cuts and the onion falls into dice.

Simone Beck, Louisette Bertholle and Julia Child, *Mastering the Art of French Cooking*

DEBUTANTE

FANNY CRADDOCK WAS ONE OF THE FIRST TV COOKS, and the one most people of a certain age remember, in her evening dress with her gormless husband Johnny in his white tie and tails. She was wonderful television, affected, ghastly, overblown. She took herself deeply seriously, and also wrote dreadful novels about an affected family, the Lormes of Castle Rising. The books were interspersed with recipes, thus: 'When William the Conqueror visited the castle he dined on "tripe à la mode de Caen" asterisk, recipe at the bottom of the page' – which was actually the best tripe à la mode recipe I have come across. Fanny eventually destroyed her career by being unutterably nasty to a very nice woman who had won a competition on TV. Everyone remembers her public persona, but what people don't remember is that she wrote exquisitely funny prose and very good recipes, as this piece on the prawn cocktail shows. The prawn cocktail itself was a strange phenomenon that swept England in the 1960s, so much so that they were known as 'the Prawn Cocktail years'.

PRAWN COCKTAIL

ONE of the most sordid little offerings is the ubiquitous Prawn Cocktail with a good old ground padding of lettuce cut with a knife and darkening at the edges, a tired prawn drooping disconsolately over the edge of the glass like a debutante at the end of her first ball and its opposite number – a piece of lemon tasting of the knife – clutching the opposite side of the rim like a seasick passenger against a taffrail during a rough Channel crossing. This kind of presentation almost invariably confirms that the mayonnaise will be that bottled stuff, further sharpened by bottled tomato sauce, that the incidence of prawns will be low, of over-cooked diced potatoes high, whereas if we have not put you off them for life by this time, Prawn Cocktails can be delicious.

Start by tearing crisp heart of lettuce and using the pieces to line the base and sides of a glass or bowl, so that when the prawn mixture is filled in all the lettuce does not have to be excavated from the base. Then make up a mixture which comprises 4 oz. fresh, freshly shelled shrimps or prawns (halve the latter), 2 oz. small diced hothouse cucumber with the skin left on, 2 oz. real mayonnaise perked up with a few drops of Tabasco and an additional teaspoonful of strained lemon juice – and absolutely no potato salad at all.

Mix the given ingredients in a bowl with 1 tablespoonful thick whipped cream and add the merest flick of sherry or dry Madeira to it. Place about 3 dessertspoonsful in each portion on the lettuce. Sprinkle the top first with paprika, then with chives and drive a single, shelled prawn with the head left on, tail end downwards, into the centre so that the head can be lifted out by the diner, the flesh nibbled off and the head discarded easily. Now fringe the glass all round the dome with very thinly sliced unskinned cucumber rounds in overlapping lines and place a very small lemon basket at the side of the glass on the plate, on which you will send it to table. Then the lemon basket can be picked up easily and additional lemon juice squeezed over as desired without getting your fingers in a filthy mess.

Fanny Craddock, *Daily Telegraph's Sociable Cook's Book by a Bon Viveur*

DELICATESSEN

I LOVE DELIS: there is always something exciting in the anticipation of what one might find in them, some new product or cheese or a made dish. If I have been away from Edinburgh I can spend a whole day in Valvona & Crolla eating, drinking and shopping and making friends. I think this piece shows something of what I am trying to say. In the last quarter of this century delis have become one of the few remaining bastions against the supermarkets, and are to be supported and encouraged in the new millennium.

SWEET AND SOUR

MY great boyhood ambition was to own a delicatessen. I had shown only erratic enthusiasms for such run-of-the-mill juvenile pleasures as electric trains, fire engines, chemical laboratories,

magician's kits, and a Schaubek postage-stamp album with interchangeable pages – a necessity in 1919 when kingdoms were folding up like badly managed night clubs. At that time I lived with my widowed mother and my seven-year-old brother Max in one of the few four-storey stone buildings in my home-town, Moravská-Ostrava, a fast-growing coal and steel centre in eastern Czechoslovakia. The house was right in the middle of the business district, near the City Hall square, a convenient and fashionable location. Most merchants and department-store owners lived in their own houses, above their business premises; doctors and lawyers had their offices next door to their apartments.

We lived on the top floor of our house; two uncles and their families had the second and third floors. The street floor was occupied by the family bank, A. Wechsberg and Co., which was founded by my grandfather. I was twelve years old and not particularly impressed by the capitalistic grandeur of the bank, though I liked to watch my cousin Nellie, the bank cashier, whose nimble fingers could count banknotes with incredible speed, and it was pleasant to draw on the bank's supplies for my steady needs of fresh pencils, erasers, coloured envelopes and paper clips. But on the whole I was delighted when my mother told me, in great excitement, that we had lost the family bank and that a delicatessen would move into the premises.

I didn't know then that we had become bankrupt almost overnight. In the wake of defeat and post-war depression many small, privately owned banks were wiped out, or, like ours, were swallowed up by one of the big trusts. Of course, I didn't understand this. I thought that the change from bank to delicatessen in what I still considered 'our' house was a definite improvement. It also undermined my belief in capitalism. If banks could be replaced so readily by delicatessens, I said to myself, they couldn't be much good. I had this theory confirmed in later years. During the big depression a lot of people would have done better if they had put their money into delicatessens instead of into banks.

One of the important aspects of the new delicatessen in our house was that it would add to my social prestige in school. Otto, one of my classmates at the local *Gymnasium*, a combined senior and junior high school, was the son of the man who owned the other delicatessen in town. For years Otto, by virtue of his father's smoked eel and paprika bacon, had maintained a hold upon our classmates which I had tried in vain to break. I owned the only available soccer ball and had consequently been elected captain of the class team; even so, Otto's prestige was greater than mine. The boys were doing papers; he had set up a formidable system of enslavement that ran from a slice of goose liver for the difficult algebra exercise to a small piece of imitation-Emmental cheese (only small holes) for a Czech theme. Otto even managed to bribe the Latin-and-Greek professor, a poor, shrivelled, coughing man who suffered from tuberculosis. He would bring him sweet butter, which was a rarity in those days.

I was watching in fascination the transformation of our premises from bank to delicatessen. The wreckers and builders, masons and painters worked simultaneously and enthusiastically. The smoke-stained oakwood panels came down and the walls were painted snow-white, an audacious undertaking in a town notorious for its dirt and coal dust. The bank's wooden counter for customers, covered with pencil marks and ink spots, disappeared and a shiny, silvery aluminium showcase went up. The dark chandeliers were replaced by modern tubes of functional design which radiated a strange, cold, bluish light. Where Cousin Nellie's cashier's booth had stood, I saw a white enamel-covered table with a new-fangled cutting machine, two round, razor-sharp steel blades – moving against each other with swishing, grinding sound – that cut ham and meats into slices as thin as paper. The machine somehow made me think of self-destruction; I wondered what would happen if I put my fingers between the swishing blades, and a shiver went down my spine.

By now there was nothing left of the bank but the old, familiar shield with our name above the entrance, and one day it came down and was replaced by a modern gold-and-black sign that read, S. BITTER, and underneath, *Lahudky-Delikatessen*. The shelves at the rear wall were filled with glass jars and cans; sausages were hung up against the wall. They didn't have refrigerated counters in those days, and the meats, cheese, rows of rollmops, fish, pâtés, hams, ragouts, fowl, and fruits were kept on the counter and behind glass-covered shelves. On either side of the entrance door stood a big barrel, one containing dill pickles, the other sauerkraut. A big wooden spoon was lying across the top of each barrel, and a hand-written sign above them said,

FREE FOR OUR CUSTOMERS

Soon everybody was talking about Mr. Bitter's new delicatessen and his 'American business methods.' Mr. Bitter had once visited an uncle who owned a barbershop in Cleveland, a town in America, and thus was the uncontested local authority on matters American. Mr. Bitter was a small, baldheaded man with a long, tired face, and a drooping lower lip which he would snap up with a gasp at the end of each sentence as though he were afraid of losing it. He wore a beautiful white chef's outfit, a white apron and a battered grey derby, presumably because he was afraid of catching a head cold. According to my classmate Otto, whose father was Bitter's competitor, Mr. Bitter was simply self-conscious about his baldness. This I failed to understand: I would have gladly traded in all my hair for Bitter's delicatessen.

The truth was that Otto was envious and frustrated. His father's shop window showed a dusty, dreary pyramidal arrangement of inferior sardines and anchovy cans, and a couple of mouldy Hungarian salamis. Bitter's window, on the other hand, had been transformed into what I assumed to be a fancy champagne supper in a chambre separée. There were two chairs and a table. On the table, covered with beautiful white linen, stood a magnum of French champagne in a silver bucket, a big can of finest Beluga caviare (French label), another with whole natural goose liver truffée (French label), and a big wheel of cured Edam cheeses, with the original Dutch label. The shop window could not be opened from inside the store, and when a customer wanted a piece of expensive Edam cheese, which happened infrequently, Mr. Bitter had to go out on the sidewalk, open the window, remove the cheese, take it inside, cut off a piece, and go out again to put the cheese back in the window. A printed sign above the champagne magnum said,

FINEST IMP. SPECIALITIES SOLD ONLY HERE

The imp. (short for imported) was a clever bit of publicity. It wasn't considered ethical for a merchant to advertise his wares in one of the daily papers; the general opinion in town was that a good merchant didn't have to advertise, and that if he did, he was probably stuck with some inferior merchandise. The imp., however, gave the matter a different aspect. No one in town except Bitter had any imported specialities; the best the other delicatessen could do was Hungarian salami and Polish ham, neither of which had any exotic imp.-appeal.

Mr. Bitter was an unusual man in many ways. His only daughter Lilya, a pretty, dark-haired girl about my age, was going to school in a French-language pensionnat in Lausanne, Switzerland, and came home only for the summer vacations. This caused raised eyebrows among the other merchants, doctors, and bank directors, all of whom sent their children to local schools. Mr. Bitter proclaimed that he wanted to give Lilya all the advantages in life which he himself had been denied. That seemed a lot of rubbish to me: what better could a man expect from life than a practically unlimited choice of pâtés, pickles, carp (sweet and sour, and in aspic), meats, and finest imp. specialities?

Joseph Wechsberg, *Sweet and Sour*

DISGUSTING

ANOTHER GREAT BRITISH ECCENTRIC FAMILY were the Mitfords, and Nancy's books on her family's behaviour in the period between the wars give us a fascinating if bizarre view of upper class life. Contemporary literature is one of the surest and safest ways of discovering what people's food was actually like, and here we learn how disgusting British food could be in even the most elevated social circles.

'SADIE, dear,' said Davey, 'I am going to do an unpardonable thing. It is for the general good, for your own good too, but it is unpardonable. If you feel you can't forgive me when I've said my say, Emily and I will have to leave, that's all.'

'Davey,' said Aunt Sadie in astonishment, 'what can be coming?'

'The food, Sadie, it's the food. I know how difficult it is for you in wartime, but we are all, in turns, being poisoned. I was sick for hours last night, the day before Emily had diarrhoea, Fanny has that great spot on her nose, and I'm sure the children aren't putting on the weight they should. The fact is, dear, that if Mrs. Beecher were a Borgia she could hardly be more successful – all that sausage mince is poison, Sadie. I wouldn't complain if it were merely nasty, or insufficient, or too starchy, one expects that in the war, but actual poison does, I feel, call for comment. Look at the menus this week – Monday, poison pie; Tuesday, poison burger steak; Wednesday, Cornish poison –'

Aunt Sadie looked intensely worried.

'Oh, dear, yes, she is an awful cook, I know, but Davey, what can one do? The meat ration only lasts about two meals, and there are fourteen meals in a week, you must remember. If she minces it up with a little meat – poison meat (I do so agree with you really) – it goes much further, you see.'

'But in the country surely one can supplement the ration with game and farm produce? Yes, I know the home farm is let, but surely you could keep a pig and some hens? And what about game? There always used to be such a lot here.'

'The trouble is Matthew thinks they'll be needing all their ammunition for the Germans, and he refuses to waste a single shot on hares or partridges. Then you see Mrs. Beecher (oh, what a dreadful woman she is, though of course, we are lucky to have her) is the kind of cook who is quite good at a cut off the joint and two veg., but she simply hasn't an idea of how to make up delicious foreign oddments out of little bits of nothing at all. But you are quite, absolutely right, Davey, it's not wholesome. I really will make an effort to see what can be done.'

'You always used to be such a wonderful housekeeper, Sadie dear, it used to do one so much good, coming here. I remember one Christmas I put on four and a half ounces. But now I am losing steadily, my wretched frame is hardly more than a skeleton and I fear that, if I were to catch anything, I might peter out altogether. I take every precaution against that, everything is drenched in T.C.P., I gargle at least six times a day, but I can't disguise from you that my resistance is very low, very.'

Aunt Sadie said: 'It's quite easy to be a wonderful housekeeper when there are a first-rate cook, two kitchenmaids, a scullerymaid, and when you can get all the food you want. I'm afraid I am dreadfully stupid at managing on rations, but I really will try and take a pull. I'm very glad indeed that you mentioned it, Davey, it was absolutely right of you, and of course, I don't mind at all.'

But no real improvement resulted. Mrs. Beecher said 'yes, yes' to all suggestions, and continued to send up Hamburger steaks, Cornish pasty and shepherd pie, which continued to be full of poison sausage. It was very nasty and very unwholesome, and, for once, we all felt that Davey had not gone a bit too far. Meals were no pleasure to anybody and a positive ordeal to Davey, who sat, a pinched expression on his face, refusing food and resorting more and more often to the vitamin pills with which his place at the table was surrounded – too many by far even for his collection of jewelled boxes – a little forest of bottles, vitamin A, vitamin B, vitamins A and C, vitamins B_3 and D, one tablet equals two pounds of summer butter – ten times the strength of a gallon of cod-liver oil – for the blood – for the brain – for muscle – for energy – anti-this and protection against that – all but one bore a pretty legend.

Nancy Mitford, *The Pursuit of Love*

69

FOOD

DIXIE

WHAT IS THE DRAW of the Deep South to British hearts? My mother lived and breathed Frances Parkinson Keyes, so here is Dixie in her memory.

'Case cookin's lak religion is
  Some's 'lected an' some ain't
An rules don' no mo' mek a saint
  Den sermons mek a saint

Howard Weeden, from *Bandanna Ballads*

THE natural geographic and climatic advantages of the different sections of the sunny South have played an important part in Dixie cookery. The fertile fields, plentiful fruit trees and waterways have each contributed bountifully. Every part of the Southland is individual and distinctive in its cookery. The 'Creole Dish' of New Orleans has nothing to do with racial origin but rather indicates the use of red and green peppers, onions and garlic. Oranges, grapefruit and avocados play an important part in Florida cookery. Maryland is famous for its fried chicken and its delicious sea food recipes. One thinks of Virginia, its hot breads and its sugar-cured hams. Kentucky is known for its corn 'likker' and its flannel cakes. Only one thing is universally true: Every corner of the South is famous for its fine cookery . . .

Fine
Old Dixie
Recipes

The very name 'Southern Cookery' seems to conjure up the vision of the old mammy, head tied with a red bandanna, a jovial, stoutish, wholesome personage . . . a wizard in the art of creating savory, appetizing dishes from plain everyday ingredients. But it should be remembered that not all the good cooks of the Southland were colored mammies . . . or folks who lived on plantations. Southern city folks are also famous for their hospitality, their flare for entertaining and the magnificence of their palate-tickling culinary efforts. Most of the recipes in this book were gathered from this latter source, though they undoubtedly in many cases owe their origin to the colored mammies who rarely bothered to write down their recipes . . . for they were good cooks who most often could neither read nor write . . . didn't have to . . . you just put 'em in front of a stove with the fixin's and they created somethin' grand . . . even if they couldn't always 'splain you jus' how.

Fine Old Dixie Recipes

KENTUCKY BURGOO

(THIS RECIPE MAKES 1200 GALLONS)
'KENTUCKY BURGOO' is the celebrated stew which is served in Kentucky on Derby Day, at Political Rallies, Horse Sales and at other outdoor events. This recipe is from a hand-written copy by Mr. J. T. Looney, of Lexington. Mr. Looney is Kentucky's most famous Burgoo-maker and it was for him that Mr. E. R. Bradley named his Kentucky Derby winner 'Burgoo King'. Mr. Looney uses a sauce of his own in the preparation of this truly amazing concoction.

Mr. Looney is invited to all parts of the country to prepare Burgoo for large gatherings. This is not a dish to be attempted by an amateur though it can be prepared in smaller quantities. It is a very picturesque sight to see Mr. Looney, aided by many negro assistants, preparing this dish over open fires and huge kettles which are kept simmering all night.

600 pounds lean soup meat (not fat, no bones)	24 ten-pound cans purée of tomatoes
200 pounds fat hens	24 ten-pound cans of carrots
2000 pounds potatoes, peeled and diced	18 ten-pound cans of corn
200 pounds onions	Red pepper and salt to taste
5 bushels of cabbage, chopped	Season with Worcestershire, Tabasco,
60 ten-pound cans of tomatoes	or A#1 Sauce

Mix the ingredients, a little at a time, and cook outdoors in huge iron kettles over wood fires from 15 to 20 hours. Use squirrels in season . . . one dozen squirrels to each 100 gallons.

'Burgoo is literally a soup composed of many vegetables and meats delectably fused together in an enormous caldron, over which, at the exact moment, a rabbit's foot at the end of a yarn string is properly waved by a colored preacher, whose salary has been paid to date. These are the good omens by which the burgoo is fortified.'

Carey's Dictionary of Double Derivations

Kentucky, oh Kentucky,
How I love your classic shades,
Where flit the fairy fingers
Of the star-eyed Southern maids:
Where the butterflies are joying
'Mid the blossoms newly born:
Where the corn is full of kernels.
And The Colonels Full of Corn!

WILL LAMPTON

Fine Old Dixie Recipes

Carry dat load on your head
De Lord will bless your good corn bread.

DRIPPING

I WONDER IF THE ARMY STILL SAVES DRIPPING? Probably not: they will all be on low fat chemicals. But what an eye-opener this piece is on the Service economy and the difficulties of cooking within large organisations.

DRIPPING should all be removed from the cookhouse and weighed into store. The receptacles should be carefully ticketed, showing the quality and the purpose for which the dripping is intended.

Issues whether for cooking, in lieu of margarine, or for sale, will be made from the store. A convenient form of keeping a check and record of recoveries will be found . . . If this by-product diary is systematically entered up, the figures required in AB.48 and for the monthly economy return will be readily accessible.

A chart is given . . . showing the source and method of treatment and disposal of products which should be recovered in the treatment of the meat ration from the time it reaches the unit to the point where it is finally disposed of.

Under (A) it should be noticed that as meat is issued in sides or quarters, it follows that in the process of cutting up the meat considerable quantities of fat will be left over. This fat is known as 'butcher's fat,' so called because the ordinary butcher disposes to the trade of this surplus which arises in the reduction of meat bought wholesale to the joints and stewing meat which are sold to the general public.

It is of importance that roasting joints should not be denied of fat; on the contrary, such joints should have plenty of fat to assist the process of roasting, and to prevent the meat from becoming dried up.

The surplus collected should be cut up into small pieces, the smaller the better, or passed through a mincer, then put into a dish or pot, barely covered with water, and placed in an oven or

over a fire and allowed to boil rapidly until the water has evaporated and the pieces of fat become a light brown colour, then allowed to partly cool, strained through a colander into a clean dish, allowed to harden, turned out and scraped clean.

First-class dripping should be firm, and vary in colour from white to pale straw. If dirty or dark brown in appearance, it has either been indifferently clarified or burnt. Fat that is the least scorched should not be accepted, as it will taint everything it may be mixed with.

In Section (B) of the chart, a description of some of the sources of fat recovered during the process of cooking is given. Naturally, such a chart cannot, without undue length, give particulars of all such sources.

The liquid fat that accumulates on the surface of stocks, stews, bakes, pies, &c., and that which settled on the bottom of the dishes when roasting, must be carefully removed before the dishes leave the kitchen, not only to provide dripping, but to render the food appetising, palatable and easily digested. Dripping is clarified in the following manner:-

The liquid fat, when skimmed off the dishes, is put into a dish to cool and harden into a solid cake. It is then cleaned, broken up into pieces, put into a dish with about one quart of water, placed in an oven or on a hot plate, and allowed to boil rapidly, all scum being removed as it rises to the surface. When the water has evaporated, and the fat becomes clear, strain it into a clean dish and allow to cool; when firm, turn it out in a solid block and carefully scrape away any particle of dirt or impurity that may be adhering to the bottom.

In section (C) the method of recovering fats from refuse is given.

Precautions must, of course, be taken that fats recovered from plates, &c., do not come into contact with those destined for re-issue for cooking or edible purposes. Materials that are in any way offensive must not be treated in the cook-house.

Extra men must not be employed on the work of recovering by-products. The extra payment of cooks (A.C.I. 348 of 1916) was sanctioned on the basis of the existing establishment, and on the understanding that cooks would receive extra payment for extra duty on this work.

It should be borne in mind that it is not financially sound from the national point of view to carry out work laboriously by elementary methods, when such work can be done quicker and better by the contractors' machinery.

For instance, second-rate material may produce a brown dripping which can readily be sold as such. It may be possible by the expenditure of labour and fuel to produce an article which will pass for white, and realise a higher price, but actually it will be found that the extra money realised by the unit will be outweighed, from a national point of view, by the extra expenditure of labour and fuel involved.

Under Section (D) of the Chart Bones are dealt with. All meat must be removed from raw bones. No bones are to be sold raw ('Green'), unless there is plenty of good stock for soup and for stews. It should seldom, if ever, be necessary to make stews with water. As a general rule bones should be removed before the meat is cooked, but when this is found to be impracticable, as with mutton, they should be used for stock before being sold. This does not refer to bones collected from the men's plates after the dinner meal. All cooked bones should be collected and sold; first from the stock pot and afterwards from the dining-rooms. Under no circumstances are bones of any description to be put into the refuse (swill) tubs.

Bones awaiting despatch or collection by the contractor should be stored away from the cookhouse, in a cool airy place. Stacking or covering up will cause heating and decomposition. If bones are kept in the dark they will not be attacked by flies.

Schedule 'J'
Method of Collecting Fats from Washing-Up Water, Cook-Houses, &c.

As in the majority of Winter Quarters the water from the cook-house and wash-ups, &c. has to go into drains, it is necessary to remove as much grease as possible, for the following reasons:-

(1) The grease blocks the drains.

(2) When collected, the sale of the grease is entirely for the benefit of the men.

(3) The country requires all available grease and fats for Munition purposes.

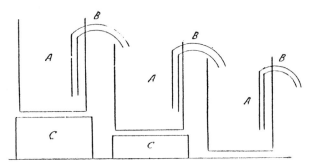

A. Represents discarded oil drums, or barrels.
B. Lengths of ½-in. gas pipe.
C. Bricks.

(The gas pipe is soldered or plugged round the hole in the receptacle.)

The apparatus acts as a water-cooler and grease collector, the greasy water is slowly poured into the top receptacle, in which most of the grease is retained, the water flowing from the bottom of the drum or barrel into the next.

When there is a reasonable amount of grease in the top receptacle. It is removed, emptied and placed at the bottom, the other two being moved up one step.

Sufficient grease being collected, it is clarified and sold.

It is strongly urged that these apparatus be established wherever possible.

Manual of Military Cooking and Dietary, 1918

DRUGS

ALICE B. TOKLAS WAS THE LOVER AND COOK of Gertrude B. Stein, and wrote this cookery book for her. It is a strangely written little book, but an interesting example of its time.

Hashish Fudge

(which anyone could whip up on

This is the food of paradise – of Baudelaire's Artificial Paradise: it might provide an entertaining refreshment for a Ladies' Bridge Club or a chapter meeting of the DAR. In Morocco it is thought to be good for warding off the common cold in damp winter weather and is, indeed, more effective if taken with large quantities of hot mint tea. Euphoria and brilliant storms of laughter; ecstatic reveries and extensions of one's personality on several simultaneous planes are to be complacently expected. Almost anything Saint Theresa did, you can do better if you can bear to be ravished by *'un évanouissement reveillé'*.

Take 1 teaspoon black peppercorns, 1 whole nutmeg, 4 average sticks of cinnamon, 1 teaspoon coriander. These should all be pulverised in a mortar. About a handful each of stoned dates, dried figs, shelled almonds and peanuts: chop these and mix them together. A bunch of *Cannabis sativa* can be pulverised. This along with the spices should be dusted over the mixed fruit and nuts, kneaded together. About a cup of sugar dissolved in a big pat of butter. Rolled into a cake and cut into pieces or made into balls about the size of a walnut, it should be eaten with care. Two pieces are quite sufficient.

Obtaining the *Cannabis* may present certain difficulties, but the variety known as *Cannabis sativa* grows as a common weed, often unrecognised, everywhere in Europe, Asia and parts of Africa; besides being cultivated as a crop for the manufacture of rope. In the Americas, while often discouraged, its cousin, called *Cannabis indica*, has been observed even in city window boxes. It should be picked and dried as soon as it has gone to seed and while the plant is still green.

Alice B. Toklas, *The Alice B. Toklas Cookbook*

Duck

One of the uses of photography in cookery books is as an aid to the technique. Properly used, a strip of photographs can tell as much as a thousand words. Ann Willan is a most remarkable woman. Born in Yorkshire, she set up La Varenne Cookery School in Paris, and earned the respect and admiration of the anglophobic anti-feminine French food world. When I moved to Scotland nearly six years ago I could only take one book with me (the rest were being shipped), and I unhesitatingly picked her *Complete Guide to Cookery*. Here is a sample on the preparation of duck.

FOOD

THE meat of a duck varies greatly from one breed to another, and so does the best method of cooking it. Some varieties, notably the American Long Island or Pekin and the British Aylesbury, have rich meat with a good deal of fat secreted under the skin. This fat must be dissolved, so thorough cooking is important.

Barbary or Muscovy ducks, and the Nantais breed popular in France, are less fatty. The Barbary is large, with generous amounts of firm breast meat; Nantais are smaller, more tender and delicately flavoured. In the United States, smaller varieties of duck can be found in Chinese markets. A new *Mulard* crossbreed is one of several offering leaner meat than the common Long Island duck. Unique to France is the Rouen duck, which resembles a game bird in taste and texture, and is killed by smothering so that its meat is dark from the blood.

Opinions differ on how well-done a duck should be. Many connoisseurs insist that the breast meat should remain pink, though the legs should always be thoroughly cooked, but this is hard to achieve with fattier breeds. For a roast bird, one common solution is to serve the breast first, while rare, then continue to roast or grill the legs.

Duck is not an economical bird as the weight of bone is high in proportion to the meat. A duckling of around 4 lb/1.8 kg serves only two people, while a 5-6 lb/2.5 kg serves six to eight people, although other breeds sometimes reach that size. A duckling or *canette/caneton* is under two months old, while a duck or canard may be up to three months. As ducks are rarely kept to lay eggs, there is no large supply of older birds. Only where they are bred for foie gras are you likely to come across them. However, foie gras producers are on the increase; there are even some in the United States. Tougher, fatty birds can be stewed, but it is better to preserve the legs *en confit*, the companion product to foie gras. The leftover fat makes wonderful fried potatoes. The breasts are boned as *magrets* and cooked rare like steak, with green peppercorns, blackcurrants or roast garlic.

Ann Willan, *Reader's Digest Complete Guide to Cookery*

ENDIVES

THE 1990S SAW A FURTHER EXTENSION of the chef/author in the form of chefs who were actually erudite, extensively read and wrote well without a ghost. One such is Simon Hopkinson, who finally left hands-on cheffing altogether for a very successful career in writing and journalism. In his beautifully written first book, *Roast Chicken and Other Stories*,

there is a great deal of autobiographical material, and this charming passage on endives with recipes illustrates very well the point I am trying to make.

Monsieur Yves Champeau of the Normandie Restaurant et Bar, in Birtle, Lancashire, would not countenance the fact that I detested the taste of endives – or chicory as it is called in England, and witloof in Belgium. Aged 16, I had taken my first holiday job at the Normandie, to decide whether this was to be my chosen career – and also to see whether M. Champeau thought that it *should* be my chosen career. A memorable statement he made to my parents one night after they had eaten dinner, was 'I shell mek 'im or brek 'im'. Encouraging words.

At lunch-time (for the staff and other members of the Champeau family, at 11 a.m.), a meal was put together and distributed to all parties. Hearing of my hatred for endives, M. Champeau decided that on this occasion I was to lunch with him and his wife Toni (she was English and at the time I thought it comical that the husband should be called Yves and the wife Toni). It transpired that, unbeknown to me, a lunch consisting of pretty well every conceivable component of the chicory family had been prepared in my honour. There were braised endives; endive salad (the leaves raw with a mustardy dressing – this was the worst); a further salad of curly endives (frisée) with fried bread croutons and garlic; and endives au gratin, for which some more previously braised endives had been wrapped in ham with sauce Mornay, dressed with cheese, topped with breadcrumbs, and browned under the grill.

It may come as no surprise to learn that I did actually come to enjoy these new tastes. I hadn't much choice. It is an adjustment of the palate that is necessary. Bitter is the taste of chicory – the French of yesteryear still miss it in their coffee – but the taste buds enjoy a 'pucker' from time to time. Rocket – that most fashionable of salad leaves – is a prime example.

When cooking endive, it is absolutely essential that you do not use water. The endive itself is pretty well all H_2O. Also, you need lemon juice to counteract the bitterness. This may sound daft, but it is true.

The Normandie's braised endives were cooked in plenty of butter, which was heated until light brown before the endives were added, gently coloured, seasoned and finished with lemon juice. They were then covered, and cooked in a moderate oven for a couple of hours. The resultant vegetable was golden brown, almost gooey, and had an aroma that was very agreeable.

M. Champeau knew his endives.

Simon Hopkinson, *Roast Chicken and Other Stories*

Enthusiasm

Ambrose Heath's books are valued today more for their William Bawden drawings, but he was very big in his day. Here he writes the introduction to Madame Prunier's *Fish Book*. Mme Prunier's Restaurant in St James's Street brought a degree of French excellence into Club Land, and was a stalwart home during the war when such delicacies as oysters and lobster were unrationed.

WHEN Madame Prunier asked me to edit and translate this book, I was not only greatly flattered, but very excited. It is not often the lot of what I may perhaps call a professional gastronomer to come across a really thrilling cookery book, but here was one at last. I read it with the avidity of a novice, and with the approval of an adept!

It is a remarkable book. Fish books are few and far between, and here is one that puts all the rest I have seen to shame. It is naturally not absolutely encyclopaedic, but there are enough recipes in it to keep all the cooks in England busy for some time to come before they have tried them all.

It is an odd thing that to an island race, used perhaps to eating fish more than most other European nations, a French-woman should have come to teach us how to prepare it, but perhaps not so odd after all, since it was a woman bearing a name which is a household word in Europe for fish. Emboldened perhaps by the revival of interest in food which has been taking place during the last few years, Madame Prunier opened her restaurant in London, and immediately set about teaching us what we could do with the fish that all our shores shower upon us. And she hit the spirit of the time, by beginning to popularise the cheaper sorts of fish, herring, mackerel, gurnard, skate – fishes which we had been used to look at askance. And she accomplished what was almost a miracle by inducing fashionable diners-out to ask for herrings, and like them, too!

Ambrose Heath, foreword to *Madame Prunier's Fish Cookery Book*

EXCELLENCE

IT IS TRULY STRANGE TO ME THAT MARCEL BOULESTIN, whose little books I have enjoyed so much, should have been the first food writer for *Vogue*. He is so essentially French, and the magazine so English – but I suppose at the time France was perceived as the culinary capital of the world and the home of chic.

CONCERNING THE ORDERING OF A PERFECT DINNER

THERE are many types of perfect dinners according to people's different ideas of what this meal ought to be. For the Abbé Morelet, the famous gourmand, it was a simple affair: *'Pour manger une dinde truffée,'* says he, *'il convient d'être deux. Je n'en use jamais autrement. Ainsi, j'en ai une aujourd'hui: nous seron deux, la dinde et moi.'*

Our modern appetites do not reach these heights and our meals are at the same time longer and shorter. Then there is the ideal dinner according to that marvellous person, 'the connoisseur of bad food.' Everything, of course, is perfect: the soup, which is thin and anaemic, full of nondescript flotsam and jetsam of doubtful origin and of faded flavour; the fish, which is upholstered with a white sauce trimmed with parsley and lined with flour; the bird or joint, desiccated (if a chicken, belonging to the sporting variety, with muscular legs) and swimming in a brown sauce which might have been a gravy soup the day before, and surrounded by homely potatoes and French beans fresh from the Turkish bath; the sweet, something jellified and mysterious the secret of which is only known to a few members of the household; the savoury, cheese straws made of bricks; then, oceans of unripe figs, of opaque grapes, of hard *marrons glacés*, of gritty chocolate; and the coffee . . . one can only say of the coffee that it leaves one speechless.

Well, as I have said before, a perfect dinner, but a perfect bad dinner. Though there is some kind of superior and perverse satisfaction in tasting that kind of perfection, it is somewhat distressing prosaically to have to stop at the coffee stall on the way home for an honest sandwich and a cup of 'white' coffee.

It comes to this: the ordering of a meal – unless you have a first-class cook who thinks about everything – is not such a simple matter as it seems. It means a certain amount of knowledge and a little consideration. A few rules should be observed: if you have a cream soup do not have afterwards a fish with a white sauce; do not make two dishes with a sharp taste follow each other; arrange your menu in a way which means the maximum of effect on the dinner table and the minimum of work in the kitchen; do not, for instance, have several things fried or two dishes which require an oven at two different temperatures. Having observed these rules you have played the game, and neither your guests nor your cook should have any ground for complaint.

Soufflé aux Huitres. – Open some oysters (say, about two dozen for four or five people) and poach them for two minutes in dry white wine. Cook two whitings in a well seasoned *court bouillon*, remove carefully the skin and bones and put the flesh in a saucepan, add a piece of butter and not quite a quarter of a pound of grated cheese, Parmesan and Gruyère mixed (more Gruyère than Parmesan); cook on a slow fire, stirring well with a wooden spoon till well melted and smooth.

To this mixture you then add your poached oysters and three whites of eggs whipped to a stiff froth. Put it into a soufflé dish and cook in a moderate oven for about a quarter of an hour. (Cover with a piece of buttered paper if the top is getting too brown.) Serve at once; in fact, as Mme. Aglate Adanson earnestly says: '*Serves le en courant.*'

Croquettes de Dinde. – One gets tired of everything, even of the best cold turkey; this is a very good way of using up the remnants. Scrape off the white flesh, trim it and cut it in small slices, also cut in the same way some good ham (about quantities, if you have half a pound of turkey you should use a quarter of a pound of ham). Peel three ounces of mushrooms, chop them finely and cook them in butter: add a cupful of consommé and let it reduce by about half. Put in a little more butter, salt, pepper, chopped parsley and spices; cook slowly for ten minutes, pass through a sieve and bind with a yolk of egg. Then pour the sauce over the pieces of turkey and ham, mixing well. The mixture, which you let grow cold, should be of such a consistency that you can then, when quite cold, make croquettes with it, but it must be fairly soft all the same. Beat an egg well, drop the mixture by small quantities at a time, roll in egg, then in breadcrumbs, again in egg and finish by another coating of breadcrumbs. Fry in very hot fat, drain well and serve with a good *jus* made with the brown of the turkey or with some other sauce, according to taste. A sauce Madère with chopped truffles in it would go well with these croquettes, but a tomato sauce would be overpowering.

Salade de Pissenlits aux Betteraves. – The humble dandelion is not to be despised as salad. It has a pleasant bitter taste and is very nice mixed with a few slices of beetroot and plainly dressed with oil, vinegar, pepper and salt. If you live in London you can get it at greengrocers, if you live in the country you have a chance of improving it by putting a flat stone or a tile over it – it then becomes white and very tender in a few days. It grows all over the place. Apparently the French and the English have different ideas about the dandelion. I have the evidence in front of me, laconical over-powering, badly printed evidence; not the evidence of scientific books or literary treatises, but that of two unbiased popular dictionaries. I have looked up the plant in both languages: the French dictionary, true to racial characteristics, says: *'genre de composées qui se mangent en salade,'* but the English work sharply and scornfully brushes aside the dandelion: 'A common plant with a yellow flower.'

Crème de Bananes. – Is a very simple and useful winter dish, being made of bananas. Peel the fruit and cut it into slices and soak them in rum for an hour. Then arrange them in a fireproof dish, sprinkle with brown sugar, add the rum. Stir lightly with a fork and bake in a moderate oven for about twenty minutes. Serve, if you like, with a rum-flavoured whipped cream.

Marcel Boulestin, *Vogue*, January 1925

EXCESSES

NOT ONLY DID THE CENTURY see great changes in cookery books, it also made a huge change in the way writers treated historical recipes. Where heretofore they had ignored them, or held them up for ridicule, it dawned on certain people that if our ancestors produced fine buildings, beautiful artifacts and exquisite tableware, they might just have eaten delicious food too. The great Maggie Black, one of our finest historical writers, was one of the forerunners of this genre. Here is a piece from her *Medieval Cookbook* on clerical excesses, which just goes to show not a lot changes!

CLERICS made up a sizable portion of the population for they included parish priests and wandering friars as well as cloistered monks and nuns. Even after the huge loss of life during the plague of the Black Death in the mid-fourteenth century, a large proportion of the population was still committed officially to celibacy and the dietary rules for clerics. But in the next hundred years, the number of clerics dwindled and their moral force waned considerably. Many monks and even more nuns became frivolous fashion-followers or unashamed gluttons, and the more literate spent hours developing subtle arguments to 'get round' such diet restrictions as remained. The main one that most clerics and laymen alike strove to avoid was the ever-repeated 'fysshe' day diet of salt herring.

Some of the recipes cooks created to titillate the palates of wealthy diners were intriguing and amusing: for instance, the mock hard-boiled eggs made of coloured almond paste dripped into the blown shells and eaten in Lent. But some of the arguments and excuses had cruel conclusions: bustards (large, swift-running birds) and beavers became extinct in early modern England because of men's greed for 'grete fowles' and the specious reasoning that beavers used their tails for swimming so they counted as fish!

Maggie Black, *The Medieval Cookbook*

Sweet-sour Spiced Rabbit
Serves Six

Egurdouce. Take connynges or kydde and smite hem on peecys rawe, and fry hem in white grece. Take raysouns or coraunce and fry hem. Take oynouns, perboile hem and hewe hem small and fry hem. Take rede wine and a lytel vynegur, surgar, with powdour of peper, of gynger, of canel, salt; and cast therto, and lat it seeth with a gode quantite of white grece; & serue it forth. (Cl.IV.23.)

6 wild rabbit joints (hind legs or saddle)
3 medium onions
75 g/3 oz pork dripping or lard
50 g/2 oz currants
275 ml/10 fl oz/1¼ cups red wine
25 ml/1 fl oz/⅓ cup red wine vinegar
15 g/½ oz granulated sugar
¼ teaspoon ground black pepper
⅓ teaspoon ground cinnamon
⅓ teaspoon ground ginger
Salt to taste
1½ tablespoons soft white breadcrumbs
          for thickening (optional)

Although the old recipe starts with a fry-up in plenty of fat, oven browning (a less fatty method than frying) suits our taste better today. Other recipes for this dish add a breadcrumb thickening, so I have provided that choice too.

Pre-heat the oven to 230°C/450°F/Gas Mark 8. Meanwhile trim the rabbit joints neatly. Peel the onions and put them in a pan of cold water. Bring to the boil on top of the stove, cook for 3-4 minutes, then drain. Chop and set aside.

Arrange the joints in one layer in a pot-roasting pan, and smear with the fat. Place the pan in the oven and sear the meat for 15 minutes or until well browned, turning once. Add the chopped onions and the currants for the last few minutes and turn them in the fat.

While browning the meat, mix together the wine and vinegar and stir in the salt, sugar and spices.

Pour off any excess fat in the pan, then pour the wine mixture over the meat and onions. Reduce the oven temperature to 180°C/350°F/Gas Mark 4. Cover the pan and cook for 30-45 minutes or until the rabbit is tender; uncover and baste occasionally with the wine mixture. Shortly before serving, stir in the breadcrumbs, if you are using them.

If you prefer, you can transfer the contents of the pan to a flameproof casserole before adding the wine, and do the low-temperature cooking on top of the stove.

Maggie Black, *The Medieval Cookbook*

FASCIST/FUTURISM

WHILST I EXPECT MARINETTI the Italian Futurist painter and ardent Fascist was the worst sort of pompous bigot in real life, I enjoy his verbal extravagances and far-fetched notions on paper.

AGAINST PASTA

FUTURISM has been defined by the philosophers as *'mysticism in action'*, by Benedetto Croce as *'anti-historicism'*, by Graca Aranha as *'liberation from aesthetic terror'*. We call it *'the renewal of Italian pride'*, a formula for *'original art-life'*, *'the religion of speed'*, *'mankind straining with all his might towards synthesis'*, *'spiritual hygiene'*, *'a method of infallible creation'*, *'the geometric splendour of speed'*, *'the aesthetics of the machine'*.

Against practicality we Futurists therefore disdain the example and admonition of tradition in order to invent at any cost something *new* which everyone considers crazy.

While recognizing that badly or crudely nourished men have achieved great things in the past, we affirm this truth: men think dream and act according to what they eat and drink.

Let us consult on this matter our lips, tongue, palate, taste buds, glandular secretions and probe with genius into gastric chemistry.

We Futurists feel that for the male the voluptuousness of love is an abysmal excavator hollowing him out from top to bottom, whereas for the female it works horizontally and fan-wise. The voluptuousness of the palate, however, is for both men and women always an upward movement through the human body. We also feel that we must stop the Italian male from becoming a solid leaden block of blind and opaque density. Instead he should harmonize more and more with the Italian female, a swift spiralling transparency of passion, tenderness, light, will, vitality, heroic constancy. Let us make our Italian bodies agile, ready for the featherweight aluminium trains which will replace the present heavy ones of wood iron steel.

Convinced that in the probable future conflagration those who are most agile, most ready for action, will win, we Futurists have injected agility into world literature with words-in-liberty and simultaneity. We have generated surprises with illogical syntheses and dramas of inanimate objects that have purged the theatre of boredom. Having enlarged sculptural possibility with anti-realism, having created geometric arthitectonic splendour without decorativism and made cinematography and photography abstract, we will now establish the way of eating best suited to an ever more high speed, airborne life.

Above all we believe necessary:

a) The abolition of pastasciutta, an absurd Italian gastronomic religion.

It may be that a diet of cod, roast beef and steamed pudding is beneficial to the English, cold cuts and cheese to the Dutch and sauerkraut, smoked [salt] pork and sausage to the Germans, but pasta is not beneficial to the Italians. For example it is completely hostile to the vivacious spirit and passionate, generous, intuitive soul of the Neapolitans. If these people have been heroic fighters, inspired artists, awe-inspiring orators, shrewd lawyers, tenacious farmers it was in spite of their voluminous daily plate of pasta. When they eat it they develop that typical ironic and sentimental scepticism which can often cut short their enthusiasm.

A highly intelligent Neapolitan Professor, Signorelli, writes: 'In contrast to bread and rice, pasta is a food which is swallowed, not masticated. Such starchy food should mainly be digested in the mouth by the saliva but in this case the task of transformation is carried out by the pancreas and the liver. This leads to an interrupted equilibrium in these organs. From such disturbances derive lassitude, pessimism, nostalgic inactivity and neutralism.'

AN INVITATION TO CHEMISTRY

PASTASCIUTTA, 40% less nutritious than meat, fish or pulses, ties today's Italians with its tangled threads to Penelope's slow looms and to somnolent old sailing-ships in search of wind. Why let its massive heaviness interfere with the immense network of short long waves which Italian genius has thrown across oceans and continents? Why let it block the path of those landscapes of colour form sound which circumnavigate the world thanks to radio and television? The defenders of pasta are shackled by its ball and chain like convicted lifers or carry its ruins in their stomachs like archaeologists. And remember too that the abolition of pasta will free Italy from expensive foreign grain and promote the Italian rice industry.

b) The abolition of volume and weight in the conception and evaluation of food.

NOCTURNAL LOVE FEAST

A TERRACE in Capri. August. The moon pours a stream of curdled milk straight down on the tablecloth. The brown-skinned, heavy-breasted native mama enters carrying an enormous ham on a tray and speaks to the two lovers who are lying stretched out in the two deck chairs, uncertain if they should renew the fatigues of the bed or begin those of the table:

'This is a ham that contains a hundred different pork meats. In order to sweeten it and free it from any possible bitterness and virulence I have soaked it for a week in milk. Real milk, not that illusory milk of the moon. Eat as much of it as you like.'

The two lovers devour half the ham. Large oysters follow, each with eleven drops of Muscat wine from Syracuse mixed into its sea water.

Then a glass of Asti Spumante. Then the *War-in-Bed*. The bed, vast and already full of moonlight, fascinated, comes to meet them from the back of the open room. They get into it, toasting each other and sipping from the War-in-Bed. It is composed of pineapple juice, egg, cocoa, caviare, almond paste, a pinch of red pepper, a pinch of nutmeg and a whole clove, all liquidized in Strega liqueur.

Formula by the Futurist Aeropoet **MARINETTI**   F. Marinetti, *The Futurist Cookbook*

FOOD

FASHION

SOME PEOPLE THINK THAT FASHIONS IN FOOD are a new thing, but I suspect that since apples became the *dernier cri* in the Garden of Eden each generation has had its particular food fad. However, the post-war years of the century have seen it increase an hundredfold. The 1980s saw the rise of the sun-dried tomato, which swept the London restaurant and deli scene as if it had not been the peasant preserve of the Mediterranean since Columbus discovered America. Now of course we have moved on, through kiwi fruit to lemon grass and cranberries, and now on again to the sun-blushed tomato! This piece from Linda Brown recalls the good old day of the sun-dried tom. Linda is not only a great cook but a brilliant gardener, and I shall never forget the barbecue I had at her house one September, when we went mad rushing round the garden slinging everything on the barbi, and discovered how good vegetable marrow is cooked in this way.

SUN-DRIED TOMATOES

SUN-DRIED tomatoes have their place, but not in everything. Usually you get what you pay for. If you can, buy them loose and insist on trying one – if you don't like it raw, think what it will do to your dish.

Good quality sun-dried tomatoes are soft, pliable and bright or magenta red in colour. The flavour is sweet and tomato-rich, tempered by a little saltiness. Poor sun-dried tomatoes are tough, leathery, dark and look more like shrivelled prunes. They have a strong, over-salty, rather unpleasant taste, reminiscent of overripe tomatoes on the verge of going mouldy.

Like dried mushrooms, a little of the rich, concentrated flavour of sun-dried tomatoes goes a long way. For this reason they should not be thought of as a substitute for fresh tomatoes, but as an ingredient in their own right.

They should be stored somewhere cool and dark. A good way is to keep them in a jar covered completely with olive oil. This makes them plump, juicy and soft. Stored like this, they will keep well for 6 months or longer, and are ready to eat as a snack on bread, or to add to pasta dishes, salads and salsas. The oil, meanwhile, takes on the flavour of the tomatoes, and can be used for cooking. They can also be bought ready bottled in ordinary olive oil, but these are more expensive, which is why it is better to do your own. Loose sun-dried tomatoes can be snipped with scissors and added directly to dishes, or rehydrated first in a little hot water. Use within 6 months.

Linda Brown, *The Modern Cook's Manual*

FISH

I SOMETIMES THINK REFRIGERATION is something of a false friend to food and flavours. We have given up so many old ways of preserving in exchange for the rather dubious and chancy preservation of chillers, and many of the outbreaks of food poisoning have been due

89

FOOD

to faulty chilling procedures. As to flavour in America, they serve food so cold it hurts the teeth and tastes of nothing. Salting, especially of fish, once one of the staples of our exports, has died away except in Portugal and the Caribbean. Elizabeth Luard, who gave up writing her wonderfully researched books on European food during a personal tragedy, was to my mind at her finest in her award-winning book *European Peasant Cookery*, and here she writes on salt fish.

STOREHOUSE SALT FISH

THE Lofoten Islands, a wild and beautiful outpost off the Norwegian coast, lapped by the warmth of the Gulf Stream, have been a centre for the preparation of dried and salt cod for at least a thousand years and probably much longer. A rocky archipelago two hundred miles inside the Arctic Circle is a long journey from the hills of the Mediterranean, but the Norwegians sprang from Viking stock and their long ships went where they pleased. It is from the cod fishermen of the North Atlantic that the peasant farmers of the Spanish, French, and Italian olive groves get the raw material for many of their favourite dishes.

Recipes for salt cod are so deeply rooted in the southern kitchen that they appear as festival food – an *aioli* with *morue* is the fast-dish traditionally prepared in France for the Christmas Eve supper. Salt cod has such excellent keeping qualities that it became one of the few items for which inland peasant communities were prepared to barter – a storeroom staple which has a high nutritional value.

The traveller, Paul du Chaillu, was much interested in the salt cod on his visit to Henningsvaer on the Lofoten in 1872:

> The warehouse of my host was a sight worth seeing: long deep rows of freshly salted codfish, six feet high, were packed together, to be afterwards laid on the rocks and dried. There are three different ways of curing the cod.
>
> The first, and the most common, is to cut the fish open, flatten, and salt it, putting it afterwards on the rocks to dry. The second is to open the fish, tie them two and two, without being salted, and hang them on frames. The third is to divide each in halves, connected only by the gills; the spine is then taken out, and the fish hung upon the frames; this method is much the quickest, as the air now operates directly on the exposed flesh of the fish, soon making it as hard as wood. It takes one to two months to dry the fish according to the season.

Every year towards the end of February, while the snow is still lying in drifts on the pebbled beaches, the cod shoals travel from the Barents Sea to spawn off the coasts of the Lofotens. From early February onwards the seaside-dwellers keep watch on the headlands and in the crow's-nests of their boats for the darkening patch of troubled water, which heralds the arrival of the fish. When the news breaks, hundreds of fishing boats scramble to sea to reap the harvest. In the old days the boats were small and sturdy single-sailed smacks, painted in combinations of green and blue, and red and ochre, which the fishermen built and patched themselves during the long winter months. Today they have company on the waves and have to compete with big ocean-going trawlers supplying modern factory conveyor belts.

Most of the fishing settlements on the wind-scoured Atlantic coast of the Lofotens have long been abandoned. Today they are ghost villages of single-roomed *rorbu*, fishermen's huts, built on wooden stilts to fringe the shoreline as close as the incoming tide would allow. Their former inhabitants can afford to build new wooden dwellings and stilt-raised boat-houses on more sheltered inlets, where the gales of the long Arctic night do not beat down their doors. These modern fishing hamlets now punctuate the islands' inshore coasts, strings of pastel-painted wooden walls stretching up the long fingers of the inlets, and petrol engines have replaced the muscle power once vital to get the boats swiftly out to sea after the shoals.

The original method of preserving fish was by wind-drying – a technique admirably suited to the cold, clean northern climate and long used by Atlantic fishermen to dry their catch on board. Scots fishermen used to hang it on the yardarm, and naturally enough it became known as 'yardarm fish'. Wind-cured in the sea air, the fish picks up a natural salt content – a good selling point for the traders since salt, after gold, was for centuries the world's most prized trading item. The resulting stiff planks of protein, which remained edible seemingly for ever, were eagerly bartered in every market from the Bosphorus to the Bight of Benin – even today shops in Ghana take annual deliveries from the north Atlantic.

During the Middle Ages the dried cod trade became so valuable that it came to the attention of the powerful Hanseatic League, a consortium of Lubeck burgers that dominated the European commodity markets of the time. The League took the trade over and ran it for two centuries from their base in Bergen in southern Norway.

Drying racks for *torrfisk* still dominate the fishing harbours of northern Norway – forests of pearl-grey wooden poles, triangular or rectangular stacks of slats that tower over the houses. As soon as the boats return, the villagers set to work preparing the catch. *Torrfisk* requires that the fish are cleaned, gutted, and tied together by the tails in pairs. These are then hung over the poles to dry – with the nets that fished the cod flung over the whole edifice to frustrate the ever-hungry gulls. By June the racks have been cleared, and the fish, now stiff and dry, are on their way for export.

Salt was not imported in quantity into Norway until relatively recently. This was perhaps because the natural preserving agents in the climate made it less important than elsewhere. In Sweden, however, the Hanseatic League wielded great power throughout the Middle Ages as the suppliers and controllers of the import of salt into the Baltic ports. Salt was vital for the preservation of the herring catch, the Skanesild, and Stockholm itself was originally a Hanseatic town. In Norway the Hansas traded grain for stockfish, and in Sweden salt for cured herring.

Norwegian exports of dried fish flourished even more when salt, largely produced from evaporated sea water, was added to the wind-drying process. Mediterranean countries soon came to prefer the salty flesh of these *klippfisk* – named after the rocky cliffs on which the cod was laid out to dry. The triangular kite-shaped sheets of fish, coated with coarse grey salt and layered in wooden crates, are still annually despatched to village shops around the Mediterranean. Today they also reach other more distant destinations whose immigrant communities long for the taste of home. Salt cod has a potent nostalgia value. A particularly pungent odour announces the arrival of the *klippfisk* to coincide conveniently with the year's first pressings of olive oil. The best Mediterranean salt-cod recipes marry the two ingredients – the harsh, pale flesh of the northern ocean and the rich, gold fruit of the southern hill slopes make a perfect union.

Portugal and Britain entered the trade during the Middle Ages. Today Newfoundland is the major source, and salt cod is now exported by Canada as well as Norway and Iceland.

Elizabeth Luard, *The Rich Tradition of European Peasant Cookery*

ALL OF US IN THE CATERING PROFESSIONS know that somewhere there exist truly horrible books of instruction, prepared to give food a bad name in the industry. Here George Lassalle proves us right.

COCKTAIL SAVOURIES FISH CANAPÉS

UNFORTUNATELY, fragments of various fish, sicklied o'er with various substances and resting on limp toast, are still to be found at official receptions and at cocktail parties serviced by caterers. Why have they survived?

I well remember (when I was working at a foreign embassy in London in the late 1940s) a reception at which a famous caterer had excelled himself with his piping bag and in the construction of every shape known to aspic geometry. Unfortunately, so crowded was the scene that very few people could, without drawing unwelcome attention to themselves, partake of the jewelled morsels. Also, a great deal of the food was so cunningly placed as to be quite out of reach. When I pointed this out to a waiter (supplied by the caterer) he gave me a solemn wink such as one expects to see on the impassive face of a hired mourner at a Connemara funeral, and said, 'It's all in the game, sir.' I was too busy then to take the matter further, but later, when all the guests had left and the fragments (of which there were considerably more than twelve baskets) had been packed up and taken away, it occurred to me that a study of the migratory habits of the *canapé* in diplomatic circles might be of some interest. On a subsequent occasion, therefore, I conspired with friends to mark a number of *canapé* with golf tees, embedding them deep in the aspic so that they appeared to be part of the decoration. These peregrinating *canapé* were later sighted at various receptions around London, and for a week or two provided an 'in' joke which relieved the tedium of these pointless functions.

The confection of these miniature masterpieces for the cocktail hour is not congenial to my temperament, nor do I propose to encourage their production in the home. As far as food to accompany cocktails or aperitifs is concerned, it seems to me that the only dividing line between this food and the *hors-d'oeuvre* should lie in the amount served of each delicacy and the 'vehicle' on or in which it is conveyed to the mouth. If you are going to serve smoked salmon as a first course at a meal, you will probably settle for fish pâté on *croûtons* with the drinks. If serving a pâté as a first course, then small pieces of smoked salmon will be in order with the cocktails.

George Lassalle *The Adventurous Fish Cook*

FOOD

Hilaire Belloc, one of the great Catholic humorous poets, wrote this charming verse which I remember so well from my childhood.

On Food

Alas! What various tastes in food,
Divide the human brotherhood!

Birds in their little nests agree
With Chinamen, but not with me.
Colonials like their oysters hot,
Their omelettes heavy – I do not.
The French are fond of slugs and frogs,
The Siamese eat puppy-dogs.
The nobles at the brilliant Court
Of Muscovy, consumed a sort
Of candles held and eaten thus
As though they were asparagus.
The Spaniard, I have heard it said,
Eats garlic, by itself, on bread:
Now just suppose a friend or dun
Dropped in to lunch at half-past one
And you were jovially to say,
'Here's bread and garlic! Peg away!'
I doubt if you would gain your end
Or soothe the dun, or please the friend.
In Italy the traveller notes
With great disgust the flesh of goats
Appearing on the table d'hôtes;
And even this the natives spoil
By frying it in rancid oil
In Maryland they charge like sin
For nasty stuff called terrapin;

And when they ask you out to dine
At Washington, instead of wine,
They give you water from the spring
With lumps of ice for flavouring,
That sometimes kill and always freeze
The high plenipotentiaries.
In Massachusetts all the way
From Boston down to Buzzards Bay
They feed you till you want to die
On rhubarb pie and pumpkin pie,
And horrible huckleberry pie,
And when you summon strength to cry,
'What is there else that I can try?'
They stare at you in mild surprise
And serve you other kinds of pies.
And I with these mine eyes have seen
A dreadful stuff called Margarine
Consumed by men in Bethnal Green.
But I myself that here complain
Confess restriction quite in vain
I feel my native courage fail
To see a Gascon eat a snail;
I dare not ask abroad for tea;
No cannibal can dine with me;
And all the world is torn and rent
By varying views on nutriment.
And yet upon the other hand,
De gustibus non disputand
-Um.

Hilaire Belloc, *Food for Thought*

FOODIES

ONE OF THE STRANGE CREATIONS of the second half of the century is the Foodie. More public than the gourmet, more disciplined than the gourmand, more driven than a society hostess after today's Lion, they were first unmasked by Rosalind Mann and Paul Levy in *The Foodie Handbook*, and here we find them in a restaurant.

DINING in a good restaurant is to a Foodie what a marvellous party is to a teenager, a big deal to a businessman, a great opera to a buff. Dozens of elements must play their parts faultlessly or the Foodie's hopes will be dashed.

The Foodie enters into a higher state when going into a restaurant. The level of response from your nose, tongue and teeth is raised, so that encountering a scented deodoriser in the restaurant's lavatory, for instance, is like being mugged. Perhaps a physical change takes place in you, as with religious fanatics who can dance on hot coals without getting burnt. It is noticeable that Foodie's tolerance of caffeine is much lower than normal people's. Normal people can drink coffee at night, but you dare not expose your sensitive blood to it after three in the afternoon, and must ask for decaffeinated (made from beans of course – not instant) after dinner, or a tisane.

As you sit in the restaurant, three of your senses are as vulnerable as an open sea anemone, and your mind is occupied by awe and the wish to worship. Like a believer in church, you do not resent the other people you see there – though they are ordering all the wrong things, and *not paying attention to the food*; you know that a restaurant needs business, even if it's from a swinishly gross plate.

Are you distinguishable to the waiters and the maitre d'hôtel? (Foodies don't say metter D) – that's Businessman's talk.) You'd better be. It is a three star restaurant, you have put aside enough money to cover the most expensive meal, you have probably travelled several thousand miles, and here you are, at the shrine, palpitatingly eager, childishly vulnerable to disappointments or slights.

Do not worry. The waiters spotted you as a Foodie as soon as you walked in. You had that air of expectancy. You treated them with the respect due to their noble profession. To you they are not minions, but men who can get dozens of people's different food on to their tables at its moment of perfection, and a succession of different wines into their glasses at the correct temperature, meanwhile dressing and redressing the table unobtrusively – all the little services to eating that you try at home and know are fiendishly difficult.

But if you have come a long way to a three-star restaurant, you are secretly hoping for some special mark of favour. And most Foodie pilgrims *are* welcomed at the shrine. Either the head waiter spots you, or more likely the proprietor was alerted when you booked, by such phrases in your letter as 'Dr Zof of Chicago asked to be remembered to you'. The restaurant does not remember Dr Z from Adam, but the keen-bean tone of your letter warned them that another Foodie approaches. They can recognise you from a telephone booking – the punctilio, the emotion. A Foodie booking at a restaurant is the nearest thing to a sex call.

When you appear in person, they make you a free apéritif or digestif ('offert' it says on the bill), or a tiny extra course you did not order, or an invitation to go around the kitchens. At the

Troisgros, at least three tables of Foodies have to be shown round the kitchens at every meal. But the restaurants are tolerant of the fans. They need a knowledgeable audience. It is not generally recognised that cooking is like acting – the chef has to feel up to the performance, he has to hear rumours of applause through the swing doors – a waiter reports that the people at table nine are overjoyed by the écrevisses, a plate comes back that has been polished to a shine by bread. A great chef is quite capable of marching into the dining-room and asking why you hardly touched a dish. Of course, Foodies have already sent a humble explanation via the waiter.

BEHAVIOUR AT A RESTAURANT

Booking

Always. Sometimes weeks or even months ahead. But you don't go on Monday – the fish might not be fresh . . .

Numbers

Two or four. Six is the maximum. Six has the advantage of only one possible placement for three couples – Foodies don't want to have to bother their heads with social niceties – but the disadvantage that none of the six can reach all the other five plates with a questing fork.

Decor

Doesn't count. Most three stars are done up hideously in specifically French bad taste. What are invariably handsome are the plates, cutlery and glasses . . .

Water

You don't want iced tap water as in America – Foodies travel such a lot they got used to drinking mineral water. Some like Perrier, others consider the bubbles vulgarly big and prefer the discreet bubbles of Badoit. (Foodie children all prefer the Perrier big bubbles and some call the other 'bad water'.)

Children

Foodies take their children to restaurants in France. The baby sits on the annuaire (telephone book) in a pink sling tied to the back of a chair. Most Foodies have been to four three-star restaurants by the age of two. British and American Foodies, like French, Italian, Chinese and Spanish parents, take their children because, one, you consider it is never too young to start. Two, Foodies are 'new' people and you don't believe that 'children should be seen and not heard'. So you push foie gras into the baby's mouth and are shocked that it picks out the chocolate among the friandises although as far as you know it has never tasted chocolate. Is this what is meant by original sin?

Rolls and bread

Yes. You believe the bread of the country is an essential element of most cuisines. Your eye whizzes like a bee over the basket the waiter offers: you take the brown, black or local roll and reject French

FOOD

bread in England (except at the Quat' Saisons – they bake their own in a French oven). You eat the roll with butter or chew even more virtuously because you eschew butter – many Foodies don't eat it because the French don't put it on the table . . .

Amuse gueule (gullet tickler)

At a three-star restaurant you are keen to see what tiny titbit will be given you first – usually a taste of the region: a weeny onion tart (Georges Blanc), a slice of saucisson de Lyon in brioche (Bocuse), or a mouthful of Welsh rarebit Gruyère (the Dorchester) . . .

What to order

Foodies discuss which of them will order which of the menus of the day. It is made plain who is the subordinate Foodie by who has to have the menu the others didn't choose. You may not be able to resist something from the carte as well, but you don't order a meal from the carte – this would be to disregard the chef's plans. You honour the chef by trying his menu. If it's a famous chef's tasting menu, a menu dégustation, you may all have it, instead of testing different dishes as Foodies are usually honour-bound to do.

Adjectives on the menu

No no no! 'Small' and 'fresh' are the only ones Foodies allow on a menu. 'Tender' rings the alarm bell hard.

In a nouvelle cuisine restaurant, the real menu is the waiter, who comes and explains the written word. He doesn't let you off a detail of what it is, where from, how cooked, how special . . .

Petits fours and friandises

Another taste treat to postpone your smoking. But most Foodies have given up cigarettes, in pursuit of the perfect palate. Actually, several famous chefs smoke.

Rosalind Mann and Paul Levy, *The Foodie Handbook*

FRUSTRATION

WE HAVE ALL SUFFERED AT THE MERCIES of a dim waiter or waitress who seems unable to comprehend a basic instruction in simple English. I remember being with my mother once in the 1960s, when Trader Vic's had just opened at the Hilton, and the restaurant was very hot. All her efforts to get the air conditioning turned up fell on deaf ears. Finally she tore a £5 note in two, handed half to the waiter and sent for the engineer. It worked. I often wonder how she would have dealt with the idiot waitress in Victoria Wood's brilliant sketch 'The Trolley'.

THE TROLLEY

Restaurant – lunchtime – businessmen. Two completely straight businessmen, waiting for pudding.

Alan Well, those figures sound very promising, Tim – how's Plymouth looking?

Tim *(waggling hand)* Plymouth? Either way, Alan, either way – it's on hold – I feel personally Plymouth could be another Exeter.

Alan Really? That's interesting.

Tim We're very much keeping an ear to the ground with Plymouth.

Alan I think what the regional boys tend to forget -

He breaks off as extremely dim waitress arrives with sweet trolley.

Tim?

Tim Alan?

Alan Just coffee thank you – yeah, the regional boys -

Tim Yes, just coffee for me too please – regional boys?

Alan Is that we have to consider the Isle of Wight as well.

They notice the waitress is still there with the trolley.

Two coffees, yes?

Waitress Coffees what?

Alan What?

Waitress Have you seen it?

Alan *(completely lost but trying not to lose face)* Erm -

Waitress Have you seen it on the trolley?

Alan Just two coffees, no sweet.

Waitress Just two coffees, no sweet?

Alan That's it. What was I – the Isle of Wight -

Waitress Have you seen it on the trolley?

Alan *(no idea what she's talking about)* No, yes, thank you.

Waitress Is it a sorbet?

Alan Just the coffees, thank you. Now, er, Plymouth -

Waitress Can you point at it?

Alan No, we don't want anything on the trolley.

Waitress Oh, anything on the trolley.

Alan No, just take the trolley away dear, thank you, and we'll just have coffee, thank you.

She wheels it away.

Tim *(to cover a sticky moment)* I must give you the print-out from Expo – it came out pretty much as you predicted -

The waitress wheels the trolley back.

Alan Yes, so I believe . . .

Waitress They're good castors, aren't they? I been right over to cutlery.

Alan We don't want a pudding, we have a lot to discuss -

Waitress You don't want a pudding.

Alan Right.

Waitress But you're having a sweet.

Tim Er love – we're just having the old 'café', coffee.

Alan I'll handle this Tim, thanks very much.

Waitress Coffee.

Alan Coffee.

Waitress Is it on the trolley?

FOOD

Alan   I asked you to take the trolley away.

Waitress   I did do.

Alan   Then you brought it back.

Waitress   Then I brought it back.

Alan   Now – take it away -

Waitress   Take it away what?

Alan   The trolley.

Waitress   The trolley. Take it away, the trolley.

Alan   And don't bring it back.

Waitress   What? The trolley!

She wheels it away

Tim   That sorted that out anyway, Alan.

Alan   Yes, well, just don't butt in next time OK, promotion's not automatic, you know.

Pause.

Yes, there, er, Expo figures – Colin, phoned them through to the top floor -

Tim   Now I didn't know that.

Alan   Oh yes, that's fairly automatic since the shake-up -

She wheels it back in.

Waitress   What did you say after take the trolley away?

Alan   Get me the bill.

Waitress   Get me the bill. No, it wasn't that.

Alan   I want the bill.

Waitress   Can you point at it?

Alan   Listen to me.

The waitress listens intently.

Are you listening to me?

Waitress   I was just then – have I to carry on?

Alan   I am not going to stand up and make a scene. Please fetch, to this table, now, the headwaiter, the man in the dark jacket pouring the wine. Just bring him here, please.

Waitress   Can you mind my trolley?

Alan   Yes.

She goes. They sit in tense silence. The head waiter arrives, suave Italian.

Head waiter   Is everything all right for you, sir? I trust the meal was to your liking, and how can I be of assistance?

Alan   I would like the bloody bill, please.

Head waiter   The bloody bill. *(In waitress's voice, with her expression)* Is it on the trolley?

Victoria Wood, *Barmy*

FRYING PANS

WHEN I WAS A LITTLE GIRL, a sweet man with a beard, who was a patient of my father's, used to come to the house. On one occasion, to amuse me, he came into the kitchen and asked me if I thought he could made a sponge cake in a frying pan. I said 'no' – I knew about sponge cakes, and they were made in cake tins. He then asked for a frying pan, and demonstrated the following recipe. The man was Philip Harben, the first of the television chefs; and when the BBC force their worst excesses on me I think – well, at least I don't have to dress up in a ruff and make a castle – yet! What Philip did teach me is that nothing is ever cut and dried in cooking, there is always another way, and if you don't have one utensil improvise.

SPONGE CAKE

IT SOUNDS fantastic, but you can in fact make a perfectly good sponge cake – or a sponge sandwich – in a frying pan. Not that I am suggesting the frying pan in preference to the oven; but if you have no oven, or have an oven, but don't want to light it just to make a sponge cake, then the frying pan will do the job to perfection.

For a sponge sandwich you will need *for each half*: 2 large eggs; 2 oz (4 dessertspoons) of *caster* sugar; 2 oz (4 rounded dessertspoons) of plain flour. In other words, for the whole job you want 4 eggs; ½ lb each of caster sugar and flour.

Grease the pan and put it on to heat very moderately. Put 2 eggs and 2 oz sugar into a bowl and beat them together until the mixture is definitely thick and frothy, no mistake about it, and holds the trace of the whisk. How long this will take depends upon the tools at your disposal. With a wire whisk it may take all of 5 minutes. With a good rotary whisk, e.g. the Prestige job, probably less than 3 minutes – and these times will be shortened if you can keep the bowl over very hot water whilst you beat. A good electric mixer will easily do it in 1½ minutes, and no need for hot water.

When you are satisfied that the mixture is unquestionably thick, add the flour (through a sieve) and mix it carefully but thoroughly in. A palate knife is a good tool for the purpose, but nothing is better than your own bare hand (but of course, the phone is sure to ring).

Scoop the mixture into the hot (not too hot) greased pan and cover it with a lid of some sort.

Keep the heat very low under the pan: what is called a head of gas will do it, or the very lowest setting on an electric hotplate.

The sponge should take 11 minutes to cook; and you can tell that it is cooked by the fact that there is no (or hardly any) sound of hissing and bubbling and the top is dry to the touch.

It is a good idea to turn the sponge out – underneath side down – onto a wire rack to cool.

As soon as the first sponge is made, do another one with the other half of the ingredients. Spread the top of the first one liberally with good jam, clap the second half on it (upside down this time, the two 'white' sides together).

And there you are. A perfectly good sponge made in a frying pan. Frankly the only tricky part is getting the pan at the right heat, for if it is too hot the surface of the sponge in contact with it will be too dark, perhaps even burned. The correct temperature is 350°F – if you are lucky enough to possess a contact pyrometer – otherwise it is a question of judgment and trial and error – but there is, luckily, a fairly wide margin for error.

For a sponge cake, such as you would serve whole – iced perhaps – use 3 eggs; 3 oz caster sugar; 3 oz flour in an 8-inch pan. And allow 15 minutes.

Philip Harben, *Imperial Frying with Philip Harben*

101

FOOD

GAME

EVER SINCE THE NORMANS set up game preserves with their brutal game laws, there has been a strong tradition of 'huntin', shootin' and fishin'' in the British Isles. This is now under attack from urban sentimentalists, the 'fluffy bunny brigade', who fail to recognise that shooting and conservation go hand in hand, or that what was once the pursuit of the gentry and the poacher is a valuable source of foreign income. Julia Drysdale's *The Game Cookery Book* is still, to my mind, the best book on the subject.

PIGEON

WE never seem to have the right number of pigeons. It is either one or 26, and when you have one you are told that you can get 15p for them at the butcher, and when you have 26 the butcher says he doesn't want them. They are the easiest birds to pluck, the feathers almost float off, but then they go on floating and get into everything. Pigeons are definitely best plucked out of doors. If you are suffering from a glut, the quickest thing to do is to peel back the unplucked skin from the breasts and take out the breasts with a sharp knife. It sounds extravagant, but most of the meat is on the breast and often there isn't the time for a mammoth plucking session, and butchers are not always cooperative. It must be so much more inspiring to be one of those French housewives of whom we are always reading. They go to a market, buy a plucked squab all trussed and barbed and start from there. I normally start from a sack full of birds costing goodness knows how many cartridges, and I feel guilty because I should have done something about them yesterday.

There is no close season for pigeons, but as they are more plump and fat when they have been living off the farmers' fields, they are best between May and October. A young pigeon has softer, pinker legs than old ones, and a round plump breast. Wood pigeons make the best eating and may be distinguished by the white ring around their necks, except when immature. A pigeon does not need to be hung, though the crops should be emptied out as soon as possible.

Julia Drysdale, *The Game Cookery Book*

THE TUAN OF the British raj had few leisure activities beyond polo and shooting. It must have been mortifying to watch what Indian staff did with the fruits of his shikari! (See also pages 220–21.)

THE Indian cook does not in the least understand the treatment of game. When it goes into the kitchen, it is either left lying in a heap on the ground, or hung up in a bunch, most likely by the legs. At the first moment of leisure the cook-boy is set to work to pluck and disembowel the whole game larder, which is then either put to dry in a strong winter wind, or laid out carefully as a fly-trap. When ordered to prepare any for the table, the cook invariably chooses the freshest-looking, and thereafter comes to say, with clasped hands and a smirk, 'The rest, by the blessing of God, has gone bad.'

A sportsman, therefore, who desires to eat of the sweat of his brow without making experiments on his teeth and his stomach, will, when in camp, have regular *shikar* sticks for each day of the week, and strict orders should be issued that the birds are not to be touched without a reference to supreme government. It stands to reason that if a bird is plucked and clean, it will dry to a chip; while if it is hung up by the legs, the parts most liable to go bad are forced into the breast, and are likely to taint it. If it is necessary to draw the birds, this should be done without plucking them, and a bit of charcoal may be put inside the bird with advantage. All game birds, except snipe, should before dressing be thoroughly washed out with scalding hot water to which some charcoal has been added.

Grace Gardiner and Flora Annie Steel, *The Complete Indian Housekeeper and Cook*

GENTLEMEN

I THINK GENTLEMEN'S CLUBS are splendid institutions, and have never understood the feminists' objection to them. If your man has gone off to his club it's rather like fishing: he's not out womanising or worse! It's a safe haven, and if he feels he's ruling the world from his own group, well where's the harm? I suppose it's the Just William–Violet Elizabeth syndrome. I had a friend whose ultra-controlling wife wished to be his only advisor, and the result is that his children eschew him, his friends and acquaintances are disastrously chosen by her, and you can write the rest yourself. Far better if he had gone to his club – and he'd be less likely to run off too! The food in such clubs is very specific, and rather reminiscent of the Edwardian country house nursery. These dishes are a phenomenon which may not long survive the century, and are here encapsulated by Robin McDouall in his *Clubland Cookery*.

ASPARAGUS SOUP

THIS, in a club, will be called Crème Argenteuil, even if the asparagus comes from Hampshire, Worcestershire or Norfolk – part of our snobbism of nomenclature. The gospel according to Escoffier says:

'Parboil for five or six minutes one and one-half lb of Argenteuil asparagus, broken off at the spot where the hard part of the asparagus begins. Drain them and set them to complete their cooking gently in one and one-quarter pints of previously prepared Béchamel.

Rub through tammy; add the necessary quantity of white *consommé*, and heat without allowing to boil.

⁂
UN AN
Paris et Départements, 10 fr.
Étranger, 14 fr.

SIX MOIS
France, 5.50 — Étranger, 7.50

Le Rire

JOURNAL HUMORISTIQUE PARAISSANT LE SAMEDI

⁂
Félix JUVEN, Directeur
122, rue Réaumur, 122
PARIS

VENTE ET ABONNEMENTS
9, rue Saint-Joseph, 9

— Et Alice ?
— Elle est aux cabinets.
— ... Rien de grave ?
— Non... elle a été se mettre de la poudre.

Dessin d'Abel FAIVRE.

Finish with cream when dishing up.

Garnish with two tablespoonfuls of white asparagus-heads and a pinch of chervil *pluches*.'

Far be it from me to suggest that I can improve on the old master, but my way is, I think, simpler and gives a stronger taste of asparagus – to be done late in the season when asparagus is not too expensive.

2 bunches asparagus	salt and pepper
1 pint milk	¼ pint cream

COOK one bunch of asparagus and the hard parts of the stalks of the other in salted water so as to make an asparagus stock. Strain. Cook the tender parts of the other bunch of asparagus in this stock. When soft, put through a blender (asparagus stock and asparagus). Reheat with the milk, correct the seasoning and, just before serving, add the cream.

Equally good cold.

JOCKEY CLUB EGGS

I DOUBT if I shall ever get inside the Jockey Club (in Paris, I mean). Equally. I doubt if I shall ever make the dish of this name, from Escoffier:

'Cook the eggs in an omelette-pan; tilt them gently on to a dish, and trim them with a round fancy-cutter. Place each egg upon a round, thin piece of toast, and then cover them with foie gras purée. Arrange them in the form of a crown, on a dish, and pour into the middle a garnish of calf's kidneys cut with dice and *sautéd*, and truffles similarly cut, the latter being cohered by means of some dense half-glaze.'

See what I mean?

NEW CLUB PÂTÉ

THIS comes from the New Club, Edinburgh

2 lb pig's liver (must be fresh)	small clove of garlic
1 lb fat bacon (ask for waste ends) – remove rind	small pieces of onion
¾ lb streaky bacon to line casserole	black pepper, salt

REMOVE tubes and waste matter from liver, cut up into small pieces, cut fat bacon into small pieces, add salt, pepper, onion and garlic and put all this into the mincing machine. Repeat three times using finest cutter, then beat mixture to blend into smooth texture (if one has a liquidizer this would save a lot of time).

Line a 10 in. casserole with bacon (without overlapping rashers) right to the rim. Place mixture in casserole. The mixture must reach about ½ in. higher than the rim of the casserole so that one may be able to press when cooked. Cover the top of the casserole with more bacon, sealing the mixture completely. Place in Bain Marie (pie dish of water). Put in oven (regulo 3 for about 1½ to 1¾ hours).

Should yield slightly to the touch when ready (holds heat for some time while cooling). Remove from oven. Place tray on top and cool under pressure. When cold put it in refrigerator; 12-18 slices.

To remove from casserole, heat outside of casserole under hot water for a few minutes.

A tablespoon of vegetable oil added to the mixture will keep it from getting too dry.

Robin McDouall, *Clubland Cookery*

GLUTTONY

THIS WAS ONE OF THE FIRST BOOKS I bought after I got sober in 1987. How could I resist the title! We all know a true gourmet is never a glutton – that's a gourmand – but it's nice to have it reiterated.

WINTER is the time for substantial, solid meals.

Cold makes one feel hollow and gives one a big appetite.

I must confess I have no great esteem for such a thing.

A true gourmet is never a glutton, and to appreciate cooking, one need not feel perpetually famished. Anything is good enough for those suffering from this infirmity and I am not going to trouble myself about them.

I have no advice for them. Let them stuff themselves with bread and swallow slices of more or less cooked meat. For them, it is only quantity that matters.

The civilising art is not meant for ostriches, for mouths that will take and swallow blindly whatever is thrown to them.

Many proverbs lie, but the one that says 'a hungry man has no ears' pleases me greatly. It is, however, not complete. A hungry man has neither hearing, smell, nor taste.

My late master's acquaintances were very exclusive, but I have heard that there are people who, at table, ask for a second helping of a dish they like.

How crude and how mistaken!

True epicures occasionally let themselves be caught in this trap, and then swear they will never let it happen again.

A certain dish may have seemed perfect and they have enjoyed it as they should have done. It has been offered again and they have let themselves be tempted, but hardly has the plate been refilled than they have bitterly regretted their action.

The piece which they first took was excellent and the one they fished out later is not so good, for the flavour of a stew or grill does not last. To take a second helping is like seeing a bad performance of a play that one has already seen acted by a first-rate company, or like re-reading a book the interest of which is exhausted; it nearly always means disillusion and a meal spoilt.

Winter is the time for big dinners, but I have not wiped my spectacles and filled my inkpot for the duchesses whose receptions are religiously described in the fashionable papers, nor for the bankers who entertain their shareholders or their board of directors.

Such a meal is not a dinner, but a banquet or a debauch.

You understand, of course, that I can only speak of these feasts from hearsay, but I am, nevertheless, aware how such things are done.

My good master, to whom I am always referring, and who was sometimes obliged to be present at these gala festivities, declared that even the most elementary rules of decorum were not observed. Long-legged rascals of lackeys, he used to tell me, with a confidential smile, were allowed to pass behind the guests, murmuring in their ear when they offered them wine: 'Chambertin 1911, Musigny 1906 . . .'

The good man was of a peaceable disposition, but this way of treating guests exasperated him.

'It is an insult,' he would assert, slightly raising his quiet voice, which I can still hear, 'a deep insult. A hostess ought to trust the taste and knowledge of those she invites to dine. Those solemn servants, whispering the name of the wine while pouring it into your glass, seem to be saying: "Doubtless you have never drunk anything but wretched wine, so we have been told to warn you every time you are honoured by being given something to drink. Left to yourself you would certainly never know the district or recognise the vintage . . . Make no mistake . . . This comes from Bordeaux and this from Burgundy . . . You would of course never even think of it, and swallow it all indiscriminately like a boor . . . Next time, perhaps, we may be ordered to tell you the price of each bottle, so that nothing shall be left to your imagination." '

To boast of the menu or to draw attention to the things one offers is in deplorably bad taste, but we do not always find those in the highest places setting the best example and the art of living is not given to all millionaires. This reminds me of a charming little tale that I read in a book of Banville's.

A country parson once unexpectedly entertained his bishop who was on tour in his diocese, and the maid-servant apologised for having nothing to offer his lordship but a pie and an omelette.

The bishop accepted the position quite cheerfully, and when the omelette arrived, he tasted it, praised it enthusiastically and complimented the cook.

'Oh,' said Maguelonne, shyly, 'it is only an omelette made with shrimps and carp's roe, over which I have simply poured the gravy of a partridge and a quail.'

I quote this sublime sentence, pronounced so humbly by the old cook, to show that even a servant can possess true refinement.

Anonymous French Connoisseur, *Clarisse or The Old Cook*

GOLDFIELDS

MY MOTHER WAS FIFTH-GENERATION AUSTRALIAN, which will mean nothing to you unless you too are Australian. The family were mostly engineers, and my great-grandfather went to Gympie in Queensland for the gold. I was raised on stories like those contained in this splendid book *When Mabel Laid the Table*. Australia is a harsh continent and raises strong brave women, and I am proud of my maternal inheritance.

109

FOOD

L<small>ATE</small> in the nineteenth century, the bush rang with tales of James Tyson better known as 'Hungry' Tyson. Tyson (1823-1889) was an Australian-born pastoralist and millionaire landowner, who reputedly deserved his reputation as the meanest man in Australia. One tale tells of Tyson employing a young ward of the state to work in his household. When a girl arrived it was discovered that she was suffering from sandy blight, a common disease causing diminished eyesight. Even though the girl could hardly see, she was immediately put to work. It was Tyson's habit to carve the meat for the evening meal so as to limit the amount of rations provided.

One evening, as he passed the plate to the young girl he quizzed. 'And how are your eyes, young lady?'

She replied, 'Poorly, sir, I can hardly see the meat on my plate.'

Next evening, as he passed the thin slice of meat, he questioned, 'And how are your eyes this evening?'

'I think they're getting better, Mr Tyson,' replied the girl, 'I can now see the plate through the meat!'

Another Hungry Tyson yarn concerns Tyson telling his stockhand he had arranged to feed them both while they were out fencing. At lunchtime Tyson produced two eggs which he boiled and proceeded to eat. As he scoffed the eggs down his worker protested, 'But Mr Tyson, you said you'd bring my lunch!'

'And I certainly have,' snarled the squatter, as he pointed to the water that had boiled the eggs, 'Egg soup!'

The pioneers devised all sorts of ways to keep flies from spoiling food. They cleaned their windows with a cloth soaked in Kerosene or paraffin oil, they moistened an old rag with oil of lavender and left it near the open windows, cloves were hung from the candle-holders and pots of fennel were placed in strategic places. If all that failed, they made a fly paper by cutting strong brown paper into strips and soaking them in alum, allowed them to dry then coated them with a mixture of boiled linseed oil, resin and honey.

The rush to the diggings in the early 1850s created large tent cities where food was generally in short supply, controlled by goldfields merchants who set up 'tent stores'. Native foods were far cheaper than potatoes and flour, but the goldfields store owner usually made more money than the miner. These stores offered a wide range of merchandise, including baking powder, imported tea, chicory, preserves and condiments as well as clothing, household furnishings and books. Still, the Australian goldfields saw the extremes of starvation and excess; jubilant miners on the Victorian goldfields would drink champagne while lighting their fat cigars with a five-pound note while at the same time, miners were starving to death on the way to the remote Palmer River in Queensland. A common story in gold-crazed Melbourne concerned miners striking it rich and hitting the finest restaurants, where they would order two slices of bread and then proceed to put a ten-pound note between them and eat it.

As gold strikes were announced, the rush would move from site to site, state to state, leaving a trail of tracks that became roads, shanties that became hotels and miners who became farmers. It was the discovery of gold that really opened up Australia, increasing the demand for an organised communication and transport system. By the 1880s there was a workable network of roadways and riverways that transported the wool, beef and wheat down to the cities and returned laden with supplies for the station owners.

Flour was the most important ingredient in the bush pantry and Australians made a culinary artform out of the wheat 'dust'. Bread, damper, Johnny cakes, puftaloons, doughboys, pikelets, scones and many other foods owed their existence to flour, water, salt and not much else.

Warren Fahey, *When Mabel Laid the Table*

Guilt

IN THE DARK DAYS OF THE 1970S, when English cooking had few friends and fewer followers, the late Michael Smith was a lone voice in the wilderness crying its praises and reworking some of the better historical recipes. As a pragmatic Yorkshireman he had few illusions, however, about his fellow countrymen and their attitude to food, as is seen here in a piece on guilt. I have never understood food-guilt, and I suspect neither did Michael. It is a curious phenomenon seeded, I suspect, by the food shortages of the two world wars, nurtured by American puritanism and brought to parturition by the health faddists.

AFTER the French Revolution many of the great French chefs fled to England, and the fashion to employ them in English kitchens grew. Their style, with their 'tricks and kickshaws', rapidly eclipsed the simple elegance so unmistakable in English cookery then. About the same time our own Industrial Revolution, responsible for so many social changes in this country, was creating a period of enormous wealth amongst the upper and middle classes, who were only too happy to jump on the bandwagon of French cookery. It was this, together with the new 'below-stairs' attitude to cooks and cooking fostered by the Victorians and the Edwardians, as well as two world wars and periods of depression, which brought English cooking into disrepute.

We are guilt-ridden to this day at the mere thought of half a pint of thick, thick cream or half a pound of rich butter which, together with a Victorian hangover of nursery food and the birth of home economics, has done little to help us regain our indigenous style. Why, even I can remember what a social crime it was to discuss food at the table; the very word was almost as taboo as the word sex! It is tempting to go into long arguments and delve further into our social history and even to doubt Isabella Beeton's efficacy. But this would bog us down and most certainly destroy any spontaneous enjoyment of the recipes.

There will be those who perhaps find my choice arbitrary. There will also be some who only think well of dishes from the 'stoves of France' and to whom anything not from the French kitchen is anathema. But I feel sure there are enough chauvinistic English men and women who, like myself, enjoy showing what our great country has to offer, but may have a somewhat damp wicket when the batting is at the kitchen end and feel they must resort to 'foreign' parts for a worthy dish.

Regional dishes, as we call them, have not suffered the fate of the many richer and more elegant English recipes. But even these are somewhat difficult to link with their origin at times, so much have they changed face. I have used some few of these and, where necessary, have restored them to one version of their original content – I say one version, for opinions have always differed on minor points, as is healthy, justifiable and regional!

Michael Smith, *Fine English Cookery*

HAGGIS

HAGGIS IS A WORD WE ALL ASSOCIATE WITH SCOTLAND, but unless we are Scots or have been tempted to try it it is also synonymous in our minds with something unpleasant or unmentionable except as a joke. This passage from Marian MacNeill's famous *Scots Kitchen* expresses the outsider's view on our cuisine. I of course choose to live in Scotland, and not just for the breakfasts.

'WHEN shall I see Scotland again?' writes Sydney Smith, the witty English divine, who spent five years (1798-1803) in Edinburgh. 'Never shall I forget the happy days I spent there amidst odious smells, barbarous sounds, *bad suppers*, excellent hearts, and the most enlightened and cultivated understandings.'

This view was shared by the average peninsular Englishman. One anonymous writer tells us that he was so disgusted at the mere sight of haggis and sheep's head that he could not bring himself to taste them. True, the 'honest sonsy face' of the haggis is hardly calculated to inspire an appetite in the uninitiated (though it did inspire Burns to an ode), and a singed sheep's head, to the eye, is no lovesome thing, God wot (though we have Dorothy Wordsworth's word that 'Coleridge and I ate heartily of it'), but Dr. Johnson's comment is more sagacious:

'Their more elaborate cookery, or made dishes, an Englishman, at the first taste, is not likely to approve, but the culinary compositions of every country are often such as become grateful to other nations only by degrees.' And Professor Saintsbury, another Englishman, and a distinguished critic of food and wine, as well as of letters, writes:

'Generally speaking, Scotch ideas on food are sound. The people who regard haggis and sheep's head as things that the lips should not allow to enter them, and the tongue should refuse to mention, are, begging their pardon, fools.'

Breakfast, however, is the meal upon which we Scots particularly pride ourselves.

'In the breakfast,' says Dr Johnson, 'the Scots, whether of the Lowlands or mountains, must be confessed to excel us. The tea and coffee are accompanied not only with butter, but with honey, conserves and marmalades. If an epicure could remove by a wish in quest of sensual gratification, wherever he had supped, he would breakfast in Scotland.'

Florence Marian MacNeill, *The Scots Kitchen*

HAREMS

RAFAELLA LEWIS'S IS ONE OF THE MOST FASCINATING BOOKS on the *mores* of the harem, an institution which has sadly and surprisingly survived the century.

EXCEPT on ceremonial occasions the food in Turkish houses was very simple and the drink was water, and little time was spent on eating. The master of the house, if he had no guests, would sometimes choose to eat with his wife and children in the harem, and he was always served first, either by his wife or by a servant. The family stood around him, and no one would sit or take a mouthful until he had begun and given them permission to join him. The dietary laws had few but rigid taboos, which forbade the eating of any animal that had not been slaughtered 'In the name of God'; its throat cut near the head, severing the windpipe, gullet and carotid arteries. It was forbidden also to eat animals found already dead, or the meat of pigs.

Breakfast, which was taken very early in the morning just after the dawn prayer, consisted for the poor of bread, curd cheese, olives and, especially in cold weather, soup. The wealthier had white cheese, fruit, jams and preserves with bread, and drank glasses of tea. The main cooking for the evening meal was done in the afternoon, and lunch at home consisted of what was left from the day before. The poorer people ate a great deal of onion and garlic to flavour their coarse bread, as well as sheepsheads and tripe and the other offal of those beasts who supplied the rich with meat. Cheap vegetables made their thick soups, and rice was their staple starch; milk and buffalo yoghurt were popular and inexpensive, and these foods were consumed with dispatch in the late afternoon when they came home from work. Artisans and labourers who could not get home for lunch took a little helva, or an onion and a piece of bread tied in a kerchief, and this, with a little water, was their midday meal. Those who sent out for food from the cookshop usually had a dish of stew and a little rice, or else some milk dish such as rice-flour pudding, or junket from the pedlar with the tray of bowls on his head.

In better homes, and particularly if there were guests, the evening meal consisted of several dishes of pilaffs, soups and stews, always served consecutively and in quick succession. Everybody washed before all meals, particularly the right hand which was reserved for clean occupations, especially eating. A tray was brought in and placed on a low stool to form a table. It was laid with spoons and metal plates, or with large flat pieces of bread, either leavened or unleavened, which were used as plates and themselves consumed at the end of the meal. The diners sat on the floor round the tray, the right knee raised and the left flat on the ground, and in this way as many as twelve people could sit round a 'table' three feet wide. The right arm was bared to the elbow and the hanging end of sleeve tucked up, and each diner had a napkin or shared a long narrow towel draped round to cover everyone's lap. The master of the house said 'Bismillah' – 'In the name of God' – and the meal began.

Spoons were only used for soup and other liquids; all other food was picked up in the fingers, and for this reason it was always prepared in pieces of suitable size, and large joints of meat, or fowl, were served boned and so well cooked that they were easily broken up at the table. To eat rice, a portion was taken from the dish between the thumb and fingers and pressed into a wad, to be conveyed neatly to the mouth. Water, or sometimes sherbet, was drunk at the end of the meal. Great decorum was observed throughout: fingers were never licked, there was no belching or lip-smacking. Then the hands were washed again under water poured, by the wife or a servant, from a tall ewer into a copper bowl with a perforated cover.

All Turks, and indeed all Muslims, had a great taste for sweet things, but these were never eaten with the meal except at wedding parties and banquets. The sweetening was provided by honey or a thick molasses made from grape sugar, called pekmez, and these and a variety of flavourings were used for dozens of sweet dishes and pastries, sometimes served with thick heavy buffalo cream and eaten at any time of the day, both in the selamlik and the haremlik.

In larger households food was stored according to the season, and tremendous supplies were laid in, in the autumn, of the season's oil, onions, honey and pekmez, preserved meats and fish, pickles and jams and fruit syrups, rice and cracked wheat and flour, nuts and dried fruits and cheeses. Fat-tailed sheep provided lard for cooking as well as oil for lamps, and baskets of fuel for the stoves and fodder for the animals were stacked in the courtyard. In the spring and summer an enormous variety of fresh fruit and vegetables and salads were available in Istanbul, where food from all corners of the empire was both cheap and plentiful, and in many other towns; in the country the variety was limited by the local quality of the soil and standard of husbandry, as well as by the very low gastronomic standard and the scant social importance attached to meals.

115

FOOD

Whatever one's resources, however, the entertainment of a guest was a sacred duty, no matter how unexpected his arrival. Food and drink, of the best that could be provided, were at once offered, as well as a bed if the visit were protracted, and while he was under the family roof the guest's needs and preferences were accorded overriding importance. If, when he left, he had a considerable way to go, he was supplied with food for the journey.

Casual visitors, no matter how familiar with the family, would in no circumstances enter a house unannounced, or without calling 'Destur' to warn the ladies of the household to retreat into the harem. A certain formality characterised the social relationships of all classes, and even the conventions of greeting were rigidly observed. Thus, a person riding saluted a man on foot, a man walking by greeted those sitting or standing still, a small party gave the first salutation to a larger party, the young to the old, the one entering a house to those within. Between Muslims the greeting was 'Peace be on you', and the reply 'On you be peace, and the mercy of God and His blessings', both said with the right hand on the breast, or raised to lips and forehead. Within the household, a son kissed his father's hand, a wife her husband's, and a slave or servant his master's, or, to show great humility, the sleeve or hem of his robe.

It was the observance of these and many other conventions of behaviour and manners that gave such solemnity to the pace of public life; their civilising effects combined with the innate humanity of the Turkish character to bring dignity as well as pattern to their domestic life.

Rafaella Lewis, *Everyday Life in Ottoman Turkey*

HAUTE CUISINE

THE CENTURY SAW THE GROWTH OF THE GREAT HOTELS and the intricacies of French *haute cuisine*, which have translated so execrably into the British system. One name shines above all the rest, August Escoffier, rescued by the great César Ritz after he was sacked from the Savoy for fiddling the books. He was the chef of whom Edward VII said 'where Escoffier cooks I dine', thus nearly ruining the Savoy, establishing the Ritz and incidentally tranferring the *demi-monde* to the Cadogan Hotel just long enough for Oscar Wilde to be arrested there!

SAUCES

THE preparation of sauces requires a great deal of care. One must not forget, in fact, that it is through the subtlety by which our sauces are constructed that the French cuisine enjoys such a world-wide supremacy.

I will not enter here into the details which the preparation of sauces requires in the large kitchens of restaurants and hotels. This would be superfluous.

On the contrary, the object of this work is to simplify formulae, to make them as clear as possible, to bring them within the grasp of everyone and to make the housewives' task an easy one.

In our cuisine we have three fundamental sauces, which are:

The so-called 'sauce espagnole', which is in fact just a brown roux bound with a brown stock.

The thick white sauce, or 'velouté', which only differs from the espagnole by being made with white stock, bound with a roux kept as white as possible.

Sauces prepared with these brown and white juices or stocks are used in various preparations of fish, meat, poultry, game, etc. Being added to these, they heighten their flavour.

Béchamel sauce. This sauce, from the economic point of view, may be considered the queen of sauces. It lends itself to many delicious preparations and harmonises as well with eggs, fish and meat as with poultry and different kinds of game and vegetables. An additional advantage is that its preparation takes little time.

Following this, we have tomato sauce, which also plays an important part in modern cookery.

Then there is meat glaze, which is not always appreciated at its true value and which, nevertheless, when it is carefully treated can occasionally be of the greatest use.

In the large kitchens of hotels and restaurants, these basic sauces are prepared every morning, and it is only in this way that a rapid service, in the best conditions, can be secured.

These 'mother sauces' allow, at a moment's notice, the preparation of all the small compound sauces, recipes for which will be found farther on.

SAUCES DE BASE
BASIC SAUCES
Les roux
THE ROUX
The roux are the bases of most sauces.

Roux brun
BROWN ROUX
Roux to bind 2½ – 3 pints (U.S. 6¼-7½ cups) brown stock: 1½ oz. clarified butter, slightly more sieved flour

Place the butter in a saucepan of convenient size, blend with the flour and cook slowly. Once cooked, the brown roux should be nut-brown in colour and very smooth.

Roux blond
LIGHT BROWN ROUX
The ingredients are the same as for brown roux, but cooking must be done very slowly, and discontinued as soon as the roux begins to turn colour.

Georges Auguste Escoffier, *Ma Cuisine, A Guide to Modern Cookery*

HEALTH

THE CENTURY HAS BECOME MORE AND MORE THREATENED by the wholesale use of chemicals in farming and agriculture. It was not really a problem before, as the chemicals were expensive and not easily obtainable. Lady Evelyn Balfour, the great organicist, foresaw the problem very early, and we who are reaping the whirlwind can only admire her vision.

IF 'FAULTY FOOD' is the correct reply to our question, 'Why so much sickness?' – if we are, in fact, what we eat – then the logical next question is: 'What is the matter with our food?' For while it seems clear that much of the blame must rest on our often ill-chosen diet, the complete answer must go deeper than this. In the U.S.A., for example, a very great deal of attention is paid to the proper balancing of diet, and milk, green leaf vegetables, and raw salads (McCarrison's 'health foods') are eaten in large quantities, yet America's '100 million illnesses a year' does not suggest that her people are markedly healthier than we are on that account. Dr. Alexis Carrel states that 'modern man is delicate'. If the primary cause of this decline in vigour is faulty nutrition, then the natural conclusion is that there must be something lacking in the quality of our foods themselves; something which was not lacking in the foods of our more robust forefathers.

In this chapter I shall present the evidence supporting the view that this conclusion is correct. Some part of this deterioration in food is, indeed, readily demonstrable and is due to the commercial development of 'processed food' wherever this has involved submitting it to treatment which profoundly alters its bio-chemical constitution.

The case of white flour is an outstanding example of such alteration. In removing the germ, modern methods of milling have removed those parts of the wheat berry which contain the vitamins B and E, a removal which, until the introduction of the National loaf and except for a brief period during the last war, has been complete since 1872. The everyday results of this are well illustrated in the following anecdote from Adrian Bell's *Men of the Fields*.

'I found a man of over seventy cutting up a fallen tree. . . . He used a curious phrase to justify the conditions under which the men of his father's generation had worked. "Well, they had their life," he said. "Mind you, I couldn't work to-day like they worked – not if I was young, I couldn't work like I worked as a young man. The bread to-day hasn't got the stay in it. I know, because I've worked on it. When I used to go to work and we baked at home, when I'd had my breakfast that'd stay by me to dinner-time. But when we took to bakers' bread, why, after you'd worked for an hour that'd be gone and you'd feel faint inside." '

. . .

'Note. The insecurity of reliance upon orange juice to correct the damage done to milk by heating it (pasteurizing, boiling, or drying) is rendered more obvious by the common use of cold storage for oranges, as, according to Professor Plimmer, vitamin C is slowly destroyed by freezing.'

'Dr. Evelyn Sprawson, London Hospital, stated that children in the institution in which he worked, who were fed on raw milk had perfect teeth, whereas others in circumstances identical in all respects except that their milk was pasteurized, had defective teeth.'

This is a point worth underlining in view of the present agitation in favour of compulsory pasteurization. There would appear to be some, as yet undefined, harm done to foods by long storage of any kind, whether frozen, heated and tinned, or dried (probably least by drying).

McCarrison states:

'There is something in freshness and quality of foods which is not accounted for by the known chemical ingredients of food: proteins, fats, carbohydrates, minerals and vitamins.'

. . .

Viel mehr Milch, Butter, Käse!

HEALTH

The loss to the livestock industry caused by such complaints as mastitis, contagious abortion, Johne's disease, foot-and-mouth disease, swine fever, swine erysipelas and white scour – to mention only a few – runs into millions of pounds annually and is on the increase. I well remember, for example, that when I was an agricultural student in 1915 we were told by our lecturer on animal hygiene that foot-and-mouth disease need not concern us, since the disease was obsolete in this country. It is commonly held that the prevalence of foot-and-mouth in the last decade is due to imported meat. Col. G. P. Pollitt, in his little book *Britain Can Feed Herself*, expresses this view. 'The repeated outbreaks in this country,' he states, 'are primarily, if not wholly due to our imports of uncooked meat.' I find this explanation unconvincing; the imports of meat into this country in 1913, shortly before the disease was said to be obsolete, amounted to 1,163,911 tons. In 1936, when it was most emphatically not obsolete, imports were 1,404,069 tons, only 240,158 tons more, while in the summer of this war year of 1942, when imports must have been very much less, there were nearly 700 outbreaks of foot-and-mouth. When the prevalence of this disease is considered in conjunction with the increase in most other diseases, it is impossible to avoid the conclusion that our livestock is less robust than it used to be.

. . .

It seems that it is not only desirable for our own food, whether animal or vegetable, to be as fresh as possible, but for those foods themselves also to be nurtured on a living diet. Until the war forced us to look once more to our own soil for the sustenance of our farm animals, this all-important element of 'freshness' has to a large extent been eliminated from the feeding of our livestock by the introduction of crushed seed cakes, and other imported processed foods. And the crops which we grow, whether for direct human consumption or as food for our livestock, are likewise being fed on substitutes for their natural diet of living organic matter. This change has resulted in our soil being seriously denuded of its humus content, with a consequent loss of fertility.

History suggests that a decline in soil fertility is always accompanied by a corresponding decline in the vigour of the people who dwell upon it.

To those who doubt this, I recommend a study of the fall of the first Roman Empire. The point was stressed quite recently in a broadcast by the Minister of Agriculture who affirmed that the basis of a strong nation lay in the fertility of its soil. The necessity to-day is to re-define the word fertility. I would remind you of a sentence in the Survey of Soil Erosion, quoted in the first chapter, that 'Increase of production must not be confused with increase of fertility. Increased production for human use can be, and usually is, secured by cashing in on existing fertility and using it up with the disastrous effects described.'

This is what has been happening throughout the world, but in this country the process did not really begin in a way that was serious until about 100 years ago, when chemical fertilizers were introduced. Before that time soil fertility was maintained by a combination of suitable crop rotations, bare fallows, and the application to the land of various forms of organic matter, principally farm-yard manure. In 1840 the famous German chemist, Liebig, published an essay, 'Chemistry in its application to Agriculture and Physiology', which has profoundly affected Western civilization. In

FOOD

this he propounded his theory of mineral plant foods. Roughly this rather naive theory is that everything required by a living plant is to be found in the mineral salts present in the ash of such a plant after all organic matter has been destroyed.

It seems a curious thing that this theory should have gained such ground as to overthrow all the experience and practice of the ages.

This can only have come about through the confusion of thought with regard to fertility mentioned above. Man's understanding was blinded by the increase in production which the application of this theory at first brought about. Only the true peasant, the man who, despite all modern agricultural science, still has a truer understanding of the soil than any theorist, was not taken in. He shook his head and foretold the evils which were to come. Once more his views are well expressed in Adrian Bell's *Men of the Fields*:

'He had further ideas about food. "If people ate more of what's grown with muck, there'd not be half the illness about. People say that what's grown with artificial manure does you as much good as what's grown with muck. But I know that's wrong. What's grown with chemicals may look all right, but it ain't got the stay in it." '

But the age of science had dawned. Intuitive judgements were 'unscientific' and 'old-fashioned'. Liebig's theory could be 'proved'. Ocular demonstration was what counted. A given quantity of these new fertilizers produced the promised increase in yield. The methods of our forefathers were clearly out of date. 'There is a prevailing popular tendency to seek to replace "intuitive" which is treated as though it were simply baseless speculation, whereas mere planned communicable routine often glories in the name of 'science'.' This tendency may have helped to establish the new soil science, in any case it was steadily gaining ground when it received a greatly quickened impetus after World War No. 1, through the necessity which faced those manufacturers of explosives, whose factories were equipped for the fixation of atmospheric nitrogen, to find other markets for their products. This resulted in the manufacture and use (assisted by a vast advertising campaign) of huge quantities of sulphate of ammonia and other synthetic fertilizers.

For some time, while the original supply of humus in the soil lasted, all seemed to go well, and in the difficult days of cut-throat competition that intervened between the two wars, when quantity rather than quality became the standard of efficiency, cultivators generally formed the habit of basing their manurial programmes on the cheapest forms of nitrogen, phosphates, and potash on the market.

All this time the 'man of the fields' remained unconvinced. 'Wait', he said, with that patience only close contact with the soil can give, and now the indications are mounting that the day of his vindication is at hand, for there are signs that yields are declining, and that increasing quantities of fertilizers are required to produce a given return. But this is not all; quality is declining even quicker than yields. Fertility, as will presently be shown, depends on humus. The accelerated growth induced by chemical fertilizers has the effect, among others, of speeding up the rate at which humus is exhausted. As this depletion of humus proceeded, troubles began. Parasites and diseases appeared in the crops, and epidemics became rife among our livestock, so that poison sprays and sera had to be introduced to control these conditions.   Lady Evelyn Balfour, *The Living Soil*

HEROISM

IN THE DAYS WHEN THE SUN NEVER SET on the British Empire and the map of the world was coloured pink to show our power, young officers in the country's service were expected to perform all manner of derring-do in the course of their duties. This did not always take the form of simple *Boy's Own* heroism, as Sir Harry Luke shows in this passage from *The Tenth Muse.*

I HAVE, as I say, chosen for this collection some of the dishes I have encountered in a long lifetime of (I hope) intelligent eating and drinking which have pleased me the most. But there is another, less agreeable aspect of the practice of eating internationally. Writing as a former member of the Colonial Service, I venture to utter the conviction that the paymasters of British Government officers stationed in foreign parts have little or no realization of the nastinesses we are sometimes called upon to swallow as part of our official duty in order to avoid giving just offence to our hosts. And more particularly is this the case with those who have attained a seniority requiring them at times to be the guest of honour at, say, an Oriental feast.

My years in the South Seas would certainly have been gastronomically pleasanter did I not dislike the taste of the coconut in whatever form it is eaten or drunk. That is a small matter; but a bold man is the Occidental who will swallow without flinching that morsel so honourable in Arab lands, the eye of a sheep or goat, even if he is constrained to do so *ad majorem regis gloriam.* I for one would certainly have preferred the brain of a barbecued squirrel, which is, or used to be, the portion of the guest of honour at picnics in the Deep South of the United States.

Some truly revolting substances have been set before me in the course of my career in the Near East and Far West, although seldom anything worse than the New Caledonian dinner recorded by J. C. Furnas as consisting of roast flying fox (a large bat), white grubs dug out of rotting tree stumps and uncleaned pigeon guts stewed with rice. I can take Kangaroo Soup with pleasure (especially if cold and jellied), and cherish nostalgic recollections of Toheroa from my five visits to New Zealand; but I never really fancied, while serving in the South Pacific, the broth made of the roe of the sea-slug or *bêche-de-mer* . . .

My own introduction to the processes of eating, so to speak, on duty took place as far back as the winter and spring of 1907-8, in the last months of the reign of Abdul Hamid II as absolute ruler of Turkey. With my Oxford friend Harry Pirie-Gordon and his parents, with whom I was making a prolonged caravan tour in the eastern provinces of the Ottoman Empire, I was staying in the most magnificent of the Crusaders' Syrian castles, the noble Krak des Chevaliers which the Arabs call Qalat al-Hosn.

Our host was the Qaimaqam (Commissioner) of the District, whose capital and residence were within the castle *enceinte.* When the two sheep killed in honour of our arrival had been cooked (which meant boiled for so long that they could be dismembered with the hand, as no eating utensils were then used in those parts), we squatted on the floor round the vast brass dishes on which the animals were served whole. Our host having pulled the best (i.e. the fattest) pieces off the carcasses

FOOD

for his guests, and then helped himself, he proceeded to pick out the juiciest morsels of the mutton off his own plate, roll them into gigantic pills with the rice, onion, pine-kernels, cinnamon and garlic with which the sheep were stuffed, consolidate them in the fat and then place the resultant bolus firmly in our mouths. I must admit that when later we entertained the Qaimaqam in our camp we amused ourselves, and apparently pleased the Qaimaqam, by popping suitably kneaded bits of bully-beef, which was all we had to offer from our plates, into his mouth.

Another embarrassing feature of Oriental hospitality is the belief entertained in parts of the East that politeness requires the host to stuff his guests to the verge of suffocation. Politeness similarly requires the guest to absorb what is pressed upon him. The following story used to be told of the Oriental sweetmeat *baqlawa*, a rather sticky confection of pastry and honey highly appreciated in the Levant. In the reign of Queen Victoria an Ottoman Grand Vizier once gave a dinner in Constantinople to the British Ambassador of the day. The dinner was ample, and by the time the sweet had arrived – it was *baqlawa* – the Ambassador could eat no more.

'Supposing,' asked the Grand Vizier with apparent irrelevance, observing that his guest had passed the dish, 'that you were in a very crowded apartment and that your King wished to enter what would you do?'

'I would press against the others,' said the Ambassador, 'and make room for him somehow.'

'That is exactly what you must do,' retorted the Grand Vizier, 'for the *baqlawa*, who is the King of Sweets.'

But there is a limit to even the Turk's capacity for politeness. When a Turkish guest had been gorged to the extent that he can chew but no longer swallow, he will gasp a final plea for mercy in the terse and homely saying: '*Yemek sizin, qarn bizim* – the food is yours but the belly is mine.'

Sir Harry Luke, *The Tenth Muse*

HOPE

I AM NOT REALLY VERY SURE what this poem says about the author, her generation, or indeed the object of her expectations, but it seems to me very indicative of a particular 1980s-90s state of mind, which is why I have included it.

ONE DAY HE'S GONNA COOK ME A MEAL

one day he's gonna cook me a meal
a big meal
a big monster of a meal
with perfectly roasted crispy potatoes
and succulent garden-grown baby carrots
nesting like sneaky little surprises
beneath some richly flavoured sauce

one day he's gonna cook me a meal
and for once his timing will be perfect

he will go to all that trouble
of scraping and slicing and peeling and dicing
of reaching boiling point
and taking care not to burn
and taking time over all those little details
and stirring and blending and caring and
    worrying
breaking down over the creme caramel
but not wanting any help or instructions
and never, no never
giving up and instead making pilchard
    sandwiches
with stale bread

he will arrange everything
like an exuberant Egon Ronay
on a willow-pattern dinner plate
swirling with dancing tongues of curling steam
and offer it to me like some long lost treasure

and I'm not going to say thank you
I'm not going to say aren't you having some
I will eat it, insatiable
sucking it up like an empty whale
my head stuck right in there
cramming my mouth with a vegetable paradise
grunting over the creamy white horseradish
gobbling like some hysterical piglet
slopping it everywhere
my face mottled with dark ripples of gravy
which run unstoppable down my chin
my neck my breasts
and congeal
in a brown solid stain
right where my heart is

one day he's gonna cook me a meal
and I'm gonna run my hands through it
feel the squelch of steaming mash
squeeze those pretty little peas till they pop
cram my ears full of pulpy swede
burrow into the thick nest of buttered cabbage
gorge and wallow and swim around
in the sweet-smelling juices
till the cows come home
till I burst with greed
till I can't breathe any more
I'll probably die
but it'll be worth it
cos hell
I've been waiting for this meal
a long time

Ann Ziety

Now's the time for

JELL-O
BRAND
GELATIN DESSERT

SIX DELICIOUS FLAVORS

Having a little trouble, Mac? Buck up! You still can surprise the little woman and the kids with a swell Jell-O gelatin dessert! It's an absolute cinch to make . . . and we guarantee they'll love every bit of it!

Collection Citron N

4 Francs

Les HORS-D'ŒUVRE

Hors d'oeuvre

AMERICA'S MOST FAMOUS cookery book is *The Joy of Cooking*, an excellent and comprehensive book which has remained with them and changed through many editions and fashions. This piece on *hors d'oeuvre* is so reminiscent of the worst excesses of 1960s cocktail parties, but still provides most useful information on their service at the time.

ABOUT WAYS TO SERVE HORS D'OEUVRE AND CANAPÉS

FOOD often looks more dramatic if some of it can be presented on several levels. This old dodge has been manifested in some really frightening ways. Look at the complex, inedible architectural underpinnings by which the glories of ancient chefs used to be supported and still are today, on celebratory occasions, in some large hotels and restaurants. Artificial coloring, rigid aspics, fussy detailing abound. These techniques for presenting food in fancy form are unpleasantly obvious and eating quality is sacrificed. Don't torture the food. Instead, play up its gustatory highlights and allow its natural subtle colors and textures to shine. Keep in mind what the platter will look like as it begins to be demolished. For this reason, it is often wiser to arrange several small plates which are easily replaced or replenished than one big one which may be difficult to resurrect to its pristine glory.

First described are some mechanical aids to give platters a lift. Here are a few of the simplest: cut a grapefruit in half or carve a solid base on an orange or apple, place cut-side down on a plate, stud with hors d'oeuvre – and surround with a garnish or canapés. You may also cut a melon or use a small, deep bowl or a footed bowl as a receptacle for hors d'oeuvre and surround it with canapés.

Stud a pineapple to make this highly decorative fruit a focal point.

Try cabbages, especially savoys, among whose beautiful curly-veined, velvety leaves small shrimp can cascade down onto the plate surface. The center can be hollowed out to hold invisibly a glass container for a dip, or use red cabbages, whose color can be picked up with stuffed beets and modified with artichokes and pâté slices. Even plain, everyday cabbages can be made interesting if you persuade your green-grocer to let you have one from which the outer leaves have not been hacked or if you can get one direct from a garden. Then curl the leaves back carefully, so as not to bruise them and cut a cavity into which you can insert a sauce bowl, deep enough so the curled leaf edges will conceal its rim.

Just by the placement of food on the platter you can bring about height variations and attractive color relationships. On an oblong plate, center some dainty triangular sandwiches, peaks up like a long mountain range. Alternate sandwiches of a fine ham spread or thinly sliced ham with others made of caviar or mushroom spread or with thin buttered bread. Place small, well-drained marinated shrimp along the base of the range, on either side, and accept the water cress garnished edge of the platter with French endive or celery filled with Guacamole and smoked salmon, wrapped around asparagus tips.

Try to choose an edible garnish for hors d'oeuvre trays. You may want to use beautifully cut vegetables. Should the vegetables for garnish or hors d'oeuvre be watery, like tomato or cucumber, be sure to rid them of excess moisture by draining well.

127

FOOD

If platters are not passed and you want a table accent, place hors d'oeuvre directly on crushed ice, on a layered tray or on a simple epergne.

If you use a silver or metal tray, you may want to protect it from food acids by an under-garnish of lettuce, grape leaves or croutons.

We saw a chef friend rapidly arrange a tray almost entirely from stored foods – a gala quickie if you feel suddenly convivial when an unexpected mob descends on you with short warning. Garnish a large platter with lettuce. For the center, make a large mound of Russian salad using canned drained vegetables of shrimp salad or of Spiced Cabbage Mound. Garnish it with slices of tomato with hard-cooked egg slices on them – topped with a tiny tip cluster of tarragon, thyme or parsley; or, cut the eggs and tomatoes into wedges and border the mound by placing the wedges against it, with the yolk side against the salad.

If you want something less rich, you might use a mound of cottage cheese decorated with tender stalks of burnet pressed into the mound to resemble coarse fern fronds and accented with borage blossoms. You may also make a double spiral of overlapping radish discs and fill the interspace with chopped chives. Place at each end of the platter sardines or asparagus tips held by onion or lemon rings. Prepare onion cups to hold caviar and surround them with a good cheddar or Liptauer, or Cucumber-Cheese Spread. Even a can of good white meat tuna, unmolded and coated with mayonnaise and attractively garnished with ripe olives or capers, looks well with canned drained artichoke hearts or hearts of palm. Fill in with shrimp or mussels.

Irma Rombauer, *The Joy of Cooking*

HOSPITALITY

I HAVE ALWAYS FOUND the late Gerald Durrell one of the most entertaining writers of my generation. Very few writers of this half of the century make tears of laughter stream down my face. He also possesses a family almost as eccentric, though much nicer, than mine own. I find this piece on the dangers of excessive hospitality incredibly funny, and I hope you will too.

THE first course that Demetrios-Mustapha set before us was a fine, clear soup, sequinned with tiny golden bubbles of fat, with finger-nail size croutons floating like crisp little rafts on an amber sea. It was delicious and the Countess had two helpings, scrunching up the croutons, the noise like someone walking over crisp leaves. Demetrios-Mustapha filled our glasses with more of the pale, musky wine and placed before us a platter of minute baby fish, each one fried a golden brown. Slices of yellow green lemons in a large dish and a brimming sauce-boat of some exotic sauce unknown to me accompanied it. The Countess piled her plate high with fish, added a lava flow of sauce and then squeezed lemon juice lavishly over the fish, the table and herself. She beamed at me, her face now a bright rose pink, her forehead slightly beaded with sweat. Her prodigious appetite did not appear to impair her conversational powers one jot, for she talked incessantly.

'Don't you love these little fish? Heavenly! Of course, it's such a pity that they should die so young, but there we are. So nice to be able to eat all of them without worrying about the bones. Such a relief! Henri, my husband you know, started to collect skeletons once. My dear, the house looked and smelt like a mortuary. 'Henri,' I said to him, 'Henri, this must stop. This is an unhealthy death wish you have developed. You must go and see a psychiatrist'.'

Demetrios-Mustapha removed our empty plates, poured a red wine out for us, dark as the heart of a dragon, and then placed before us a dish in which lay snipe, the heads twisted round so that their long beaks could skewer themselves and their empty eye-sockets look at us accusingly. They were plump and brown with cooking, each having its own little square of toast. They were surrounded by thin wafers of fried potatoes like drifts of autumn leaves, pale greeny-white candles of asparagus and small peas.

'I simply cannot understand people who are vegetarians,' said the Countess, banging vigorously at a snipe's skull with her fork so that she might crack it and get to the brain. 'Henri once tried to be a vegetarian. Would you believe it? But I couldn't endure it. "Henri," I said to him, "this must stop. We have enough food in the larder to feed an army, and I can't eat it single-handed." Imagine, my dear, I had just ordered two dozen hares. "Henri," I said, "you will have to give up this foolish fad".'

It struck me that Henri, although obviously a bit of a trial as a husband, had nevertheless led a very frustrated existence.

Demetrios-Mustapha cleared away the debris of the snipe and poured out more wine. I was beginning to feel bloated with food and hoped that there was not too much more to come. But there was still an army of knives and forks and spoons, unused, beside my plate, so it was with alarm I saw Demetrios-Mustapha approaching through the gloomy kitchen bearing a huge dish.

'Ah!' said the Countess, holding up her plump hands in excitement. 'The main dish! What is it, Mustapha, what is it?'

'The wild boar that Makroyannis sent,' said Demetrios-Mustapha.

'Oh, the boar! The boar!' squeaked the Countess, clasping her fat cheeks in her hands, 'Oh lovely! I had forgotten all about it. You do like wild boar, I hope?'

I said that it was one of my favourite meats, which was true, but could I have a very small helping, please?

'But of course you shall,' she said, leaning over the great brown, gravy-glistening haunch and starting to cut thick, pink slabs of it. She placed three of these on a plate – obviously under the impression that this was, by anyone's standards, a small portion – and then proceeded to surround them with the accoutrements. There were piles of the lovely little golden wild mushrooms, chanterelles, with their delicate, almost winy flavour; tiny marrows stuffed with sour cream and capers; potatoes baked in their skins neatly split and anointed with butter; carrots red as a frosty winter sun and great tree trunks of white leeks, poached in cream. I surveyed this dish of food and surreptitiously undid the top three buttons of my shorts.

'We used to get wild boar such a lot when Henri was alive. He used to go to Albania and shoot them, you know. But now we seldom have it. What a treat! Will you have some more mushrooms?

No? So good for one. After this, I think we will have a pause. A pause is essential, I always think, for a good digestion,' said the Countess, adding naively, 'and it enables you to eat so much more.'

The wild boar was fragrant and succulent, having been marinaded well with herb-scented wine and stuffed with garlic cloves, but even so I only just managed to finish it. The Countess had two helpings, both identical in size, and then leant back, her face congested to a pale puce colour, and mopped the sweat from her brow with an inadequate lace handkerchief.

'A pause, eh?' she said thickly, smiling at me. 'A pause to marshal our resources.'

I felt that I had not any resources to marshal, but I did not like to say so. I nodded and smiled and undid all the rest of the buttons on my shorts.

During the pause, the Countess smoked a long thin cheroot and ate salted peanuts, chatting on interminably about her husband. The pause did me good. I felt a little less solid and somnolent. When the Countess eventually decided that we had rested our internal organs sufficiently, she called for the next course and Demetrios-Mustapha produced two mercifully small omelettes, crispy brown on the outside and liquid and succulent on the inside, stuffed with tiny pink shrimps.

'What have you got for sweet?' enquired the Countess, her mouth full of omelette.

'I didn't make one,' said Demetrios-Mustapha.

The Countess's eyes grew round and fixed.

'You didn't make a sweet?' she said in tones of horror, as though he were confessing to some heinous crime.

'I didn't have time,' said Demetrios-Mustapha. 'You can't expect me to do all this cooking and all the housework.'

'But no sweet,' said the Countess despairingly. 'You can't have a lunch without a sweet.'

'Well, I bought you some meringues,' said Mustapha. 'You'll have to make do with those.'

'Oh, lovely!' said the Countess, glowing and happy again. 'Just what's needed.'

It was the last thing I needed. The meringues were large and white and brittle as coral and stuffed to overflowing with cream. I wished fervently that I had brought Roger with me, as he could have sat under the table and accepted half my food, since the Countess was far too occupied with her own plate and her reminiscences really to concentrate on me.

'Now,' she said at last, swallowing the last mouthful of meringue and brushing the white crumbs from her chin. 'Now, do you feel replete? Or would you care for a little something more? Some fruit perhaps? Not that there's very much at this time of the year.'

I said no, thank you very much, I had had quite sufficient.

The Countess sighed and looked at me soulfully. I think nothing would have pleased her more than to ply me with another two or three courses.

'You don't eat enough,' she said. 'A growing boy like you should eat more. You're far too thin for your age. Does your mother feed you properly?'

I could imagine Mother's wrath if she had heard this innuendo. I said yes, Mother was an excellent cook and we all fed like lords.

'I'm glad to hear it,' said the Countess. 'But you still look a little peaky to me.'

I could not say so, but the reason I was beginning to look peaky was that the assault of food upon my stomach was beginning to make itself felt. I said, as politely as I could, that I thought I ought to be getting back.

'But of course, dear,' said the Countess. 'Dear me, a quarter past four already. How time flies.' She sighed at the thought, then brightened perceptibly.

'However, it's nearly time for tea. Are you sure you wouldn't like to stay and have something?'

I said no, that Mother would be worried about me.

'Now, let me see,' said the Countess. 'What did you come for? Oh, yes, the owl. Mustapha, bring the boy his owl and bring me some coffee and some of those nice Turkish delights up in the lounge.'

Mustapha appeared with a cardboard box done up with string and handed it to me.

'I wouldn't open it until you get home,' he said. 'That's a wild one, that.'

I was overcome with the terrifying thought that, if I did not hurry my departure, the Countess would ask me to partake of Turkish delight with her. So I thanked them both sincerely for my owl, and made my way to the front door.

'Well,' said the Countess, 'it has been enchanting having you, absolutely enchanting. You must come again. You must come in the Spring or the Summer when we have got more choice of fruit and vegetables. Mustapha's got a way of cooking octopus which makes it simply melt in your mouth.'

I said I would love to come again, making a mental vow that, if I did, I would starve for three days in advance.

'Here,' said the Countess pressing an orange into my pocket, 'take this. You might feel peckish on the way home.'

As I mounted Sally and trotted off down the drive, she called, 'Drive carefully.'

Grim-faced I sat there with the owl clasped to my bosom till we were outside the gates of the Countess's estate. Then the jogging I was subjected to on Sally's back was too much. I dismounted, went behind an olive tree and was deliciously and flamboyantly sick.

Gerald Durrell, *Birds, Beasts and Relatives*

HUNGER

IT SEEMS STRANGE TO US, at our end of the century, where poverty simply means no designer trainers for the children and a cardboard box is a matter of choice, to think that the Great Strike and the hunger marches of the 1920s were driven by a real threat of starvation and a terror of joblessness. One of the strangest sights must have been the confrontation at the Ritz when the Jarrow Marchers faced the bejewelled rich.

IT WAS not the New Gentlemen who invaded the hotel but some of the Jarrow hunger marchers; today such a protest would have taken place at the Houses of Parliament but at that time the Ritz was seen as the target. Barbara Cartland was having tea in the Palm Court and is able to give an eye-witness account of what happened when the marchers came into the Ritz: 'The poor things were in rags; they looked tired and exhausted. They didn't make a sound; they just gazed around in disbelief, overwhelmed by the fountain, the opulence, the atmosphere. The people having tea just sat there, still, looking upper-class; nothing was said. There was an uncanny silence. Then the marchers were politely asked to leave, which they did without any fuss or bother.' Recalling the deprivation that some people had to suffer in the 1930s Miss Cartland paused, and then said, with considerable dramatic effect: 'We deserve everything we get from the unions now, quite frankly, everything we get.'

The General Strike of 1926 had coincided with an unsettling time for the Ritz as various new hotels were being built, providing many more bedrooms in the capital. Taxation had risen sharply since 1918, and continued to rise; the 1920s saw the destruction of the great London mansions like Devonshire House, Grosvenor House and Dorchester House. The competition from the new hotels, the Dorchester and Grosvenor House, was expected to be fierce and the major overhaul of Piccadilly in the late 1920s when the street was relaid caused a disturbance that many guests at the Ritz found intolerable. The year 1929 was said to be a difficult one for trading 'due to the severe winter and the critical illness of His Majesty The King'.

As the effects of the depression began to sink in there was inevitably a very serious drop in business at the Ritz, and in the summer of 1931 staff wages were reduced. In an attempt to cheer people up, dancing in the Restaurant was tried again, this time under the baton of Lord Vivian's son, Anthony, the brother of Lady Weymouth. The Tony Vivian Band's engagement only lasted a month in spite of his offer to continue playing for a reduced fee. Times were hard and the cashier who was imprudent enough to cash a cheque for £100 given to him by a Mme de Toledo was required to repay the debt at a rate of £4 per month. The free supplies of staff beer were stopped to all save those who worked in the kitchen and the directors themselves took a 25 per cent cut in their fees. This year – 1931 – was the most trying and difficult yet experienced by the Ritz, and the slump in the United States resulted in a serious reduction of American visitors.

Hugh Montgomery-Massingberd and David Watkins, *The London Ritz*

ICE CREAM

ACCESSIBILITY TO ICE CREAM, once a preserve of the rich, is very much a feature of the century that we take for granted. In Robin Weir and Caroline Liddell's splendid book *Ices* we find not just recipes but history and enthusiasm.

TASTING ICE-CREAM AND ICES

'. . . smell and taste form a single sense, of which the mouth is the laboratory and the nose is the chimney; or, to speak more exactly, of which one serves for the tasting of actual bodies and the other for the savourings of their gases.'

Jean Brillat-Savarin, *The Physiology of Taste*, 1825, translated by M. F. K. Fisher

'WHAT is a good ice cream?'

'What are the qualities you look for in an ice cream?'

These are the two questions we are most commonly asked and yet books on ices, other than those written for the industry, ignore this most important feature, which is how to assess quality. Since our book is concerned with the production of quality ice cream, this chapter describes the guidelines that we used to judge whether a recipe was good enough to be included.

More importantly this chapter is particularly addressed to the hapless British who within living memory have no heritage of quality ice cream and little or no knowledge of how good ice cream should taste.

Part of the explanation must be that almost a whole generation was deprived of ice cream during and for some years after the Second World War. (Food rationing did not cease until 1954.) This, coupled with the British tolerance of poor-quality food, has enabled manufacturers to take advantage of the situation and sell us ice cream which, as Jane Grigson said, is 'largely air and fakery'.

It is a curious fact that childhood memories of ice cream, whether recalled accurately or not, remain the basis for adult judgements on taste. Obviously the British start off at a disadvantage compared with other nations.

But what also have to be taken into account at this stage are the differing national characteristics of ice cream. For example, the Americans will prefer ice cream that is sweeter, richer and softer than the Italians, who would look for a milkier, dense and colder ice, whereas the French would want a rich, very smooth ice cream with more sophisticated flavour.

FOOD

However, the rise of the multi-national ice-cream companies is blurring these distinctions. For example, in Italy, a wide range of restaurants offer a dessert menu comprising an identical range of ice creams, all from identical freezers supplied by the company who makes the desserts. We hope this monotonous diet will begin to pall, and in order to win back jaded diners restaurateurs will have their chefs produce their own ices again. Some of the lost characteristics and qualities of differing flavours and textures will happily be restored.

The problems of tasting are compounded by the fact that the image of ice cream promoted in magazines, books and advertisements is of rock-hard, frozen scoops of ice; never shown melting, which is the ideal state for tasting. Frozen hard, even the best ices are nearly inedible, and quite flavourless as the taste buds are anaesthetised at this temperature.

Ice cream should ideally be eaten between −15 to −8°C/4 to 18°F. The ideal temperature according to Arbuckle (*Ice Cream AVI*, Westport, Conn, 1986) is −13°C/8°F.

Sorbets and sherbets should be eaten below −13°C/8°F and granitas when they are ready, straight from the freezer.

So, given the ice served at the correct temperature, how do we judge an ice cream? There are five criteria.

1. APPEARANCE

The colour of the ice cream should be appropriate to the flavour. Any whole fruit, nuts etc. that have been added to the ice cream should be evenly distributed. There should be no ice crystals on the surface and no evidence of shrinkage from the sides of the container.

2. BODY

We consider the body of the ice cream to be everything you can detect with the eye before tasting. As it is scooped from the container to a plate, note the resistance of the ice cream. If it is too firm to scoop it will be uncomfortable to eat and too cold to taste. The body of the ice cream should not be waxy, gummy, crumbly, soggy or fluffy.

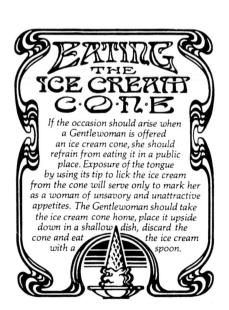

EATING
THE
ICE CREAM
C·O·N·E

If the occasion should arise when a Gentlewoman is offered an ice cream cone, she should refrain from eating it in a public place. Exposure of the tongue by using its tip to lick the ice cream from the cone will serve only to mark her as a woman of unsavory and unattractive appetites. The Gentlewoman should take the ice cream cone home, place it upside down in a shallow dish, discard the cone and eat the ice cream with a spoon.

3. TEXTURE

Taste a sample; the initial texture should be smooth. Push it with the tongue on to the roof of the mouth. If it is rough but rapidly clears as the ice cream melts in the mouth the ice crystals are too large. If however a sandy roughness persists it is due to lactose crystallisation, caused by too much M.S.N.F.

4. FLAVOUR

Is the flavour appropriate to the mix? Is it too elusive or too overpowering? Flavour should be identifiable for what it is, and the ice cream should not be so rich that it swamps the flavour, nor the flavour so rich that you cannot eat more than one or two spoonfuls.

Sweetness is the element which most commonly offends; it is highly subjective, and in our experience it is the flavour that people comment on first. Since sugar is one of the cheapest ingredients in commercial ice cream, it is the one that is most likely to be overdone. Beware oversweetness killing the freshness of flavour, especially in fruit-based ice creams.

The flavour should not stop when the ice is swallowed. Does it leave a pleasant aftertaste? There should be neither cooked-milk flavour, nor any metallic or rancid flavours detectable in the ice cream.

5. Melt

The ice cream should melt to a creamy liquid. It should not remain like shaving foam, or separate, or curdle.

Caroline Liddell and Robin Weir, *Ices*

IGUANA

BRITAIN HAS ALWAYS HAD A GREAT LINE IN STYLISH ECCENTRICS, but between the wars it was difficult to compete with those great self-publicists the Sitwells. The amount of attention they attracted to themselves vastly outweighed in most instances any little talent they possessed. However, Osbert was far and away the best, and to my mind very funny. The Sitwells always sought the most eccentric adventures as part of their self-promotion, and 'Iguanas in Guatemala' fits that bill very well. In today's bland, conformist world, where all that passes for extraordinary is sexual misadventure, I rather yearn for the simple eccentricity of the Sitwells and their age.

A CLEAN feeder, the creature lives in the tree-tops of the steaming jungles on sea-level, and subsists on the green leaves round it. The iguana-catcher is trained to net his prey, a difficult profession that needs a long schooling in these swamps and forests; or again, it may be shot – sitting, I apprehend – and in these tropical regions 'a day's iguana shooting' is a popular sport, comparable to 'a day's partridge shooting' here . . . Now it may be that the iguana is no pleasant object to look at. Its small eyes, pail-shaped snout and shark-like jaws, lined with a saw's teeth of steel, are, I know, repellent to many. Even the reptile's best friends, indeed, will be obliged to admit that at first sight it presents a somewhat case-hardened exterior, and that its saurian countenance bears an unpleasing expression, both sarcastic and ferocious. But it is good, *very good*, to eat: and its cost does not amount to more than the equivalent of a shilling; two facts which must both tell in its favour. The ways of cooking it are many, but the best seemed to me to be roast saddle, cooked with herbs, and served in a circle of its own eggs with a rich brown sauce, flavoured with madeira or port. The saddle is white and tender as the best capon, and the eggs, too, are a suitable, and even delicious, concomitant, once you have grown accustomed to the idea of them.

If, then, iguana, sauté or roast, is the great indigenous delicacy of Guatemala, *tortillas* and *tamales* constitute the country's most ordinary dish. You can see them everywhere, in market, hotel and restaurant, in house and hut. The sight and smell of them is as common in town and village and jungle settlement as is the music of the *marimba*, the liquid-tongued national instrument of Guatemala, which sounds out in *plazas*, in crowded streets, in wattle-built villages, and in clearings between the jacarandas and flamboyant trees . . . But the word *tortilla* is deceptive. First you must clear your mind of its Spanish significance, for here is no flattened-out omelette, sprinkled with flat strips of tomato and pimento, but a bastard pancake, resembling the sole of a boot fashioned of oatmeal, or some substance like it, instead of leather – though certainly leathery enough. *Tamales*, on the other hand, are more interesting; small flat, hot, square packets of savoury maize, of a brown colour. The varieties are endless, but they are always very hot and aromatic, always square or rectangular, and always cooked and served in a neat green casing of banana leaf, which the consumer himself has to unwrap (this, perhaps, psychologically, is one of the secrets of all tempting food: it must give its consumer trouble, not make things too easy for him; that is why a cold lobster should never be separated from the shell except by him who eats it). In addition, *tortillas* and *tamales* seem in every instance to be permeated by a subtle and curious flavour, difficult to identify, but akin to the smell of incense – perhaps due to something used in the fires upon which they have been cooked.

Osbert Sitwell, *Sing High Sing Low*

ILLUSION

BRITAIN ALSO HAS A GREAT TRADITION of unconventional female explorers, who set out into worlds where they were unwelcome and uncomfortable for no other reason than curiosity. Freya Stark was one of these, and this piece sums up for me the essence of her writing.

IT WAS a small colony of four tents, the first of the Arkwaz land, and there was no chieftain to entertain us. The people were so poor that they had neither meat nor fowl nor eggs, milk, rice, tea, nor sugar: nothing in fact but the essential bag of flour and a tiny patch of tomatoes and cucumbers, of which they proceeded to pick every one with the noble hospitality of their code.

There were three charming women. I left the men outside and came to them by the fire, out of the night wind. An older woman, with a sweet and gay face, was mistress of the tent; it was her daughter, and a daughter-in-law, and a friend, who had brought us in, and showed us off as a delightful find picked up by rare good fortune. I soon discovered that I carried a kind of radiance about me, a magic not my own, derived from the city of Baghdad from where I came. The two young women had spent a few months there when their husbands worked as coolies, and the memory lived with them in a glorified vision. They stroked my city clothes with a wistfulness pathetic to see.

'Kahraba,' electricity! I lit my torch and they murmured the word as if it held a whole heartful of longings. The worship of the East for mechanical things seems to us deplorable and shallow; but seen here against so naked a background, the glamour of the machine, of something that gives comfort without effort in a place where bare necessities themselves are precarious, and every moment of ease comes as a boon and a miracle; seen here by the fire in the tent that swayed in the cold night, the light that sprang at will from the palm of my hand did indeed hold a divinity about it – a Promethean quality as of lightning snatched from heaven and made gentle and submissive to the uses of man. So their eyes saw it, more truly, perhaps, than ours, who buy the thing as soulless glass and wire.

I watched the beauty of the two girls – a fine beauty of an old race, with small hands and thin lips and long oval faces. On their heads they wore little skull caps embroidered with beads round which they wound the voluminous dark turban. There were beads round their ankles too, where the scarlet trousers were fastened tightly and ended in a woollen fringe over the little bare heels. This is a good and decent costume for women who sit about on the ground all the time. Over it they wore loose gowns of printed cotton, like the flowery affair I carried in my saddle-bag . . .

I wondered if among their poets, who still sing in the old manner about the things they know, there is not someone who has told the splendour of his beloved's hands with their silver bracelets, as she tosses the bread from one to the other with swift and lovely movement in this most beautiful of household tasks. When the flour was kneaded, a sort of convex shield of metal called the saj was laid above the flames, the pancakes of dough were thrown upon it one at a time, and the bread, warm and rather sodden, was ready in a minute or so.

But this was not all our supper. The tomatoes were cooking in a pot while our hunger in the meanwhile was being stayed with raw cucumbers. Our meal was evidently looked on in the nature of a banquet. Every now and then the mother of the family gave it a stir, tasted it, and nodded with an appreciation beyond mere powers of speech. Four little boys, subdued with expectation, sat in a silent row, while a smaller infant amused himself with two lambs, tied up in the tent near the fire out of the way of wolves, and evidently used to being treated as members of the family. The little daughter, the prettiest woman's eldest child, busied herself with household jobs, knowing well that her chance of the feast was remote.

And presently the dinner was cooked: the tomatoes were poured out steaming: they had dwindled, alas, and now only just looked presentable on three small pewter plates, one for me, one for the Philosopher, and one for the two muleteers.

Such as they were, they were put before us, while the family looked on in admirable silence: only one boy, unable as yet quite to control his feelings, followed the plates with his eyes: his tears rose slowly, the corners of his little mouth turned down. His mother, ashamed, gave him a small slap and then, surreptitiously, offered him her fingers to lick, on which some savour of tomato still lingered.

I myself was hungry enough to have demolished all three dishes at once with the greatest ease; but who could withstand so heart-rending a spectacle? To say anything was impossible: our hostess would have been humiliated beyond words: but one could leave part of the dinner on one's plate. I pretended to be satisfied half-way through the microscopic meal, and the four little boys lapped up what remained. As for the daughter, she had learnt already what is what in this world. She neither got nor expected a share.

Freya Stark, *The Valley of the Assassins*

INSECTS

PROFESSOR BODENHEIMER, in his fascinating book *Insects as Human Food*, reminds us that there is one protein source we are not tapping into. I have yet to eat insects, but have nothing against this in principle. Certainly they are best removed, and why not to the table?

H. NOYES compares the welcome of the rainy season with its termite flights in Central Africa to the hailing of the advent of the oyster season by the British gourmets. The Baganda like the winged sexuals, alive. When these leave the nests, a contingency which has long been foreseen, they often rise only to collide with a sheet of bark-cloth spread over the summit of the termite hill by the natives. The impact breaks off their wings at the sutures and they fall to the ground within the curtain in white, struggling masses; their wings are swept aside by human hands, when they are sifted out from the cloth. Men and women scoop them up in handfuls, eating a few occasionally, savouring the flavour; naked children, shrieking with delight, vie with all the birds of the neighbourhood, wild or tame, in chasing and collecting stragglers, munching as they run, stuffing themselves to repletion, heedless of the acute diarrhoea which will presently disorganise their interiors.

Professor F. S. Bodenheimer, *Insects as Human Food*

INTREPID

I WAS BORN INTO A WORLD in which the sun never set on the British Empire, and most of my atlas was coloured pink to designate this empire. Before I was old enough to vote it had all gone, but this piece of Mrs Bartley's reminds us how intrepid our quite recent ancestors were. We are armchair feminists pontificating from the comfort of home about the courage and ingenuity of women. How many of us could undertake the challenge of being transported from suburban England to a strange and barbaric land to cope with the sort of exigencies implied in this piece?

KITCHEN REQUISITES
OUR KITCHENS, we must allow, lack comfort as well as convenience. Possibly, if they were oftener within the reach of the mistress, matters would improve. Things lie all about, and articles that should

be far apart are seen to be close neighbours. St. Clair's kitchen was a king to ours, and Aunt Dinah compares favourably with the heads of local kitchens. It would be indeed something wholesome to have her 'claren' up times here! However it is not all the fault of our cooks. Our kitchens have not sufficient accommodation, and the fact is that there is no place for everything, and hence nothing is in its place.

The first arrangement of these matters lies perhaps more in the hands of the master than the mistress, but when once the necessary fixtures are made, the latter must see that things are clean and kept in their places. The kitchen floors are mostly dirty and damp, through being built low, – the fact is quite lost sight of, that the kitchen is, very often, the dwelling place by day, and the sleeping place at night, of the servants of the household, and not only a place where kitchen fires are lighted. To avoid the dampness and dirt of the floors, the servants are forced to throw themselves down to sleep at night on boxes of different heights or on the kitchen table, while others manage to make a bed of a single mat, thrown on the bare floor.

About the *Kitchen Requisites*, the most important are Chatties or Saucepans, varying in size from the largest, – a foot or more in diameter and a foot or more deep, – to the smallest which would be half that size. One should quite fit into the other, and thus be conveniently moved. Every chatty should have a close fitting cover, both made of copper and well tinned; when the work of the day is over, they must be scrubbed well, washed, drained and placed away on shelves.

Besides the chatties abovementioned, a copper Fry-pan and Kettle are required. In order to have a *good supply of Clean Water*, have two or three large *Earthenware Jars*; these must be well scrubbed on alternate days to have the water clean and fresh.

In connection with the water jars, have large and small tin pots renew them when leaky, as the leakage will damp the floor.

Our kitchen spoons are made by Nature's own hand, and no art could make them better adapted for their work. The shell of the cocoanut cut in halves gives at once two cups requiring nothing more than a wooden handle, fixed into natural holes which are found at the bottom of the cup. They are sold in the market for a trifle, and, if taken care of, they last quite a while and are easily cleaned.

A *Smooth Black Stone*, sixteen or eighteen inches long and about twelve broad with a *Round Stone Roller*, is needed for the daily grinding of the curry paste; and every Indian kitchen has one of these. The stone must be tough and hard so that particles may not break off during the process of grinding. It needs to be 'tankeed' or chipped at seasons, and stone masons call at the kitchen doors for that purpose. When the work of grinding is over, both stones should be well and carefully washed.

For *Scraping the Cocoanut* into flakes there is a simple instrument – a circular piece of iron, edged with teeth, and fixed to an oblong piece of wood pointed at one end; this can be put out of the way, when not required, and hung on a nail on the kitchen wall.

The *Roasting of Coffee and Mussala* is done on an iron plate called a 'Thoa;' the thicker the metal, the better it is for many reasons; when done with, it is merely washed or wiped dry, and, as some have a ring attached, it can be hung up on a nail.

An *Iron Mortar and a Pestle* are required for the pounding of coffee, spices, &c., and these must be strong and durable, as they are never renewed.

For *Chopping Meat* two things are necessary; a foot or so of a log of hard wood, sawn smooth across the grain, and a large *knife called a 'Koitha.'*

For *the making of Pastry*, a smooth board is necessary, about two feet square, with a wooden pin for a roller. The latter is called by the cook 'Bellen.'

The Kitchen Table is made of Teak and is about five or six feet long, and three or a little less broad, and is used for the standing of dishes and plates. A small board two feet long and one foot broad is required for preparatory work – the mincing of herbs, &c.

Scales and weights must not be forgotten – they are most useful for weighing and proportioning your materials.

For the kitchen salt, pepper and other things, provide tin canisters or something suitable, and a small supply of cups and plates are needed to hold the meat, cocoanut milk and tamarind pulp; and when you have a place for everything, and everything in its place, your servants will not fail in the end to admire so good an arrangement.

Mrs J. Bartley, *Indian Cookery 'General' for Young Housekeepers by an Anglo-Indian*

IRELAND

MY FATHER CAME FROM an Anglo-Irish Ascendancy background. His mother lived in a tent in her own drawing room, which was not regarded as eccentric in Ireland. I love this book, and the description of Mrs Knox's dinner party is one that could as easily happen in rural Ireland today as in 1910. When this book was first written an aged colonel wrote that he had read it three times with enjoyment and enthusiasm, and 'then, and thank God only then, did he discover the book was written by women'. I suppose he was paying the highest compliment he could manage.

OLD MRS KNOX received us in the library, where she was seated by a roaring turf fire, which lit the room a good deal more effectively than the pair of candles that stood beside her in tall silver candlesticks. Ceaseless and implacable growls from under her chair indicated the presence of the woolly dog. She talked with confounding culture of the books that rose all round her to the ceiling; her evening dress was accomplished by means of an additional white shawl, rather dirtier than its congeners; as I took her into dinner she quoted Virgil to me, and in the same breath screeched an objurgation at a being whose matted head rose suddenly into view from behind an ancient Chinese screen, as I have seen the head of a Zulu woman peer over a bush.

Dinner was as incongruous as everything else. Detestable soup in a splendid old silver tureen that was nearly as dark in hue as Robinson Crusoe's thumb; a perfect salmon, perfectly cooked, on a chipped kitchen dish; such cut glass as is not easy to find nowadays; sherry that, as Flurry subsequently remarked, would burn the shell off an egg; and a bottle of port, draped in immemorial cobwebs, wan with age, and probably priceless. Throughout the vicissitudes of the meal Mrs Knox's conversation flowed on undismayed, directed sometimes at me – she had installed me in the position of friend of her youth, and talked to me as if I were my own grandfather – sometimes at Crusoe, with whom she had several heated arguments, and sometimes she would make a statement of remarkable frankness on the subject of her horse-farming affairs to Flurry, who, very much on his best behaviour, agreed with all she said, and risked no original remark. As I listened to them both, I remembered with infinite amusement how he had told me once that 'a pet name she had for him was 'Tony Lumpkin', and no one but herself knew what she meant by it'. It seemed strange that she made no allusion to Trinket's colt or to Flurry's birthday, but, mindful of my instructions, I held my peace.

E. O'E. Somerville and Martin Ross, *Some Experiences of an Irish RM*

JAM

I CAN NEVER DECIDE whether it is the weather or the opportunity for unconventionality that drives the British to live abroad. The tone of slightly xenophobic affection that accompanied such a move before the war is very well shown in this piece from *Perfume from Provence*. Today so many British have moved abroad that Chianti has become Chiantishire and one is pushed to find an Italian there. Whole areas have become ghettos, affection has gone while the xenophobia remains.

JAM-MAKING is their greatest sport. When the harvest of orange-blossom is plucked and the wild oranges turn golden, everyone picks them for *confiture d'oranges*, a delicious bitter marmalade.

Neighbours this year vied with each other in showering these wild oranges upon us until Emilia, grown desperate, announced her intention of making marmalade at once. From that moment everything in the house became sticky. Emilia and Lucienne were up to their eyes in marmalade. The kitchen table and all that was laid thereon became coated with it. Forks, spoons, and knives stuck to our hands; plates clung to the tablecloth. The smell of cooking oranges pervaded the whole house; every casserole and kitchen vessel was filled with soaking oranges; the stove completely covered with preserving pans, some of them borrowed from an obliging American neighbour. Even

our *lingerie* was stiffened with marmalade after the sticky hands of Lucienne had ironed and folded it; for in Provence the maids do all the household ironing as part of their job.

When a mass of pots were filled and I had soaked papers in brandy to preserve the marmalade, and we had tied on the covers and labelled the jars, Emilia proudly invited *Monsieur* to enter her 'jam-shop.' When he made his enthusiastic exit, his feet stuck to the parquet in his study. He had been paddling in marmalade.

The cherry season is even funnier; for when the stones are all taken out of the fruit preparatory to making jam, our two maidens are stained crimson all over. Emilia dramatically informs me that she and Lucienne are murderers, and that their victim is stewing in the preserving pan. But, though a messy occupation, the resulting jam is quite excellent, and the jam-makers have had great fun.

That is the joy of Provençal servants; they are so joyous. They may lack method; they may often be slovenly in their ways – they generally are – but they work like little willing slaves from early morning till night, and they never sulk. They may have volcanic outbursts of temper, but, as they always express what they feel at the moment, they get rid of the thing fermenting within their minds and hearts in one explosion, instead of letting it turn sour within them. And they are so perfectly natural that one cannot take offence or be shocked when they do unconventional things.

The Hon Lady Fortescue, *Perfume from Provence*

JELLYFISH

WHY NOT?

Particularly in China and Japan jellyfish are dried and prized as food. In the Gilbert Islands even highly venomous jellyfish called sea wasps are considered a delicacy. Their ovaries are dried and deep-fried and are said to taste rather like tripe.

Basic Preparation

Soak a sheet (approximately 4 oz.) of dried jellyfish (purchasable in oriental stores) in cold water in the refrigerator for a week, changing the water daily. Wash it thoroughly under running water to remove all adherent sand or dirt.

PICKLED JELLYFISH (*Alu alu*) / SAMOA

Fresh jellyfish are cut into pieces, marinated briefly in lemon juice or vinegar, and then eaten raw.

JELLYFISH (*Sueh tin yue*) / CHINA

Cut well-drained, presoaked jellyfish into long, thin strips about $1/8$ in. by 4 in. Add a little light soy sauce, 1 T sesame oil, a dash of sugar, and a dash of Ajinomoto. Mix well and serve cold.

Shredded cucumbers may be added as a variant.

JELLYFISH AND WHITE TURNIP SALAD (*Sueh tin yue lopo sala*) / CHINA

Cut the jellyfish as above. Peel and chop into a fine Julienne 2 medium-sized Chinese white turnips (or Japanese Daikon), sprinkle them with salt, let stand an hour, and squeeze them dry between paper towels. Mix the turnips, the jellyfish, and a little coarsely chopped green onion. Pour over this about 4 T of hot vegetable oil. Mix and add 3 T light soy sauce, 1-1½ T sesame oil, ½ T sugar, and a dash of Ajinomoto. Mix, chill, and serve.

Calvin W. Schwabe, *Unmentionable Cuisine*

JEWISH

TO ME CLAUDIA RODEN is one of the five great food writers of the century. I first came to know her in Thessalonika, where we went on a church crawl on the feast of St Michael – although she is Jewish and I am Catholic, and Thessalonika is firmly Greek Orthodox. Ever since I have known her she has been involved in her life's work, *The Book of Jewish Food*, a fantastic book which quite rightly won every prize in its year. Jewish food has, in all its variants, to be one of the most complex and exciting food cultures to investigate, and one of the most difficult to write a book on coherently. My step-grandfather was a Manasseh from Calcutta, so I was brought up with some knowledge of the Sephardic food traditions; and my father had many friends and patients in the Ashkenazim culture. So I know quite a lot about Jewish food – but I shall be for ever grateful for this book.

THE early pioneers and the first immigrants from Europe to the newly established state were happy to abandon the 'Yiddish' foods of Russia and Poland as a revolt against a past identity and an old life. Zionism's early desire had been to leave the shtetl behind and to break with everything it stood for. The new state lived by a vision of the future and looked with distaste at the foods that represented exile and martyrdom. There was no place in the Promised Land for food that smelled of persecution and anti-Semitism. Anyway, it was not suitable in the hot Mediterranean climate.

The new Hebrew type, the antithesis of the old passive Jew, looked for his identity in the Bible, and it was assumed that the Yemenites and Oriental Sephardim were closest to the early Jews of Biblical times. The European immigrants learned from the old, established Sephardim how to use the local produce, especially vegetables such as courgettes, peppers, aubergines and artichokes, which were new to them. The food of the local fellahin (villagers) and Bedouin Arabs had a strong appeal for the early Zionists. They were shepherds and dressed like the Biblical figures depicted by nineteenth-century painters, and represented their forefathers in appearance and way of life. Arab and Oriental food like hummus and falafel, both of which are based on the indigenous chickpea, exerted a powerful pull on the young. It was very tasty and cheap, and it was offered by street vendors, at a time when eating a cheap snack on the go was becoming a way of life.

The first ten or more years after the establishment of the state in 1948, when the country was isolated and at war with all her neighbours, have left their mark in the kitchen. Many refugees lived in absorption camps; apartments were small and sometimes had three families sharing. People cooked on tiny oil stoves in pots called sirpella (we called them *casseroles palestiniennes*), which are still used today to save on fuel. There were no refrigerators, only iceboxes, and at mealtime dining tables had to be dragged from under school-books and sewing. The Tzena period, as it is called, was a time of rationing, of making do from nothing, from what you got with coupons. And close memories of the Holocaust were not conducive to inspired cooking. A legacy of those times of scarcity and austerity is a repertoire of mock or simulated foods which are the popular butt of humorists. They were ingenious ways of making something out of something else – chopped liver from aubergines, apple sauce from courgettes, radish jam as a substitute for cherry jam, semolina pudding instead of whipped cream, and turkey as a substitute for veal schnitzel or for lamb in kebabs. Restaurants at the time also served a ubiquitous fish 'fillet' – an unidentifiable compressed fish mixture imported from Norway – nondescript 'white' cheese, yogurt and salad, bean and vegetable soup, mushy pasta with a little goulash. You only went to the restaurant if your mother was sick and there was nothing to eat in the house. Pioneers and volunteers never went; by their standards, only decadent people spent time in restaurants.

Part of the normalization process in the late 1970s – explained as the euphoria of finally emerging from the trauma of deprivation and austerity and the constant threat of war into a new affluence with greater travel facilities and the peace with Egypt – was an explosion of interest in food, from French cuisine and the exotic dishes of China, Hawaii and Bali, to cooking with wine and herbs and healthy vegetarianism. Eating out in restaurants became a popular recreation.

At home today, people still on the whole eat according to their background. In street markets, as in the frozen and chilled food sections in the supermarket, you see a variety of foods of different origins. You find Bulgarian yogurt and cucumber salad and Bulgarian palamida (marinated bonito), Iraqi kubba and Syrian kibbeh, Turkish borek, Yemeni flaky and spongy breads and hot peppery zhoug, Moroccan cigars, Polish lokshen pudding, Russian piroshki, Hungarian blintzes and Viennese tortes. Every group of immigrants has made an impact, and the repertoire of foods at people's disposal is forever growing.

The greatest impact has come from the large Sephardi migration, and most particularly from Morocco, which forms the largest single ethnic group. The Sephardim are seen as knowing and caring more about food. A young Moroccan cook explained: 'The Ashkenazim are more concerned with getting on, studying and going to university. We want to enjoy our life. We like to keep the family together round the table with friends chatting and joking. The mother cooks so that the children come back on Shabbath, even when they are married.'

For years, the kitchens of the land – from the army, schools and hospitals to restaurants and hotels – have recruited their staff from the working-class population of Oriental Jews, from countries like Morocco, Tunisia, Turkey, Iraq, Kurdistan and Yemen, and Israeli Arabs. Caterers too are from the Middle East. But despite its predominance, North African and Oriental food is seen as low-class, poor food. As Israelis often complain, it is the poor Sephardim who settled in Israel, while the rich and educated have gone elsewhere.

When I express my appreciation of Moroccan dishes to some of my Israeli friends, they look surprised, to say the least. The truth is that the cooking standards of Moroccan immigrants have deteriorated in Israel more than in other countries. One catering manager explained it in this way: 'The cooks have rejected their mothers' cooking, because they see it as part of a humiliating backward culture. Yet, after learning the basics at the army catering school, they fall back on what they vaguely remember from home.' In the early days of their massive immigration, the Sephardim were labelled backward and primitive. It was believed that the way to transform them into modern Israelis was to make them forget their backward Oriental past and assimilate them into the dominant Ashkenazi culture. The 'melting-pot' policy was at the expense of Sephardi cultural pride and identity. It has a lot to answer for in the state of the kitchens.

Claudia Roden, *The Book of Jewish Food*

WHEN FLORENCE GREENBERG WROTE her *Jewish Cookbook* there was little written on the subject in the English language. Jews were still considered a strange and alien race, still outcast and ostracised. In 1954 my sister married an American Jew, and before they returned to the USA my father took her aside and warned her that because of her husband she would be refused entry into certain places because of his race. When Florence's column first appeared in the *Jewish Chronicle* in 1934, Hitler was but newly Chancellor of Germany. By the time it was published as a book in 1947, many millions of men and women had been horribly butchered simply because they were Jewish. Nothing changes if nothing changes, and Florence's book broke down much of the ignorance and misconceptions about Jewish food and Kasruth, which can only help to ensure it will not happen again.

TO KASHER MEAT AND POULTRY

The meat or poultry should be put into a bowl (especially reserved for this purpose), entirely covered with cold water and left to soak for half an hour. Wash every particle of blood from the meat before removing from the water. Then place it on a smooth wooden board with holes in it, and lightly sprinkle with salt. Let it drain for one hour, then rinse thoroughly in cold water.

Poultry must be drawn before being kashered. Liver must be cut through and washed thoroughly. Sprinkle with salt and broil or grill for a minute or two on each side, then wash thoroughly and use in any way required.

These instructions are according to ritual requirements and should be carried out independently of and before those given for the preparation of individual meat recipes.

Hindquarter Meat

According to the Jewish dietary laws hindquarter meat may only be eaten if correctly porged.

Until recent years this was available in the British Isles and some other countries and recipes have been included in this volume for such time as it may once more become available.

THE SEDER TABLE

The following are required for the traditional *Seder* table:

Three Matzot. For the *Seder* Service it is customary to have specially prepared *Matzot*, known as *Shemura Matzot* (and sometimes referred to as *Mitzvot*). If not available, ordinary *Matzot* may be used. In the absence of a special *Matzot* cover, fold a large napkin in four and place one *Matza* in each of the three folds, making sure that the *Matzot* do not touch each other. Then put on a plate.

Roast Shank-bone of a Lamb, representing the Paschal Lamb.

One Roasted Egg, representing the Festival offering.

Bitter Herbs. Some small pieces of horseradish are normally used.

The shank-bone, the egg, and the horseradish are put together on a dish or plate which is then placed next to the three *Matzot*.

Charoseth

Parsley or Lettuce, accompanied by a small bowl of salt water.

All the items listed above are placed in front of the man conducting the service.

Wine. Sufficient wine should be provided for four full glasses for each person present.

Elijah's Cup. This is a spare goblet of wine which, though placed on the table, is not used during the ceremony. It is a guest cup set aside for any visitor who may enter the family circle unexpectedly.

STUFFED NECKS

(Gefillte Helzel)

Remove the skin from the neck of the chicken (or goose). Tie up one end, fill with the stuffing, and sew up the other end securely. Put in a small baking dish with a sliced onion and a little water, and bake in a moderate oven until crisp and brown – ¾ to 1 hour, basting occasionally.

Or it can be cooked in the tin with the chicken.

For the Stuffing. 1. Use veal forcemeat, adding the finely chopped heart and liver of the bird.

2. Chop finely a little of the raw fat from the chicken (or goose). To each tablespoonful of fat add 3 tablespoonfuls flour and a teaspoonful of finely grated onion. Season with salt and pepper, and mix thoroughly.

HALIBUT STEWED WITH EGG AND LEMON SAUCE

Head and shoulders of halibut	*Egg and lemon sauce*
2 onions	*Chopped parsley*
Liver balls	*Salt and pepper*
Oil 2 tablespoonfuls	

Cut up the fish into convenient sized pieces for serving. Slice the onions. Put the oil in a stewpan, add the onions, and fry gently till just coloured. Then lay in the fish, sprinkle with salt and pepper, and pour over sufficient warm water to barely cover. Put the lid on the saucepan, and continue to simmer slowly for another 15-20 minutes.

Lift out the fish with a fish slice, put in the centre of a dish with the liver balls around, pour over the egg and lemon sauce, and serve cold sprinkled with finely chopped parsley.

Liver balls. Boil $\frac{1}{2}$-$\frac{3}{4}$ lb. cod's liver in salted water, then strain and chop finely. Add a little chopped parsley and a beaten egg, then sufficient fresh breadcrumbs to bind. Season with salt and pepper, and with hands dipped in flour roll into small balls.

Egg and lemon sauce. Mix 2 teaspoonfuls cornflour or arrowroot smoothly with the strained juice of 2 lemons, add $\frac{3}{4}$ pint of the hot fish stock, and stir over a gentle heat till boiling, and simmer for 3 minutes. Remove from the heat, and when slightly cooked pour on to 2 lightly beaten eggs. Turn into a double saucepan and stir till it thickens but do *not* reboil or it will curdle.

Florence Greenberg, *Jewish Cookbook*

JUNK FOOD

TO ME ONE OF THE TRUE HORRORS OF THE CENTURY has been the growth of the American fast junk food market. It has killed so much that is good in our eating habits, and is now shown to be damaging to our health. Here the brilliant American humorist and food writer Calvin Trillon gives his views.

I NOW realize, though, that before restaurant newsletters came along we were in the position of people who had to argue about the latest film without having a collection of film critics to cite with approval or dismiss with contempt. Just after one newsletter, *The Restaurant Reporter*, had criticized the prices and service at the Palm steak house, for instance, some zealous *palmistes* I know took Alice and me there and presented an impassioned two-hour defense over dinner – a defense that did not, in fact, include everything they wanted to say on the subject, since their mouths were often too full of steak or home-fried potatoes to permit articulation. At the end of the evening, they remained unpersuaded by my argument that a diner who is presented a bill at a restaurant – such as the Palm – that has no menu and therefore no announced prices has no choice but to negotiate. I still think that if a man tells you for the first time that the lobster you just ate costs eighteen dollars, the only sensible response is to offer him six.

I am now so accustomed to *The Restaurant Reporter* that I would probably subscribe even if I lived in Kansas City, just on the chance that I might fall into a conversation with a visiting machine-tools drummer about Japanese restaurants on the Upper West Side. (The other New York newsletter I have seen, *The Craig Claiborne Journal*, devotes more space to recipes than to restaurants, and is therefore of less use to me, since my cooking skill does not extend past a special way of preparing scrambled eggs so that they always stick to the pan. I do enjoy Claiborne's use of the editorial we, such as 'We remember the first time we ever dined at Le Pavilion . . .' It has the effect of making me think that he is eating double portions of everything.) I like *The Restaurant Reporter* for the writing as well as for the tips. The ordinary restaurant reviewer might express his displeasure over a dish of spinach by saying that it was limp or tasteless or not in conformity with the classic dish of spinach. *The Restaurant Reporter* described the spinach served at one midtown restaurant as tasting like 'new-mown artificial lawn.' Reviewing Mr. & Mrs. Foster's Place, a small expensive restaurant on the East Side, *The Restaurant Reporter* said, 'After overcharging 25 patrons twice a night, six nights a week, for a couple of years, Mrs. Foster, the sole proprietor, apparently still cannot afford larger quarters for her establishment, or the elimination of a couple of tables, so that the remaining diners could eat comfortably.' Talking about a steak restaurant that had every characteristic of those out-of-the-way, informal little places New York restaurant samplers are always touting except good food, *The Restaurant Reporter* said, 'You have heard of a tourist trap? This restaurant is a New Yorker trap.'

One spring evening in New York, I happened to run across a friend of mine who was on his way to Chinatown but seemed to lack the look of gleeful anticipation I associated with the beginning of such a journey. What concerned him, I quickly learned, was that an excellent new restaurant he had been patronizing for a while had just been reviewed in the *Times*. We were both familiar with an uptown Chinese restaurant that had been Sokoloved a year or so before – having transformed itself within a few days of being praised in the *Times* by Hess's predecessor, Raymond Sokolov, into an approximation of what might have happened during the more antic phases of the Cultural Revolution if someone had tested out his new authority by ordering every single soldier in the People's Army to eat at the same mess hall. 'It was a very good notice,' my friend said glumly. It had even mentioned the cold-kidney appetizer, his favorite dish. He admitted that complete lack of publicity also had its perils: He said he had once managed to keep a perfect Chinese restaurant pretty much to himself for six months, until it closed, apparently having maintained an exclusivity that was inconsistent with paying the rent. But as he started off toward his first post-review dinner, I could tell he was haunted by expectations of having a harried waiter bob up from a shoving mass of new customers after a forty-minute delay only to announce that the chef had been forced to turn to canned shrimp for the Shrimp With Brown Sauce and had, regrettably, given up trying to make the cold kidneys altogether.

'Cheer up,' I wanted to say. 'Maybe they'll be listed in the *Times* tomorrow for a health-code violation.' But he seemed inconsolable.

Calvin Trillon, *American Fried*

KEROSENE

I DON'T KNOW IF YOU FOLLOWED the adventures of *Swallows and Amazons* as I did, but this passage is very close to reality for me. A school friend's brother had a camp with a fire, and

I volunteered to cook fried potatoes with the aid of some kerosene for the fire. How we swore that they were the best fried potatoes we had all ever eaten, how we made no allusion to the taste of kerosene, comes back to me whenever I read this passage.

IT grew darker and darker:

'What about a lantern?' said Pete.

'In a minute,' said Bill, who was holding a big tin in a damp rag that kept slipping and letting the heat get at his fingers while he was trying to use the tin-opener.

'You can't see what you're doing,' said Tom.

'Joe, you get the grease off them plates,' said Bill. He had got his tin open and emptied its contents, black and shiny, out on a frying pan.

'Shall I lend you a torch?' said Dick.

'No, thanks,' said Bill and turned his back on the party, taking the frying pan with him into the fo'c'sle.

They heard the striking of a match, which lit up the little fo'c'sle, though Bill's body was in the way and they could not see what he was doing. They heard him strike another, and yet another.

'What's gone wrong, Bill?' said Joe.

'Drat it, there ain't nothing go wrong,' said Bill. 'You wait, can't you.'

Another match flared in the fo'c'sle and went out. Then, after a dark pause, they heard the gobble, gobble of liquid pouring from a bottle.

Another match was lit, and the next moment Bill was coming backwards into the cabin, bearing the Christmas pudding in a sea of blue flames.

'What about that?' said Bill.

'I say,' said Dick.

'It's lovely,' said Dorothea. 'Oughtn't you to slop the flames all over it and get some of it burning on each plate?'

Bill hesitated a moment.

'Better not,' he said. 'Wait till that die down.'

He put the frying pan with the flaming pudding on the table and turned to the lighting of the lantern. The lantern, burning brightly, was hanging from its hook under the cabin roof by the time the sea of flame round the pudding had shrunk, died away, flamed up again and gone out. There was a most decided smell of methylated spirits.

Bill carved his pudding and served it out, a helping each on three plates, and a helping each on the three saucers. He watched anxiously the faces of the visitors.

'That want a lot of sugar,' he said.

People helped themselves to sugar again and again and in the end the helpings of pudding disappeared.

'It did burn beautifully,' said Dorothea.

'That's the way to make it,' said Bill, much relieved. 'That don't fare to light without you have a drop of spirit.'

They washed it down with ginger beer, and finished up with oranges, the juice of which took away the last traces of the methylated, which had hung about in people's mouths in spite of all the sugar. Everybody agreed that it had been a first class feast.

Arthur Ransome, The Big Six

IN AFRICA INGENUITY seeems to have known no bounds when it came to cookery, as Miss Williams' book shows.

THE KEROSENE TIN COOKER

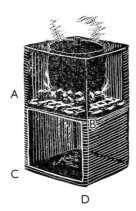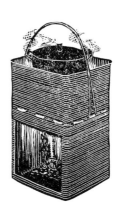

A FAIRLY satisfactory cooker can be made out of an empty kerosene tin following these instructions. See Picture.

(a) Cut off the top of the kerosene tin.

(b) Cut off the bottom half of one of the long sides. This is shown as A, B, C, D in the picture.

(c) Make holes round the middle of the kerosene tin, and pass strong wire through these holes. On this the fire is made. The bottom part which is open will allow for inrush of air, and the bottom of the tin will collect the ash.

(d) Finish off by putting a handle to facilitate easy carrying. The above are cheap stoves commonly used in Nigerian homes but none is smokeless.

Miss Williams' Cookery book

KILLING

MINE WAS THE FIRST GENERATION this century not to know war. I was born in 1947, so my older siblings held up their experiences like badges of merit. My father, though he seldom spoke of it, came through World War I. I know that war brings changed attitudes, and food also takes on a different perception, as seen here in this piece from Laurie Lee on his experiences in the Spanish Civil War.

AN ALMOST wolf-like hunger, too, was now part of our lives, sharpened by the winter cold and idleness. At last, wearying of our acorn coffee and thin donkey soup, a half a dozen of us pooled our pay – over a thousand pesetas in fresh-printed notes – and persuaded an old farmer to part with three chickens, each of which looked as hungry as we were. These bony birds we took to two widowed sisters who lived with their old father on the other side of the town. They had one of those bare stone kitchens which were still almost medieval – a paved floor, high roof, brick and tiled stove by the wall, a few chairs, a table, a twist of olive wood in the corner, and hanging from the rafters an old ham-bone and some harness.

The sisters were wispy, watchful, bright-eyed, sunken-cheeked, their bodies almost mummified in their widow-black. The father sat on a high-backed chair near the stove, his limbs as lean as a whippet's. He slipped to his tiny feet as we came crowding in and raised a wrinkled fist.

'Your house,' he said. 'José, at your service. And my daughters – Doña Anselm – Doña Luisa . . .'

The sisters bridled at this, but lost none of their watchfulness. They took the birds we had brought with us with little clucks of the tongue. 'Come back in two hours,' they said.

So we walked around in the snow, and when we returned Doña Anselm swept our boots with a broom. The old stove blazed with a mixture of wood and refuse, and a great iron pot stood bubbling upon it. The entire kitchen simmered and was awash with steam, a steam banked on the long-forgotten juices of real home-cooked food, swimming aromas of tomatoes, dried beans, and garlic sausage, and boiled chicken peeling on the bone. How the widows had done it seemed a miracle. We stood there in a swoon of hunger. A hunger more blest in that it was about to be appeased. The widows could have asked us another thousand pesetas.

I'd been hungry before, and had also known the simple, voluptuous appetite of youth when taste was never jaded. I remember as a boy being so in love with bread and butter and the cloudy meat of a new-boiled egg that I could hardly wait to go to sleep at night so that morning breakfast should come again. So it seemed now, that long moment of delayed consummation, as we sat round the table while the sisters fussed and quarrelled by the stove and carried us at last the stew in a great earthen dish. We had brought our slabs of grey bread, our metal knives and spoons, and the plates we had were of curved polished wood. The farmer's three birds, who must have been survivors of at least two long winters, now swam brokenly in a thick soup of beans and sausage, splendidly recharged with succulence. Doña Anselm guarded the dish while her sister spooned out our portions, one squashed steamy limb to each plate.

A jar of thin reedy wine was passed around, a brew strangely flavoured with sage and cinnamon – a lacy, fastidious old woman's drink which hinted at secluded and secret comforts.

'Eat!' snapped Doña Anselm, and we broke our grey bread with solemn ritual under her scaring eyes. Six young strangers at their private table, for whom they had cooked three old and irreplaceable hens; we were guests, visitors, but also the enemy in possession. The sisters clearly took no sides in this war, which had occupied their land and must be endured. They served but did not join us as we plunged into our food, while the old man by the stove stared at the floor and waited.

Lopez, a late arrival, and the only Spaniard among the six of us, set himself up as a surrogate host.

'Three in one pot,' he said, beaming round at us proudly. 'Few of you could have eaten better.'

Carried away by the majesty of the moment, he began to pick out pieces from the dish with his stubby fingers and hand them to us with a bow. Doña Anselm hit him with a spoon.

'What are you doing?' she cried. 'Have some culture, man.'

'At my brother's wedding,' said Lopez, 'we had two birds and a rabbit – stewed in wine. I have never forgotten.'

Doña Luisa sniggered. 'Yes. The bride, the bride's mother and the groom.'

Lopez lowered his face to his plate. We others were now deep in our meal, skewering, spooning, using our fingers, awash with flavours and greed. Few of us, I think, had been long from home; none of us, except perhaps Lopez, were married. Instead of great chunks of swede and donkey thrown into a rusty bucket and boiled by some lout in the barrack bath-house, we were now eating food prepared by the hands of women, especially and particularly for us.

In reality, it must have been a poor and scratch-me-down meal. But it was a memorable banquet in that winter of war. In the end it cost each of us several weeks' pay. We were bullied, cursed, perhaps even despised by the sisters, but we were not cheated. There was enough on the stove for all of us. Sprawled at the table, feet up, near repletion, chasing the pimply chicken skins through the thinning soup, digging out the last bits of sausage with our bread, we wallowed now, wheedled more wine, sipped it slowly and grew sentimental. As the afternoon passed, even the sisters softened a little, and found us some beech nuts and raisins.

We gave them the rest of our money, and the old man in the corner said, 'Now you'll be able to buy that clock.'

When we'd finished all there was, we sang, sleepy-eyed, while the sisters cleared the table and put all the chicken bones on a plate and set them down on the old man's lap. Slowly, one by one, he picked them up and passed them between his naked gums, dwelling on each with a delicate bliss as though he was sucking asparagus. He had waited five hours for this moment and now his time had come. He tasted his portion of bones with the absorbed grace of a prince.

Laurie Lee, *A Moment of War*

KING

THE NEW CENTURY SAW THE FADING OF VICTORIAN ENGLAND and that full flowering of hedonism and luxury that was Edwardian England. Britons ruled the waves and the sun never set on the land of the King Emperor, the shrewd, spoilt, immoral and much-loved Edward VII. He had waited a long time for his coronation, and when it came an attack of appendicitis made him wait still longer. He did not reign long – three short years – and when the peacemaker died the peace died with him in the horror of World War I. However, the country that loved him gave him a great coronation and a great feast for the gourmet-monarch.

155

FOOD

CORONATION BANQUET MISHAP

IT HAD not been a good week. Everyone knew King Edward was not well, and special light dishes had been prepared for him separately at lunch and dinner, which meant extra work. It was quite hot for June, and the younger ones amongst us felt restless and impatient to escape from the heat of the kitchens into the cooler evening air. M. Menager sensed this, and because he appreciated how irksome all the early preparations for such a large banquet can be he disliked insisting that everyone worked harder than usual and became irritable simply because it was necessary to insist. There are bound to be small hitches in arranging a big royal banquet, and one of the most annoying of these had delayed some of the cooks. The order for caviare from Russia for the banquet had arrived, and in some inexplicable way the checking of it was overlooked. When it came to be needed we found that through an error of calculation there was only half the quantity necessary. M. Menager was very angry, and the Clerk of the Kitchens denied that the error was his. Eventually the matter was sorted out and the extra amount obtained, but this small hitch did not make things any easier amongst the staff.

At last almost everything was ready. The jellies had been made to take the cold quail and other dishes, some flavoured with claret and brandy, and some to be used as dessert with liqueur. They filled almost every available dish in the kitchens which could be set aside for coronation banquet use, and we were looking forward to the time when the kitchen routine settled down to normal again. I had been working on the *Consommé de faisan aux quenelles* with which the banquet was to begin. It had been clarified and awaited only the red, white and green quenelles or forcemeat garnishing which were to give it the appropriate banquet touch. Almost half the kitchens had been taken over for coronation dishes.

Once again on the night before the coronation we were to work late on the sauces and croquettes needed for the following day. We were about to begin, when word came to us that the King's doctor Sir Frederick Treves had been summoned hurriedly to Buckingham Palace, and consultation with the Master of the Household, Lord Farquhar. He in turn had hurried to see the Clerk Controller, and there were rumours that the King was very ill and might not be able to attend Westminster Abbey for his crowning after all. M. Menager grew pale, for he was an old Palace servant and deeply devoted to the King, but as we had heard nothing official we decided to carry on with our work. About a quarter of an hour later the Clerk Controller sent for the Royal Chef. When he returned we learned that King Edward had been taken very ill that day and was to undergo an operation as soon as possible. As a result the coronation and banquet were to be postponed until his health had recovered.

The staff listened to the news in silence. It took a little time to get used to the fact that the King, who was no longer a young man, was in such serious health. But once we had adapted ourselves to the change in plans a problem faced us. What was to be done with the food for the banquet of two hundred and fifty guests?

Some of it could be kept in the ice-boxes, but a lot of it was perishable and would not keep. There was also the difficulty of storing all the jellies, which could not remain in the dishes which were filled to overflowing. These days at Buckingham Palace such a problem would not arise, for

FOOD

they could be stored in screw-top jars indefinitely. But such modern preserving utensils did not exist in King Edward VII's reign, and we had never faced such a large-scale storing operation before. Finally the Clerk of the Kitchens redeemed himself in everyone's eyes by coming up with a solution. The jellies could be melted down and stored in magnum champagne bottles until such time as the coronation banquet took place. When they were needed they could be remelted by being put in front of the fire and then returned to moulds. We spent the next few hours carrying out this course of action, and eventually there were two hundred and fifty champagne bottles of claret and liqueur jelly ranged along the wall in one corner of the kitchens.

This was by no means an end to the problem. The caviare could be kept on ice, and it was possible to preserve the two thousand five hundred quails. But there were huge amounts of cooked chicken, partridge, sturgeon and cutlets, not to mention all the fruit and cream desserts which would not keep. A little could be put aside for the staff, but the rest, it was decided, would have to be given to charitable organisations dealing with the poor.

We were in touch with a good many of these charities, who had literally thousands of hungry and homeless families on their books, and the Buckingham Palace staff often passed on to them broken or spoilt food. In this case they would be receiving something a little different – six or seven courses from the coronation banquet of a King – and from all the many charities it was hard to choose one which could be relied on to handle the disposition of the food fairly and discreetly. Finally we stored the food in hampers for the Sisters of the Poor, and, without any explanation of how it came to be passed on, gave it to them to distribute to poor families around Whitechapel and the East End. It was sad to think we would never know how the dishes we had laboured over for more than a fortnight had been received, and in the Household disorganisation caused by the King's illness few people gave a thought to the coronation banquet and what had happened to the food prepared for it. But on June 26, the date the banquet was to have been held, it was the poor of Whitechapel and not foreign kings, princes and diplomats who had the *Consommé de faisan aux quenelles*, *Cotelettes de bécassines à la Souvaroff* and many of the other dishes created by the Royal Chef and his staff to grace the King's coronation.

Gabriel Tschumi, *Royal Chef*

KITCHENS

KITCHEN DESIGN IS OF GREAT IMPORTANCE to the cook, if only because most modern kitchens are clearly designed by people who don't cook. Here is a 1960s piece (an age which saw the lowest ebb of the art) on the subject.

BUT first, Mrs. Scoop, you want to show me your kitchen. Yes, *please*. I always think people's kitchens are so . . . ouch! No, nothing at all. I didn't know this beautiful lino-parquet was waxed as much as that. No, I assure you. Only very slightly dislocated. Be right as rain in a month or two.

180 LITRES , A GROUPE HERMETIQUE

FRIGEAVIA

Yes, it *is* a kitchen isn't it? I don't think I've ever seen such an expanse of spotless white enamel and brilliant chromium. What inexhaustible cupboard space! I envy you that. Yes, I see. That lets down and that pulls up and you just open this, and the whole thing turns into a laundry. Very convenient. Everything electric? Yes, I'm sure, only I've never got used to the rings. One seems to me to wait so long for the effect of turning down or up that things get burnt or frozen before the heat has adjusted itself. Yes, I see there's a thermometer on the oven but I can't remember whether they're Fahrenheit or Centigrade and anyhow have no idea about the heat of ovens unless I watch the things in them. Of course there are charts, but who the hell . . . I beg your pardon. Still, as you say, I'm sure electricity's much *cleaner* than gas or anything else.

So that's the pressure cooker. Wonderful! Five minutes for a chicken? The only thing is, suppose you don't like chicken steamed? Yes, I know you can brown it in the oven afterwards. You find it the same thing, Mrs. Scoop? And think of having a sirloin of beef ready in twenty minutes? Yes, I am thinking of it. What happens to the steam? I mean isn't the thing pervaded with the vapours of previous meals? You don't think so. I expect your palate's more delicate than mine. You can tell the difference between the various things that come out of the pressure-cooker. I can't. I never know whether it's pork or veal. But of course it's a wonderful invention.

And these are your utensils. Your daily woman must be a treasure because they're all brilliant. Oh, you have three daily women? Yes, I daresay you need them for this lot. Four steamers on one saucepan, too. It look like the Tower of Pisa, only straight up, doesn't it? And you don't find the taste affected if you're using two or three at once? The one I tried must have had something wrong with it because the steamed pudding tasted of Brussels sprouts. Then those measuring jugs. How clever you are! All I know is a pint glass when I see one. Eight wooden spoons in a row according to size. I'm afraid I've only got two, large and small, and they've been with me for years. What do you call this? A spatula. Oh, I see. What a magnificent set of kitchen knives! All your three dailies could be cutting at once, couldn't they? And this? A doughnut cutter. No, I've never seen one before. Pastry cutter? Biscuit cutter? Set of icing pipers? Juice extractor? It's really wonderful. What will they invent next? A waffle iron, too. A sterilizer. A palette knife. Vegetable shredder. Cream maker which can also be used for mayonnaise? Don't you think . . . Oh, but here's your electric mixer. Four speed with a silver polisher attached. I congratulate you.

I see you have five frying-pans. That one is specially for omelettes? Then why has it got such deep sides, I wonder? And why is it so burnished clean? Please don't be offended. I know that's Mrs. Riddle's way of doing things. I was only remembering an old friend of mine who kept her omelette pan (less than an inch deep so that she could get something under the omelette without breaking it) from year to year without doing more than wipe it with a piece of paper. If someone had cleaned it with boiling water she would have had to start all over again, a five years' task of getting it how she wanted. Unhygienic? I don't know. She made delicious omelettes.

But you've lots more gadgets. I won't ask what all those things with handles are, I'm sure they peel and mince and shred and pound and pulp and liquefy splendidly. But I don't see a chopper for bones. No? You should. It will be a new gadget for you and really useful this time. A special chopper and block to cut large bones into two or three for soup. You will find they give twice as much marrow and 'goodness'. But perhaps you're right. It would look rather out of place in this kitchen, wouldn't it? And where's your pestle and mortar? Frankly, I couldn't cook for a day without one.

Yes it's a fine collection of utensils and gadgets. Mrs. Beeton's was rather more comprehensive but then it included beetle-traps, butlers' baize aprons, banister brushes, cucumber slicers, ivory marrow scoops, and putty powder.

No, I'm afraid I've nothing like this. My principle is a rather haphazard one in the matter of utensils – I just go on till I find I need one, then go out and buy it. I feel that if you are going to start by trying to provide for every contingency that might arise you would need more cupboard space than even you have here. My way really seems to work out quite well. I've never been stopped in the middle of making something for lack of a case of larding needles or a dozen ornamental tart pans.

So your kitchen table is enamelled. Very germfree, I'm sure. No, I'm afraid I don't like cutting or messing about on metal. Rather reactionary, but I have a well-made wooden table which is scrubbed every day, and the top of an old marble washstand at one end of it for making pastry. Wood seems to me the only thing to work on.

Rupert Croft-Brooke, *English Cooking*

THE WHOLE AREA OF KITCHEN DESIGN has been revolutionised in this century. The absence of servants, the increase in family cookery involvement, the saving of heat have all led to the kitchen as the main room in the house – with the consequent attention to design. Here Johnny Grey, in his excellent book on the subject, talks about Elizabeth David's kitchen.

ELIZABETH DAVID'S KITCHENS

THE first visit I can recall to my aunt, Elizabeth David's house was at the age of five to receive instructions on how to cook a chicken! The extraordinary atmosphere of the kitchen was intensified by a wide range of exotic aromas from those dishes currently in preparation, as well as smells lingering from previous dishes, other fragrant spices, strong French cigarettes, and the various fruits on display. The room abounded with interesting objects, fascinating to a young child. The presence of three overladen dressers, a cramped main table and two smaller circular ones, two ancient cupboards, quite a few chairs and a chaise-longue allowed for plenty of parking surface for her many objects, both culinary and otherwise – and that didn't include a sink cabinet with generous draining boards.

The kitchen didn't seem peculiar to me. Our own one at home shared some of its features although it was a lot smaller. I enjoyed it because it was a bit like exploring a treasure chest. Mrs David, as she was affectionately called by the family, was equally fascinated by food and the objects connected with cooking and beyond. She talked to me as a child about her recent 'discoveries' and her interests without condescension – and with a lot of enthusiasm. I could not help but be interested. Later on when I was older, I realized that conversation was something she desired as she lived on her own. Although her sister Felicite lived upstairs, she worked in her bookshop during the day and they always rang each other up before invading the privacy of each other's part of the

house, especially the kitchen because that was where Mrs David lived. Apart from early in the morning when she wrote in bed, the majority of her writing was done in the old kitchen. To all intents it was a study kitchen. More often than not when you called on her, books and papers were stacked on the table. When guests were invited to lunch, she would only have one dish ready, the ones to follow would be prepared over a lengthy pre-lunch conversation and guests were usually asked to assist at least in some minor way. All of this was done at the main table, with a scrubbed pine top. On occasions it received a tablecloth, but it was the working centre of the kitchen. She had no worktops as such.

All her recipes were thoroughly tested before being finally included in her manuscripts, and there were written notes, research books, peculiar new gadgets she was trying out and cooking equipment ever ready. If you were lucky and some experiment had taken place the previous day, she would offer it to you in a matter-of-fact way and ask you to try it. Invariably it would be delicious. She never boasted about her cooking skills – her whole attitude to cooking was one of interest, enquiry and very occasionally genuine pleasure when a dish turned out well. Her emphasis on the quality of raw ingredients and on simplicity was evident in the kitchen – despite the clutter. The dresser that stood next to the entrance door always had an abundant collection of white bowls displaying her recent food purchases or gifts ... semi-dried dates from California, Italian plum tomatoes, wild figs brought by a friend from Spain, giant yellow quinces from Greece and even free-range eggs piled up neatly. She owned a painting by Cedric Morris in which eggs are enchantingly arranged on an earthenware dish: it was used on the front cover of her anthology of writings, *An Omelette and a Glass of Wine*. Many other less exotic fruits of the season – humble things like walnuts, pears or shallots – were also in residence.

Johnny Grey, *The Art of Kitchen Design*

Lettuce

One can of course write a poem to anything but lettuce!

Poem for Lettuce

I know
you don't want to be eaten
anymore than a cow or a pig or a chicken does but they're the vicious
vegetarians
& they say you do
Gobbling up the innocent green beings who gladden
any reasonable person's heart
I'll tell you little lettuce
you'll see them in cowskin shoes & belts
& nobody can make sense of that
Those virtuous vegetarians they'll look at you with prim distaste
while you enjoy your bacon
Makes me want
to buy some cowboy movie blood capsules
Imagine an introduction
I'd like you to meet Lily, she's a non-smoking non-drinking
vegetarian separatist Pisces with choco-phobia
& I smile
while secretly biting down on the capsules concealed in my cheeks
then shake her hand drooling blood
I whisper
Hi I'm a flaming carnivorous double Scorpio who'll eat anything
& as she wilts in dismay trembles with trepidation
hisses with disgust
Ah then little lettuces
we'll have our moment of laughing revenge

Chrystos

FOOD

LIBERAL

THIS PIECE FROM DAVID LLOYD GEORGE, the 'Welsh wizard', I find a curiously revealing bit of history. He wrote it as an introduction to the Vicomte de Mauduit's book *They Can't Ration These*, from which I have quoted elsewhere (see page 213). See also Rationing, page 221.

THE British nation, which once contained a thriving and prosperous peasantry, has within the last century become a race of townsmen, banished from the fresh air, the sunshine, and the green fertility of the countryside, to the confined spaces, the grimy bricks and mortar, the slums and mirk of crowded cities.

We have lost much by the change: the tough, sturdy health of country life, the infinite interest and variety of natural surroundings, the urge to resource, craftsmanship, and self-reliance, the homely and frugal but nourishing country fare. Our people have grown more sophisticated, but less wise; intellectually more elaborately taught, but practically less widely competent.

It has long been one of my ambitions to help in restoring a juster balance between town and country; to bring back to the empty fields and villages of Britain some part at least of the exiles in the towns, and to establish them in that healthiest and most satisfying of all tasks – the winning of food from the soil. For years past I have tried to induce successive Governments to take this work in hand – but in vain.

But what reason and peaceful persuasion have been unable in long years to accomplish, war is now bringing to pass. Under its stern compulsion, scores of thousands of our children have been thrust hurriedly into the country-side for safety, and very many of them are now learning for the first time the lore of Nature which ought to be the birthright of all. Not a few, let us hope, will form a purpose to seek there a permanent home and career.

Under that same compulsion, belated efforts are being put forward to stimulate the production of food from our own land, so as to reduce our piteous and dangerous state of dependence on supplies from overseas. During the coming months, we may hope to see a swift growth in the numbers of people engaged in agriculture, a large increase in the output of our farms, and a big expansion of allotment cultivation and of the growing of vegetables in domestic gardens.

That will be all to the good, socially and physically, for the nation. It will be of more than military advantage, for the best and healthiest food is fresh-grown food, not the dried and desiccated stuff you can purchase in cans. But the growing of such food is only half the battle. If you are able to get the full benefit from it, alike in nourishment and in palatability, you must know how to prepare it for the table. Here we have as a nation a great deal to learn, especially from our French neighbours, who with their highly developed culinary technique can make a dinner of herbs more delicious than the stalled ox of the British roast-beef tradition.

In this region the Vicomte de Mauduit, son of a valiant French General, whose acquaintance I made in the Great War, is an expert. He knows how to translate, not only the more familiar plants of the field and cottage garden, but even unpromising weeds of the hedgerow, into dainty dishes.

Under his skilled guidance, you may find food all around you, and the most unlikely plants will yield you appetising fare.

I need not stress the timeliness of this guide-book which he has written. It is a valuable contribution towards our national defence. Days may lie ahead when it will be a matter of life and death to secure the maximum food supply from those things which grow in our country-side. For that art our town-bred generations have long lost such skill and wisdom as their forebears possessed; and I doubt whether kitchen-lore of this order was ever brought by us to so high a degree of perfection as by our neighbours across the Channel.

Here is, in sort, a cottage cookery-cook. But it is also a good deal more than that. It is a guide to the simple riches of the garden and the field, alike for food and drink, for healing, craftsmanship, and adornment. Not the least of its merits lies in this, that it offers to restore to us the old forgotten kinship with Nature, a familiarity with her secrets, and a sapience in their practical application.

Foreword by D. Lloyd George to Vicomte de Mauduit, *They Can't Ration These*

LIVESTOCK

OUR WHOLE ATTITUDE TO BUTCHERY AND ANIMAL HUSBANDRY has changed enormously over the century, and I feel I am not alone in thinking not always for the better. Excess hygiene and Disney-fed anthropomorphism have not helped the industry, any more than factory and/or intensive farming. This is a piece that some among you may not like, but I hope you will read it and look for its message. We have more food poisoning and *E. coli* and less resistance to it now in these days of super-hygiene than we ever had in simpler times. It reminds me of the passage in the New Testament about the seven devils.

DO NOT believe for one minute that everyone who works in the meat industry here in Britain believes in what they produce. Although not all of them will admit it, their senses and sensibilities have been harnessed often against their better judgement, and they have succumbed to the direction of some authority or other which has decreed the sort of meat that we will be able to buy. We have not been given a choice. In fact, choice has been removed from us, for those who want a bit of fat on their bacon can go and whistle for it if it happens to be no longer the taste of the trade. It is not as though they can take their custom elsewhere, for those with the most influence have ensured by ruthless use of economic force that there can never be any competition, and so no choice. If it were politics we would be living in a totalitarian state, but since it is only food and we do not care much for making a fuss, we have let it slide. And so we have got what we deserved, and the pig has ended up with what it does not deserve, which is an often miserable life, lived in vain to produce an inferior kind of food. What a way to treat a loyal servant of centuries.

So on my travels I did not bother to go to the big factories. I never had to don the white wellingtons or the hair net, for I was never in the mood for smooth-talking platitude, condescension,

the stink of profit before all else. Instead, for my final foray, I went back to the north to meet men who knew how a pig should be treated, and who know how to take the care needed to produce the glorious and varied foods only the pig can give us.

I started in an unlikely spot, on the outskirts of Leeds, in a small house on a modern housing estate, which, luckily for Trevor Gamble, has a 40-foot garage. It is in the garage that Trevor cures his own sides of bacon, fat pieces of belly, to give him the sort of bacon on his plate without which his weekend would not be complete. It was pitch dark as I drove round a web of newly built Crescents, Avenues, Closes and Streets, looking for a man who knew what to do with a pig.

Trevor is in his mid-forties but the pig culture was sufficiently alive in recent years for his wife to remember regularly using lard for the chip-pan, stored in a pig's bladder: 'Yer just cut it in half and used it when you wanted some more fat.'

'My father was a butcher, an old country butcher,' Trevor told me. 'We used to do a lot of pig killing; it went on till the late sixties, I suppose, goin' out, killin' pigs. But not so much for cottagers in later years, more for farmers. There was one old chap I remember, in Barwick in Elmet, he were. He always used to buy a runt from a litter an' feed it up. He treated it like a pet. Well, we used to go up there and kill it for him and when we had, he used to go in the house and cry his heart out, he was that upset. Well, it used to upset us too because we then had to put his pig on a sort of stretcher and cart it away, then we'd cut it up for him and one pig would nearly last him two years. But we used to go all over, killin' pigs. We'd dress 'em in washhouses, foldyards sometimes. The only mistake I remember making was when I did one on oat straw once, and the pig went yeller. Yeh, I remember that.'

I had been introduced to Trevor by a vet, Geraldine Hale, who worked alongside him in an abattoir where he had a job as a meat inspector. She wrote to me, sharing my view about the depths to which our treatment of pig meat had sunk:

'It would be a pity if the sound knowledge of the likes of these men were lost, as it has already been to some modern bacon factories which may take only the best pigs and slaughter them cleanly and humanely but then treat the meat produced in a manner which could almost be described as profane.'

. . . I bid him farewell and watched him close the door on the innocent semi-detached house where no one would guess Trevor's porky secret, hidden in the garage. It was a long way from Romania where everyone kept a pig, and a big step from the days when the Yorkshire Dales could boast a pig in most back-yards; but it was a start. Trevor Gamble may be showing connoisseurs of real ham and bacon the way forward, and not the way back.

Paul Heiney, *Ham and Pigs*

167

FOOD

L UNCHEON

SOMERSET MAUGHAM IS NOT ONLY ONE OF THE GREAT SHORT-STORY WRITERS of all time: he is the definitive record-keeper of a way of life which two world wars and the passing of an empire have killed off. Like all great men he has his imitators, as Lord Archer's piece (of which I quote part) will show. We still do lunch of course, and many of us will have similar experiences.

THE LUNCHEON

I CAUGHT sight of her at the play and in answer to her beckoning I went over during the interval and sat down beside her. It was long since I had last seen her and if someone had not mentioned her name I hardly think I would have recognised her. She addressed me brightly.

'Well, it's many years since we first met. How time does fly! We're none of us getting any younger. Do you remember the first time I saw you? You asked me to luncheon.'

Did I remember?

It was twenty years ago and I was living in Paris. I had a tiny apartment in the Latin Quarter overlooking a cemetery and I was earning barely enough money to keep body and soul together. She had read a book of mine and had written to me about it. I answered, thanking her, and presently I received from her another letter saying that she was passing through Paris and would like to have a chat with me; but her time was limited and the only free moment she had was on the following Thursday; she was spending the morning at the Luxembourg and would I give her a little luncheon at Foyot's afterwards? Foyot's is a restaurant at which the French senators eat and it was so far beyond my means that I had never even thought of going there. But I was flattered and I was too young to have learned to say no to a woman. (Few men, I may add, learn this until they are too old to make it of any consequence to a woman what they say.) I had eighty francs (gold francs) to last me the rest of the month and a modest luncheon should not cost more than fifteen. If I cut out coffee for the next two weeks I could manage well enough.

I answered that I would meet my friend – by correspondence – at Foyot's on Thursday at half past twelve. She was not so young as I expected and in appearance imposing rather than attractive. She was in fact a woman of forty (a charming age, but not one that excites a sudden and devastating passion at first sight), and she gave me the impression of having more teeth, white and large and even, than were necessary for any practical purpose. She was talkative, but since she seemed inclined to talk about me I was prepared to be an attentive listener.

I was startled when the bill of fare was brought, for the prices were a great deal higher than I had anticipated. But she reassured me.

'I never eat anything for luncheon,' she said.

'Oh, don't say that!' I answered generously.

'I never eat more than one thing. I think people eat far too much nowadays. A little fish, perhaps. I wonder if they have any salmon.'

Well, it was early in the year for salmon and it was not on the bill of fare, but I asked the waiter if there was any. Yes, a beautiful salmon had just come in, it was the first they had had. I ordered it for my guest. The waiter asked her if she would have something while it was being cooked.

'No,' she answered, 'I never eat more than one thing. Unless you had a little caviar. I never mind caviar.'

My heart sank a little. I knew I could not afford caviar, but I could not very well tell her that. I told the waiter by all means to bring caviar. For myself I chose the cheapest dish on the menu and that was a mutton chop.

'I think you're unwise to eat meat,' she said. 'I don't know how you can expect to work after eating heavy things like chops. I don't believe in overloading my stomach.'

Then came the question of drink.

'I never drink anything for luncheon,' she said.

'Neither do I,' I answered promptly.

'Except white wine,' she proceeded as though I had not spoken. 'These French white wines are so light. They're wonderful for the digestion.'

'What would you like?' I asked, hospitable still, but not exactly effusive.

She gave me a bright and amicable flash of her white teeth.

'My doctor won't let me drink anything but champagne.'

I fancy I turned a trifle pale. I ordered half a bottle. I mentioned casually that my doctor had absolutely forbidden me to drink champagne.

'What are you going to drink, then?'

'Water.'

She ate the caviar and she ate the salmon. She talked gaily of art and literature and music. But I wondered what the bill would come to. When my mutton chop arrived she took me quite seriously to task.

'I see that you're in the habit of eating a heavy luncheon. I'm sure it's a mistake. Why don't you follow my example and just eat one thing? I'm sure you'd feel ever so much better for it.'

I am only going to eat one thing,' I said, as the waiter came again with the bill of fare.

She waved him aside with an airy gesture.

'No, no, I never eat anything for luncheon. Just a bite, I never want more than that, and I eat that more as an excuse for conversation than anything else. I couldn't possibly eat anything more – unless they had some of those giant asparagus. I should be sorry to leave Paris without having some of them.'

My heart sank. I had seen them in the shops and I knew that they were horribly expensive. My mouth had often watered at the sight of them.

'Madame wants to know if you have any of those giant asparagus,' I asked the waiter.

I tried with all my might to will him to say no. A happy smile spread over his broad, priest-like face, and he assured me that they had some so large, so splendid, so tender, that it was a marvel.

'I'm not in the least hungry,' my guest sighed, 'but if you insist I don't mind having some asparagus.'

I ordered them.

'Aren't you going to have any?'

'No, I never eat asparagus.'

'I know there are people who don't like them. The fact is, you ruin your palate by all the meat you eat.'

We waited for the asparagus to be cooked. Panic seized me. It was not a question now how much money I should have left over for the rest of the month, but whether I had enough to pay the bill. It would be mortifying to find myself ten francs short and be obliged to borrow from my guest. I could not bring myself to do that. I knew exactly how much I had and if the bill came to more I made up my mind that I would put my hand in my pocket and with a dramatic cry start up and say it had been picked. Of course it would be awkward if she had not money enough either to pay the bill. Then the only thing would be to leave my watch and say I would come back and pay later.

The asparagus appeared. They were enormous, succulent, and appetising. The smell of the melted butter tickled my nostrils as the nostrils of Jehovah were tickled by the burned offerings of the virtuous Semites. I watched the abandoned woman thrust them down her throat in large voluptuous mouthfuls and in my polite way I discoursed on the condition of the drama in the Balkans. At last she finished.

'Coffee?' I said.

'Yes, just an ice-cream and coffee,' she answered.

I was past caring now, so I ordered coffee for myself and an ice-cream and coffee for her.

'You know, there's one thing I thoroughly believe in,' she said as she ate the ice-cream. 'One should always get up from a meal feeling one could eat a little more.'

'Are you still hungry?' I asked faintly.

'Oh, no, I'm not hungry; you see. I don't eat luncheon. I have a cup of coffee in the morning and then dinner, but I never eat more than one thing for luncheon. I was speaking for you.'

'Oh, I see!'

Then a terrible thing happened. While we were waiting for the coffee, the head waiter, with an ingratiating smile on his false face, came up to us bearing a large basket full of huge peaches. They had the blush of an innocent girl; they had the rich tone of an Italian landscape. But surely peaches were not in season then? Lord knew what they cost. I knew too – a little later, for my guest, going on with her conversation, absentmindedly took one.

'You see, you've filled your stomach with a lot of meat' – my one miserable little chop – 'and you can't eat any more. But I've just had a snack and I shall enjoy a peach.'

The bill came and when I paid it. I found that I had only enough for a quite inadequate tip. Her eyes rested for an instant on the three francs I left for the waiter and I knew that she thought me mean. But when I walked out of the restaurant I had the whole month before me and not a penny in my pocket.

'Follow my example,' she said as we shook hands, 'and never eat more than one thing for luncheon.'

'I'll do better than that,' I retorted. 'I'll eat nothing for dinner tonight.'

'Humorist!' she cried gaily, jumping into a cab. 'You're quite a humorist!'

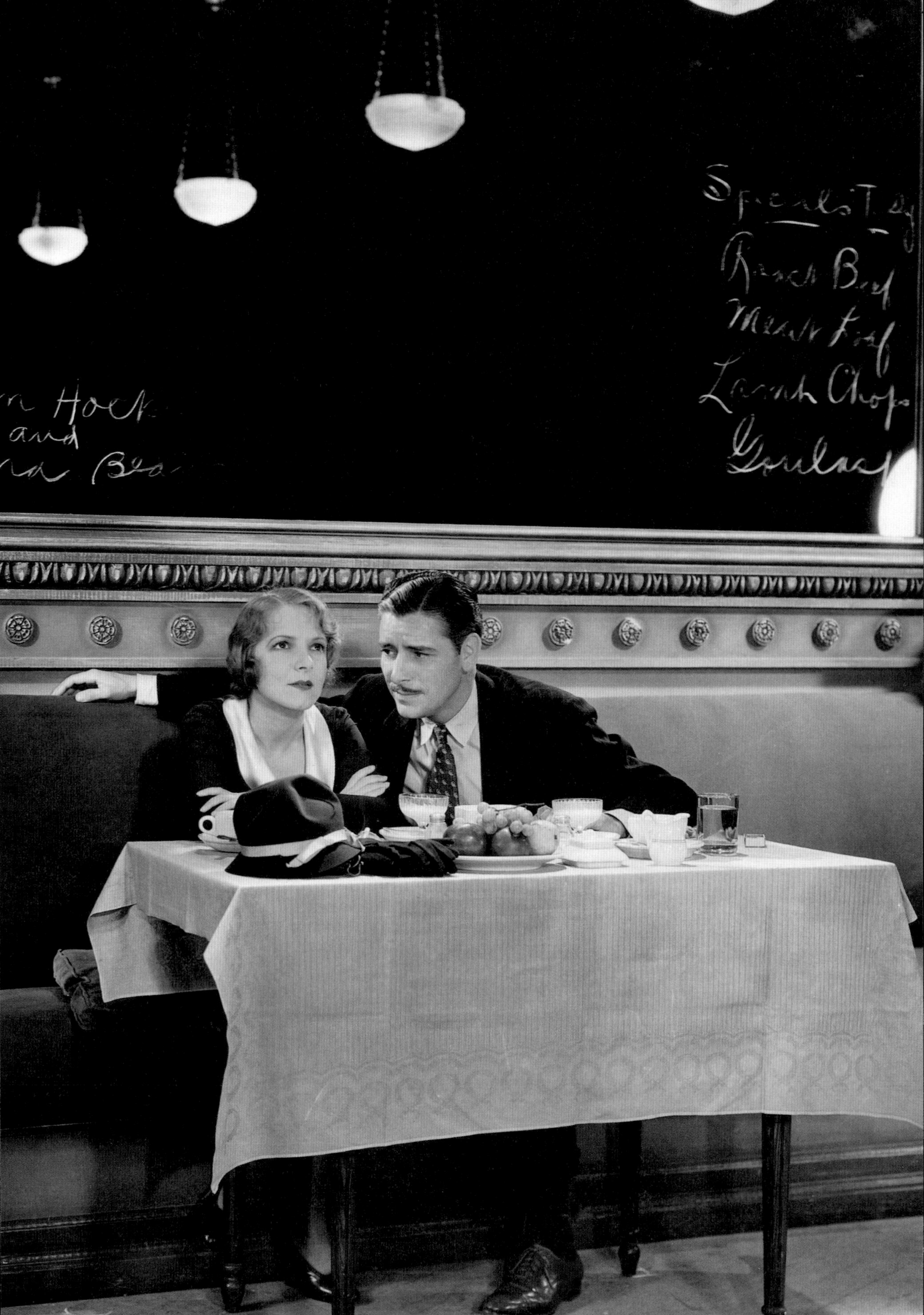
Roast Beef
Meat Loaf
Lamb Chops
and

But I have had my revenge at last. I do not believe that I am a vindictive man, but when the immortal gods take a hand in the matter it is pardonable to observe the result with complacency. Today she weighs twenty-one stone.

Somerset Maugham, 'The Luncheon'

JEFFREY ARCHER'S STORY, also entitled 'The Luncheon', follows much the same plot, though the setting is updated and moved from Foliot's in Paris to the St Regis in New York.

THE LUNCHEON

SHE WAVED at me across a crowded room of the St Regis Hotel in New York. I waved back, realising I knew the face but unable to place it. She squeezed past waiters and guests and had reached me before I had a chance to ask anyone who she was. I racked that section of my brain which is meant to store people, but it transmitted no reply. I realised I would have to resort to the old party trick of carefully worded questions until her answers jogged my memory.

'How *are* you, darling?' she cried, and threw her arms around me, an opening that didn't help as we were at a Literary Guild cocktail party, and anyone will throw their arms around you on such occasions, even the directors of the Book-of-the-Month Club. From her accent she was clearly American, and looked to be approaching forty, but thanks to the genius of modern make-up might even have overtaken it. She wore a long white cocktail dress and her blonde hair was done up in one of those buns that looks like a cottage loaf. The overall effect made her appear somewhat like a chess queen. Not that the cottage loaf helped, because she might have had dark hair flowing to her shoulders when we last met. I do wish women would realise that when they change their hairstyle they often achieve exactly what they set out to do: look completely different to any unsuspecting male.

'I'm well, thank you,' I said to the white queen. 'And you?' I enquired as my opening gambit.

'I'm just fine, darling,' she replied, taking a glass of champagne from a passing waiter.

'And how's the family?' I asked, not sure if she even had one.

'They're all well,' she replied. No help there. 'And how is Louise?' she enquired.

'Blooming,' I said. So she knew my wife. But then, not necessarily, I thought. Most American women are experts at remembering the names of men's wives. They have to be, when on the New York circuit they change so often it becomes a greater challenge than the *Times* crossword.

'Have you been to London lately?' I roared above the babble. A brave question, as she might never have been to Europe.

'Only once since we had lunch together.' She looked at me quizzically. 'You don't remember who I am, do you?' she asked as she devoured a cocktail sausage.

I smiled.

'Don't be silly, Susan,' I said. 'How could I ever forget?'

She smiled.

I confess that I remembered the white queen's name in the nick of time. Although I still had only vague recollections of the lady, I certainly would never forget the lunch.

I had just had my first book published, and the critics on both sides of the Atlantic had been complimentary, even if the cheques from my publishers were less so. My agent had told me on several occasions that I shouldn't write if I wanted to make money. This created a dilemma, because I couldn't see how to make money if I didn't write.

It was around this time that the lady who was now facing me and chattering on oblivious to my silence telephoned from New York to heap lavish praise on my novel. There is no writer who does not enjoy receiving such calls, although I confess to having been less than captivated by an eleven-year-old girl who called me collect from California to say she had found a spelling mistake on page forty-seven and warned that she would ring again if she discovered another. However, this particular lady might have ended her transatlantic congratulations with nothing more than goodbye if she had not dropped her own name. It was one of those names that can, on the spur of the moment, always book a table at a chic restaurant or a seat at the opera which mere mortals like myself would have found impossible to attain given a month's notice. To be fair, it was her husband's name that had achieved the reputation, as one of the world's most distinguished film producers.

'When I'm next in London you must have lunch with me,' came crackling down the phone.

'No,' said I gallantly, 'you must have lunch with me.'

'How perfectly charming you English always are,' she said . . .

Jeffrey Archer

And so on . . . Need I say more?

LUXURY

ANDRÉ SIMON'S DESCRIPTION of the Savoy in World War II is a fine example of the great entrepreneur's work, as well as an insight into how it really was.

THE OPENING of the Savoy Restaurant under the famous Mr. Ritz, in 1888, marks a new era in the history of catering in England. It shifted to a higher plane the standard of luxury and refinement, a standard which left no room for heavy drinking and gross feeding. The Savoy – and a number of other great hotels were conceived in the same spirit, which have been built since by the same and by other financial groups – was from the beginning, and has remained ever since it was opened, a model of *grand luxe* and *bon goût*; it has also been a remarkable nursery for *restaurateurs* who made their reputation when at the Savoy, and made or lost their fortune when they launched out on their own.

A little later, in the nineties, another brilliant constellation rose in the catering firmament, one which was destined to achieve greater financial importance and success than any other in the catering business. Its chief star was Joseph Lyons.

J. Lyons & Co., Ltd., was registered in 1894, with a capital of £120,000. It may be said to have been 'born' in 1887, at the Newcastle Jubilee Exhibition, where Joseph Lyons supplied light refreshment at 'popular' prices at a stall by a shooting gallery. Less than ten years after, on October 5th, 1896, the *Trocadero* was opened, and not many years later the firm of J. Lyons & Co., Ltd., had grown to such unheard-of dimensions that they could, and did, purchase from one of the leading champagne shippers 20,000 dozens of one particular vintage, irrespective of smaller, yet considerable quantities of the same vintage which they purchased from a number of other shippers!

At the opening of the twentieth century, London hotels and restaurants had reached a remarkably high standard of excellence as regards the quality of the meals served, the variety of wines stocked and the reasonableness of their charges.

Then came the war, conscription and restrictions: and then came demobilisation and the home-coming of many 'temporary' gentlemen. Then came the far larger army of men who had made money – lots of money – by luck, work or roguery, and who had never yet had a chance to let other people know how rich they were and how foolish they could be. They descended upon the hotels and restaurants ready and willing to pay the price of fresh cream for milk, and the price of Champagne for any well-advertised gas and sugar in a bottle. Food and drink were as Greek and Latin to them; all they cared about was brilliant lights and loud music. They demoralised the catering trade, but, happily, only for a time. The generation that was just too young to take part in the war are now coming into their own: they have an idea of their own of life's real values: the mere wasting of money for the sake of show does not appeal to them: the long dinners with course after course: the ladies leaving the table when the Port has been once round the table, the men sitting on and on, drinking on and on, and being expected to laugh at 'drawing-room' stories or stale jokes: all these things belong to another age altogether.

Cocktails and jazz belong to a nearer but now passing age: they belong to the previous generation – the one that went through the strain and anxiety of the war and lost their sense of balance, harmony and art. The young people of to-day found cocktails and jazz holding the stage when they first set timidly their foot upon it. They did what they saw others – their elders but not their betters – do. But they do not like cocktails nor jazz. They crave for something that is better balanced, more harmonious, more artistic; for well-cooked food enjoyed in peace with a real wine selected with care; they long for a meal which is both stimulating and restful, for body and mind alike; a meal such as can be enjoyed only by those who understand the art of good living.

The art of good living is above all a matter of appreciation, the appreciation of what is good, of what is best among food and drink, and also the appreciation of the happiest combinations of both food and drink: it is a matter of understanding values.

To cultivate the art of good living requires a little time and a little common sense: it is well worth being granted both.

Quite a common heresy is the 'every man to his own taste.' Many a man or a woman who ought to know better will not blush to say: 'I know what I like, but that's about all. I have really no taste and no time to bother about what is best to order: I leave it to cook – she knows!'

It is perfectly true that we all have, and should cultivate, our own individual tastes in food and

ARRIVAL OF 1909 AT THE SAVOY

SAVOY HOTEL

Menu.

PETITE BOUCHÉE WLADIMIR

CONSOMMÉ AUX NIDS D'HIRONDELLES

SUPRÊME DE SOLE NANTUA

CAILLE ROYALE AU RAISIN DE MUSCAT

NOISETTE D'AGNEAU À LA MASCOTTE.

PÂTÉ DE FOIE GRAS DE STRASBOURG

SALADE ISABELLE AUX ASPERGES

PLUM PUDDING FLAMBÉ AU RHUM

FANTAISIE PARISIENNE

FRIANDISES.

New Years Eve 1908, Savoy Hotel, London.

drink, just as in painting, books or music. But, above all individual tastes, there are general rules which are the frame upon which hang individual tastes: when those rules are broken there are no individual tastes left – merely a nondescript heap of rubbish.

André Simon, *The Art of Good Living*

Macroneurotics

EVERY CENTURY HAS ITS PERIODS OF FOOD FADISM, a product of peace and plenty. Hungry people may have religious taboos which they hold to even in adversity, but they don't have time for fads. As an African friend of mine said, 'We don't adopt Third World diets like vegetarianism in Africa – we are trying to get away from them.' Macroneurotics is macroneurotics, and when you have read this you will know as much as I do!

MACRONEUROTICS

AN OBSCURE food cult, which came from Japan in the 1950s and gained a considerable following among reformed drug dealers in the USA. Macroneurotics holds that food is the only important thing in the universe. The three main foods, held to be able to create total health, happiness, success, fulfilment and enlightenment, are brown rice with miso soup, brown rice with seaweed, and brown rice on its own.

The ultimate text is, of course, the Macroneurotic Bible; and the key passages are found in the Letters of St George O'Sawa to the Constipated. Chapter 7, Verses 1-29 contains the very core of Macroneurotics and its comparison with other 'paths':

CARROT CIRCLE

Though I speak with the tongues of men and of angels, and have not Macroneurotics, I am become as a sounding bell or a tinkling cymbal.

For though I have the gift of prophecy and can do Tarot readings, and understand all earth mysteries and oracles, but I have not Macroneurotics, then I am nothing.

And though I bestow all my goods to Oxfam or to the jumble sales of Guru Maharaji, and have not Macroneurotics, then it profiteth me nothing.

For I say unto you, Macroneurotics suffereth long, in fact is very much into suffering; Macroneurotics envieth not, and is not puffed up, unless by excessive consumption of rice cakes.

Macroneurotics never faileth. But whether there be vegetarians, they shall fail. And whether there be vegans, they shall be wrong too. And whether there be proponents of Food Combining, yeah verily, they shall all vanish away.

But when that which is perfect comes (ie brown rice), then that which is in part (white rice) shall be done away. For when I was a vegetarian, I spoke as a child; and when I became a vegan, I understood as a child; but when I became Macroneurotics, I put away childish things, and learned how to use chopsticks.

For now we see through a Cooking Class darkly, but then face to face. Now I know Macroneurotic Studies, but then shall I know Total World Domination.

And now abideth vegetarianism, veganism and Macroneurotics, these three; but the greatest of these is Macroneurotics.

Gerry Thompson, *Astral Sex to Zen Teabags*

MAHARAJAHS

FOR THOSE OF US RAISED IN THE SHADOW of empire, one of its great fascinations was the exotic and the dramatic. The world of the Indian Maharajah was as far as one could get from the Home Counties, and even after we had imposed cricket and the old school tie, usually Etonian, on the incumbents it remained a source of tantalising romance.

MEANWHILE the others too had been surprised with Indian costumes, Malcolm looking very fine in pink with a sword, and the other man in purple. The ladies went as themselves. At last we were ready, and really it was a glorious sight when the Goodalls were perched on the elephant, sitting on real cloth of gold with torches around them and above splendid starlight. The band played, the children cheered, and the Darlings' nice old Ayah stood in the veranda invoking blessings from Heaven. We went each in a carriage with Sirdars: I had two old men and one fat one, all gorgeous, but conversation not as good as our clothes. An elephant being pensive in its walk, we didn't reach the New Palace for a long time, though it is close to the Guest House. Hideous building! But it was too dark to see it. After the Rajah had welcomed us we went to the Banquet Room. This again I must try to describe to you.

177

FOOD

We all sat on the floor, cross-legged, round the edge of a great hall, the servants running about in the middle. Each was on a legless chair and had in front a tray like a bed tray on which was a metal tray, on which the foods were ranged. The Brahmans ate no meat, and were waited on by special attendants, naked to the waist. The rest of us had meat as well as the other dishes. Round each man's little domain an ornamental pattern was stencilled in chalk on the floor. My tray was arranged somewhat as follows, but 'Jane, Jane, however shall we recollect the dishes?' as Miss Bates remarked.

1. A mound of delicious rice – a great stand-by.

2. Brown tennis-balls of sugar – not bad.

3. Golden curlicues – sweet to sickliness.

4. Little spicy rissoles.

5. Second mound of rice, mixed with spices and lentils.

6. Third mound of rice, full of sugar and sultanas – very nice.

7. Curry in metal saucer – to be mixed with rice No. 1.

8. Sauce, as if made from apples that felt poorly. Also to be mixed with rice, but only once by me.

9. Another sauce, chooey-booey and brown.

10, 11, 12. Three dreadful little dishes that tasted of nothing till they were well in your mouth, when your whole tongue suddenly burst into flame. I got to hate this side of the tray.

13. Long thin cake, like a brandy snap but salt.

14. It may have been vermicelli.

15. As for canaries.

16. Fourth mound of rice to which I never came.

17. Water.

18. Native bread – thin oatcake type.

Some of these dishes had been cooked on the supposition that an elephant arrives punctually, and lay cooling on our trays when we joined them. Others were brought round hot by the servants who took a fistful and laid it down wherever there was room. Sometimes this was difficult, and the elder dishes had to be rearranged, and accommodate themselves. When my sweet rice arrived a great pushing and squeezing and patting took place, which I rather resented, not knowing how attached I should become to the newcomer. Everything had to be eaten with the hand and with one hand – it is bad manners to use the left – and I was in terror of spoiling my borrowed plumes. Much fell, but mostly into the napkin, and the handkerchief that I had brought with me. I also feared to kneel in the sauces or to trail my orange scarf in the ornamental chalk border, which came off at the slightest touch and actually did get onto the Jodpores. The cramp too was now and then awful. The courtiers saw that I was in pain, and told the servants to move the tray that I might stretch, but I refused, nor would I touch the entire English dinner that was handed round during the meal – roast chicken, vegetables, blanc mange etc. As each guest finished, he sang a little song from the Vedas in praise of some god, and the Rajah was, as usual, charming. He made the Goodalls feed each other five times and pronounce each other's name aloud. These are among their marriage customs. Afterwards he, his brother, the Dewan, and all of us went onto the Palace roof, where was champagne and betel-

FOOD

nut, and we danced in our grand clothes and our socks to the music of the band which was playing down in the square. This suited me very well. We were interrupted by a message from the Rani — she desired to see us. This was a great surprise to me. The two ladies went first, and then we, and had a lovely vision. She was extraordinarily beautiful, with dark 'gazelle' eyes. Having shaken hands all round, she leant against the door-post and said nothing. There was an awkward if respectful pause, and after Malcolm had talked a little Urdu and received no answer, we went. Her dress was on the négligée side, but she had not been intending to receive. The Rajah was pleased she had sent for us. He longs to modernize her, but she remains a lovely wild creature. We returned to the hall below, sitting on the floor again and hearing a little singing from nautch girls. We drove back to the Guest House to find Mrs D. and Mrs G. in the most magnificent Indian dresses: the Rani had dressed them and sent them back in a Purdah carriage. – So ended a very charming evening, full of splendour yet free of formality.

E. M. Forster, *The Hill of Devi*

MEAT

I HAVE LONG SUSPECTED that the only joy in being a vegetarian is that which results when one returns to the carnivorous fold.

RE-EMBRACING FLESH

IT HAPPENED overnight. Abruptly, I stopped talking to foodie friends about the best Marcella Hazan recipe for lamb and turned into a timorous nibbler of vegetables.

This was a dramatic rejection of my carnivorous past. I tried not to think about the Paris restaurant where I used to eat steak melting with Roquefort, or about roast guinea-fowl in Gubbio and lamb *cous-cous* in Fez. Instead, I resigned myself to a diet of pasta, vegetables and more pasta.

'I don't mind,' I insisted to dismayed and disbelieving friends. 'After all, I never really liked meat that much.' They groaned, complained about the awkwardness of producing vegetarian meals and compromised by serving endless quantities of poached salmon, my remaining concession to flesh.

I don't even *like* fish, so I should have known something was wrong. Towards the end of this ludicrous period, I began to cheat: a sliver of *prosciutto* here, a hunk of *luganega* there, as though Italian meat was somehow in a different category. Then, on the evening of my birthday last year, I went with friends to an Italian restaurant in Chelsea and ordered a huge plate of *fegato alla veneziana* – calves' liver with onions. No starter, no pudding, just meat: I abandoned vegetarianism as wholeheartedly, though not as impulsively, as I had embraced it.

I half expected a hostile reaction, assuming that such a large and unaccustomed quantity of offal might be an unwelcome shock to my gastric juices. But the next day, I felt exceptionally well and incredibly cheerful; over the next few weeks I binged on Toulouse sausages, venison pâté, pork with dried *porcini* and juniper berries.

FOOD

I completed the re-entry process by spending New Year's Eve at a hotel in Burgundy that served a nine-course meat extravaganza – one of those French feasts which seem expressly designed to challenge the whimsical notion that any part of an animal could possibly be inedible.

I don't really approve of such fanatical carnivorousness, but it did bring home the fact that I had engaged in a major act of self-deception: I love meat and the event which apparently prompted my vegetarianism – a sighting of a terrified fox with the local hunt in pursuit – was actually a cover for a much more arcane motivation.

This strange conversion happened at one of the lowest points in my life: I was writing a book which was not going well, I was so physically run-down I caught every cold that passed through Oxfordshire, and I was very, very unhappy. I am far too greedy to become anorexic but, like many women writers and artists, I fell into the trap of making a sinister deal with myself: if I gave up something I really liked, I would be able to go on working.

I am not elevating myself to the level of Emily Brontë or Gwen John, two prime exponents of creative self-starvation. But I had unknowingly joined those women whose tortured relationship with food is inextricably linked with their gnawing need for self-expression. Vegetarianism, like anorexia, brings with it an illusion of control, turning every mealtime into a ritual of calculation, denial and self-congratulation.

I am surprised at how long I allowed this absurd state of affairs to continue. What is now obvious is that, as I began to get my life back under some sort of control and my writer's block evaporated, my pretence at being a committed vegetarian became more and more untenable.

As I finished my last novel, completing the final chapters with my private life in turmoil but enjoying the writing more than anything I had ever done, I realised I would soon start eating meat again. But I needed to understand why I had taken such an unaccountable decision in the first place.

The link with my writing was the easy bit. As I wrote with greater confidence than before, I thankfully accepted that I no longer had to make self-punishing deals with myself. But the other part of the puzzle involved a more painful realisation which centred on the double meaning of the world 'flesh'. It finally dawned on me, as I considered this earthier, more carnal synonym for meat, that in my case the decision to become vegetarian had been a side-effect of feeling miserably and involuntarily cut off from my sexuality.

It embarrasses me to think I ever imagined I was going without meat out of concern for animals; I am soft-hearted about fur, paws and tails, but that did not stop me eating meat for the greater part of my life. And I have always been relatively unsqueamish about handling meat, baulking at only the most grisly jobs like chopping the feet off pheasants (dead ones, I hasten to add).

This is not to deny that many people become vegetarians and even vegans for purely ethical reasons. Leonardo da Vinci and Piero di Cosimo liked animals too much to eat them; George Bernard Shaw wrote of 'the enormity of eating the scorched corpses of animals', a phrase I often quoted in my vegetarian period.

I understand their revulsion but it no longer has sufficient force to make me turn down a dish of tender lamb with apricots. I have re-embraced flesh and, like Piaf, I have no regrets.

Joan Smith, *Observer*, 8 May 1994

MEMSAHIBS

THE BRITISH OCCUPATION OF INDIA which gave rise to the strange admixtures of the Anglo-Indian Cuisine – the first east-meets-west, pan-Asian cooking if you think about it – created some curious problems of its own. Various pundits tried to advise the memsahib, as is shown in this piece from the 1920s. (Sind always reminds me of that clever telegram from the general who took the town, 'Peccavi'.)

COOKING! At home in England the word conjures up visions of a buxom rosy cheeked lady, polished white tiles and a spotless range. In India a not over-clean Aryan, two bricks and a tumble down outhouse. Put our buxom lady in an Indian cook-house and she would have to be removed to the nearest Asylum babbling the while of her Trades union and apple tarts. Put our Aryan in an English kitchen and he would put his *lakri* in the oven, his *huqqah* on the range, and revert to his two bricks in a corner of the coal cellar. In gastronomic India what the eye does not see the heart does not grieve over and the fact remains that an Indian cook can produce from his two bricks dishes that could not be excelled with the aid of the most perfect of modern culinary appliances. His greatest fault is his lack of creative power. To invent a new dish is a matter entirely outside his scheme of things. At composing a menu he is useless. At cooking his bazar accounts he is supreme. Each mistri (for a few brief moments one suspects the race in general of a sense of humour and a capacity for punning by the coining of the word 'mistri') has his own idiosyncrasies and his own successes. One is a master of the succulent soufflé, another lord of the enticing entrée, a third a successful producer of the sauce that your soul desires. But never yet have we found all these virtues combined in one man. However, far be it from us to disparage the arbiters of our destinies and all in all, a good Indian Cook is little short of a marvel. The extent to which he is able to show his skill depends to a considerable degree on his mistress. The reason one so often partakes of a bad dinner in India (perhaps it would be better to say a dinner that might be improved upon rather than a bad one) is not because the cook is to blame but because the lady of the house has not herself chosen the menu. Before we go any further we venture to lay it down as an axiom that a dinner for English people must be chosen by an Occidental. After all it only stands to reason. An Indian cook does not eat our food nor can he know anything of our tastes. Could the most expert of Swiss or English Caterers successfully choose the menu for an Indian dinner given by a Raja? For this reason we have endeavoured in these notes rather to be of use in indicating palatable dishes and suggesting menus than in dealing exhaustively with the higher gastronomic art. Therefore, oh gentle hostess, we pray you do not leave your menus to your cook and remember that more divorces are brought about by bad cooking than by the mental effect on the ages of Eve persuading Adam to partake of the tree of knowledge. 'Feed the beast' should be your motto and after all perhaps Adam's apple was a bad one. Therefore we exhort you purchase some good cookery book (this one for choice – Advertising Manager) and choose your own menus.

We are very firmly convinced that one of the surest roads to health in India in general and in a plain station in particular during the hot weather is to eat and drink heartily. 'Never fall out with yer wittals' as Sam Weller would have said. In order to eat well it is essential for most people that their food should be attractively set before them. Take the cook who sends up the residue of last night's chicken for tiffin 'slabbed' on a dish, possibly even the same dish it was sent up on last night. When the shade temperature is in the hundreds even the hardiest appetite will quail at this. Take the same chicken cut into small slices and place in the centre of an attractive salad garnished with aspic so that even to look at it makes you feel cool and what a different story. More senses than the sense of taste are brought into play when eating and the sense of sight is by no means the least important. At a certain dinner party we attended in Karachi not long since the last course was intended to be Pêche Melba. When this was served everything appeared to be in order. The taste was slightly acid but by no means unpalatable and every single person at the table finished their portion.

It was then that the Butler whispered to the Hostess his fears that the Sauce was bad. On demanding to see the bottle she discovered that the Cook had used Sauce Robert instead of Sauce Melba. But if she had discovered the Cook's mistake before how many of her guests would have partaken of the dish? As it was they saw nothing wrong.

C. C. Lewis, *Culinary Notes from Sind*

JENNIFER BRENNAN, descended from a long line of the said memsahibs, recalls her grandmother's adventures.

MY grandmother, born and raised to become a *burra mem*, took the command of the household in her stride. Her large bunch of keys was necessary both as a prevention against theft and as a symbol of her status; indeed, most Indian and some English women wore them hanging from chatelaines on their belts. Every morning after breakfast, her household duties began. She met the *khansamer* (cook) outside the store cupboard near the pantry, unlocked the room and, with due ceremony, gave out measured quantities of flour, tea, sugar and other imperishables in the amounts required for the meals of the day. Earlier that morning the *khansamer* had done the shopping for the day's requirements of perishables, meats and vegetables, hailing a passing *tonga* – a horse-drawn, two-wheeled carriage for hire – for the several-mile journey to the native bazaar. There was an understanding between mistress and cook that a perquisite of his job was to be allowed to purchase at a discount from the Indian merchants and charge her retail price, with the proviso that his profits did not become too exorbitant. The *khansamer* presented his accounts book, or *hissab*, to my grandmother, who scrutinized it carefully. The menus for the following day were then discussed and she gave him a sum of *rupees* for his future shopping requirements.

Meals were elaborate in framework but simple in content. The majority of the British in India came from middle-class homes with straightforward tastes in food. There were always several courses to a meal. This concept even extended to breakfast which, whether taken buffet-style from hot-plates on the sideboard or cooked to order, contained a choice of dishes.

The cooks were talented, mostly. Goanese, Nepalese, Madrassi or Bengali, they had served long apprenticeships with a variety of families and were well used to the idiosyncrasies of British tastes. The more accomplished *khansamers* acquired a repertoire of French dishes and all could, naturally, produce a wide range of Indian food, accented by the regional tastes of their home provinces. In truth, I suspect that the talents of most cooks were somewhat under-utilized. Individual tastes, preferences and methods of preparation were transmitted back and forth between mistress and cook so the resultant complexion of the fare reflected many cross-cultural influences. However, once a meal was ordered, it was not done for any *memsahib* to interfere in the kitchen.

Dinner, the crowning meal and signal event of the day, was served late, around 9 p.m., and normally consisted of soup, followed by fish, then meat. Desserts were predictable and were mostly puddings, sometimes a trifle or a fruit salad. Our family was particularly fond of Indian food and so curries were served very frequently either at lunch or at dinner. Vegetables were only available seasonally, owing to lack of refrigeration, and we celebrated with a variety of squashes, 'ladies' fingers'/okra (*bhindi*) and leafy greens during the hot weather, while the more traditional peas, beans, cauliflower and cabbages were winter produce. Sometimes the *mali* would nurse a particularly handsome specimen to gargantuan proportions and proudly show it at the annual agricultural fair for the district. If it won an award, he would be allowed to eat the exhibit in celebration while we had to be content with his certificate of merit.

Meat was mostly lamb or chicken (pork was prohibited in the Muslim areas in which we lived), frequently varied with game, such as partridge or pheasant. As there were many shoots during the cold season, little time elapsed before someone presented the family with a brace of birds or even a dressed deer. Mutton, the principal meat of northern India, came from the *dumba*, or fat-tailed sheep, aptly named for their rear appendages which hung like padded plates, thickly layered with fat. The *khansamer* bought meat in bulk, then butchered it into pieces for individual meals. He also rendered the sheep's tails for cooking fat. (There were no bottled cooking oils available except for olive oil, and that was used for dressing salads.)

In the Punjabi winters, when the frost crackled on the grass and the temperature occasionally dropped to 19°F (−7°C), the meat was stored outside in *dooleys* – wooden boxes with mesh-screened sides – which were hung from the branches of trees, out of range of any prowling animals. In the warmer weather perishables were put in the icebox, which was made of wood and lined with tin sheeting. The large blocks of ice for this were purchased from the icehouse by the bearer, wrapped in gunny sacks and placed into the box together with saltpetre. The bearer was also responsible for the non-edible household shopping, candles, cleaning materials, etc., and he presented his daily accounts book in the same manner as the cook.

Cow's milk was delivered daily in large metal churns. When families had children, it was often the practice to own a cow and have it milked daily so that the source of the milk could be checked for contamination. In any event, the milk was always boiled. The dairy also supplied semi-soft farmer's cheese called *paneer*. One of my early memories of my grandmother was of her churning buffalo milk into creamy white butter, which we would spread on *chapattis* and eat with marmalade for breakfast.

Jennifer Brennan, *Curries and Bugles*

MENUS

I SUPPOSE IT IS THE ABSENCE OF SERVANTS that has done away with the menus element in cookbooks. I know from personal experience that one can't get a publisher to look at a menu layout, which I think is a pity. In 1902 almost every householder had at least one servant, and no doubt *Please M'm, the Butcher* was a useful tool to any stressed mistress. Note how the menus reuse every leftover, a form of economy lost to us in our disposable world.

SUNDAY, MAY 14TH.

BREAKFAST.　Kidneys on Toast, Savoury Eggs, Rhubarb Jam.

DINNER.　　　1. White Macaroni Soup.

　　　　　　　2. Roast Rolled Ribs of Beef, Horseradish Sauce, Yorkshire Pudding, Browned
　　　　　　　　　Potatoes, Cauliflower.

　　　　　　　3. Boiled Gooseberry Pudding.

　　　　　　　4. Gruyère Cheese.

　　　　　　　Dessert — Melon, Figs, Oranges, Sultana Cake.

SUPPER.　　　Cold Salmon, Beaufort Sauce, Cold Beef, Gruyère Sandwiches, Mixed Salad,
　　　　　　　Cucumber, Chocolate Custard, Jamaica Cream, Cheese.

KITCHEN BREAKFAST.　Potted Meat.

　　,,　　DINNER.　　Roast Beef, Potatoes, Cauliflower, Boiled Gooseberry Pudding.

　　,,　　SUPPER.　　Yorkshire Pudding, Salad, Cheese.

Beatrice Guarracino, *Please M'm the Butcher*

NASTY

MARGARET VISSER'S BOOK *It All Depends on Dinner*, written thirteen years ago, was an unheeded cry for sanity against the destruction of our food by the commercial world. My godfather was the Jurgens who married the van den Berg and thus founded Unilever, and he made me promise never to eat margarine. I have broken most promises in my life, but never that one.

FROM the very beginning, nowhere was margarine allowed to be called by a name remotely resembling the word butter. Fear of the consumers being fooled was the reason, as well as the

jealous guarding by dairy interests of butter's semi-sacred status. The United States had 180 applications for butter-substitute patents after margarine first arrived in the 1870s. The names of some of these were 'oleoid,' 'creamine,' 'butteroid,' and 'butterine.' 'Butterine' was the name by which the product was first known in England. Legislation was passed in the United States in 1886 forbidding every echo of 'butter,' and making 'oleo-margarine' the generic name – which it remained for sixty-four years. The British changed 'butterine' to 'margarine' by law in 1887.

Margarine, being factory made, has always been a brand-name product in the west, with fierce competition between the brands for the best, that is the most butter-like, taste. These names like to suggest nostalgia (Blue Bonnet), the regal (Imperial), the childlike and natural (Stork, Flora, Country Crock) – whatever might participate in something of the prestige of butter. Relatively rarely is the modernity of margarine stressed, as in L'Avenir (The Future) in France.

Handcuffed as it is to the concept of butteriness, margarine launched in the twenties a long-lasting series of advertisements in many languages, which showed blindfolded people trying both spreads and pronouncing, 'You can't tell the difference.' a judgement which no one who heard it at the time would have thought himself sufficiently insensitive to make. Butter, forced into publicity which has insisted more and more neurotically on its own ineffable singularity, had ended up with slogans as lame as 'Only butter is butter.' In Russia, where state-controlled margarine production has grown to surpass butter production in volume as the country becomes industrialized, there are two kinds available: kitchen, and better-quality table margarine. The latter is marked with a cow on its wrapper, 'to indicate the product's uses.'

Butter's meanest punches in the battle with the upstart began as early as 1902 in the United States, even before hydrogenation technology became available. Margarine was called a 'harmful drug,' and stores had to be licensed to sell it. Butter producers primly and cunningly insisted that, since margarine was not butter, it should be prevented by every means from resembling butter. Above all, it should be denied the golden colour which, as butter had good reason to know, proves irresistible to buyers, no matter what the substance actually tastes like. Unless it wanted to bear a heavy tax, margarine had to be sold lard-white. Five of the states went so far as to have all margarine dyed pink, presumably so that no one could take it seriously, let alone eat it as a daily basic food or cook anything in it without turning the stomachs of their family and guests.

Margarine countered first of all by including in packages a tube, bag, or tablet with yellow colouring matter in it. You kneaded the dye into the white fat by hand – often imperfectly, so that the finished product had a streaky look. The job was accepted as something a man could do in the kitchen without endangering his self-esteem – like emptying garbage and sharpening knives. Presumably it did not drag him too inextricably into the 'female' activity of actual cooking.

By the 1920s, when hydrogenated vegetable oil had become almost exclusively the raw material of American margarine, yellow oils had become available; if not deprived of all their colour, these could make margarine 'naturally yellow,' and the tax had been circumvented. But the American dairy industry kept fighting, and in 1931 a tax was slapped on all margarine containing yellow oils; in 1934 it became illegal to use any kind of unbleached oil in margarine. Meanwhile, the role of 'purity' in the butter myth was turned against it in 1923, when Congress forbade the addition to butter of any other ingredients, including those enhancing spreadability; margarine, less 'pure,' rushed to embrace spreadability, which has remained perhaps its greatest advantage (apart from cost and the cholesterol scare) in consumer preference over butter.

Further good fortune arrived for the margarine industry when the Second World War began: war is always bad for butter. During the war millions of people in Europe were forced to eat margarine rather than butter. They grumbled, but made the substitution. A butterless world was seen to be possible.

In 1950 the discriminatory taxes against margarine were lifted in the United States and the long and greasy word *oleomargarine* was officially changed to margarine. (Pronunciation of the *g* had long been softened in popular practice – presumably on an analogy with the way in which a hard *g* becomes soft in the name *Marjorie*, a derivative of *Margaret*. The British shorten the word to *marge*, with connotations which include familiarity, boredom and contempt.) Margarine, allowed to 'float' freely on the market, swiftly caught up with butter sales, especially when the 'quality' and higher-priced margarines were first introduced in 1956.

The taste of margarine began soon after the war to be improved, by leaps and bounds. Sales grew internationally. Intensive research by Unilever in the 1950s discovered hundreds of the flavour components of butter, and ways were found of synthesizing these and adding them to margarine. Lecithin, which increased plasticity, was added originally as egg yolk; later, cheaper chemicals were substituted for the egg. Margarine can now be provided with spreadability at almost any temperature, to order.

All the manipulations to which margarine is subjected make it very prone to flavour reversion. Soy bean oil, for instance, may quickly develop an interesting, but in margarine undesirable, smell of freshly cut green beans. Autoxidation because of exposure to air and light is common. The precursors of a host of persistent 'off-flavours' had to be pinned down, and anti-oxidant additives to block them. This extraordinarily complex process of analysis and correction is known as hydro-refining.

Deprivation of butter, in the populations of the north, has always been known as one of the causes of eye problems, skin diseases, kidney stones, and rickets. The reason is butter's richness in vitamin A, which is in short supply if few fresh vegetables and little sun are available. Vitamins A and D are now added, by law in many countries, to margarine.

The colour of butter was endlessly studied, until it was found that the addition to margarine of an orange-yellow dye with a pink tinge gave a good approximation. Margarine was often provided in North America with a pronounced yellow hue – much yellower even than coloured butter. This is usually the case where the law still prevents margarine from looking like butter – in Ontario, for instance. When margarine is permitted to resemble butter it tries to do so – and greatly gains in sales as a result. Butter generally sticks to paleness, denoting thereby the fastidious restraint of the Real Thing, which does not need to strive for effect. Margarine is not entirely defenceless, however, with its carefully cultivated shiny appearance and the obvious and immediate consumer-appeal of gold. Many aroma scientists say they are convinced that margarine is now in no respect inferior to butter, and even that it surpasses butter in colour, in plasticity, in 'lustre,' and in taste. It keeps longer, and it still costs less.

Margaret Visser, *It All Depends on Dinner*

IF GEORGE BERNARD SHAW had simply stuck to writing plays, we would all have been happy for he was a splendid playwright; but he was self-confessedly obsessed with a high moral stance and what he termed his unconventional ideas. He was also a vegetarian and a nudist, though as Mrs Patrick Campbell once said: 'One day, George, you'll eat a pork chop and then God help all women!'

BUT WHATEVER the initial stimulus Shaw maintained his vegetarianism on both ethical and health grounds. 'Meat is poison to the system,' he said. 'No one should live on dead things.' And again, 'Animals are our fellow creatures. I feel a strong sense of kinship with them.' And further, 'It is beneficial to one's health not to be carnivorous. The strongest animals, such as the bull, are vegetarians. Look at me. I have ten times as much good health and energy as a meat eater.' He was certainly extremely healthy, always fit, energetic both mentally and physically, and lived to be within sight of his ninety-fifth birthday. He once revealed his vision of the happy scene at his funeral. 'My hearse will be followed not by mourning coaches but by herds of oxen, sheep, swine, flocks of poultry and a small travelling aquarium of live fish, all wearing white scarves in honour of the man who perished rather than eat his fellow creatures.'

Shaw not only refused to eat flesh but also did not want meat fat, meat cubes or meat essences to be used in the cooking of his meals and, being a teetotaller, he would not allow alcohol in any form to be incorporated in any dish.

His mother, who was the provider of his specialised meals during the seventeen years he continued to live with her as a vegetarian, did not, as I have mentioned, involve herself at all with what went on in the kitchen. Shaw ate such vegetables as were prepared to go with the meat courses served to the others, and he had to use his powers of persuasion with the cook to prevent her from using meat fat in their preparation.

He constantly complained about the cost. 'I'm a poor man,' he used to say. But he never denied himself anything. Alice Laden remembers the following incident: 'He asked me once if I had enough money to pay the bills. 'Yes,' I said. 'I change your cheques at the butcher's.' He exploded. 'What?' he gasped. 'At the butcher's? You know I don't eat meat! I don't want the butcher to handle any of my cheques.' I explained that his cheques had always been cashed at the butcher's – even in Mrs Shaw's time. 'You must stop that,' he said. 'I shall open an account for you at the bank. You must cash them there in future.' I was glad of that because the butcher was not always able to cash a £50 cheque.' Even after the war was ended, Shaw's food remained very expensive – in contrast to his earlier days when vegetarian restaurants had saved him money – because of his insistence on having the very best butter and cream, varieties of excellent cheese and a large assortment of the finest nuts. Food had become very important to him and a great deal of time was spent over meals. Shaw's breakfast occupied two-and-a-half hours of the morning, and lunch two-and-a-half hours of the afternoon! Dinner, a relatively light meal, was over in an hour-and-a-quarter.

Alice Laden, *The George Bernard Shaw Cookbook*

I am always at a loss to understand the horrible things people do to food in the interests of economy. Such people should all be sent to a desert island together with endless inedible things, where they would undoubtedly die happy and I suspect quickly.

To increase the Quantity of Margarine or Butter

> 1 lb. of margarine.
> 4 ozs. of flour, or 2 ozs. of cornflour.
> 1 pint of milk.
> Salt if necessary.

Mix the flour smoothly with the milk, stir until it boils; allow to boil five minutes, stirring well. Remove from the fire, add the margarine; cut into pieces, and well stir with a whisk, until it blends and begins to set. The more it is whisked the more creamy it tastes.

The flour, now being brown, makes the butter rather dark, half quantity of maize flour may be used.

When cornflour is used, it must be well cooked, and the margarine rather quickly whisked in, or it may turn lumpy.

It is an improvement to add an egg; this should be well beaten with a dessertspoonful of the milk, and dropped in, after the flour has cooked, stirred over the fire for a few seconds, and finished as above.

The bulk is increased from 1 lb. to 2 lbs. 3 ozs. to 2½ lbs. If part of the allowance were treated thus, the remainder could be utilized for cooking.

A quarter of a pound of margarine may be treated as above, it will then weigh from 7¼ ozs. to 7¾ ozs.

M. Mitchell, *Cookery under Rationing*

NAUTICAL

As I learned the hard way, cooking at sea requires a different set of skills, as well as an insulation from *mal de mer*. I wish I had had this little book with me in those days.

WITH the great changes which have taken place for the better in the conditions of a sailor's life whilst he is at sea and especially with regard to his food, the need arises for a work dealing particularly with the simpler methods of sea cookery. The old saying that 'Anything is good enough for Jack' is rapidly becoming a dead or forgotten phrase; or, strictly speaking, one finds that Jack's tastes are becoming more critical. He requires his food, plain though it may be, to be served to him properly, and palatably cooked; not, as in days gone by, to be dished out to him in a take-it-or-leave-it style, sometimes half-cooked, sometimes not cooked, but never with the least regard to his taste. So long as the men received their daily allowance, it used to be a matter of indifference to those in authority in what condition it left the cook's hands in the galley. 'If the captain and steward are indifferent to Jack's comfort, why should I trouble myself about him?' asks the cook. To avoid this, the galley should be inspected every day, and a responsible officer should see the men's food served from the galley.

But this indifference is not always intentional on the part of the cook or steward. One finds the same condition of things prevailing at the cabin table; tasteless dishes, indifferently cooked, supplied in abundance may be, but nothing on the table fit to eat, and merely because one or the other, and sometimes both, are ignorant (not incapable, mind) of anything but the very simplest methods of preparing the simplest of dishes.

To remedy this evil as far as possible has been my idea in publishing this book, which is not an elaborate treatise, needing master chefs, unlimited stores, and paraphernalia innumerable, but a book adapted to the requirements of the ordinary merchant ship, be she liner, or the meanest tramp that sails the seas. Those palatial floating hotels that now traverse the waters may have no need for this work, and it is not for them the *Nautical Cookery Book* is intended, but, as I have said before for those vessels whose stores are limited, and whose cooks are so much less experienced.

LIVE STOCK
Directions for Keeping, Killing, and Jointing.

Ducks

Ducks do not bear the confinement on board ship as well as fowls. They also should be kept clean and fed regularly, and if possible, a shallow tin of water should be kept in their coop, so that they may keep themselves clean. They require moister food than fowls, all potato peelings should be boiled for them with barley meal, and any pea soup that is left over from meals can be mixed in. The ducks on board ship should be eaten before the fowls, as they seldom gain flesh at sea, but lose it rapidly. To kill ducks lock their wings, press the bill down to the neck, and cut with a sharp knife right across the back of the head. Hold the duck over a bucket to prevent making a mess.

Fowls

Most ships carry a few fowls. The principal point to be noticed in the care of them is to keep the coops clean and feed the fowls regularly. Avoid putting too many fowls in one coop. Whitewash the coops once a week. The steward should provide a bag of fresh (not sea) sand with which to strew the floors; ashes should not be used in the coops as the sulphur gets into the fowls' eyes and blinds them. In fine weather the fowls should be let out on deck, and some ashes put down in which they can clean themselves; it will be necessary to clip their wings before putting them out, but after a few days they will not attempt to fly overboard. Fowls will always repay trouble taken in looking after them. The mangy ones should be killed off first, so that they may not infect the rest. The best way to kill fowls is to wring their necks.

Geese

These, like ducks, seldom put on flesh at sea. They must be well looked after and have plenty of barley meal. They must be killed in the same way as ducks.

Lamb

Kill and skin it like a sheep, but cut it only into quarters, fore and hind. The head must, of course, be cut off.

Pigs

The pigstyes should be kept very clean and washed out every day, and the hose should be played over the pigs, who like it and learn to look out for it. They can be fed on anything, and will eat all the refuse from the galley. If you have a cargo of coal and the captain will allow you to litter the styes with it do so, and the pigs will thrive wonderfully well; ship-fed pork is better than any other. It is rather a difficult matter to kill a pig at sea, especially if the ship is rolling; it is best done in this way: Tie a rope round the pig's hind leg and haul it up the rigging, let the head hang over a bucket or tub, then take one fore-leg in your left hand and get the other fore-leg held by another man. Just under the pig's throat you will feel a little lump like a button. Stick the knife into that and force it straight up; by doing so you will touch the heart; if you cut to either side you will touch the shoulder and will not kill the pig. When it has ceased to struggle, drop it into a steep tub of scalding water (salt water will do), and scrape it all over with the back of a knife or a large iron cooking spoon; do not let the water get cold. When the pig is well scraped, scrub it with a hard brush, then put a gamble in the sinews of the hind legs and hang it up. Cut it open, take out the inside, and wash the interior of the carcase well.

To cut up the pig, while it is still hanging up, cut right round the neck just below the cheek and screw the head off, then mark straight down the back for a guide in cutting it up; saw it right in half, saw off from the front. Then joint each part thus:- Cutting off the hind legs, cut off the belly-flap all the way down, then the loin, hand and spare-rib, cut off the hocks and feet; take the flare (inner layer of fat) from the belly. Clean the small gut and use it for sausages, and the larger ones for black puddings.

Thomas F. Adkins, *The Nautical Cookery Book*

NOSTALGIA

SO MUCH OF FOOD WRITING has it roots in nostalgia, and come to think of it so much about food has that self-same base. I wonder if the crabs I boiled up in a bucket of sea water as a child in Donegal really tasted that much better, or the eggs really had that much more flavour, or if I have spent so much energy and enthusiasm fighting to save ephemera for the next generation. But no matter. The fight is worth a shilling anyway, and a better world is always worth the seeking. This beautifully written piece from Rena Saloman's *Greek Food* is probably half the reason her recipes are as good as her writing. Rena once told me her theory that the great cooks of the Ottoman Empire were the inherited Greek cooks of Byzantium, and opened my eyes to one of my favourite theories: that the barbarian comes over the wall, kills the men, spears the babies, rapes the women and then looks round for something to eat – at which point up pops the cook from behind his oven and survives to cook for his new masters and preserve the train of nostalgia.

LENT, of course, with its fasting and churchgoing, is a build-up for the major occasion of Easter. Each household reaches an almost frenzied level of activity in preparation for Easter Sunday and the first celebratory meal after the week's fasting, which takes place after the midnight liturgy on Saturday night celebrating the resurrection of Christ. Various shapes of *koulouria* (small cakes of the shortbread variety) will be made during Easter week and sent to the local baker's in huge, flat, shallow dishes which are lent out by the baker. Always there will be some made specially for the children in the shape of rabbits or hens or fish, with shiny bright red eggs stuck in the middle of their tummies. These hardboiled and dyed red eggs are traditionally prepared on Good Friday, but they should never be touched before Saturday midnight.

On Easter Saturday, we would walk to our local church, St George's, with our next-door neighbours, in time to find a good place in the square in front of the church, so that we could watch the celebratory liturgy at midnight. Everyone carried a white candle, plain for the adults, but particularly large and pretty fluted ones, with large pink and white or gold-threaded ribbons tied in bows around the top of the candles, for the children. Everyone also had a red egg in their pockets, specially selected from among the pyramid of red hardboiled eggs at home.

A little before midnight, the assembly of richly gold-draped priests and their faithful congregation would come out to celebrate the Resurrection in the open air. The first words of *Hristos Anesti* (Christ has risen) would be sung by the priests in the warm spring night on the specially erected wooden platform in the middle of the square. At midnight, the bells of the church would join in a pandemonium of excitement. Everyone would start singing, fireworks would be lit, people would light their candles from each other's (the original light having come from the special candles of the priests on the platform), friends and relatives hugged and kissed each other on both cheeks and finally cracked each other's eggs and ate them. Everybody would then walk home in small groups, carefully carrying their lit candles, and before entering the house the head of the family

FOOD

would mark the sign of the cross on the lintel of the front door with the flame of the candle which would leave a smoked mark of a cross.

My grandmother would always stay behind, fussing about her cooking and having everything ready for our arrival. The table would have been prepared, covered with the best white linen tablecloth, and on it a small feast would have been laid: various *meze*, to be followed by a traditional soup called *mayiritsa*, made by boiling the cleaned intestines of the young spring lamb and adding to it a large quantity of fried spring onions and dill and a few small fried pieces of the liver. This would have an *avgolemono* (egg and lemon) sauce added to it at the last minute, just before it was served. *Mayiritsa* would be followed by plates of freshly fried liver and lights, as well as the heart of the lamb, and large bowls of salad, with thinly shredded cos lettuce, spring onions and dill, dressed with olive oil and lemon.

One can imagine what wonderful moments these were for the children! The whole colourful ritual would be awaited, talked about and dreamed of for the rest of the year. This is the evening I missed most when I left Greece.

Rena Saloman, *Greek Food*

NUTRITION

I HAVE ALWAYS BEEN AMAZED that children ever grow up to adulthood, as they seem to survive on sausages and ice cold drinks, with the odd chip or crisp thrown in. However, it seems they survive better without too much adult interference, which is usually faddy and designed to either destroy their health (as in Vegan or low fat) or their palates, and doom them to a life of nursery food – or its even worse modern equivalent, junk food. Here we find Mrs Leyel on the subject in 1925.

COOKING FOR CHILDREN
MANY CHILDREN listen to the story of Cinderella with their sympathy for the heroine warped by the reflection that at any rate she was given the free run of the kitchen when the family departed for the ball. Most children prefer the kitchen to the nursery or drawing-room. If the cook is an Irish-woman, she will welcome the society of five or six children in the kitchen at all hours, if she is any other nationality she will probably prefer them one at a time or not at all. But it is a pity when a child is debarred from all contact with the practical affairs of the home during its impressionable years, and anyway, the time to interest children in cookery is when they are under twelve, when their education cannot or should not be all book work, and when it is undiluted bliss to be allowed to shell peas, to pick currants, and whisk eggs. By the time they are eighteen the glamour of life will be re-oriented. But when we are very young there is romance in the oven and the singing kettle.

A child in a kitchen is an alchemist learning the properties of those mysterious elements – fire and water. A saucepan is a crucible in which anything may happen. Cooking is sheer magic to the

FOOD

child, the purest white magic. A child watches the kneading of flour and water into dough and the transmutation of the pale dough into crusty loaves and brown cakes with the delighted wonder with which the cherubim and seraphim must have looked on at the creation of the world.

It is easy to give children the natural primitive pleasure of making things themselves. They can make or help to make their own toffee and ginger beer; they can cut out their own gingerbread ducks and whales. Not all the following recipes are intended to be made by children themselves. The 'ostrich-egg' calls for some skill, and the point of others is their surprise. But they have been chosen because they will appeal to children by providing that combination of the familiar with the unexpected which is the real zest of pleasure to children all over the world.

TO MAKE AN OSTRICH EGG

GET A PIG'S BLADDER, boil it and cleanse it thoroughly. Break about a dozen eggs, separating the whites and the yolks. Half-fill the bladder with some of the white, and plunge it into hot water and allow it to boil, shaking the bladder so that the whites form a coating to the lower part of the bladder. Then beat the yolks and pour them into the centre of the bladder, shaking it so that the yolks, as they cook, form a ball in the middle. Lastly, pour in the rest of the whites, so that the yolks are covered and a complete egg is formed.

Cut away the bladder and serve the enormous ostrich egg in a Béchamel sauce.

Mrs Leyel, *The Gentle Art of Cookery*

OFFAL

M. F. K. FISHER WAS AMERICA'S ANSWER TO THE WRITING of Elizabeth David. In an incredibly brave book called *Dubious Honours*, she revisited the work of her youth and wrote a critique of it. Here is an extract from this.

So, except for one ugly experience, I was never made to reread anything I had written. Once I went for a while to a psychiatrist in Beverly Hills, and early on in our work together he asked me what I thought of what I wrote, and when I said I never looked at it, he said in real amazement, 'But that is sick!' So I agreed to read a few pages of anything I wanted to, and I think I picked up *The Gastronomical Me* and got to about page eight before I was forced to run to the nearest bathroom and throw up . . . dark spots swimming ahead, and wambly legs, and of course a violent gut reaction.

So the next time I saw the doctor I told him with embarrassment what had happened, and he looked at me with even more astonishment and said, 'But that is *sick!*' 'Yes, I certainly am,' I said, and we agreed that I would never have to do it again.

. . .

One way to horrify at least eight out of ten Anglo-Saxons is to suggest their eating anything but the actual red fibrous meat of a beast. A heart or a kidney or even a sweetbread is anathema. It is too bad, since there are so many nutritious and entertaining ways to prepare the various livers and lights. They can become gastronomic pleasures instead of dogged voodoo, so that when you eat a stuffed baked bull's heart, or a grilled lamb's brain or a 'mountain oyster,' you need not choke them down with the nauseated resolve to be braver or wiser or more potent, but with plain delight. [I believe this more firmly than ever, but am years wearier in my fight. Now, when I want to eat what English butchers call 'offal,' I wait until everyone has gone to the Mid-South Peoria Muezzins' Jamboree and Ham-bake, and then make myself a dainty dish.]

I must admit that my own first introduction to *tête de veau* was a difficult one for a naive American girl. The main trouble, perhaps was that it was not a veal's head at all, but half a veal's head. There was the half-tongue, lolling stiffly from the neat half-mouth. There was the one eye, closed in a savory wink. There was the lone ear, lopped loose and faintly pink over the odd wrinkles of the demi-forehead. And there, by the single pallid nostril, were three stiff white hairs.

At first I thought the world was too much with me, and wondered how gracefully I could leave it. Then what I am sure was my good angel made me stay, and eat, and finally ask for me, for *tête de veau*, when it is intelligently prepared, can be a fine exciting dish. ['I don't go much out,' as a German-American friend of mine says, but even so I have lived about three-fourths of my life in the United States and I have never been served anything even faintly suggestive of the undisguisable anatomy of a boiled calf's head, in this my homeland. The nearest I have ever come to it was, when I was little, delicious cold shaky slices of Head Cheese for summer lunch, and even that was genteelly called 'cold shape' by my English aunt who had the courage to make it for Southern Californians . . . until I grew up enough to make it myself. I give her basic recipe, to be flavored to differing tastes, and then my own version of the classic rules of Tête de Veau: Escoffier, for instance, dictates using a 'white court-bouillon,' but I like a less subtly delicate broth to cook the meat in . . . I like it cooked in halves, *à l'anglaise* but served with a vinaigrette sauce instead of the proper 'boat of parsley sauce' . . . and so on.

. . .

Why is it worse, in the end, to see an animal's head cooked and prepared for our pleasure than a thigh or a tail or a rib? If we are going to live on other inhabitants of this world we must not bind ourselves with illogical prejudices, but savor to the fullest the beasts we have killed.

People who feel that a lamb's cheek is gross and vulgar when a chop is not are like the medieval philosophers who argued about such hairsplitting problems as how many angels could dance on the point of a pin. If you have these prejudices, ask yourself if they are not built on what you may have

FOOD

been taught when you were young and unthinking, and then if you can, teach yourself to enjoy some of the parts of an animal that are not commonly prepared.

Sweetbreads of course are in somewhat snobbish repute, and are indeed worthy of their reputation. Unfortunately they are expensive.

The same is true of liver, which is supposed to be one of the best things in the world to eat if you are anemic. It should be beef or calf liver, since pork liver is fat and heavy to the taste, and according to some authorities actively impure.

There are many fine recipes for preparing liver, but it should always be cooked swiftly so as not to be toughened. It is good the next day, cooked with other left-overs with some sherry added to the sauce, and brown rice to eat with it. (It is also delicious cold, with a glass of beer and some fresh-ground pepper, and a few sprigs of parsley, if you're of the same turn of mind as I am.)

Tongue is of course more acceptable socially than some of the other functional parts of a beast's anatomy. Its main trouble as an economic thing to prepare is that it takes a long time to cook. It is a deceptively mild meat, and needs some characterful sauce well laced with condiments or wine to stand by it.

Brains are, to my mind, unfortunately coupled with scrambled eggs on most menus. The combination is an unpleasant one, because of the similar textures of the two things. Instead, I think brains should be cooked so that they are crisp, and should be served with crisp things, to offset the custard-like quality of their interiors.

M. F. K. Fisher, *Dubious Honours*

OLIVER TWIST

QUITE THE BEST FOOD song ever written. Farewell dear Lionel, you enjoyed my cooking so much. I hope the grub is as good in heaven.

FOOD, GLORIOUS FOOD
Boys
Is it worth the waiting for?
If we live 'til eighty-four
All we ever get is gru...el!
Ev'ry day we say our prayer –
Will they change the bill of fare?
Still we get the same old gru...el!
There's not a crust, not a crumb can we find,
Can we beg, can we borrow, or cadge.
But there's nothing to stop us from getting a thrill
When we all close our eyes and imag...ine.
Food, glorious food!
Hot sausage and mustard!

While we're in the mood –
Cold jelly and custard!
Pease pudding and saveloys!
What next is the question?
Rich gentlemen have it, boys –
In-dye-gestion!
Food, glorious food!
We're anxious to try it.
Three banquets a day –
Our favourite diet!
Just picture a great big steak –
Fried, roasted or stewed.
Oh, food.
Wonderful food.

Marvellous food.
Glorious food.
Food, glorious food!
What is there more handsome?
Gulped, swallowed or chewed –
Still worth a king's ransom.
What is it we dream about?
What brings on a sigh?
Piled peaches and cream, about
Six feet high!
Food, glorious food!
East right through the menu.
Just loosen your belt
Two inches and then you
Work up a new appetite
In this interlude –
Then – food.
Once again, food.
Fabulous food.
Glorious ... food.
Food, glorious food!
Don't care what it looks like –
Burned!

Underdone!
Crude!
Don't care what the cook's like.
Jut thinking of growing fat –
Our sense go reeling –
One moment of knowing that
Full-up feeling!
Food, glorious food!
What wouldn't we give for
That extra bit more –
That's all that we live for.
Why should we be fated to
Do nothing but brood
On food?
Magical food.
Wonderful food.
Marvellous food.
Fabulous food.
Oliver
Beautiful food.
Boys
Glorious food.

Lionel Bart, *Oliver!*

ONE WORLD

THE CENTURY HAS SEEN the world shrink, and travel expanded beyond all imagining. This has brought us contact with all forms of different food styles and ingredients. When I was a child London boasted a few Chinese restaurants and a few Indian, all cooking dishes which bore no resemblance to the food eaten in their homelands. I knew this because I had been there, but I was unusual among my friends. Today London boasts almost every style and nationality of restaurant, and even my small town of Musselburgh sports a Thai restaurant because my fishmonger has a wife from Phuket, and the next generation of Clarke Brothers will be Scots-Thai. However, there is a down side to all this world shrinking: the other side of the world is now where we were when I was young, adopting the worst of our – or rather America's – food culture as we once enthused over Chop Suey and Chicken Madras.

Sri Owen is a great cook, and the leading writer on Indonesian food. She has won innumerable prizes for her brilliant books, and so I feel a real chill when I read her frightening account of one world in Indonesia.

ATTITUDES TO FOOD
THIRTY-FIVE or forty years ago, Indonesia was a Third World country. Today, though it still has problems, its economy is growing quickly and it is confident of being one of the giants of Asia, or

indeed of the world, in the next century. Indonesian life has become more confident, more outgoing, more cheerful and much noisier. People are taller and broader because they eat better than their parents did. And in the cities they live better, too – perhaps.

It is this confidence, expressed in the universal determination to trade and make money, that most strikes the returning exile. I write to a friend, a teacher in a provincial town, to tell him we are coming to visit and will charter a car to bring us from the capital. 'Why do you want to go all that way by road?' he asks in reply. 'I think you had much better fly.' When we get there, I telephone another old friend and ask the family to come and have traditional Javanese fried chicken with us at the place we used to go to years ago – it is still there. There is a moment's hesitation. 'Of course,' she says, 'we'd love to. Well – there's a Kentucky Fried just over the road from there; wouldn't you prefer that?'

I have to admit that I can remember when the Javanese chicken restaurant was a new business, with a new recipe. The pressures on people's eating habits today are powerful and complex. It is not just a matter of Coca-Colanization, though this plays a part. The change comes from within Indonesia as much as from without. In part, it betrays a failure of nerve; where food is concerned, national confidence seems to falter. The same ten or twelve dishes appear on every Indonesian menu; these are the ones foreigners are supposed to recognize, almost as if a gastronomic treaty had been negotiated. It is difficult for Indonesians, especially in the provinces, to offer their own local food to visitors, partly because they know that however good it tastes it doesn't always look very appetizing.

Genevieve Harris, who is now a chef in Sydney but spent a year with one of the Aman Resort hotels in Bali, told me that in Bali she spent a lot of time working with her local staff on dishes that they cooked at home every day but did not think worthy of being offered to hotel guests. All that was needed was to write down an exact recipe, so that the dish came out the same way every time, and to work out an attractive presentation. I couldn't help remembering my husband's old Javanese cook, who used to prepare bachelor suppers for him of solid Dutch dishes heavily laced with margarine. As a new wife, I asked her if she could cook a few Central Javanese sambals occasionally, give us some fresh salad with the delicious local watercress . . . 'Do you really think,' she said coldly, 'that I would give the white tuan Javanese food? As for watercress, it grows in every ditch. I hope you do not expect him to eat *that*.'

She was a good-hearted old lady, and was persuaded graciously to accept a pension. That was years ago, but the attitude is still common. When I was in Jakarta in 1981, I mentioned to the editor of a women's magazine that I wanted to write about regional food. 'Regional food in this country is uneatable,' she told me. It was to be another ten years before I could travel and test the truth of this assertion; and I have to say that she was not entirely wrong. But when bad food has been set before me, its badness has been the result of careless and uncaring cooking and sloppy serving, and these vices in turn derive surely from a lack of pride in the kitchen.

This is part of a more general belief that what comes from abroad must be good. Indeed, this is a universal human trait, and contains much truth, and greatly benefits international commerce. But there is an uncritical acceptance of imported food, and ideas about food, that is having rather mixed results. Indonesians have been taking foreign ideas and beliefs and knowledge on board with enthusiasm throughout their history. Among them, in the 1920s and 1930s and still influential today, were vitamins and vegetarianism – biftek teosofi used to mean a nut cutlet. People are still very health-conscious. In taking to Western food, they are following not only the example of their own past but that of contemporary Asia; every rice-growing country that can afford it is eating less rice, more bread, more milk and butter and cheese, more fast food and convenience foods, above all more meat. What Americans eat is surely what we should eat too. Steaks, fried chicken, hamburgers, ice cream, milk shakes and cola are the staples of the urban middle class, with Japanese fast food running strongly in second place.

Crossing on the ferry from Surabaya to Madura, you have a fine view of the Bogosari flour mills, one of the biggest wheat-milling complexes in the world. A Jakarta businessman told me how its owners contracted with the government to grind flour at cost if they could keep and sell the screenings. 'They sell the screenings for animal feed all over the world,' he said. 'It's like having a bar of gold extruding from the mill, 365 days a year.' But bread, as a result, is relatively cheap and is certainly plentiful.

Even outside the cities, even in the remote islands, change is accelerating. Far more foods are now factory-processed and branded, so that basic foods like noodles are marketed nationwide. In quite small provincial towns, supermarkets are rising, old-fashioned markets disappearing and taking with them the sociable habit of haggling over unfixed prices. It will be many years of course before the pasar vanishes altogether, and changing circumstances may bring it back, but for the moment the supermarket offers standard goods, standard prices, speed, hygiene and bright lights, things which appeal to tourists as much as they do to the locals.

Sri Owen, *Indonesian Regional Food and Cookery*

ONIONS

THE DATA RECIPE BOOK, for want of a better term, on a particular dish or ingredient is a product of the century, but Lindsey Bareham (an excellent cook) has turned it into an art. Onions evoke rustic comfort and cosy kitchens to me. The recent onion riots in India showed how necessary this allium is. I agree with Eric Weir that an onion is a cheerful thing, and should be so honoured.

WITH EGGS

'LET US have a dinner-party all to ourselves! May I ask you to bring up some herbs from the farm-garden to make a savoury omelette? Sage and thyme, mint and two onions, and some parsley.'

Beatrix Potter, *The Tale of Jemima Puddleduck*, 1908

EGGS and onions were made for each other. They're two of the most versatile and widely used ingredients it's possible to cook. Both act as support systems for other ingredients but come into their own in a number of different ways. When they're cooked together they complement each other in more ways than I have room to explore here.

Many of my favourite recipes, including Leeks Vinaigrette with grated hard-boiled eggs, Aioli, Pickled Eggs and Spaghetti Carbonara. I've shunted off to other more obvious sections of the book. This selection gives eggs the starring role – all those soufflés, omelettes and frittatas, the pancakes and scrambled egg dishes, but it's the allium and the way it's been cooked that makes the dish.

Take Jemima Puddleduck's omelette. I imagine those onions being young, juicy and sweet-flavoured. Perhaps they were spring onions that didn't need much cooking before they were mixed with the herbs and folded into the eggs. Perhaps they were white onions used raw, or boiled first in milk, or caramelized in turn the omelette filling a deep chestnut brown.

Chives and raw onion behave oddly with eggs. Chives will turn scrambled egg rancid within half an hour, and cut onion and shallot turns sour almost as quickly, giving cooked egg an odd taste. Most of the time this doesn't matter, because egg dishes tend to be eaten as soon as they're cooked. But the problem is avoided by a brief blanching in boiling water.

Lindsey Bareham, *Onions without Tears*

Onion Soup, or Soupe à l'Oignon

THIS soup is good at any time, but it tastes best at 2 o'clock in the morning after a hectic night.

HARASSED HOUSEWIFE. We never have such things. My husband gets into his bedroom slippers directly after dinner and listens to the wireless.

AUTHOR. I'm so sorry, but I can do nothing to help you. You must have brought him up that way. Haven't you a boy cousin or somebody who can take you out occasionally?

The peculiar thing about this onion soup is that it should be taken in cheerful company. It will lose all its charm if you swallow it in the company of a bunch of frousty aunts and uncles from the provinces. Somehow or other the grated cheese gets round their beards and makes them even more depressing.

THERE is a little restaurant in Montmartre where one can eat it (there is a good deal of 'eating' attached to it) in a most cheerful, disreputable crowd, to the sound of an asthmatic concertina, up to any hour of the morning.

HARASSED HOUSEWIFE. I don't think it sounds a nice soup at all.

AUTHOR. Peel six or eight onions . . . not the Spanish football variety but ordinary onions. Cut them into thin slices and fry them gently in butter until they are a nice golden colour, but not brown.

Put sufficient stock into a saucepan that will go into the oven. Bring the stock to the boil and put in your fried onions. Add some thin slices of bread that you have cut into squares and sprinkle on top four ounces of grated Gruyère cheese.

Put the soup in a hot oven or under a grill flame until the pieces of bread and the cheese begin to brown, then serve and enjoy the fun of watching your friends trying to get the cheese strings into their mouths gracefully.

Eric Weir, *When Madame Cooks*

OXFORD

MY SISTER JUNE, who is far better read than I am and should have been an Oxford don, asserts that Virginia Woolf is the greatest literary influence of the age. Certainly she is a great essayist and a fine wordsmith, as this essay shows.

A LUNCHEON AT OXBRIDGE

IT IS a curious fact that novelists have a way of making us believe that luncheon parties are invariably memorable for something very witty that was said, or for something very wise that was done. But they seldom spare a word for what was eaten. It is part of the novelist's convention not to mention soup and salmon and ducklings, as if soup and salmon and ducklings were of no importance whatsoever, as if nobody ever smoked a cigar or drank a glass of wine. Here, however, I shall take the liberty to defy that convention and to tell you that the lunch on this occasion began with soles, sunk in a deep dish, over which the college cook had spread a counterpane of the whitest cream, save that it was branded here and there with brown spots like the spots on the flanks of a doe. After that came the partridges but if this suggests a couple of bald, brown birds on a plate you are mistaken. The partridges, many and various, came with all their retinue of sauces and salads, the sharp and the sweet, each in its order; their potatoes, thin as coins but not so hard; their sprouts, foliated as rosebuds but more succulent. And no sooner had the roast and its retinue been done with than the silent serving-man, the Beadle himself perhaps in a milder manifestation, set before us, wreathed in napkins, a confection which rose all sugar from the waves. To call it pudding and so relate it to rice and tapioca would be an insult. Meanwhile the wineglass had flushed yellow and flushed crimson; had been emptied; had been filled. And thus by degrees was lit, half-way down the spine, which is the seat of the soul, not that hard little electric light which we call brilliance, as it pops in and out upon our lips, but the more profound, subtle and subterranean glow which is the rich yellow flame of rational intercourse. No need to hurry. No need to sparkle. No need to be anybody but oneself. We are all going to heaven and Vandyck is of the company – in other words, how good life seemed, how sweet its rewards, how trivial this grudge or that grievance, how admirable friendship and the society of one's kind, as, lighting a good cigarette, one sunk among the cushions in the window-seat.

Virginia Woolf, *A Room of One's Own*

PONG

WE ARE ALL ACUTELY AWARE OF the place smell plays in the enhancing of food. There are, however, occasions when what draws us is not fragrance but the peculiarly stimulating odours of decay. Almost every country or civilisation uses fermentation or just plain rot as a means of both preservation and the production of different flavours. Alan Davidson not only is the most erudite food writer of the 20th century but has the rare facility of combining knowledge with entertainment. I love his piece on *Surströmming*, that curious rotten fish from the north of Sweden which actually shimmers on the plate. I have never been brave enough to try it, as I only came to know of it when the required *schnapps* intake was no longer an option for me, but I did once have a tin of it which bulged and grew until I threw it into the bin, failing to remember the crushers on the dustcart!

SURSTRÖMMING

THIS celebrated (or should one say notorious?) kind of fermented herring is produced in the region of Nordingrå, in the north of Sweden, where the clear, dry atmosphere is just right for the process.

Dr Alander of Göteborg used to work in the surströmming region and was told by a local fishery inspector how the practice began. It seems that in the sixteenth century the inhabitants of Gävle on the Bothnian coast were wont to sail forth every spring in search of herring, which they would salt at sea. Their vessel, the *Haxe*, accommodated wives and children as well as goats, empty barrels and a store of salt. Having fished all summer, they would come back and sell their catch at Älvekarleby.

One year they caught more herring than they had salt for; so some of their herring began to ferment and could not be sold to their regular customers. Luckily they found some guileless forest people, of Finnish stock, to whom they were able to sell the faulty produce, confident that they would never see them again. Next year, of course, they took ample salt with them and came back with perfect produce. However, the forest men were waiting for them, and demanded 'the same as last year'.

So the men of Gävle began to ferment herring deliberately for these special customers and thus established a new little industry. Nowadays the fermentation is very exactly controlled. The herring are placed, whole, in closed barrels with about half the normal amount of salt, and the barrels exposed to the summer heat until about 20 August. Then they are opened, to be readied for repacking. Five days later, the surströmming can be sold and there is a stampede all along the coast to get at it.

FOOD

Another fishery official recalled that as a young man he was in the harbour of the island of Ulvön on the August day when 200 barrels of surströmming were opened. As the smell billowed upwards, birds began to drop dead from the sky. Moreover, the wind carried the fumes over to a distant convoy of tugs hauling barges of limestone along the coast; whereupon every single tugmaster changed course for Ulvön. The small harbour was soon a solid tangle of barges and tugs, from which the crews leaped in a frenzy of desire to secure some of the delicacy.

Cans of surströmming bulge slightly, to accommodate the fermentation. A Swedish naval officer told me that when they ate surströmming on board his ship the cans were always opened on deck, because of the smell. The procedure thereafter is to drain and rinse the fish; to sprinkle some chopped, small red onion over them, to reduce the smell; and to lift off the fillets. These are then served with the small oval potatoes which the Swedes call almond potatoes; thin slices of a special bread, tunnbröd, which the northerners carry about in their wellington boots; and butter.

Alan Davidson, *North Atlantic Seafood*

POSH

JOHN BETJEMEN WAS THE VOICE of the British middle class, the villas of suburbia were his metier, the nuances of the tennis club and the lounge his stock in trade. This is perhaps one of his most famous poems, and almost all of us know at least the first line. It gently mocks the mores of the bourgeoisie who 'phone for the fishknives.

HOW TO GET ON IN SOCIETY
Originally set as a competition in Time and Tide

PHONE for the fish-knives, Norman,
As Cook is a little unnerved;
You kiddies have crumpled the serviettes
And I must have things daintily served.

Are the requisites all in the toilet?
The frills round the cutlets can wait
Till the girl has replenished the cruets
And switched on the logs in the grate.

It's ever so close in the lounge, dear,
But the vestibule's comfy for tea,
And Howard's out riding on horseback
So do come and take some with me.

Now here is a fork for your pastries
And do use the couch for your feet;
I know what I wanted to ask you –
Is trifle sufficient for sweet?

Milk and then just as it comes, dear?
I'm afraid the preserve's full of stones;
Beg pardon, I'm soiling the doilies
With afternoon tea-cakes and scones.

John Betjeman, *A Few Late Chrysanthemums*

POST-PRANDIAL

HOW WELL I REMEMBER THE RITUAL of after-dinner coffee! I really felt that when I was allowed to remain for this after dinner it marked a right of passage towards adulthood, of which I am reminded when I read this piece on coffee from *The Unharried Hostess*. After dinner coffee, still such an anxiety for the hostess, is very much a feature of the century, and surprisingly, given all the modern technology, much of the coffee is still filthy.

AFTER-DINNER COFFEE

COFFEE should never be served with dinner. It should be served after, and it should be much stronger than breakfast coffee. Follow these pointers and your coffee will be a fitting finale to your dinner.

5 rules for perfect after-dinner coffee

1. Use a rich roast. Combine Italian after-dinner roast with your breakfast coffee, half and half. Or use all Italian or all French roast, if you prefer.

2. Use a fine grind. Regardless of the roast you use, always choose drip or filter grind. Gives far more flavour than the coarser percolator or all-purpose grind.

3. Use any coffeemaker you like. You can even use a saucepan, as is suggested in *Last-Minute Coffee* below. In fact you get most flavoursome coffee by this simple last minute process. To use filter grind coffee in a percolator, place a paper filter at base of coffee compartment. Will keep coffee clear and help you get every bit of flavour.

4. Start with fresh cold water. (To retain flavour, keep coffee tins in refrigerator once they have been opened.)

5. Measure both water and coffee carefully; I well-rounded Tbsp. coffee for each cup or use more, as you find you like it.

Last-Minute Coffee

FOR each cup you wish to serve, measure into saucepan I coffee cup of running cold water. Heat just to the boiling point. Throw in I heaping Tbsp. of filter or drip grind coffee for each cup of water. (Use combination of breakfast blend and Italian after-dinner roast if you like it.) Let all come to a quick boil to top of pan, stirring coffee gently with spoon to create a pretty foam as it comes to top. Watch carefully; pan can boil over in a minute. Turn off heat; let stand a minute or more so grounds settle. Pour through a small sieve into a warmed pot or directly into cups. (To warm a coffee pot, fill with hot water and let stand a few minutes.)

Festive coffees

Coffee Brûlot

HAVE each guest lay a lump of sugar into his spoon and hold over his cup of hot black coffee. Saturate sugar with some cognac or brandy; ignite it with a match. When flaming is finished, sugar

207

FOOD

is dropped into coffee, giving it a tasty flavour. Pass some slivered orange and lemon peels so each guest can twist a piece of each into his cup.

Caffé Poncino

AN Italian invention made with filter grind Italian roast coffee (Medaglia d'Oro or another good brand). Looks delightful in a stemmed glass.

Into each serving of hot black coffee, pour 1 Tbsp. rum. Add a twist of lemon peel, and serve. Pass sugar for those who may want it.

Irish Coffee

SOMETIMES called 'James Joyce' coffee. This is one of the most delightful special coffees.

To each cup or glass of sweetened hot black coffee, add 1 or 2 Tbsp. Irish whisky (not Scotch whisky), depending on size of cup. Float a teaspoon of cold heavy sweet cream on top by pouring it over the reverse side of spoon, ie, the convex side. Do not stir in. Contrast of cool cream over hot coffee is what counts – to say nothing of the Irish whisky.

Rebecca Reis, *The Unharried Hostess*

POVERTY

THE SCOTTISH AUTHOR CATHERINE BROWN is fascinated by poverty, and is probably the only writer I know who can tint it with a degree of romance so that one longs to taste the mince and dumplings of her grandmother's Glasgow tenement. The poor, says the Bible, we have always with us and having been both very rich and very poor I know which I prefer. However, I have no doubt from tales of my grandfather's medical practice in the poorer areas of Glasgow that if one had the choice it was a better place to eat on the bread line than any other – a belief that is borne out by Catherine's evocative piece from *Broths to Bannocks*.

FOR dinner at one o'clock there is a plate of thick meaty broth: ham bone with lentils, or the stock from a boiling chicken thickened with leeks and rice, or Scotch Broth made with pearl barley and a piece of nineholes (flank) of beef: always the cheapest cuts of meat, always the threepence-worth (1½p) of vegetables and parsley, always a warming plateful.

Meat and potatoes are for Sundays: an oxtail stew, tender meat sliding of its own accord from sculptured bones left on the plate; or rich brown oniony mince with misshapen mounds of grey-white suety dumplings, or chewy tripe in milk and soft boiled onions – all cooked in the pot which sits on the black iron range in the cramped kitchen of my Glasgow tenement-living grandmother.

Through two World Wars, and the subsequent repercussions on food supplies, through a Depression which hit hardest at this urban population, it was quite astonishing that these

fundamental Scottish cooking traditions should have been so well preserved in this tenement lifestyle which I grew up with in the 1940s and 50s.

Of course much was lost. But the old habits of Scots frugality saw this generation through their difficulties, some better than others, their powers of ingenuity stretched by the relentless scrimping and saving which went on to make ends meet. Their attitude to waste as a criminal offence also helped them to survive. It developed their hard-headed approach, which made them so splendidly thrifty – valuing occasional luxuries, but always realistic of the horrors around the corner which were all too visible on suffering faces in city streets.

To say that the Scots can't cook, but are nevertheless quite good bakers, always seems to me to dismiss too lightly the ancient tradition of cooking in a pot, which survived despite serious obstructions, if the things which came out of my urban grandmother's and my mother's pots were anything to go by.

Their ideas on cooking were quite sound. They had an intuitive talent for making good things out of a little, which requires clever cooking skills rather than just the ability to slap out a scone for the girdle or make a crisp round of shortbread. How much easier, also, to stick a roast in the oven, fry up a steak, grill a lamb chop, than gently coax the flavour from meat and vegetables, blending with patience and discretion the delicate combinations.

This was clever economy cooking, using the least amount of fuel, extracting the maximum amount of flavour. It is a more advanced method of cooking than primitive roasting on the spit. It is a method understood in the higher echelons of gastronomy. In France, more than in any other country perhaps, there is a long history of respect for the pot on the fire, the *pot-au-feu* – the foundation of the cooking.

There were other food influences around, of course, for the young generation who played the streets and back courts of Glasgow tenements at the end of the Second World War, but there is no doubt that for the fortunate the focal point of the eating day was the cooked dinner from the pot. We never saw such things as roasts. Vegetables went into broths or were cooked in the stews, but hardly ever appeared separately, except sometimes a cabbage, or a tin of peas. It is, I fancy, the main reason why so many Scots of this generation have a mental block about eating vegetables on their own.

Street food, if it wasn't a 'piece in a poke' (white bread and jam in a paper bag thrown out of the window to hungry children in the back court), was from 'chippies' (fish and chip shops) or 'Tallys' (Italian ice cream cafés) or there was always the baker selling hot pies, sausage rolls and gravy.

At the ancient street-market complex where people eked out a living selling from barrows there was more street food for hungry children along with second-hand clothes and books, rusty mincers, crystal wireless sets and all the clamjamphry of odds and ends that makes up the 'Barras'.

Developed as one way of fighting poverty and unemployment in the nineteenth century, it later became an established part of the city life, which it remains today: a pantomime of fast-talking barrow men and women. Selling is the thing. Holding the attention with whatever antics are most novel and the typical Glasgow sceptic in the crowd quips back: 'See him . . . could sell the Pope a double bed, so he could.'

We indulged in toffee apples, poky hats (ice cream cones), hot peas and vinegar, pea bree (cooking liquor), hot pies and gravy, bags of whelks, plates of steaming fishy mussels with cups of mussel bree. As we lived so much of the time in constant city smoke, sulphurated air and wintertime pea-soupers, just to put our heads round the door of the Oyster Bar in the Gallowgate as the huge pans of black mussels and whelks were tipped onto wooden slats on the floor to drain, was to take us back to nostalgic salty scents of the sea.

For those who struck some sort of balance between this street/shop-cooked and home-cooked food, the diet did not lack variety. Vegetables eaten raw were certainly rare. But the city streets, especially on Saturdays, were full of fruit and vegetable barrows. Much of the produce came from the Clyde valley, a fertile source of vegetables, plums, apples and pears, tomatoes, strawberries and raspberries. Fruit was our treat in those days of post-war rationing when we never knew sweets and never missed them.

Of course there were those, inevitably, who ate more fish suppers from the chippies in the week than was good for them – like every night because their mothers were out working all day. Their diet suffered, though nutritionists have established that fish and chips make a well enough balanced meal.

While broths and stews were for dinner, shop-cooked foods were for the teatable at night. You went out to smart tearooms where a black and white uniformed waitress would ask if you wanted a 'plein or a heigh tea'. But tea was just tea at home. There was nothing 'high' about it.

White bread and marge with a huge pot of brewing tea on the hob. Fish, pies, black and white puddings were always with chips. Bacon was with eggs, or tattie (potato) scones, herrings were in oatmeal, squerr sausages (square sliced Lorn sausage) were with fried potatoes, cheese was scrambled with eggs, kippers and boiled eggs were with toast. The standbys were either sardines, or for a special treat, tinned salmon.

Salads were virtually unheard of, the only nod in that direction being a solitary Clyde valley tomato which appeared along with a plate of cold meat. The meat was invariably gammon (ham), a smoky cure which came from a grocer who sliced the cold meats with a long sharp knife.

Catherine Brown, *Broths to Bannocks*

IN CONTRAST IS THIS EXTRACT from Philippa Pullar's *Consuming Passions* on London poverty at the turn of the century, which seems chillingly nasty. However, neither of them are one half as unpleasant to my mind as what the poor eat nowadays, spending their scanty funds on cheap, frozen, pre-prepared or junk food. At least in times gone by mothers made their best efforts to see their children got the best food possible. Today nutrition has taken second place to designer gear, cynically designed for the budget market; and the dearth of cooking and misplaced nutritional information has brought about a return to pre-First War constitutions, with rickets revisited by the affluent skimmed milk dwellers of Hampstead, and the Army rejecting a third of recruits on the grounds of generally poor health.

Of course the poor have always eaten badly, and as prosperity increases it seems they eat consistently worse. It is the poor who will suffer most from unsafe meat removed from

211

FOOD

carcases with hosepipes, hormonised chickens and GM vegetables. However, one of the best additions to an inferior diet was provided by the advent of the fish and chip shop. Nutritionists who pontificate against the deep fat fryer should look realistically at what is eaten instead.

1902 saw the arrival of the fish-and-chip shops which emanated from the hot pie and cook shops. There was a growth in eating out. In London hotels and restaurants there was a remarkably high standard of food. Simpson's was well to the front with its joints 'fit for Pantagruel', its turbots, delicious pies and puddings. Forty years later Arthur Moss was to become Master Cook there – one of the three English Master Cooks – which entitled him to wear the Black Cap of the Master Cooks, made for him in black velvet by his wife. But in those days his mother had to go out to work and he spent a good deal of time with his grandmother in Brixton. He remembers sitting in her kitchen, cross-legged on the floor in front of a great Dutch oven, basting the mutton as it cooked. In 1912 he began a job at a bakery in Wandsworth, working under the skill of a superb German pastry cook. Moss remembers the wonderful smell of muffins, crumpets and buns, which costing about a halfpenny each were sold with the bread in the morning; cakes and patisseries were displayed in the afternoon. Marvellous aromas emerged from the shop in the early mornings as the cottage loaves, big and round with a smaller loaf on top, brick loaves with notched tops, and coburgs, split open during baking, came out of the ovens.

The people of Wandsworth were poor; most of them cooked on open fires with a tiny oven at the side. On Sundays they queued up at the bakery to have their joints – bought cheap at the market the night before – cooked for them, for which they would be charged 4d to 6d. And then he remembers they ran home like the wind, their joints wrapped in a warm cloth. Next door the butcher sold boiled beef, salt pork and carrots, and faggots, which were made by Moss at two o'clock each morning. The butchers still had their own slaughter houses, the milkmen kept their cows tied up in sheds so that the milk was still warm when sold: a beverage which Moss remembers with disgust, ever since he drank a warm mug of milk frothing straight from the cow. Moss's dislike was upheld generally; the unpopularity of milk probably accounted for the general malnutrition of poor children. A survey made in Sheffield, in 1900, showed that sixty per cent of mothers in working class districts were feeding their young children on quite unsuitable foods – mainly bread and jam. As a result instruction in the Board Schools was being wasted, children were often so hungry they fell asleep during the lessons. J. B. Priestley remembers that what he calls the 'lower orders' were poverty stricken. He himself was a member of the lower middle classes, and although his family lived carefully, frugally even, he was certainly well-nourished, with the main meal in the middle of the day, a colossal Yorkshire high tea and uproarious parties at Christmas time when he laughed himself in a red haze at charades. It was a life when there was none of the common anxiety there is now, it was more secure. This Mr. Priestley puts down to the fact that there were very few clever people persuading everyone to buy what they could not afford to buy, and making them discontented that they were not buying so much as their neighbours.

Philippa Pullar, *Consuming Passions*

QUEER

DEPRIVATION DRIVES US TO STRANGE FOOD and stranger habits, but the true gourmet will not sink to Woolton Pie, as the Vicomte de Mauduit illustrates here.

PREPARING A HEDGEHOG

AFTER killing the hedgehog, clean its inside. Then roll it thickly in some moist clay and put it in a moderate oven (Romany or kitchen oven) and bake till the clay is quite dry and hard. Break the clay by cracking it with a stick or hammer and the prickles and top skin, which will adhere to the clay, will come off with it. Lastly, skin the legs.

WAYS OF COOKING A HEDGEHOG

HAVING prepared the hedgehog as above, it can be cooked in different ways. Either roasted or fried as a chicken, stewed as a rabbit, or made into a paté as for Hare Paté.

THE SQUIRREL

THIS is another great delicacy, the flesh of a squirrel being more tasty and tender than that of a chicken.

GRILLED SQUIRREL

SKIN and clean the squirrel, then open it out as you would a chicken for grilling, and grill the squirrel in the same way.

SQUIRREL-TAIL SOUP

THE tail, which is put aside after skinning, can be used with haricot beans, onions, and herbs in making a delicious soup.

ROAST SQUIRREL

SQUIRREL is also most tasty roasted, and this is done in the same way as for roast chicken.

STEWED ROOKS

CLEAN, draw, and skin the rooks. Make an incision half an inch thick on each side of the spine and remove the piece which is the bitter part of the rook. Put the birds in a casserole with equal parts of water and milk sufficient to cover the rooks, add salt, pepper, 1 sliced onion, 2 sliced turnips, 2 sliced carrots, some chopped mint, or preferably chopped fennel, and stew with the lid on the pan till tender.

Vicomte de Mauduit, *They Can't Ration These*

The Sugar Plant

This, of course, is a tropical plant, but since it has been successfully acclimatised to grow indoors in temperate regions there is no reason why it could not advantageously replace the dismal aspidistra of the Victorian era in the homes of Britain today.

This plant, which goes by the botanical name of *Impatiens sultani*, grows on its branches granules which crystallise and which not only taste like cane sugar but also contain an equal proportion of sucrose and dextrose.

When these crystallised granules are gathered others grow in their place and it does not sound, therefore, such an extravagant idea, especially in times of sugar rationing, to suggest growing a sugar plant in a pot as a centrepiece for everyone's dining-room table and reach out to it for granules when wishing to sweeten our tea, coffee, or other beverages!

Vicomte de Mauduit, *They Can't Ration These*

QUINCE

The American Waverly Root wrote a splendidly quirky encyclopedia of food. Here is an extract.

The appreciation of taste is, I suspect, an artificial phenomenon acquired by education, like the appreciation of Western music, also an artificial phenomenon acquired by education, so that our ears accept a scale which is out of tune (and do not even perceive it is out of tune) in exchange for the ability to move up or down it without limit and to modulate without difficulty through the entire gamut of our keys. The infant is born with an uninitiated ear and unprejudiced taste buds, which at first transmit to the brain a message about the taste of whatever is being eaten without making any judgment about whether that taste is good or bad. The child learns quickly how to convert the measurable chemical and physical stimuli reaching it from the exterior into an esthetic estimate of quality – the transfiguration of mathematics into emotion. It discovers what it likes and what it does not like within the ecology of which it is a part – the biological ecology (the plants and animals it eats because they occupy the same habitat) and the social ecology (the eating habits of the society in which it lives). Once learned, these judgments harden into prejudices. That is why it takes so long for an unfamiliar food to be accepted in regions uneducated to appreciate it.

The subjective and artificial nature of our responses to the stimuli of taste is beautifully betrayed by the quince.

Almost all of us today would agree that the quince is too sour to eat fresh, and can be tolerated only when it is cooked with great quantities of sugar. The quince, says *The Practical Encyclopedia of Gardening*, almost brutally, is 'of a peculiar, almost guava-like flavor when cooked (useless otherwise).' Yet in ancient times the quince was eaten as a fresh fruit, and even today, in some countries, is eaten whole cooked with a minimum of sugar.

Almost all the other venerable fruits (the quince has been cultivated for more than four thousand years) have gained in favor since antiquity; the quince has moved in the opposite direction – and only since medieval times, when according to Paul Lacroix in his *France in the Middle Ages*, it was 'generally cultivated' and 'looked upon as the most useful of all fruits,' and in the Orléanais 'formed the basis of the farmers' dried preserves.' The quince does not seem to have changed during that period: it is our gastronomic education which has changed. Since the coming of sugarcane, we have learned to demand sweetness in our food. The ancient countries where the quince was eaten fresh, and Europe in the Middle Ages, were brought up on less efficient or less plentiful sweeteners, like honey or grape sugar. They could appreciate not only foods which were sweet, but also foods which were sour.

Many taxonomists were at first reluctant to believe that the quince was a separate fruit: they thought it a kind of pear, and tagged it *Pyrus cydonia*, the Cydonian pear. It does look, after all, like a pear. It is often pear-shaped (but also sometimes a flattened sphere); it is golden yellow, like many pears; and when it is cut open the cross section resembles that of a pear, but with yellowish flesh which turns a pretty dull-pink when cooked. Since 1870, most pears have been grown on quince rootstock, which holds the height of the pear tree down, making picking easier, and encourages it to bear fruit earlier. But the quince will not hybridize with the pear, which is why it has now been decided that the quince is a quince, not a pear. Its scientific name has accordingly been changed to *Cydonia oblongata* or *C. vulgaris*, the only species of its private genus, though there are several subspecies and numerous varieties.

The quince is a native of at least Persia and Anatolia, where it still grows wild, and perhaps of an even larger area, extending into the Caucasus and Greece. We hear of its cultivation in Mesopotamia first, and next in Greece, where the ordinary mainland quince was improved by grafting onto it scions brought from Cydonia, on the island of Crete, which produced the finest quinces in the ancient world. Rome imported Cydonian quinces too, and Pliny remarked that the variety he called Mulvian was the only one which could be eaten raw, which suggests that the Romans knew fruit no less astringent than ours. Columella wrote that 'quinces yield not only pleasure but also health,' and distinguished three varieties, which he called the sparrow apple, the golden apple and the must apple.

The ordinary Roman name for the quince was the Cydonian apple, hence its modern scientific label. It was also called the golden apple, and it has been suggested that it was the golden apple of the Hesperides, but it seems likelier that this was the orange, or even the lemon. I do not know whether the quinces Petronius represented Trimalchio as serving at his ridiculously extravagant banquet were raw or cooked, but it would probably have been inadvisable to eat them either way, since Trimalchio had studded them with thorns to make them look, Jupiter knows why, like sea urchins.

At a slightly later period, Athenaeus wrote that Athens was importing from Corinth quinces which were 'as delicious in taste as they are beautiful to the eye.' For the Greeks the quince was a symbol of fertility, dedicated to the goddess of love. In Athens quinces were tossed into the bridal chariot in which the groom was conducting his bride to her new home, where she would be offered a piece of wedding cake flavored with sesame, honey and, as a charm for fruitfulness, a date or a quince.

In the Middle Ages quinces were so highly esteemed in France that presents of a quince preserve called *cotignac*, a sort of marmalade which was a specialty of Orléans, were ordinarily made to kings, queens and princes in cities which were honored by their visits; when Joan of Arc arrived to lift the siege of Orléans, the first gift offered her was *cotignac*. The menu of a splendid banquet given by Pope Pius V in 1570 included quince pastries on its menu, with the meticulous specification: 'One quince per pastry.'

The best quinces of that period were held to be those of Portugal, which is why 'marmalade' comes from *marmelo*, the Portuguese word for quince, the fruit originally used to make marmalade. It was not made with oranges until 1790, when orange marmalade was first manufactured in Dundee, Scotland. A British cookbook published several marmalade recipes in 1669, but none of them used oranges: most were based on quinces. The fruit was known to Chaucer, who mentions 'coines,' a spelling which suggests that the fruit came from France, where its name today is *coing*. Baked quinces appeared on an English banquet menu in 1446.

Quinces enjoyed a period of popularity along America's eastern coast in Colonial times. The Massachusetts Bay Colony's Memorandum of March 16, 1629, listing the seeds it wanted sent to it from England, called for quince seeds, and there are at least two seventeenth-century mentions of the quince in Virginia, in 1648 and 1669, while they were reported in 1720 to be growing there abundantly. An old New England specialty were quince cheese, preserved fruit solidified by all-day boiling, and a small amount of quince was often added to apple butter. In New England especially, the quince was once common in home gardens and was also grown in commercial orchards, but today it has lost favor even there; it is now the least grown of all tree fruits in the United States.

Elsewhere the quince has remained in favor in certain countries whose cuisine contains many fatty foods: the acidity of the quince counteracts greasiness. This is true of Germany and of South Africa, for instance. In the latter the popularity of the quince has been heightened because apples, which grow well at the Cape, do badly in the interior; the quince there replaces the apple. Quince sauce is made exactly like applesauce. Fatty meats like mutton or pork are frequently accompanied by whole baked quinces, cored, and only lightly sugared. Quinces appear fresh in *sambals*, which are mixtures of raw grated, spiced fruits and vegetables, used as condiments.

I do not know whether quinces are still eaten raw in Latin America, but they used to be. When they reached this part of the New World, brought there by the Spanish or the Portuguese or both, either the new climate produced new sweeter varieties or the acidity of the quince did not disturb the natives, who may be presumed to have had a gastronomic education different from the one which shapes our tastes now. One early nineteenth-century explorer in Chile reported large quinces there which were acid and astringent but became 'sweet and good' if allowed to ripen completely. From Santa Cruz, Mexico, John Russell Bartlett, who may be presumed to have been of the orthodox American gastronomic school, wrote in 1854:

> There are two varieties of the quince here, one hard and tart like our own, the other sweet and eatable in its raw state, yet preserving the rich flavor of the former. The Mexicans gathered and ate them like apples but I found them too hard for my digestive organs.

Waverly Root, *Food*

FOOD

QUO VADIS

I LOVE THIS BOOK. I love the professional dedication it displays, and the humour of an Italian who had come to love his adopted country even though they locked him up as an enemy alien. It represents a small piece of history which in itself I find fascinating.

AN ENFORCED 'HOLIDAY'

WE reached the cell door and the policeman produced an enormous key with which he unlocked it, the corridor ringing with the clash of metal.

'What happens next?' I asked, as he pushed the heavy door open.

'You won't be here long,' he replied, standing aside to let me enter. 'As soon as we've got a coach-load we'll run you down to the Collection Centre at Wandsworth.'

The way he spoke made it sound as if the coach journey was going to be a jolly day excursion to the seaside on that fine June day, though little of the sunshine penetrated into the sombre cell-block.

'And then?'

'I don't really know. An internment camp in the Isle of Man, I believe. You're lucky, you'll be by the sea, everything looked after for you, and no worries. Ought to be some smashing grub when all you Ities get cracking on the rations. Perhaps too many cooks, though . . . Sorry, but I've got to lock you in. Got something to read to pass the time away? Don't know how long you'll be here.'

I shook my head. I didn't mind being locked in. I didn't want anything to read. I had more than enough to occupy my thoughts, and the time.

The door closed with a bang and I was alone in the bare, sparsely-furnished cell. The walls were whitewashed down to within three feet from the ground and the rest was chocolate brown, and the only light was grudgingly supplied by a narrow, barred window set high in the wall facing the door. I was used to sunshine on the whitewashed walls in my native village of Cannero, on Lake Maggiore, but there was no sun on this whitewash, scored with the initials of its countless prisoners. I went to the far wall. I am not a tall man and all I could see through the window was a drab brick wall. I felt compelled to see the sky. Taking the wooden chair, I climbed upon it and craned my neck. My reward was a small square of blue sky, patterned by the window's thick bars. Why should I, who had never been actively conscious of the sky before, suddenly feel such an urge to see it? I can't explain, but that small square of sky satisfied me. I climbed down from the chair and looked round the cell.

To say it was sparsely furnished is an understatement. Apart from the chair there was a table and a wooden platform built into the wall. This, I thought, must be the bed, for on it was an untidy tangle of rather dirty looking blankets. It was as if somebody had been torn from a nightmare sleep to be taken straight for trial. The table was of white deal. At least it had been white, but now it was stained with grease, the ring marks of mugs, and a brown stain, which could have been blood, but must have been the prison chocolate I had often heard about. I remembered my tables, with their spotless linen and shining cutlery, and that brought me back to reality . . .

Yet they went out of their way to treat us as human beings, not cattle. When we were delivered by the coach to the school in Wandsworth which was to be our temporary stopping place before we were transferred to a camp in the provinces, they were polite, courteous, but strong. They were determined to keep to International Law, as laid down for internees, but they made it clear they wouldn't stand for any funny business. They treated the ingratiating, the whiners, the pompous and the threateners who had friends in high places, with patience and tolerance. 'There,' they said in effect, 'your bed,' pointing to three coir-stuffed square objects, which I learned later to call biscuits, on which were a couple of folded blankets, 'there is your bed. It is unmade in one sense but, in another sense, it was made for you, by our country's leaders. And you must lie in it. By the way, the sooner you settle in the sooner you'll get some food. Irish stew, we believe.'

'No minestrone?' called out some wag, and there was laughter . . .

With the enamel plates with which we had been issued we queued up to collect our food. When I got back to my bed on the floor I set the plate down and looked at my watch. I was astonished to see that it was nearly six o'clock. It was almost twelve hours since I had been picked up and the time had gone like a flash. If every day of internment went as quickly as this I would be well pleased. I felt suddenly hungry. Taking my knife and fork I attacked the plate on the floor before me. Irish stew is hardly a dish I would serve in my restaurant and this was, as far as I could remember, my first acquaintance with it. That it was nearly cold didn't help my enjoyment. It was, I saw, a dish made of the cheapest joint of mutton and since the cook had not trimmed the meat of fat, it was, in its cold state, glutinous in the extreme. There were also little bits of bone which kept on getting stuck in one's throat and chunks of half-cleaned carrot and undercooked potato. I pushed it to one side and, still hungry, opened my suitcase to see what my wife had provided. There was ham, chicken, cheese, biscuits, and a pear. Taking a chicken leg in my fingers, I lay back on my narrow bed and ate it. It was delicious.

Peppino Leoni, *I Shall Die on the Carpet*

THE RAJ

HOW HARD IT MUST HAVE BEEN ON BOTH SIDES to form a mistress–servant relationship in the Raj, when all the social *mores* clashed and neither party would have held the job but for the strange social rearrangements of Empire!

FOOD

THE DUTIES OF THE MISTRESS

HOUSEKEEPING in India, when once the first strangeness has worn off, is a far easier task in many ways than it is in England, though it none the less requires time, and, in this present transitional period, an almost phenomenal patience; for, while one mistress enforces cleanliness according to European methods, the next may belong to the opposite faction, who, so long as the dinner is nicely served, thinks nothing of it being cooked in a kitchen which is also used as latrine; the result being that the servants who serve one and then the other stamp of mistress, look on the desire for decency as a mere personal and distinctly disagreeable attribute of their employer, which, like a bad temper or stinginess, may be resented or evaded.

And, first, it must be distinctly understood that it is not necessary, or in the least degree desirable, that an educated woman should waste the best years of her life in scolding and petty supervision. Life holds higher duties, and it is indubitable that friction and over-zeal is a sure sign of a bad housekeeper. But there is an appreciable difference between the careworn Martha vexed with many things, and the absolute indifference displayed by many Indian mistresses, who put up with a degree of slovenliness and dirt which would disgrace a den in St. Giles, on the principle that it is no use attempting to teach the natives.

They never go into their kitchens, for the simple reason that their appetite for breakfast might be marred by seeing the *khitmutgâr* using his toes as an efficient toast-rack (fact); or their desire for dinner weakened by seeing the soup strained through a greasy turban.

The ostrich, who, according to the showman, '*ides 'is head in the sand and thinks as 'e can't see no one, as nobody can't see 'e,*' has, fortunately, an exceptional faculty of digestion. With this remark we will leave a very unpleasant subject.

Easy, however, as the actual housekeeping is in India, the personal attention of the mistress is quite as much needed here as at home. The Indian servant, it is true, learns more readily, and is guiltless of the sniffiness with which Mary Jane receives suggestions; but a few days of absence or neglect on the part of the mistress results in the servants falling into their old habits with the inherited conservatism of dirt. This is, of course, disheartening, but it has to be faced as a necessary condition of life, until a few generations of training shall have started the Indian servant on a new inheritance of habit. It must never be forgotten that at present those mistresses who aim at anything beyond keeping a good table are in the minority, and that pioneering is always arduous work.

SALADS

'THANK YOU, I never eat salads, except at my own house,' was the inadvertent reply of a *gourmet* to his hostess. In India, at any rate, the habit is a safe one; for anything more appalling than the usual mess of flabby shreds mixed with mustard and vinegar, and decorated lavishly with hard-boiled eggs and beetroot, cannot be imagined. Yet nothing is more simple than salad-making. First, the gardener should have orders *not* to wash the lettuce. A washed lettuce is a spoiled lettuce. Secondly, lettuces should never be eaten the day they are cut, but the next. On being brought in from the garden, they should be cut with a sharp knife about one-fourth of their length from the top, so as to cut across the leaves, and just expose the white heart. They should then be stood upright, roots up, cut leaves down, in about one inch of water. The leaves will suck up the water, and become wonderfully crisp and juicy. The great Soyer never used a lettuce until it had stood two days in this fashion, and his salads were the wonder of all who ate them.

Half-an-hour before they are to be eaten, the lettuces should be pulled to pieces with the hands, dirt removed with a damp cloth, and each leaf broken into three or four. A leaf that will not break is not worth eating. Next, rub a clove of garlic round the bowl, pour in 3 units of salad oil. Add the lettuce and shake well. Then add 1 unit of vinegar – tarragon if possible – salt, pepper, and sugar, about ½ unit each, 1 unit of chopped chervil, and 1 of the green part of young onions. Mix by putting a plate on the top of the bowl and shaking. Salads may be treated with mayonnaise sauces, but the plain dressing is more wholesome.

The following salad maxims were given to the writer by a pupil of Soyer: Never let water touch the lettuce. Never let a knife touch it. Never touch it till half-an-hour before it is to be eaten. Never put mustard in a salad sauce. Never mix different kinds of salad stuffs. Never decorate your salads.

Grace Gardiner and Flora Annie Steel, *The Complete Indian Housekeeper and Cook*

RATIONING

THE WAR YEARS OF WORLD WAR II, with the home front, rationing and making-do, seem extraordinary even to me, born in their shadow in 1947. I can just remember sweet-rationing, and certainly it was a topic much discussed in my childhood. The voice of the Ministry of Food was very much the prolific author Marguerite Patten, and it is to her that I turn to recall to you the true face of wartime austerity.

THE immediate period before Victory was certainly not a peaceful one. Fighting was intense both in Europe and in the Far East.

The Home Front, as we at home were known in Britain, continued to cope with the perils of flying bombs and rockets together with more personal worries. The problem of rationing had become a familiar one and people were managing well. We also became like squirrels, hoarding summer foods for the winter.

Seasonal fruits and tomatoes were bottled. Onions were a problem, too, for shipping space was far too valuable to import onions, so people dried as many as possible to give flavour to winter dishes.

The Women's Institutes and other organisations achieved wonderfully high standards when preserving fruits. They made jam, on behalf of the Ministry of Food and to the Ministry's specifications, to form part of the rations. The jars of bottled fruit put on show by them and those of us in the Food Advice Division of the Ministry were often artistically perfect – every piece of rhubarb would be the same length and beautifully packed. You would see jars of apple rings, with blackberries nestling in the centre of each apple ring.

221

FOOD

Dig for Victory was a message observed by a very large percentage of the public. You could see vegetables growing among the roses and other plants in gardens, and some people even dug up all their flowers to plant a variety of vegetables and fruits instead.

In the country it was taken for granted that people would keep chickens, but many town dwellers decided to keep them, too, to give them fresh eggs and provide a chicken to cook from time to time. Some of my friends had invested in poultry, and a few had rabbits too. Many of the latter were never eaten, for they became family pets and no-one could bear to kill them.

The Ministry of Food

The Ministry controlled the distribution of food during the war, and afterwards, and was responsible for giving out information on food rationing, and the wise use of all foods. The recipes and Food Facts leaflets published by the Ministry of Food enabled people to make the best use of the rations available and augment them with unrationed foods, such as potatoes, flour, oatmeal and seasonal vegetables. Much of the advice was given in a light-hearted manner. In addition to recipes and suggestions for new ways of incorporating more potatoes into the daily diet, for instance, the value of the vegetable was extolled by the symbol 'Potato Pete'. Children became interested in Potato Pete's friendly figure and advice and were more inclined to eat, and enjoy, potato dishes.

A Food Advice Division was established within the Ministry of Food to help ensure that the public kept fit on the rations and enjoyed the dishes they could make with the food available.

The headquarters staff in London were responsible for nutritional information and the recipes published by the Ministry. Throughout Britain Food Advice Centres were established, staffed by home economists, of whom I was one. We gave demonstrations in the Centres, and in market squares, hospital out-patient departments, works' canteens, large stores or any place where we could come into contact with people, for it was essential that everybody knew about the rations and any additional foods to which they were entitled.

In April 1940 Lord Woolton became Minister of Food and his name soon became very well-known. Although a recipe for the famous Woolton Pie, named after him, has already been given in my book on wartime cooking, *We'll Eat Again*, I have repeated it for, since that book was published, I have found that there are several versions, all of which are interesting.

Food Rationing

Not all basic foods were placed on the ration at one time; foods were introduced gradually.

January 1940 – rationing introduced. The foods placed on ration were: bacon, ham, sugar and butter.

March 1940 – meat became a rationed food.

July 1940 – tea, margarine, cooking fat and cheese made part of the ration.

March 1941 – jam, marmalade, treacle and syrup all put on ration.

June 1941 – distribution of eggs controlled.

November 1941 – distribution of milk controlled.

July 1942 – sweets put on ration.

FOOD

WELFARE FOODS

The Vitamin Welfare Scheme was introduced in December 1941. Small children and expectant mothers received cod liver oil and concentrated orange juice (from America). These played a major part in ensuring that children grew up strong and healthy. Expectant and nursing mothers and small children were entitled to extra milk rations, too, as were certain invalids.

WHAT WERE THE RATIONS?

THESE were the basic rations for one person per week. The ration book had coupons, covering the different ration foods, which were removed as the food was purchased. The basic rations varied slightly from time to time, as more or less of a certain food was available, but on the whole they were as follows:

Bacon/Ham 4 oz (100 g) of either bacon or ham.

Meat to the value of 1s 2d (6p in today's money).

Sausages were not rationed but often difficult to obtain.

Offal was originally not rationed but when supplies of meat were difficult it formed part of the ration. Canned corned beef and products like Spam generally formed part of the points system.

Butter 2 oz (5 g).

Cheese 2 oz (50 g). Sometimes this rose to 4 oz (100 g) and very occasionally to 8 oz (225 g). Vegetarians had extra cheese, for they surrendered their meat coupons.

Margarine 4 oz (100 g).

Cooking Fat 4 oz (100 g) but quite often this dropped to 2 oz (50 g). Dripping sometimes mentioned in recipes was scrapings from every frying pan or pot to obtain every spoonful of dripping. This was not available on rations.

Milk 3 pints (1.8 litres), often dropping to 2 pints (1.2 litres). National Dried Milk (known as Household milk), which became available after December 1941, was a tin per 4 weeks.

Sugar 8 oz (225 g), which had to be used for cooking and jam-making too. When there were adequate supplies in the country the Ministry would release a little more for jam-making, this was available on the sugar coupon.

Preserves 1 lb (450 g) every 2 months, so it was very important to supplement this (jam, marmalade, with home-made preserves, golden syrup or treacle).

Eggs 1 shell egg a week, if available, but frequently dropping to 1 shell egg every 2 weeks. From June 1942 dried eggs were available and the ration was a packet (containing the equivalent of 12 eggs) each 4 weeks.

Tea 2 oz (50 g) per week. In December 1944 on extra tea allowance was introduced for 70-year-olds and over.

Sweets 12 oz (350 g) every 4 weeks.

Marguerite Patten, *Victory Cookbook*

MUCH HAS BEEN WRITTEN ABOUT OUR OWN RATIONING in World War II, but I was fascinated to come across these references to Axis rationing conditions in World War I. I know so little about how it was for the other side in this war and how they coped during it, though there is plenty of literature on their postwar hardships.

THE rationing system adopted by Germany had one major fault. It worked well so far as the distribution of flour, sugar and a few other commodities was concerned but it did not ensure an equitable distribution of all the food that was available. A vast illicit trade came into existence between the country people and disreputable tradesmen in the towns. Right through the War some foods were reasonably plentiful in the country districts but a large proportion that should have reached the markets through normal channels and been fairly distributed came into the hands of private speculators who disposed of it at a large profit to wealthy people in the towns. The magnitude of this trade (*Schleichhandel*) and the audacity of those who operated it are a blot on the record of the 'home-front' in Germany during the War. One of the charges brought against the German Jews and for which they are suffering to-day is that they were largely concerned in organizing and operating this illicit trading.

By the summer of 1916 it was known to the British authorities that our blockade of Germany had so reduced the food supply of the Central Powers that in some areas the civilian population was living on rations that were little above starvation level. In Bonn, for example, a civilian was unable openly to buy more than 10 oz. of bread, 13 oz. of potatoes, 2 oz. of meat, 1 oz. of sugar and about ½ oz. of fat daily. If, therefore, he was too poor to buy extra supplies from illicit sources he was forced to exist on a diet providing about 1350 calories and a mere 31 gm. of protein. This was slow starvation. Factory workers were permitted slightly larger rations, but even these were inadequate to sustain the labour required. Not a few factory directorates went so far as to contract with illicit dealers to supply their canteens with extra food so that production in the works would not be seriously retarded by the declining vigour and efficiency of the operatives.

J. C. Drummond and Anne Wilbraham, *The Englishman's Food*

... AT their entry into the War the Italian troops drew a ration consisting of about 4½ lb. of meat a week and a daily issue of bread, macaroni, etc., providing about 3500 calories. It was nearly 1000 calories less than our own men received and was certainly less than they required for campaigning under very arduous conditions. In February 1917 the weekly ration of meat was reduced by no less than 1 lb. and, what was even more serious, the macaroni and bread issue was also curtailed. The new diet gave the men barely 3050 calories a day; just about what would suffice a woman for a light day's work. It was an inexcusable folly on the part of the authorities because Italy was not then short of cereal foods. Resentment spread through the ranks, morale declined and the men's health began to be affected. On October 24th the Austro-German forces delivered the surprise attack in a thick mist which was the opening move of the battle of Caporetto. Within forty-eight hours the Italian front had collapsed over a wide sector and the greater part of the second Army was in headlong

FOOD

SAVE BREAD

and you save lives

SERVE

POTATOES

retreat. There is no longer any question in the minds of experts that the effect of more than seven months' subsistence on inadequate nourishment played a large part in bringing about the disintegration of the Italian resistance.

J. C. Drummond and Anne Wilbraham, *The Englishman's Food*

REFORM

EXACTLY what the heading says.

FRUITS proper; there is not the slightest doubt that fruit is a valuable item of our fare. It is not to be denied that the structure of our teeth is conclusive evidence of our being naturally fruit eaters. Fresh fruit contains a great deal of water; you think you are getting something but you are really getting very little. Were we to eat nothing but apples we should have to eat fully 13 lbs. a day to ensure absorbing the necessary 3,000 calories; with the same view, 29 lbs. of tomatoes would be required. No wonder, then, that vegetarians have failed in their attempt to live on nothing else but fruit. If dry fruit be used instead, then the result is more fortunate. The only point is that dry fruit lacks fat, but as this can be remedied by the addition of fatty fruit, spoken of in the previous group, it is evident that nothing ought to prevent us making our entire diet of fruit. It would, however, be an expensive way of living.

This group goes extremely well with cereals and fat foodstuffs, which it supplements, being very much richer in salts. This is why I mix fruit with porridge and groats, and why I eat jam, apple marmalade, stewed plums, etc., with bread and butter. The aperient effect of fruit is often very useful, but, like everything else, it can be overdone. We need but think of the frequency of stomach-ache during the plum season.

Tomatoes I recommend. Their nutritive power is slight, it is true, but as an addition to various sauces they are valuable.

TUBERS

AMONG these is to be found my favourite – the potato. It is the best article of food I know of. Nobody has so thoroughly tested the value of potatoes as I have. For ten months I have had human test subjects living entirely on potatoes and margarine. Their health and strength during this period had not only been maintained, but had even improved. Potatoes cure constipation, dissolve uric acid, etc., etc. But this is a point into which I cannot go fully in this book, and therefore refer the reader to my other work, *Protein and Nutrition*.

Badly masticated potatoes are difficult to digest and irritate the intestines. Therefore potatoes must either be mashed in the kitchen, or, what is better still, well masticated. Other roots are closely related to potatoes. Carrots can provide a good many tasty dishes which I urgently recommend. This applies to all other roots, scorzonera, and so on.

VEGETABLES

VEGETABLES are neither particularly wholesome nor cheap. The comparatively cheap kinds, such as cabbages, as a whole, must not be eaten in too large a quantity, for they would bring on indigestion, and the dearer kinds, well, they are too dear for people of small means. Added to this, vegetables have another fault, i.e., they are too satisfying. Anybody choosing to feed exclusively on cauliflower would require nearly 19 lbs. a day to absorb 3,000 calories or 40 lbs. of salad. Hence the general belief that a vegetarian diet is far too filling. One can, however, obviate such a fault by glancing over the table of foodstuffs; one will realise how many vegetable products are in reality far more concentrated as regards nourishment than lean meat. Fat meat is an exception, but it contains more fat than flesh.

It is nevertheless astonishing how much vegetables are recommended nowadays, even outside vegetarian circles. Most doctors have of late decided against eating too much meat, but none has dared to go further than to say to his patients, eat meat but with a large addition of vegetables. Such advice may be good for many people, but what about the housewife who must economise? Green vegetables, I say, are a luxury. They may hold their place on the table, but they must not form the principal part of a meal. Instead of saying with the doctors, eat meat with plenty of vegetables, I would urge people to eat meat with abundant roots.

Dr M. Hindehede, *What to Eat*, English adaptation by C. A. Bang

RESTAURANTS

HAVING BEEN TAKEN TO RESTAURANTS by my mother from a very early age, I am fascinated by their *mores*. I think this a charming piece.

'PSTRUH' is Czech for 'trout' – and trout there were! The cadences of the 'Trout' Quintet flowed methodically through hidden speakers and shoals of trout – pink, freckled, their undersides shimmering in the neon – swam this way and that way in an aquarium which occupied most of one wall.

'You will eat trout,' said Utz.

I had called him on the day of my arrival, but at first he seemed reluctant to see me:

'Ja! Ja! I know it. But it will be difficult . . .'

On the advice of my friend, I had brought from London some packets of his favourite Earl Grey tea. I mentioned these. He relented and asked me to luncheon: on the Thursday, the day before I was due to leave – not, as I had hoped, at his flat, but in a restaurant.

The restaurant, a relic of the Thirties in an arcade off Wenceslas Square, had a machine-age decor of plate-glass, chromium and leather. A model galleon, with sails of billowing parchment, hung from the ceiling. One wondered, glancing at the photo of Comrade Novotný, how a man with so disagreeable a mouth would consent to being photographed at all. The head-waiter, sweltering in the July heat, offered each of us a menu that resembled a mediaeval missal.

We were expecting the arrival of Utz's friend, Dr Orlík, with whom he had lunched here on Thursdays since 1946.

'Orlík', he told me, 'is an illustrious scientist from our National Museum. He is a palaeontologue. His speciality is the mammoth, but he is also experienced in flies. You will enjoy him. He is full of jokes and charm.'

We did not have long to wait before a gaunt, bearded figure in a shiny double-breasted suit pushed its way through the revolving doors. Orlík removed his beret, revealing a mass of wiry salt-and-pepper hair, and sat down. His hand – rather a crustacean claw than a hand – gave mine a painful nip and moved on to attack the pretzels. His forehead was scoured with deep furrows. I stared with amazement at the see-saw motion of his jaw.

'Ah! Ha!' he leered at me. 'English, he? English-man! Yes. YES! Tell me, is Professor Horsefield still living?'

'Who's Horsefield?' I asked.

'He wrote kind words about my article in the 'Journal of Animal Psychology'.'

'When was that?'

'1935,' he said. 'Maybe '36.'

'I've never heard of Horsefield.'

'A pity,' said Orlík. 'He was an illustrious scientist.'

He paused to crunch the remaining pretzel. His green eyes glinted with playful malice.

'Normally,' he continued, 'I do not have high regard for your compatriots. You betrayed us at Munchen . . . You betrayed us at Yalta . . .'

Utz, alarmed by this dangerous turn to the conversation, interrupted and said, solemnly, 'I cannot believe that animals have souls.'

'How can you say that?' Orlík snapped.

'I say it.'

'I know you say it. I know not how you can say it.'

'I will order,' said Utz, who waved his napkin, like a flag of truce, at the head-waiter. 'I will order trout. 'Au bleu', isn't it?'

'Blau,' Orlík bantered.

'Blau yourself.'

Orlík tugged at my sleeve: 'My friend Mr Utz here believes that the trout, when it is immersed in boiling water, does not feel more than a tickling. That is not my opinion.'

'There are no trout,' said the head-waiter.

'What can you mean, no trout?' said Utz. 'There are trout. Many trout.'

'There is no net.'

'What can you mean, no net? Last week there was a net.'

'Is broken.'

'Broken, I do not believe.'

The head-waiter put a finger to his lips, and whispered, 'These trout are reserved.'

'For them?'

'Them,' he nodded.

Four fat men were eating trout at a nearby table.

'Very well,' said Utz. 'I will eat eels. You also will eat eels?'

'I will,' I said.

'There are no eels,' said the waiter.

'No eels? This is bad. What have you?'

'We have carp.'

'Carp only?'

'Carp.'

'How shall you cook this carp?'

'Many ways,' the waiter gestured to the menu. 'Which way you like.'

The menu was multilingual: in Czech, Russian, German, French and English. But whoever had compiled the English page had mistaken the word 'carp' for 'crap'. Under the heading CRAP DISHES, the list contained 'Crap soup with paprika', 'Stuffed crap', 'Crap cooked in beer', 'Fried crap', 'Crap balls', 'Crap à la juive . . .'

'In England,' I said, 'this fish is called 'carp'. 'Crap' has a different meaning.'

'Oh?' said Dr Orlík. 'What meaning?'

'Faeces,' I said. 'Shit.'

I regretted saying this because Utz looked exceedingly embarrassed. The narrow eyes blinked, as if he hoped he hadn't heard correctly. Orlík's wheezy carapace shook with laughter.

'Ha! Ha!' he jeered. 'Crap à la juive . . . My friend Mr Utz will eat Crap à la juive . . . !'

I was afraid Utz was going to leave, but he rose above his discomfiture and ordered soup and the 'Carpe meunière'. I took the line of least resistance and ordered the same. Orlík clamoured in his loud and crackly voice, 'No. No. I will eat 'Crap à la juive' . . . !'

'And to begin?' asked the waiter.

Bruce Chatwin, *Utz*

RIDICULOUS

WHEN I WAS YOUNG I HEARD that Jesus mixed with publicans and sinners, and I read Chesterton's the grocer, 'that men might shun his awful shops and go to inns to dine'. I have met some great publicans and have been one of the fraternity myself, I know the bonding of the tavern and the important role it plays. I remember saying to my favourite nun, when she expressed surprise that I had kept my faith, 'where do you think Christ found the Publicans and Sinners? Down the Women's Institute?' When I discovered a biblical publican was a tax collector I was truly bemused. I would love to have met John Fothergill, the legendary landlord of the Spread Eagle at Thame. John published a portrait of himself as a beautiful young man beside one of himself in raddled middle age, under the caption 'Was this the face that launched a thousand chips!' He excelled in serving food that didn't look like its taste, such as this white beetroot soup.

Beetroot. Scrub and slice thin (with kitchen chopper for preference), and simmer with onion in stock or clear soup or water. Watch carefully so as to take it off before the beet begins to look brown. If you want brilliant colour it's best to be extravagant, i.e. more beetroot and less simmer. Drain. Mix in a milky, buttery white sauce, pepper, salt and a bit of sugar. Don't boil, and it's best kept hot in a double saucepan to retain the colour longer. Sugar beet can be done in the same way, but, being white, it loses in colour what it gains in the unexpected in taste. When serving, drop a teaspoonful of whipped cream into each plate.

Thame Innkeeper's Diary

Pre-packed foods are the norm for us nowadays, so this is an interesting little insight into their early promotion. It's strange that the century has seen such huge leaps in this department when you would think that improvements in refrigeration and gadgetry render it totally unnecessary.

Packaged Foods – A Modern Convenience

How fortunate today's housewives are! Not many years ago few foods were sold in packages. Foods, sold in bulk, were exposed to dust and handling; pantry shelves were cluttered with paper bags. Today, General Foods Corporation, among other progressive food manufacturers, is giving every housewife an opportunity to buy in packages of practical sizes and shapes, so that she, too, may have as neat and compact an array as her enviable grocer.

But not only for convenience does the modern housewife like packaged foods. She knows that they take the guesswork out of buying. When she buys the same brand she can be sure of the same type and quality of product – that coffee, with the enticing, fresh aroma, the cake flour which makes such feathery light cakes, the coconut just moist enough for her meringues and toppings and quick desserts.

It is in maintaining quality, not only in the products themselves, but in the dishes made from them, that General Foods Corporation makes one of its important contributions to the needs and desires of modern home managers. We have studied the problems of food buying and preparation and have tried to meet them, in part, by the information and recipes on the package. Each label carries a description of the product and gives suggestions or recipes, as the case may be, for some of its most popular uses. All of these recipes are thoroughly tested by food experts in our experimental kitchens.

Learning Brands, Grades, and Sizes

It will be a boon to efficient marketing when standards are established for grades of all foods. It then will be possible for the housewife to know what she may expect from her dealer when she buys meat, potatoes, fresh or canned fruits, and vegetables of grade 1, 2, or 3. Although there now

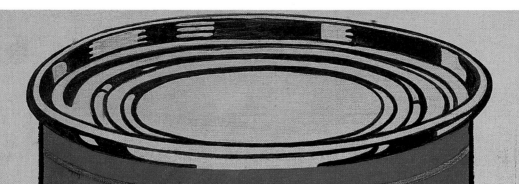

are some grades which have been established by groups of canners or manufacturers, or by growers or packers, they have not been passed on to consumers in many instances. This is partly because grades are not uniform throughout the country, and partly because of a belief among retailers that housewives are not interested in grades. Many grocers buy potatoes in the wholesale markets graded as United States No. 1 or No. 2, but very few sell them so graded to their customers.

There is, however, a growing tendency to grade foods. The wise home buyer will watch the market and become familiar with grades as soon as they come into use in retail stores. In the meantime, she can help herself considerably by becoming acquainted with canned and packaged foods by brand name and noting those which she likes best.

The General Foods Cookbook, 1932

SALT PORK

JANE GRIGSON WAS AS CORRECT THIRTY-ODD YEARS AGO as she would be today when she wrote that everyone knows about pâté but to serve a hot glazed joint of salt pork would cause a sensation. Yet it was once the most commonplace of daily foods. Salt pork can be decribed as a builder of empires, staple of the Roman world and the British Navy alike. It has circumnavigated the globe and left industries in its wake. If armies marched on their stomachs many of those digestive systems were fuelled with this versatile meat. In some ways I am almost happier with Jane Grigson's recipe-based enthusiasms than with Elizabeth David's wonderful purple prose. *Charcuterie* was her first book, and is as useful and readable today as ever. I have two salted pig's cheeks sitting in my larder waiting for intrepid dinner guests as a result of her advice.

OF ALL *charcuterie*, the most easily rewarding to make, from an English housewife's point of view, is salt pork and unsmoked ham. Everybody nowadays knows about pâté, but produce a hot, glazed joint of salt pork, or a cold dish of delicate *jambon de Paris*, and you cause a sensation.

This enthusiasm has a long historical tradition. Dumas, in his *Grand Dictionnaire de Cuisine*, tells of the not-so-stupid Emperor Claudius, Robert Graves's Claudius, who walked into the Senate one day crying, 'Pères conscrits, dites-moi, je vous prie, est-il possible de vivre sans petit salé?' To which that noble body promptly replied, 'Oui, seigneur, plutot mourir que de se passer de lard.' And from then on senators ate large quantities of salt belly of pork and cabbage to keep alive and flatter Claudius.

Or perhaps they meant it, for the Romans sustained their enthusiasm, beyond their own resources, by imports of ham from Gaul. It was Strabo who early recorded the excellence of French *charcuterie* in his *Geographia*, Book 4, written in the first century A.D.: 'Food they (the Gauls) have in very great quantities, along with milk and flesh of all sorts, but particularly the flesh of hogs, both fresh and salted. . . . And their herds of swine are so very large that they supply an abundance . . . of salt-meat, not only to Rome, but to most parts of Italy as well.' At the same time Romans in Britain were enjoying their favourite salt-pork in another Celtic area: one cremation site of the first century A.D., excavated recently near Winchester, disclosed to the diggers 'a tray set with cutlery for a meal, a pig's trotter and a Bath Chap'. A vivid but anachronistic description; or were pig's jaws cured *à l'Aquae Sulis*, even then? (The tray is on view in Winchester Museum.)

When I buy kilo bags of *sel marin de Bretagne* from our Trôo grocer, I like to reflect that Strabo's hams were cured in this same grey salt, evaporated nearly two thousand years ago from the same cold Atlantic.

Earlier still, northern meat had to be preserved by burial in pits, or by drying in the wind, because our fitful sun could not sustain a salt industry on Mediterranean lines, where, then as now, huge glistening heaps of white salt dried on low shores, in brilliant light. But with the increased technological skills and achievements of the Iron Age, Northern Europeans overcame their salt problem by artificial means. The method they used has left red fertile mounds, easily to be seen around Maldon, in Essex, where excellent sea salt is still produced. Shallow earthenware trays on legs were filled with sea water and fires were lit beneath. The water boiled away leaving a deposit of salt to be scraped off the trays. Naturally there was a high wastage of such friable equipment. New trays were set up on top of the broken pieces, and reduced in their turn to coarse red powder, betraying now, by large, slightly raised circles of red soil in brown ploughed fields, and by lumps of *briquetage* fused with jade-coloured vitrifications of sand, the sites of this ancient, essential industry.

The problem of salt is still with us (though not, in these days of refrigeration, as a means of preserving meat for winter use). The flavour of sea salt is vastly better than the flavour of refined rock salt. In London continental grocers in Soho stock good salt, and so does Elizabeth David, at 46 Bourne Street, S.W.1, but in smaller towns it may only be available in Health Food shops. Polythene bags of sea salt which keep well in a dry place, can be brought back from France. Refined rock salt is all right for brine and dry salting, but the flavour of the ham will not be quite so good; all grocers stock refined rock salt. Be careful not to buy free-running table salt, as chemicals are added, to prevent it forming lumps, which make it unsuitable for curing.

The other things needed are easily come by. A large crock, preferably of stoneware, although a plastic bucket will do. A piece of boiled wood which fits right into the crock, to keep the floating pieces of pork below the surface. Household soda for cleaning the crock. Saltpetre (to be bought from any chemist) to give the meat an appetising pink colour. Sugar to counteract the hardening effects on the meat of salt and saltpetre. A maximum and minimum thermometer is not essential, but it gives accurate information about the fluctuations of surrounding temperature, which can be deceptive . . .

White wine can be used, and flavourings of herbs and spices, but from the actual preserving point of view salt is the only absolute necessity. Brine will keep for several weeks, indefinitely if you strain it off from time to time, clean the crock, and boil up the brine again. In bacon factories the brine in huge white-tiled curing baths is eternal, perpetually being drained off and added to, but never thrown away. A vintage blend, with as many strains as a fine brandy.

Jane Grigson, *Charcuterie*

SEX

COOKING AND SEX are two of my favourite occupations, and I might be minded to disagree with Theodore Zeldin were he not so devastatingly attractive.

KRAFFT-EBING, the expert on sexual perversions and Freud's colleague in Vienna, said that hunger and love govern all world affairs. But they both forgot about hunger and concentrated on the torments of love, which was unfortunate, because sex, food and drink have always been fellow travellers in the search for pleasure. If sexology had not become a separate scientific subject, if the search for knowledge had been organised differently, if there were professors of happiness who studied the passion for pleasure as a whole, in all its forms, a different outlook might have emerged. Physical urges are not despots and have frequently been disobeyed; tastes are not fixed for ever. The way to look afresh at desire is to consider what people want at table and in bed as part of a whole.

Gastronomy is the art of using food to create happiness. There are three ways of eating, and three corresponding ways of searching for happiness. To eat until one is full up is the first and traditional way, putting faith in old recipes and well-tried methods. The aim is to become contented, to be comforted, to feel cosy, to purr. This is the cautious approach to pleasure, with the motto 'Protect yourself from foreign bodies'.

Foreign bodies are not only the fly in the soup, but also everything that is unusual, forbidden, unfashionable, threatening. It was in the process of learning to eat that humans made their fear of foreign bodies a virtue and called it taste. Mental habits developed which mimicked the patterns set by eating, and fear of foreign bodies spread to many other aspects of life; routine, however boring, appeared to be the safest insurance policy. Much of history has consisted of wars against foreign bodies, because the first kind of happiness humans sought out was that which gave security. Nothing would ever have changed if caution had triumphed, but there were always nervous and lonely people who did not feel safe, regarding themselves as foreign bodies too, strangers in their own surroundings; contentment seemed impossible to them.

So a second way of eating was invented, treating food as an amusement, a form of permissiveness, a caress of the senses. The purpose was to seduce and be seduced, with the help of romantic candlelight, to create conviviality around delicious odours. In such circumstances, one's

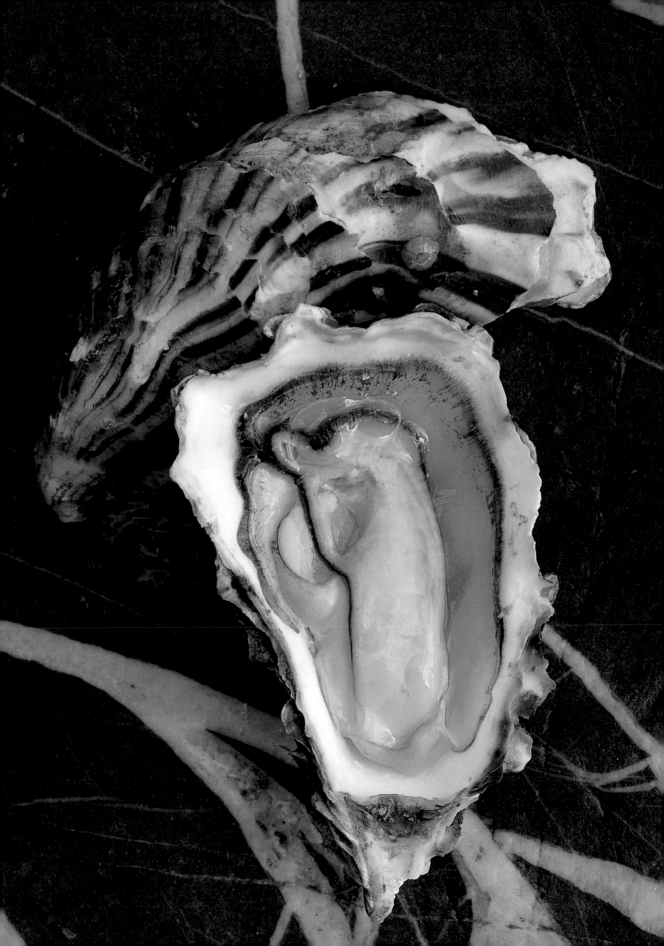

attitude to the world at large is only temporarily modified: one flirts with foreign bodies during the meal, but they do not affect how one behaves in the office. This kind of eating has suited the person who has despaired of being fulfilled by a quiet life, who yearns for distractions and surprises, who seeks a different kind of happiness in frivolity, in being jokey, cynical, ironical, refusing to be made permanently miserable by the big problems, like starvation and stupidity. The cooks who prepare food for them are like jazz musicians, improvising playful flourishes, never reaching a conclusion.

But of course it is impossible to be happy in more than a very superficial way while others are unhappy. When peace and quiet, or wit and detachment, began to pall, a different yearning was born, to make a personal, original contribution to life. The search for a third kind of happiness – which moderns call creativity – demanded a way of eating which corresponded. All invention and progress come from finding a link between two ideas that have never met, bringing foreign bodies together. For individuals who aspired to be creative, eating became part of the process of looking at the world in a more adventurous spirit. Creative cooks found qualities in food that nobody suspected were there, uniting ingredients that never used to mix. Creative diners are constantly engaged in losing their fear of strange foods, and of foreign bodies.

However, this does not mean that there are three kinds of people, each of them stuck with their habits. Creativity is the preoccupation of the master chef, consciously trying to innovate, but those who believe they are doing the opposite, endlessly reproducing the same grandmother's recipes, are sometimes creative without realising it. It is true that there are people who eat roughly the same food as their ancestors thousands of years ago, but variety creeps in all the same, however limited the menu may seem. Thus in Ghana a poor community, completely unknown to the world of culinary connoisseurs, eats 114 species of fruits, 46 kinds of leguminous seeds and 47 greens. In the Andes, a peasant can distinguish without difficulty between 300 varieties of potato, and he will cook his stew with as many as twenty to forty varieties, carefully balanced. Every time a recipe is not strictly followed, every time a risk is taken with changed ingredients or proportions, the resulting food is a creative work, good or bad, into which humans have put a little of themselves. The invention of a new dish is an act of freedom, small but not insignificant. There is still enormous scope for such acts, since humanity today eats only about 600 out of the hundreds of thousands of edible plants.

Children have usually been brought up either to be loyal to their family's taste or, more recently, to develop individual identities by asserting their own taste. But now some are being encouraged to treat tastes as they treat people, as worthy of being respected, recognised, understood, and not to erect high walls between those whom they will or will not speak to, between foods they like or do not like. The French schoolchildren whose syllabus now includes systematic lessons in the art of tasting are the pioneers of an important revolution. An open mind about food, and about the tastes of foreigners, inevitably modifies one's attitudes to one's neighbours.

The world was for long divided into three major empires, of roughly equal size, based on the three main staple foods, wheat, rice and maize. But what separated people even more was the sauce or spice they added: olive oil in the Mediterranean, soya in China, chilli in Mexico, butter in northern Europe, a whole variety of aromas in India. The Russians rioted in the 1840s when the government tried to persuade them to grow potatoes; being used to living mainly on rye bread, they suspected a plot to turn them into slaves and force a new religion on them; but within fifty years they were in love with potatoes. The explanation is that they added the same sourness – *kislotu* – which had always given savour to their food, and which was what they were ultimately addicted to. Every people puts its own scent on its food, and it accepts change only if it can conceal the change from itself, by smothering each novelty in its scent. Optimism about change, whether in politics, economics or culture, is only possible if this premise is accepted.

The Americans have used sugar as the taste which makes all novelties acceptable. Sugar, which does not smell and which has the magical power to make almost anything superficially palatable, has indeed united the world's taste more than anything else. Once a rare and divine medicine – honey was called the perspiration of the sky, the saliva of the stars – its production has increased fortyfold in the last hundred years: it is the culinary expression of democracy. Only when Latin American chocolate, previously spiced with chilli, was married to sugar (by Conrad van Houten of Amsterdam in 1828) did it capture the world's palate. In 1825 Brillat-Savarin, author of *The Physiology of Taste*, predicted that sugar was destined to be the 'universal flavouring'. At that time Goethe was paying 2.70 gold marks for one kilogram; sugar was the elixir of pleasure only for the rich, who spent more on it than on bread. Now the prophecy has been fulfilled: almost every packaged food contains sugar.

All culinary progress has been dependent on the assimilation of foreign foods and condiments, which are transformed in the process. Chinese food reached its apogee in the twelfth century thanks to the importations of adventurous merchants. The food of Europe was orientalised by the massive use of spices – it was almost Indian in the Middle Ages. Then it was Americanised by the introduction of the potato, the tomato, the Christmas turkey and other Native American produce. Fast food is neither American nor European, but an inheritance from the street vendors of the Middle and Far East. The *nouvelle cuisine* is the result of a graft of Japanese ideas on to French tradition. These importations have always been by minorities, against opposition. All innovation encounters opposition.

However, hunger is still being satisfied without full awareness of what it is one is hungry for. Some delicious foods have no nutritional value, others are disagreeable until a taste for them is acquired, others still do not stop one feeling hungry but stimulate one to eat yet more, to prolong the pleasure of eating, like a lover seeking to prolong an embrace. Trying to make sense of such behaviour can clarify a lot more than one's tastes in food – for example, how far one is interested by new sorts of pleasure, or innovation and creativity in general, whether one is willing to risk disappointment or failure, whether one wants to be brave and free more than to be applauded, whether one likes to discuss one's pleasures, whether one enjoys giving pleasure to others. Gastronomy is a branch of knowledge in its infancy, focusing not on self-indulgence but on exploration, not just on self-exploration but on the exploration of the whole of nature. It can look forward to ever-widening horizons of pleasure and understanding, even though it has its dark side, for it has done little to deal with the obscenities of famine and cruelty, and it will perhaps only receive proper recognition when it does. Nevertheless, forks and spoons have probably done more to reconcile people who cannot agree than guns and bombs ever did.

Theodore Zeldin, *An Intimate History of Humanity*

237

FOOD

SENTIMENT

JAMES BEARD IS A LEGENDARY NAME in American food circles, and like so many gay men was besotted with his mother. Here he sentimentally ascribes his love of food to her influence. Strange to think that only in the second half of the century could he legally admit he was homosexual, and that is not even yet a universal privilege.

I THINK I developed an accurate taste memory early in my life. I was not sentimentally attached to the cooking of any one person at home, and we ate in restaurants a good deal. I tried to be as objective as possible about taste and was somewhat precocious in appreciating the pleasure of blending satisfying flavors. While this meant that I learned to enjoy the delights of a good meal, it also meant that I soon grew intolerant of mediocre food. More than once, I'm afraid, my candid appraisals embarrassed a hostess or friends with whom we were sharing a meal. I often wonder why I didn't have a pie thrown at me!

Both my parents had sensitive palates, my father to a lesser degree, although Mother tended to disparage his knowledge of food. In later years he looked forward to the periods when my mother was away at the beach so he could live on his own cooking. Aside from this, he had a favorite late Sunday breakfast menu, which he produced every week, save in winter, consisting of deliciously sautéed chicken served with a bacon-and-cream sauce made in the sauté pan. With this dish there were generally hot biscuits, toasted crumpets or just good toast. In winter the menu changed to sausage, smoked fish or country ham. These expressions of my father's culinary skill were memorable indeed, and whenever friends stayed with us on weekends, they used to request his breakfast.

Mother had an uncanny sense of food and the talent to show others how to prepare it. She loved to cook, eat and talk food more than almost anyone else I have known. At the turn of the century she had an international approach to food that would have been considered revolutionary in the last ten years. She was ahead of her time socially as well. When women were still subordinate and modest, Mother was forceful and fearless. She swept through a room or down the street with an air of determination and authority, and she met men on their own terms. In any social gathering men surrounded her, and on outings she was among them, clamming, fishing, berrying. She could talk their language and used profanity on occasion, though without vulgarity. Women, as could be expected, were less drawn to her, except for those who gave her the boundless devotion often felt by the weak for the strong. Her circle of friends was colossal. Her counsel was constantly sought, and her know-how saved many an occasion.

She was always ready for an adventure – prepared to pack her bag and be off on a journey (she had never been seasick, she boasted, never missed a meal at sea). And it was probably in this same spirit that she had packed up and left England years before.

James Beard, *Delights and Prejudices*

SMELL

THE SUFFRAGETTE MOVEMENT, votes for women and finally feminism are very much 20th-century developments. Whilst I of course feel very much part of the increase in womens' influence and rights, American feminism has always terrified me. This poem epitomises why Stateside feminism has not been a great asset to culinary development. I am, after all, the woman who gave up a legal career for cooking.

WHAT's that smell in the kitchen?
All over America women are burning dinners.
It's lambchops in Peoria; it's haddock
in Providence; it's steak in Chicago;
tofu delight in Big Sur; red
rice and beans in Dallas.
All over America women are burning
food they're supposed to bring with calico
smile on platters glittering like wax.
Anger sputters in her brainpan, confined
but spewing out missiles of hot fat.

Carbonized despair presses like a clinker
from a barbecue against the back of her eyes.
If she wants to grill anything, it's
her husband spitted over a slow fire.
If she wants to serve him anything
it's a dead rat with a bomb in its belly
ticking like the heart of an insomniac.
Her life is cooked and digested,
nothing but leftovers in Tupperware.
Look, she says, once I was roast duck
on your platter with parsley but now I am Spam.
Burning dinner is not incompetence but war.

Marge Piercy, *Stone Paper Knife*

SNOEK

ONE VERY GOOD REASON for not going to war, according to my sister, is that one will never have to eat snoek again!

THERE was a great bonfire in our street that day, with fireworks, and all of us wearing red-white-and-blue ribbons pinned V-shaped to our lapels. Afterwards, we wandered through the dusk with lighted stubs of candle, ten-year-olds in solemn procession, to show that there was no black-out any more. 'The war's over . . .'

But afterwards, after the war and the victory, where was the transformation scene? We still bathed in water that wouldn't come over your knees unless you flattened them; we still wore clothes with the ugly 'Utility' half-moons on the label. Chewing carrots for sweets, we still said avidly to our parents: 'Tell us about pre-war days,' and wondered at stories of chocolate cigars and real pineapple that didn't come out of tins. For years after the war a faint aura of the miraculous seemed to hover round shops piled with oranges, lemons, grapes, bananas: all the routine-exotic fruits unknown to an island enclosed by war, and the aftermath of war. Austerity, like poverty, leaves its children with a lingering appreciation of the treat.

Of the generation in Britain which remembered vanished pre-war treats, perhaps no one in 1945 was expecting a sudden magical return of prosperity. All the same, hope was burgeoning. It was, after all, the hope of release from the long grinding privations of wartime life which had done much to put the Labour Government so resoundingly in power; release from the small, dull, makeshift meals, from darkness and drabness and making do, from the depressing, nerve-aching, never-ending need to be *careful*. For a great many people, war had meant the same kind of food, clothes, and living conditions as the Thirties; now, the vitality of Labour would whisk them out of both. The housewife knew she would have to be patient a little longer, whipping up her mock cream from cornflour and margarine; but there was a good time coming soon. Well, fairly soon . . .

In October 1947, with the butter and meat rations newly cut, the bacon ration halved, restaurants' food supplies dwindling, and potato rationing on the way, the hungry British first heard the word 'snoek'. Ten million tins of it from South Africa were to replace Portuguese sardines, whose import was restricted by exchange troubles; the new fish, said Mr. Strachey, would go on points. 'I have never met a snoek,' he added, with the Ministerial waggishness that always holds a faint sense of doom, 'so I cannot tell you much about it. It is long and slender, weighing up to eighteen pounds.'

The name, of course, was a gift. Before it even arrived in the shops this unfortunate fish was seized with cries of delight by cartoonists, sub-editors, music-hall comedians, and Members of Parliament; not least when one early consignment was found to be packed in salt, and inedible except as fish paste. Research revealed that the snoek was a large, ferocious tropical fish, like a barracuda; that it was dangerous to bathers, had rows of fearsome teeth, and when displeased hissed like a snake and barked like a dog. A Lieutenant-Colonel (retd.) wrote a long letter to *The Times* about snoek fishing, ending: 'I have the greatest respect for this notable fighter as an article of diet. It tastes like a mackerel, only more so.' *The Times*, infected by the gentle delirium, headed his letter: 'Hunting the Snoek'.

Wholesalers did not welcome snoek; they had already imported a number of tins, off points, and these had not been a success. 'People didn't like it,' said one. 'Tasteless and unpalatable,' said another. 'Abominable stuff.' The Minister, however, had not only spent £857,000 on snoek, but had eaten it: at a picnic, in sandwiches. It was, he said with rash honesty, 'good, palatable, but rather dull'.

In May 1948, when the first large consignment arrived, Dr. Edith Summerskill presided at a snoek-tasting party at the Ministry; the Government put up quantities of snoek posters (even, as an Opposition member pointed out, in fishing ports) and published eight remarkable recipes.

Snoek piquante: 4 spring onions, chopped; liquid from snoek; 4 tablespoons vinegar; ½ can snoek, mashed; 2 teaspoons syrup; salt to taste; ½ teaspoon pepper. Cook the onions in the fish liquor and vinegar for five minutes. Add the snoek, syrup and seasoning and mix well; serve cold with salad . . .

It cost 1s 4½d. for a half-pound tin, and took only one point – thirteen points less than red salmon, five points less than household salmon, and much cheaper than either. But nobody seemed quite clear whether it was being eaten. The crescendo of music-hall jokes rose. 'We can sell every tin,' said Mr. Strachey, in October 1948, and arranged to import some more. The *Daily Express* chose twenty-five Mrs. Smiths from the telephone directory, rang them all up and asked if they had bought any snoek yet. 'The name frightened me,' said one Mrs. Smith. 'Well, if I were very hard pushed,' said another. Only two, reported the *Express*, had actually bought a tin: one said it tasted terrible, and the other gave it to the cat. Grocers and distributors alike reported guardedly that snoek was 'not going well'.

The fact was that the housewife, conditioned by shortage, had learnt during the war years to regard any food publicised by the Ministry with fatalistic suspicion. She knew that its quality would probably be low, due to the austerity principle of selecting foods primarily for their capacity to 'go round', and, without the incentive of wartime effort, she was not now disposed to play ball. Also, she disliked the taste of snoek. By the summer of 1949, more than a third of the snoek imported since 1947 was still unsold: 3,270,000 half-pound tins, out of a total of 11,110,400 – with 1,209,000 still to come under existing contracts. The Ministry hopefully put out more recipes: snoek sandwich spread, snoek pasties, snoek with salad. Their leaflets were still going the rounds when in August 1949 two thousand more tons of tinned fish, in 8,960,000 half-pound tins, arrived from Australia to be sold at a shilling a tin. They called it barracuda, but it still tasted like snoek.

The Ministry began to wilt. In September 1949 they reduced the price of their South African snoek from 1s. 4½d. to 1s. 3d. a tin. By December the Minister, on a note of affectionate farewell, was referring to it as 'dear old snoek', and claiming that every tin bought from South Africa had been sold without loss. His honest incredulity was even more apparent this time. 'It was eaten, believe it or not. I ate it myself. I must say, I thought it was one of the dullest fish I have ever eaten.'

Three weeks later snoek, with tinned tomatoes and various tinned meats, came off points. The worst privations of austerity were over by then, and decently obscure mists closed round the piles of tins; there were new jokes, this one wasn't needed any more. But eighteen months later, quiet among the junketings of the Festival of Britain, a mysterious quantity of tinned fish came onto the market, labelled: 'Selected fish food for cats and kittens.' It cost tenpence a tin, and its origins were left muffled in tact. One of the distributors admitted that it might be either snoek or barracuda. 'Cats,' he said, 'are very fond of both.'

Wars end tidily in the history books, with the moment of signing a document. But there was no single finishing line for the shortages of food, clothes and fuel, and all the aspects of austerity which gave a dull grey tinge to post-war life. They slackened, gradually. When clothes rationing ended in March 1949, and the lights went up in London for the first time since the war began, the weekly meat ration was lower than it had ever been. When points rationing was abolished in May 1950 the Korean War arms programme was advancing to cut the rising supplies of cars and television sets.

Throughout 1950 controls were steadily eased; in January milk rationing was suspended, in May hotels and restaurants were freed of the five-shilling meal limit and the restriction on the number of courses they might serve. In the autumn, flour, eggs and soap were removed from control. But the process was slow, and perhaps that very slowness is one reason for the gulf which exists now between the generations of the young and the middle-aged.

For those who remembered the years between the wars, the gradual climb back to prosperity was a long, dispiriting haul, echoing with pre-war memories of better days. For the wartime children, it was different. Those years were not a return, but a revelation. They were lit by surprises; between 1945 and 1951 we saw not only the first pineapples and bananas of our lives, but the first washing-machine, the first fountain, the first television set. The world opening before us was not a pale imitation of one we had lost, but a lucky dip of extraordinary things we had never seen before. If, later, we seemed to snarl with baffled rage at the disillusionment and apathy of our elders, perhaps this is why. They treated it all as a dreary mess; they forgot that for us it could have been a brave new world.

Susan Cooper, 'Snoek Piquante', *Age of Austerity* (ed. Michael Sissons and Philip French)

Song

WE HAVE SEEN FOOD POETRY, but food is even something we celebrate in song. Any of us who have had anything to do with village fêtes or charity functions will recognise the contents of this song, and perhaps we have eaten the equivalent of this celebrated dessert. Somewhat more conventionally romantic, and probably better music, is Cole Porter's 'Tale of the Oyster'.

LIME JELLO MARSHMALLOW COTTAGE CHEESE SURPRISE
LADIES, the minutes will soon be read today.
The Garden Club and the Weaving Class I'm sure have much to say . . .
But next week is our Culture Night, our biggest, best event,
And I've just made a dish for it you'll all find heavensent:
It's my LIME JELLO MARSHMALLOW COTTAGE CHEESE SURPRISE
With slices of pimiento (you won't believe your eyes)
All topped with a pineapple ring and a dash of mayonnaise;
My vanilla wafers round the edge will win your highest praise.
And Mrs Jones is making scones that are filled with peanut mousse;
To be followed by a chicken mould that's made in the shape of a goose.
For ladies who must watch those pounds we've found a special dish:
Strawberry ice enshrined in rice with bits of tuna fish.
And my LIME JELLO MARSHMALLOW COTTAGE CHEESE SURPRISE
(Truly a creation that description defies)
Will go so well with Mrs Bell's creation of the week:
Shrimp salad topped with chocolate sauce and garnished with a leek.
And Mrs Perkins' walnut loaf that's crowned with melted cheese
Was such a hit last Culture Night, we ask: no seconds, please!

FOOD

Now you must try her hot-dog pie with candied mushroom slices . . .

Those ladies who resigned last year, they just don't know what NICE is!

But my LIME JELLO MARSHMALLOW COTTAGE CHEESE SURPRISE

I did not steal that recipe – it's lies, I tell you, lies!

Our grand award: a picture hat and a salmon-sequined gown

To any girl who tries each dish and keeps her whole lunch down.

I'm sure you all are waiting for the biggest news: dessert!

We've thought of things in moulds and rings your diet to subvert.

You must try our chocolate layer cake with a peanut brittle base

And slices of banana that make a funny face;

Around the edges peppermints just swimming in peach custard.

With luscious little curlicues of lovely yellow mustard!

If all this is too much for you, permit me to advise

More LIME JELLO MARSHMALLOW COTTAGE CHEESE SURPRISE!

I've made heaps!

Words and music by William Bolcom

THE TALE OF THE OYSTER

DOWN by the sea lived a lonesome oyster,

Every day getting sadder and moister.

He found his home life awfully wet

And longed to travel with the upper set.

Poor little oyster!

Fate was kind to that oyster, we know,

When one day the chef from the Park Casino

Saw that oyster lying there

And said, 'I'll put you on my bill of fare.'

Lucky little oyster!

See him on his silver platter

Watching the queens of fashion chatter.

Hearing the wives of millionaires

Discuss their marriages and their love affairs.

Thrilled little oyster!

See that bivalve social climber

Feeding the rich Mrs Hoggenheimer.

Think of his joy as he gaily glides

Down to the middle of her gilded insides.

Proud little oyster!

After lunch Mrs H complains

She says to her hostess, 'I've got such pains!

I came to town on my yacht today,

But I think I'd better hurry back to Oyster Bay.'

Scared little oyster!

Off they go through the troubled tide,

The yacht rolling madly from side to side.

They're tossed about till that poor young oyster

Finds that it's time he should quit his cloister

Up comes the oyster!

Back once more where he started from,

He murmured, 'I haven't a single qualm

For I've had a taste of society,

And society has had a taste of me.'

Wise little oyster!

Words and music by Cole Porter

SOUFFLÉ

I INCLUDE THIS PIECE FROM GRATITUDE. When I was a student, Robert Carrrier was the coolest thing around in the food world, opening a new and stylish restaurant in the new trendy place, Camden Passage. Some years later I took my first live-in cooking job, and on my first evening my new boss's words were 'We thought we'd have something simple, just a soufflé'. I had never made a soufflé, and I panicked. The only book on hand was Robert Carrier's *Cookbook*, and his words of wisdom saved me from the embankment – as I'm sure they will you.

SOUFFLÉ SORCERY

WHY IS IT, I wonder, that simple things seem so appallingly complicated before one tries them? And why does one often try the more difficult things first, looking with awe at the people who dare to attempt the easy?

We struggle with water-colours, never dreaming of attempting the easier oil paints; we teach our children languages, Latin and Greek for the very young, French when they are older; and the very same thing holds true when we turn our attention to the ubiquitous egg. Soufflés, for instance, hold no terrors for me. I have always found it more difficult to soft-boil or poach an egg to perfection. But a soufflé . . . give me an oven I can trust, a timer, and the requisite number of fresh eggs, and I can turn out a marvel at the drop of a proverbial hat.

That is my story . . . or at least it was until I was invited to a Paris 'pot luck' luncheon on the very last day of a trip to Paris – 'pot luck' because it was a Monday and all the shops were shut. I had been warned by my host that in all probability I would have to make do with a soufflé and that everything would be *tout-à-fait simple*. So when Monday and the hour of luncheon came, I arrived – dressed in sports jacket and slacks – to find myself in a drawing-room in the French grand manner, complete with nine floor-to-ceiling windows overlooking the Seine and the Louvre, some of the most beautiful furniture I have ever seen, and a group of sparkling Parisians, gathered for what was to be the most memorable meal of that Paris visit.

Lunch began with a superb *soufflé au turbot* . . . served with all possible pomp and pride in a large flat oval Pyrex dish on a Louis XIII silver salver . . . the smooth golden body of the soufflé broken only by the oven-crisped head and tail of the turbot visible at each end. The turbot, first poached in a white wine *court-bouillon*, had been carefully boned, leaving just the head and tail, and then gently deposited on its bed of cheese-flavoured soufflé mixture. The body of the fish was then covered with another layer of soufflé; the whole baked in the oven; and served with a delicate, pink-tinted *sauce Choron* (Béarnaise with a little tomato added for colour and flavour).

Rôti de boeuf à la périgourdine – a great platter of rose-red slices of rare beef, surrounded by stuffed *champignons de Paris* and served with a fabulously rich sauce made of beef stock, Madeira and fresh black truffles from Périgord – provided the main course of this 'hastily organised' luncheon. Then followed a great dish of *primeurs de Paris* (tiny fresh peas, baby carrots, new-season haricots verts and the smallest of *pommes rissolées),* a French salad spiked with a hint of shallot and tarragon, a platter of cheeses, and a *tarte alsacienne* (thin slices of eating apple set in spirals on a layer of *crème*

FOOD

pâtissière in a crumbly *pâte sablée* crust). Coffee was served . . . with gold spoons. The whole meal was perfection. But it is the soufflé I shall remember. And it is the soufflé that I have determined – after an unsuccessful attempt, unenthusiastically aided by my host, to extract the secret from his cook – to recreate for myself one day.

The thing that still puzzles me is how the weight of the turbot could have been supported in the soufflé, for a soufflé is built, like Ben Johnson's dream castles, of air. To transform air into a building material sounds next to impossible, but all you need for it is one simple implement – an egg beater. For after all, the most awe-inspiring of soufflés is nothing more than a simple air mixture of eggs, butter, flour, and a purée of fruit, vegetables, meat, fish or fowl. And the last – unglamorous and unpretentious as the case may be – are very often left-overs.

Soufflés, technically speaking, can be divided into three definite categories: the *soufflé de cuisine* – the famous savoury soufflé of France – makes the perfect beginning to a meal, whether it is a simple cheese affair (try a combination of Gruyère and Parmesan), a concoction of fish or shellfish, or one made with a well-seasoned base of puréed vegetables (endive, onion, or mushroom and cheese). Savoury soufflés also make light-as-air entrées to dramatise a luncheon or supper party. For here you can let your imagination run riot. I remember one superb duck soufflé, served to me in Rome, whose creamy interior was studded with olives stuffed with *pâté de foie gras*.

Why not experiment? What do you risk? The basic soufflé mixture of flour, butter, milk, eggs and grated cheese remains just the same whether you add a breakfast-cupful of diced kippers, chicken, lobster or sole.

Category number two in our soufflé line-up is the *soufflé d'entremets*. I give you a selection on the following pages; but the choice is limitless. Chocolate, coffee, vanilla; *soufflé aux liqueurs*; or the whole gamut of sweet soufflés based on purées of fresh or cooked fruits (strawberries, raspberries, cherries, cranberries, or the sharp tang of lemon and orange, and the more muted note of mandarins).

A well-known soufflé in France is the *soufflé arlequin* or *soufflé panache*. This is simply a soufflé made by combining two different variations of the basic sweet soufflé mixture – chocolate and vanilla – and spooning them in gently side by side, so that each half of the soufflé is a different colour and flavour when cooked. *Soufflé aux fruits confits* is another favourite French classic for you to try. Simply add chopped *fruits glacés* and a little coarsely chopped praline to the basic sweet soufflé mixture which you have flavoured with a little Jamaica rum.

Our third category, the *soufflé froid*, is not really a soufflé at all, but a moulded mousse made with a base of whipped cream and gelatine, and served in round moulds or soufflé dishes. Cover the bottom of the dish with a layer of gelatine, tie a strip of paper round the top of the dish to permit the mixture to be piled high above the edge, and *voilà*, when the paper is removed, it gives the illusion of a real soufflé.

Soufflés are perfectly easy to make if you follow a few basic rules.

1. A rich smooth sauce is the basis of all soufflés – a thick Béchamel Sauce for a savoury soufflé; a *crème pâtissière* for a sweet soufflé.

2. The egg yolks must be beaten one by one into the hot sauce after the saucepan is removed from the heat, or they will curdle.

3. Egg whites must be beaten until stiff but not dry. In separating the eggs, be sure there is no speck of yolk left in the whites, or you will not be able to beat your whites stiff.

4. A slow to medium oven (325° to 350° – M2 to 3) is an essential for a perfect soufflé. If your oven is too hot, the soufflé will be well cooked on the top and undercooked inside.

5. Sweet soufflés should be softer than entrée or vegetable soufflés.

6. A soufflé must never be too liquid before it goes into the oven. I find that the proportion of egg whites, when well beaten, should just about equal the bulk of the basic mixture. With the addition of the beaten egg whites you double the volume of your mixture. Cooking will double it again.

7. Finally, a soufflé must be eaten immediately.

If you are partial to soufflés – and I believe the whole world is – you will find that you can mix the major ingredients in advance and store them in the refrigerator. This is a trick used in many French restaurants. You just add the beaten egg whites before baking. I have had some wonderful soufflés made this easy way. Of course, if you are a novice cook, there are a certain number of culinary operations to master before you can be sure of turning out a perfect soufflé each and every time. You have to know how to regulate your oven heat, how to make a smooth white sauce, how to fold in stiffly beaten egg whites without making them lose their lightness, and how to keep your eggs from curdling when making a sauce. But these are the simple, everyday techniques of the kitchen. You will need them for any type of cookery.

Robert Carrier, *The Robert Carrier Cookbook*

SPAM

THE GROUP THAT made up the Cambridge Footlights in the 1960s were one of the great influences on British humour and media development. Peter Cook, John Cleese, Eric Idle, Michael Palin were the leaders of a new breed of satire and pure humour which shaped our cynical sixties minds. Spam was a key word for all that was wrong with the war generation (i.e. our parents), who had not had the advantages of our new freedoms. We did not of course acknowledge that they had won them for us – such is not the way of youth. But I offer you this piece of nonsense from my youth.

1 Spam, spam, spam, lovely spam,
    Wonderful spam, lovely spam.

Spam, spam, spam, spam,
Spam, spam, spam, spam, (etc)

Spam, spam, spam, spam,
Spam, spam, spam, spam, (etc)

3 Spam, spam, spam, wondrous spam,
    Surgical spam, splendiferous spam.

2 Spam, spam, spam, magnificent spam,
    Superlative spam.

Spam, spam, spam, spam,
Spam, spam, spam, spam, (etc)

Monty Python's Big Red Book

STAFF

ANYONE WHO WISHES TO HIRE KITCHEN STAFF knows the difficulties and pitfalls which accompany this seemingly simple task. Here is Ruth Lewinsky on the subject.

A MOST difficult task is to find just the cook one is looking for. Most of us have some drawback from the cook's point of view, such as too large or too small a kitchen – either is an insuperable difficulty – or too large a nursery. How often have I been told 'Well, madam, if you had *one* little boy, I might have tried your place.' I have always pointed out that, had the cook and I met each other earlier, something might have been done, but, with four already in the nursery . . .

It never pays even to interview the 'good plains,' and very seldom the chef-trained or 'equal to chef.' The first think that, as they called themselves plain cooks, they are entitled to boil everything and to serve it with a garnish of water. Any sweet above a trifle – there is nothing below – has no place in their repertoire.

On the other hand, the chef-trained cook is quite unable either to roast or to grill meat, though she can send up the most marvellous looking mousses. It is only by their position on the menu and the fact that they taste vaguely of sugar or salt that you know whether they be made of lobsters or of strawberries. Remember that food is not a 'still life,' but made to be eaten. Never correspond with a cook – see her, and then ask for her idea of a good menu for a dinner party. If she suggests as an inspiration that it should start with grapefruit, then goes on to *consommé a la royal*, a nice sole, and a bird, you can stop her before she proceeds to the inevitable meringues and sardines on toast. Give her up as hopeless and renew your quest.

Two very good test questions are: 'What ices do you know?' and 'Can you make a vol-au-vent?' You will be surprised to find how these two simple questions reduce the number of possible cooks.

Ruth Lewinsky, *Lovely Food*

STRINE

ONE OF THE STRONG, brave women of Australia is Joan Campbell. In the era when Australian equalled male-chauvinism as firmly as overdone lamb equalled Strine cuisine, Joan created what everyone agrees is the world's finest gourmet magazine, *Australian Vogue*. In 1998 she wrote her autobiography, and with the same gutsy devil-may-care attitude that made her famous called it *Bloody Delicious*.

THERE are only a few of us left, I suppose, who can remember *When Mabel Laid the Table* (the title of my friend Warren Fahey's book). My mother had a housemaid, a Mabel who laid and waited on the table, but her name was Katie. She arrived by ship from Scotland with hair as black as coal,

FOOD

cheeks like shining red apples and a broad Scottish accent. Katie seemed to be with us for a great deal of our childhood. I would watch her making jams, jellies and pickles and such delights as tripe and onions, pig's head brawn, boiled mutton and caper sauce, and the best bread sauce to go with roasted stuffed chicken.

MISS AMY SCHAUER'S GOOD PIG'S CHEEK AND VEAL OR BEEF BRAWN

'MISS' SCHAUER, as she was called, was a great name in food in Brisbane for as long as I can remember and, if I do remember, she cooked biscuits and cakes for people. I also remember the trotters and pig's cheek and sheep's tongues were pink, so they must have been 'corned'.

3 pig's trotters, cut in half	¼ teaspoon cayenne pepper
½ fresh pig's cheek	I blade mace
I knuckle of veal	2 bay leaves
750 g shin of beef	2 cloves
3 sheep's tongues	6 allspice berries
I tablespoon salt	12 peppercorns

Wash the pig's trotters and soak in cold water for 30 minutes. Thoroughly wash the pig's cheek. Drain the trotters, wash well under cold running water and put into a large saucepan with the pig's cheek, veal knuckle, shin of beef, sheep's tongues, salt and cayenne. Tie the remaining spices in a small piece of muslin and add to the pan. Add just enough cold water to cover, and place the lid tightly on the saucepan. Bring to the boil and simmer for 3 or 4 hours or until the meat is tender.

Transfer the meats to a large dish. Skin the tongues. Remove all the meat remaining on the bones and discard the bones. Quickly cut all the meat into cubes. Put the meats into a large basin, season to taste with salt and cayenne.

Boil the liquor in a saucepan over high heat for 10 minutes. Take ½ cup of the boiling liquor and pour over the meat in the basin. Pack the mixture tightly into wet moulds, cover and place weights on top, and refrigerate overnight. Turn out onto a platter to serve.

VOGUE BOARDROOM CHICKEN SALAD
(Serves 6)

6 medium chicken breast fillets	DRESSING
vegetable oil	I tablespoon balsamic vinegar
60 g finely sliced prosciutto, cut in strips	4 tablespoons oil from the tomatoes
¼ cup pine nuts, roasted in the oven	½ teaspoon Dijon mustard
¼ cup sliced sun-dried tomatoes	salt and freshly ground pepper to taste
2 tablespoons finely shredded fresh basil leaves	
salt and freshly ground pepper	

Preheat the oven to 200°C. Brush the chicken fillets lightly with vegetable oil and place on a baking tray. Bake in the oven for about 12 minutes, or until just cooked. Remove the chicken from the tray, transfer to a plate and allow to cool to room temperature. (Do not refrigerate.)

Slice each chicken breast into diagonal slices and arrange in a large, shallow serving dish. Cover the chicken with a layer of prosciutto strips, then add the roasted pine nuts, dried tomatoes, basil and salt and pepper to taste.

To make the dressing and serve:

Place all the ingredients in a jar and shake thoroughly to amalgamate. Drizzle the dressing over the salad and serve at once.

Joan Campbell, *Bloody Delicious*

TEA

As IMPORTANT AS AFTERNOON TEA was the Scottish meal of High Tea. This is of course not singular to Hibernia, but that country has made it firmly its own. The table groaning with a combination of scones and cakes, besides the more substantial dishes of smoked haddock or herrings, with always the pink gleaming ham and the soft Scottish voice asking 'Ye'll take an egg with your tea?' is a nostalgic memory for any who spent any time north of the border. This piece from Annette Hope's *Caledonian Feast* says it all.

GIVEN its popularity during the closing years of the 19th century and the first half of the 20th, the origins and early development of high tea are surprisingly obscure. It has been a somewhat insecure meal, clear enough in its shape yet moving from social class to social class and between different age-groups, without obvious reasons. But it is easy enough to distinguish three different sources which contributed to its development and final place as the repast which, for many, encapsulates the whole ambience of middle-class Scotland in the early 20th century.

The first of these sources was the adoption by the urban poor of bread and tea for their supper. Poverty was the chief, but not the only reason. As a popular drink, tea had long since moved near the top of the league, though it was usually of the lowest quality; and the rise of the Temperance Movement with its emphasis on the evils of drink reinforced the value given it by the labouring classes. Because it was drunk hot and had a mildly stimulating effect it replaced ale more effectively than milk – 'the cup that cheers but not inebriates' was no idle slogan. As for bread, after about

1860 the price of white flour fell below that of brown, and the introduction of roller-milling with its efficient removal of almost all the husk and germ of the wheat, leaving behind only the whitest part, put white bread within reach of all. It could be bought at every cornershop, and was the cheapest way of filling hungry stomachs, besides needing no preparation – the mere addition of butter or margarine and cheap jam made it appetizing enough.

This became the basic, unalterable foundation of the workers' evening meal. When times were good or a family prospered, 'kitchen', or relish, of other foods were added – fish, potatoes, eggs, cheese, even meat, especially in the latter half of the century when cheap tinned goods from Australia became available.

So ubiquitous did tinned food become that even home produce was supplanted by the same item, tinned from another country. Cost and ease of preparation were the initial factors; but the tragic consequence was that tinned goods came to be preferred, as anyone who observes the sale of tinned carrots in supermarkets cannot fail to notice. Neil Munro has a story in *Para Handy*, set at the turn of the century, which illustrates this enslavement of urban populations to the tin: Dougie, the ship's mate, has tricked a Glasgow woman on holiday into buying a coal-fish from him, under the impression that he was selling her cod.

> 'I'm only vexed I didna say it wass a salmon,' said Dougie, when he came back to the vessel with his ill-got florin. 'I could have got twice ass much for't.'
> 'She would ken fine it wasna a salmon when it wasna in a tin,' said the Captain.

Supper, then, was the principal progenitor of high tea. But secondary influences also played their part, notably that essentially middle-class institution, *nursery tea* (at which, paradoxically, milk was the usual beverage although cambric tea, made from hot water, milk, sugar, and a minute quantity of tea, was sometimes given as a treat). Stevenson's *A Child Garden of Verses* has many references to nursery tea, none explicit enough to quote, but leaving no doubt of its importance in the child's life. Nor was it confined to the very young. Most middle-class schoolchildren went home for a hot meal at midday until free school meals were introduced. In the evening they had their 'tea', until deemed old enough to join their parents at the dinner-table. Perhaps this accounts for the easy adoption by the middle class of what had begun as a working-class custom.

There was also farm tea. This, again, depended on the need of workers for midday dinner with another fairly substantial meal at about five o'clock. In the long days of summer, work continued after tea; in winter it was the signal for retreat to the warm shelter of the farmhouse kitchen. Either way, farm tea was rarely the lavish spread which is sometimes depicted. The good things were there, naturally: new-laid eggs, home-made cheeses, fresh-caught fish from the burn, sizzling rashers of bacon, potato cakes, scones, pancakes, potato scones, oatcakes, bannocks, fresh butter, home-made jam, and heather honey – but not all at the same meal. Rarely could the farmer or his wife afford the time for this kind of repast, unless there were visitors. Then, preparations were elaborate and the table was crowded with good things. Such a meal was the one enjoyed by Dickson McGunn and John Heritage in *Huntingtower*:

Meringue Gateau

Mushroom Cakes

Mocha Fingers

Mackerel-Soused

Mixed Medley

Macaroon Jelly

Marrow & Ginger Tart

Mousse à la Russe

Milk Jelly

Marble Cake

They were seated in Mrs Morran's kitchen before a meal which fulfilled their wildest dreams. She had been baking that morning so there were white scones and barley scones, and oaten farles, and russet pancakes. There were three boiled eggs for each of them; there was a segment of an immense currant cake ('a present from my guid brither last Hogmanay'); there was skim-milk cheese; there were several kinds of ham, and there was a pot of dark-gold heather honey. 'Try hinny and aitcake,' said their hostess. 'My man used to say he never fund onything as guid in a' his days.'

Interesting, as proof that supper in the country was still a robust collation at the turn of the century, is the fact that Buchan's heroes, returning the same evening to a late supper, are offered most of the dainties which had appeared at tea, supplemented by 'a noble dish of shimmering 'potted-head'.'

By the beginning of the present century high tea had attained its position as the evening meal of the rural classes and the industrial working classes, with a kind of optional status among those of the middle class who preferred dinner at midday – a status which rose rapidly after the First World War. From the 1930s to the 1950s high tea was the evening meal of all but the professional and upper classes. For the servantless housewife with children it made sense to have a simple meal which could be enjoyed and shared by the whole family, and saved on the washing-up. If there were visitors it became the most hospitable of occasions.

In the industrial towns, Saturday teas were specially important family events, when married daughters and sons visited or were visited, and old ties with more distant relatives renewed. On Saturdays there was often more than one main course, and an impressive array of baking.

Annette Hope, *The Caledonian Feast*

Tʜᴇ ᴍᴏᴠᴇᴍᴇɴᴛ ᴏꜰ ᴍᴇᴀʟs and the changes in their style and content is fascinating to any food historian. The last years of the century have seen virtually the abolition of the family meal, killed off by feminism and television. In the one family I know who still eat together the children's conversational skills are infinitely better than their contemporaries. Jeremy Clancy here addresses the issue, and the sad passing of afternoon tea.

Mᴏᴠᴀʙʟᴇ Fᴇᴀsᴛs

As schoolchildren, my sisters and I used to return home before four every day. Our mother would already have the kitchen table prepared with sandwiches, jam, biscuits, cake or pastries, butter-drenched crumpets, and the old maiden aunt or two. Our father would then come in from his afternoon calls. Rubbing his hands vigorously together and with a grin that aimed for each ear, he would proclaim, 'Saved another life today!' On days when he was particularly pleased, he would amaze us all and amuse himself by ending the meal with a little fruit – throwing a grape in the air and scoring a hole-in-one every time.

Afternoon tea was a light, happy occasion. It was a gentle break in the day, between calls and the evening surgery for my father, between school and homework for us children, between cooking and yet more cooking for our mother. Not a closed gathering but an open event, anyone who knocked on the door between half-three and five was invited to join the table. Tea-time was a social occasion, a simple, relaxed meal for easy conversation and good company. Family rows were saved for other times.

But these are memories and so is afternoon tea. This brief meal has since disappeared from our working days. By the late 1970s, offering an afternoon guest anything more than a cup of tea and a biscuit or slice of cake had come to seem pretentious and old-fashioned – the sort of event a Young Fogey would stage. These days, urban shoppers pausing from their toils in a 'tea-shop' hardly ever choose more than something to drink and a pastry. Even a male student trying to pick up the girl sitting opposite him in the library does not invite her to a full, cream-rich repast. The chances are that all she gets is a cup of coffee and a query about what she is doing tonight. The Ritz and other surrealist dream-palaces may still offer full-blown 'set teas' (tea, sandwiches, scones, pastries, cream-cakes – and no jeans), but their customers are mainly ageing ladies or tourists nostalgic for a past they never had. And these pricey teas, as a privileged form of 'living heritage', are so popular you have to book, two weeks in advance.

Like the twelve-course dinner, afternoon tea has disappeared into history because times have changed and there is no longer any space in the day for it. Mealtimes map the structure of our waking lives. They are the points around which our days turn because, except for snacks, we do not eat when we feel like it. We eat at certain times, and we eat certain foods at different times of the day. Who has turkey for breakfast, or scones and cream for lunch?

Other than the recent demise of afternoon tea, our present mealtimes of morning breakfast, midday lunch, and evening supper feel as permanent as the Grand Canyon and as natural as flowers budding in spring. Breakfast is to wake up and prepare us for the hours ahead, lunch is a refreshing pause in the middle of the working day, and supper is a relaxing opportunity to restore spent energies. There is, however, nothing biologically necessary about this tripartite schedule. Our gastronomic timetable is a dynamic, not a static, product of our history and continues to evolve. It only seems unchanging because the changes occur so slowly.

Anyone who goes on holiday abroad learns immediately just how their own mealtimes are. The Basques do not eat breakfast, while tourists who dine in Madrid at 8 p.m. wonder why they are the only people in the restaurants. (Local diners do not start arriving until ten.) Visitors also complain that lunch does not begin until half-past two. What they do not realize is that many urban Spaniards break from work at one, meet their friends in a bar and eat a small snack before then going home for their main meal of the day. Others work without a break: they start at eight, finish at three, and then have their lunch. The people of Zumbagua in the Ecuadorian Andes have a very light meal before dawn, a larger meal at midmorning, the same again in the late afternoon, then another very light meal, this time after dark, to end the day. This arrangement suits the local women, who need to pasture their flocks from midmorning to midafternoon without interruption. It would not suit hungry backpackers who turned up at midday, only to find nothing was to be cooked for several hours. Some African communities do not bother with set meals at all: they just nibble and pick at food throughout the day.

But even the present tripartite division of the day is under threat. Most Americans now snack rather than fast during the mid-morning and mid-afternoon, and the meals they do eat have become much more snack-like. Similarly, very few Britons now bother to cook anything for breakfast, and more and more are choosing to go to work on an empty stomach. Lunch has also declined in importance. Though in the 1950s the majority of men still went home for their midday meal, these days most just have a light meal or a quick bite in a canteen, cafeteria, or fast-food outlet. In Britain today, almost the only people who prepare their own lunch, and it is not a main meal at that, are housebound mothers and the retired.

The English might be happy following the American example, but other Europeans are holding on to their gastronomic traditions much more firmly. For the Germans and the Swiss, lunch remains the largest meal of the day, eaten either at home, in a small restaurant, or in a canteen. At the end of the day, Germans have only a light meal of cheeses and cold meats. In France, Spain, and Italy many people, though not as many as before, still go home at midday while others patronize restaurants offering three-course meals. Unlike the Americans and the British, many Continentals continue to uphold lunch as a meal worth bothering about. They are not going to overturn their culinary customs and love of food for the sake of a snatched sandwich or a Big Mac.

Jeremy Clancy, *Consuming Culture*

TEA-TIME

NO NATION IN THE WORLD HAS SUCH A TRADITION of Afternoon Tea as the English, and it has had its finest flowering in this century. The image of tea on the lawn under the cedar tree on an Edwardian afternoon must have strengthened many an empire builder or mud-sodden hero of the trenches. It is the England of which H.V. Morton dreamed lying ill on a Palestinian hillside. The hand that rocked the cradle and ruled the world dispensed politics, policy and influence from behind the tea kettle. Feminism has cut it down in the home, but if you think the plant is dead try, as I recently did, to get a table for tea at the Savoy out of season. At Lennoxlove, where I have my café, I am constantly amazed at the numbers who come out for tea and scones or even something more substantial. This piece, written by Constance Spry in 1942, yearns for the return of peace, normality and afternoon tea.

I HOPE tea time will never cease to be part of our English picture. It is associated with peaceful days and leisurely living. It has an aura of cosiness in winter, sunshine in summer. In fiction, at any rate, firelight and silver, crumpets and plum cake, boiled eggs on return from the chase, make winter afternoons sound attractive. And for summer's note there is the tea table laid in the shade of spreading branches where, coming in from unbroken sunshine, you may refresh yourself with strawberries and cream. China tea, ewers of cream, sponge cakes tasting of orange flower water, make part of the nostalgic pattern. Those were the good days.

FOOD

Nursery teas, too, are classics. Back in the Victorian days nurse-dragons, under the ameliorating influence of strong sweet tea, let up in their dragooning. Their lust for power seemed momentarily satisfied in seeing that their charges ate butter before jam and jam before cake, indifferent alike to the state of appetites or idiosyncrasies of digestion. An easy-going nursery-maid might turn a blind eye while you toasted one side of your bread and butter at the fire, a performance impressively described as 'making French toast'. There were notable days of home-made bread and beef dripping, of watercress and radishes – or one radish grown by yourself; solitary because you couldn't bear to thin out the seedlings. Later, as the horizon widened, one came face to face with those period pieces called 'At Home Days'.

These were dressy affairs in more ways than one. Tatted doilies, ribbon-bound plate-handles, and tiered cakestands, impiously nicknamed curates, gave scope for competitive ingenuity and a source of revenue for bazaars. There was a complicated ritual about cards. White kid gloves were *de rigueur*. Woman's crowning glory was her hair, and she made the most of every bit of it. Glacé silk petticoats swished, veils twisted themselves into knots no sailor would care to name, and immense feather boas framed the face in a seductive and feminine manner.

The second Tuesday or fourth Thursday or whatever the hallowed day might be had a personality of its own; you could recognize it from the moment you came downstairs in the morning. The kitchen hummed with activity. The fire had to roar, the oven get hot, and there was to be no nonsense on the part of anyone.

As possible residuary legatees, we children noted with something more than academic interest what delicacies were in course of preparation. We had to temper curiosity with discretion, for there was apt to be tension in the air. With luck, however, there might be interim solace in the shape of an imperfect piece or two, the low standard of which went unnoticed by us.

After lunch came a lull. A lull that needed tactical negotiation on our part if we were to avoid being sent for a walk. The kitchen heavyweights toiled up to their attics for a good wash. They polished their faces with yellow soap and water, dragged their hair back till the line of their eyebrows was lifted, buttoned up their black 'bodies', and showed discrimination in the matter of caps. The more important the occasion the longer the streamer. They could judge to a nicety.

The drawing-room contingent might take longer to dress, but never in our eyes achieved anything so smart as our Mary's best cap. Down the ladies came, curled and attired, and taking up a tasteful bit of work or blameless book, settled down to wait.

There was a Median law governing the time before which no well-mannered caller would arrive. From that mystic hour, however, answering the bell was a breathless affair. Hanging over the banisters we children might see the feathers and hear the *frou-frou* and get a nice sense of party goings-on. Sometimes, indeed, unnaturally clean and restrictingly dressed, one of us might be called down 'to say how do you do'. On such occasions, until observed and called to order, I have watched with unwavering concentration miracles of sleight of hand. I have seen tightly gloved women balance a cup and saucer in the air, negotiate a knotted veil, and convey a tremulous cucumber sandwich from hand to mouth without a fault. Seldom have I had the satisfaction of seeing even a bit of tomato misfire. The white gloves, in consideration of which the bread and butter had been rolled, might come to grief over buttery toast or too-soft sugar icing, but what of it? Such offerings on the altar of delicate behaviour only added lustre to a reputation for refinement.

Downstairs in the kitchen, as soon as it became reasonable to hope that there would be no more calls for thin bread and butter, you might find and even share a proper sort of tea: steps of bread and butter, home-made jam spooned out of the jar, watercress, perchance shrimps, and seed cake to fill in gaps. You might blow upon your boiling sweet tea or pour it, if you chose, from capacious cup into sensible saucer. Table manners might seem easier down here, but you would be wrong to assume they were lax. It was just that the gentility was of another brand.

That particular aspect of family life is going fast or gone. At one moment tea-time itself seemed to be going too. Cocktails were the competitor. In London and big towns the later hour of cocktails suited busy people, and even in some country houses one might find tea-time supplanted. But the ingredients for cocktails are now scarce, and tea-time comes back, I hope for keeps.

When the cocktail fashion was in full swing, there was a particular tea-table in London that remained notable. Whether you were hungry as a hunter or merely wanted tea and talk, it met the case perfectly. I must describe it because it seemed to me the apotheosis of the tea-table. Its beauty did not lie only in old silver and delicate china, but in the intelligent way the food was served. For the hungry there were different breads on a wooden platter to be cut thick or thin as you pleased. There were cheeses also on a wooden board and a long dish of lettuce hearts and radishes. There were home-made jams and exotic jams and aromatic honeys. There was dark, sticky gingerbread and cream to eat with it if you chose; there might be an ethereal orange cake. Lady Portarlington, whose table it was, has a gift for associating beauty with essentials. The combination of the elegant with the robust – the wood and silver touch – stays in my mind. Lest you should think it unseemly to describe so rich a feast these austere days, let me point out that the principle is perfectly suitable now. No food cut about, no sandwiches to go stale, nothing left to waste because it was uneaten. If you look closer you will see that even for practical politics to-day the details are not unworthy of consideration. The bread, the salads, jam, honey, even cakes, are not out of the wartime picture. They have to be modified intelligently, but that is interesting. After the war we hope to colour our lives again more vividly.

Constance Spry, *Come into the Garden, Cook*

Toast

TOAST IS ONE OF THOSE STRANGE ILLUSIONS of the mind, peculiar to the British Character. When I was at school I remember how the great sixth form privilege was to be allowed to make our own toast in our common room. Before that we had surreptitiously made it on the art room fire, at some risk of being caught with loss of privileges, for the toast in the refectory was lukewarm and rubbery. Do today's youth, I wonder, still take risks for toast rather than, as we are led to believe, for more dangerous mood-altering substances? I seldom eat bread left to my own devices, and yet even I can be overcome with an irresistible nostalgic desire for toast plus, of course, that other great British addiction, Marmite. This evocative passage from Elizabeth David says it all in her own inimitable way. Elizabeth is the doyenne of food writers, the one who transformed and marked the second half of this century into a culinary garden of literature, and made your poor editor's task all the harder, as well as more enjoyable.

'No bread. Then bring me some toast!'

Punch, 1852

'"Toast" said Berry, taking the two last pieces that stood in the rack. "I'm glad to get back to toast. And a loaf of brown bread that isn't like potter's clay."'

Dornford Yates, *Adèle & Co.*

IT ISN'T only fictional heroes to whom toast means home and comfort. It is related of the Duke of Wellington – I believe by Lord Ellesmere – that when he landed at Dover in 1814, after six years' absence from England, the first order he gave at the Ship Inn was for an unlimited supply of buttered toast.

In *The Origin of Food Habits* (1944), H. D. Renner makes an attempt to explain the English addiction to toast. 'The flavour of bread', he says, 'can be revived to some extent by re-warming and even new flavours are created in toasting.' This is very true, but leaves the most important part unsaid. It is surely the *smell* of toast that makes it so enticing, an enticement which the actuality rarely lives up to. In this it is like freshly roasted coffee, like sizzling bacon – all those early morning smells of an intensity and deliciousness which create far more than those new flavours, since they create hunger and appetite where none existed. Small wonder that the promise is never quite fulfilled. 'Village life', Renner continues, 'makes stale bread so common that toasting has become a national habit restricted to the British Isles and those countries which have been colonized by Britain.' Surely England was not the only country where villages were isolated and bread went dry and stale? I wonder if our open fires and coal ranges were not more responsible than the high incidence of stale bread for the popularity of toast in all classes of English household. For toasting bread in front of the fire and the bars of the coal-burning range there were dozens of different devices – museums of domestic life are crammed with them, Victorian cookery books show any number of designs – as many as there are varieties of electric toaster in our own day; apart from toasters for bread, there were special racks for toasting muffins and crumpets, and special pans for toasting cheese ... There were, in the nineteenth century, eminent medical men writing grave advice as to the kind of bread which, when toasted, would absorb the maximum amount of butter. That buttered toast goes back a long way in English life, and was by no means confined to country places where fresh bread was a rarity is shown by the following quotation: 'All within the sound of Bow Bell', wrote Fynes Morison in *Itinerary*, Volume 3 (1617), 'are in reproch called cochnies, and eaters of buttered tostes.'

259

FOOD

Buttered toast is, then, or was, so peculiarly English a delicacy – and I use the term delicacy because that is what in our collective national memory it still is – that the following meticulous description of how it was made, at least in theory, reads poignantly indeed. It is from the hand of Miss Marian McNeill, author of that famous work *The Scots Kitchen*, on this occasion writing in an enchanting volume, long out of print, called *The Book of Breakfasts*, published in 1932:

'Sweet light bread only a day old makes the best toast. Cut into even slices about quarter of an inch thick. It may be toasted under the grill, but the best toast is made at a bright smokeless fire. Put the slice on a toasting-fork and keep only so near the fire that it will be heated through when both sides are well browned. Move the toast about so as to brown evenly. Covered with an earthen bowl, toast will keep warm and moist.

'If very thin, crisp toast is desired, take bread that is two days old, cut it into slices about three-eighths of an inch thick, and toast them patiently at a little distance from a clear fire till delicately browned on both sides. With a sharp knife divide each slice into two thin slices, and toast the inner sides as before. Put each slice as it is done into a toast rack.

'For hot buttered toast, toast the bread more quickly than for ordinary toast, as it should not be crisp. Trim off the crusts and spread the toast liberally with butter that has been warmed but not allowed to oil. Cut in neat pieces, pile sandwichwise, and keep hot in a covered dish over a bowl of hot water. Use the best butter.'

I have my own childhood memories of toast-making in front of the schoolroom fire. Although I fancy that more toast fell off the fork into the fire and was irretrievably blackened than ever reached our plates, I can recall the great sense of achievement when now and again a slice did come out right, evenly golden, with a delicious smell and especially, as I remember, with the right, proper texture, so difficult to describe, and so fleeting. Only when it was hot from the fire and straight off the fork did that toast have the requisite qualities. Perhaps young children are better qualified than grown-ups to appreciate these points. And perhaps that is why buttered toast is one of those foods, like sausages, and potatoes baked in their skins, and mushrooms picked from the fields, which are never as good as they were.

Nowadays my toast is usually made on one of those ridged metal plates which goes over a gas flame or an electric burner. This produces crisp toast, very different from the kind made in front of the fire, but in its way almost as good. These lightweight metal toasters are very cheap. There is no need to buy an expensive iron one. Rye bread or 100 per cent whole wheatmeal bread both make excellent toast, but for buttered toast a light white bread is best. I prefer to make this kind of toast under the grill, electric toasters being machines with which I cannot be doing. In this I must be in a very small minority, for electric toasters are one of the most popular of all wedding presents, and in May 1975 *Which?* published a report on no fewer than thirteen different electric toasters. 'Some like it well done,' declared *Which?*, 'others pale brown; some like it done slowly to give a crisp finish, others done quickly so it's still soft inside.' All of these pronouncements are no doubt correct, as indeed is the statement that 'you don't want your piece of toast to be black in the middle and white round the edges'. That is to say, I don't. But I know plenty of people who actually *like* their toast to be charred. Perhaps they prefer it charred at the edges and white in the middle, and I'm not sure

how this would be achieved. Another of the report's dictums, 'however you like your toast, you want all pieces to be more or less the same', is one I don't agree with, perhaps fortunately, for it is not easy to get all your pieces more or less the same. Unless, that is, you have a caterers' toasting machine and caterers' sliced bread which between them produce what I call restaurateurs' toast, that strange substance cut in triangles and served with the pâté, and for breakfast, in all English hotels and restaurants. This English invention has in recent years become popular in France where, oddly enough, it goes by the name of toast, as opposed to real French toast which is called *pain grillé*, and is just what it says, grilled bread. That brings me back to the toast-making device I myself use, the metal plate or grill over the gas burner. Part of the charm of the toast produced on this device is that every piece is different, and differently marked, irregularly chequered with the marks of the grill, charred here and there, flecked with brown and gold and black . . . I think that the goodness of toast made in this way does depend a good deal on the initial quality of the bread, and the way it is cut. Thin slices are useless, and I don't think that white sliced bread would be very successful – there is too much water to get rid of before the toasting process starts, and steamy bread sticks to the toaster. Thickish slices are best, preferably rather small ones which can be easily turned with grill tongs. Like most other toast, this kind is best straight from the grill. 'If allowed to stand and become sodden, dry toast becomes indigestible. From the fire to the table is the thing', wrote the delightfully named Lizzie Heritage in *Cassell's Universal Cookery Book* (first published 1894). And if the toast is to be buttered, I suppose we must remember Marian McNeill's 'use the best butter'. What is the best butter? Unsalted, some would say. I'll settle for any butter that's good of its kind. The very salt butter of Wales can be perfectly delicious eaten with the right kind of toast (no marmalade for me), and here is Flora Thompson describing toast with salt butter and celery, and toast with cold boiled bacon. Toast-resistant though I am, she makes me long for that fresh hot toast and crisp celery, a wonderful combination, and how subtle:

'In winter, salt butter would be sent for and toast would be made and eaten with celery. Toast was a favourite dish for family consumption. 'I've made 'em a stack o' toast as high as up to their knees', a mother would say on a winter Sunday afternoon before her hungry brood came in from church. Another dish upon which they prided themselves was thin slices of cold, boiled streaky bacon on toast, a dish so delicious that it deserves to be more widely popular.'

Elizabeth David, *English Bread and Yeast Cookery*

TOMATOES

IN THIS PIECE FROM *LARK RISE*, Flora Thompson is writing in 1934 of her own childhood at the turn of the century. I love this piece, with its contemporary description of the arrival of a new food ingredient, and its all too familiar nostalgia for what had been ruined by the century.

IT WAS on Jerry's cart tomatoes first appeared in the hamlet. They had not long been introduced into this country and were slowly making their way into favour. The fruit was flatter in shape than now and deeply grooved and indented from the stem, giving it an almost starlike appearance. There were bright yellow ones, too, as well as the scarlet; but, after a few years, the yellow ones disappeared from the market and the red ones became rounder and smoother, as we see them now.

At first sight, the basket of red and yellow fruit attracted Laura's colour-loving eye. 'What are those?' she asked old Jerry.

'Love-apples, me dear. Love-apples, they be; though some hignorant folks be a callin' 'em tommytoes. But you don't want any o' they – nasty sour things, they be, as only gentry can eat. You have a nice sweet orange wi' your penny.' But Laura felt she must taste the love-apples and insisted upon having one.

Such daring created quite a sensation among the onlookers. 'Don't 'ee go tryin' to eat it, now,' one woman urged. 'It'll only make 'ee sick. I know because I had one of the nasty horrid things at our Minnie's.' And nasty, horrid things tomatoes remained in the popular estimation for years; though most people to-day would prefer them as they were then, with the real tomato flavour pronounced, to the watery insipidity of our larger, smoother tomato.

Flora Thompson, *Lark Rise to Candleford*

TRADE

MY DESERT ISLAND BOOK is undoubtedly *Food in England*, the work of the scholar gypsy Dorothy Hartley, who went around after the Second World War recording so much of food traditions and dishes that were all too soon to be lost to us. It was as if she knew that the supermarket, the fast food chains and the gadgetry of the new era would all too soon destroy a way of life that had lasted since the Industrial Revolution. In this piece she writes not about ancient history and traditions but of the efforts made by working men in the trades to feed themselves and improve their lot in this century. Sadly publishers don't agree with my view, as this wonderful book is more often out of print than in.

'TRADE' SPECIALITIES

IF YOU ever find some 'special' type of cooking in a district where there is no 'foreign influence' or other cause to account for it, study the local trades. It was young Watt, watching his mother's kettle-lid dancing up and down, who made steam work for mankind; and to assess the genius of the eighteenth-century engineers realise that the first Manchester to Liverpool canal was built before steam power was developed. Roads and aqueducts, all over industrial districts, show the structural thought – and that is engineering at its best – and many stone aqueducts and tunnels are as beautiful in their simplicity as any ornate mediaeval cathedral. These great feats moved a mass of specialised workers about the country, often keeping them in residence in the same district for several years together (like cathedral and castle-builders of earlier centuries).

These clusters of workmen, coming from one part of the land to another, carried their own special cooking methods with them, and in turn learnt local ideas and materials. Anyone who has to keep a large party of workpeople happy in a strange district knows how a consignment of 'food from home' will cheer the whole party; and when you study the large undertakings of *any century*, it is pleasant to find sudden consignments of unexpected food being brought, at great expense, from some remote place – to vanish, apparently, into thin air.

Sometimes it is a cargo of salt herrings by waggon, or a curious sudden bill for 'sum pygges' (that makes one think there had been complaints about the local bacon).

The same thing had happened when William the Conqueror took his castle-builders to work in Saxon land; when the Flemings came to settle in South Wales (twelfth century); when the lace workers came to the east Midlands; and the same will always happen where *sets of workers* who serve one trade work the same hours and eat the same food.

Thus clay and pottery workers cook in their own kilns – encasing raw meat, fish, game, etc., in clay to bake it. The rich carefully preserved aroma of the 'enclosed cooking' made them invent pottery jars with close-fitting lids and pottery 'cases' to save the expense of the huff paste.

Painters and workers, using certain chemicals, developed a compensating taste for salt and acid flavourings, and their natural cooking used these abundantly. Field workers in Scotland were given free barley water, slightly acid, and well-salted oat porridge to replace their 'sweating' in the dry harvest fields.

Leather workers became so impregnated with the tannin from the oak and willow bark used in dressing the hides, that their bodies did not decay after death, but shrivelled and dried up like old leather sacks.

Lime workers were issued with extra butter, grease or cream to save their skins and eyelids, and (so I have heard) developed a compensating taste for vinegar and milk.

Iron workers, by reason of the furnace heat, learnt much about light beers and strengthening ales and liquors.

All the various trades cooked and flavoured according to their special requirements. The engineer was ever a good cook under all circumstances, and what he learnt on his trade furnaces he later incorporated into the iron cooking ranges he invented.

The modern Thermos flask and 'works canteens' have put an end to much of the unofficial cooking that went on around the old factory-heating stoves. I worked for five years in a shipwright's factory heated by great coke stoves. The stoves were ridged and spaced into hollows, like a big black honeycomb, and from 6 a.m. to 6 p.m. these heated hollows would be packed full of things cooking, 'tins' boiling, tea mashing, chops, potatoes, or even bread and pie, baking! Some of the men would come 'on' direct from their allotment gardens, and big round onions baking used to scent the night shifts. (Often an apprentice boy got his 'kit' for being good at cooking.)

Quarry men, working on a 'face' a long distance from home, often became expert cooks, their 'bakestone' supplementing the iron grid-iron over the fire in their blast shelter. Slate will not stand heat, and some stones 'fly' dangerously, but some mountain men used to keep goats, or even a cow, up near their jobs. The queerest 'churn' I ever encountered was where some Arenig men took their spare milk down in a can slung below the rattling trucks; it was good buttermilk, and butter for tea by the time it reached the valley.

Foresters cooked at a wood fire, and the 'plank steak' is direct from their specialised craft cooking. They also used the slow 'buried iron oven bake' that the peat burners used on their open hearths. Lancashire mill hands, working long shifts, developed many special dishes that could be left to cook all day, and 'finished in a few minutes' on their return home. That the size and shapes of the pots and pans depended upon their owner's job is understandable, but you will also find long-boned Yorkshire sheep required a different-shaped stewpot from its neat-boned southern lamb! The 'shepherd's lambstones', the 'lambtail pies' are farming examples of 'the job and the food'. The sprouts of the buried swede turnip, and the cut tendrils of the hop, are agricultural local foods, and cod's liver and clams were discoveries of the fisherman. Such remote connection as the sawdust from York Minster flavouring York hams shows how interesting trade and craftsman's cooking can become!

Dorothy Hartley, *Food in England*

TRUFFLES

WHEN I WAS YOUNG I COULDN'T UNDERSTAND WHY something that smelled of old socks or doormice was so prized. Now that I am older and more experienced, I realise that truffles smell of sex and debauchery, and set off all sorts of exciting thought-patterns. They have a unique quality that is exotic, erotic and slightly psychotic, and not only is their own taste delicious but they enhance the quintessential flavour of whatever they are cooked with. They are also extremely energising. After a devastatingly tiring year I went to Valvonna & Crolla, our brilliant Italian deli in Edinburgh, and ate pasta & truffles twice a week until I could think again. Anna del Conti is another of my five great food writers of the century, and from her I have chosen this charming piece on truffles.

TRUFFLES – *tartufi* in Italian – are fungi, many species of which are found in northern and central Italy. The only three species that are of importance gastronomically are the *Tuber magnatum* – the white truffle or *tartufo d'Alba* – the *Tuber melanosporum* – black truffle or *tartufo di Norcia* (which the French call *truffe du Périgord*) – and the *Tuber aestivum* or *scorzone*. This last, also known as *tartufo d'estate* or *maggengo*, is not on a par with the white or the black truffle, and it differs from them in that it matures in the summer. It has a delicate and quite pleasing flavour, but is rather bland and uninteresting. It is mostly used in pâtés, sausages, terrines, truffle paste, etc. In the context of this book, I am mainly concerned with the white truffle, which is found only in Italy.

Truffles have been known in Italy since the beginning of history. The Romans were passionate about them and studied them in great detail. Pliny, Martial and Juvenal wrote treatises about truffles, while Apicius collected recipes for them. Nero ate truffles in abundance, calling them *cibus deorum* – food of the gods. After the fall of the Roman empire, truffles were ignored even by the monks, who preserved so much of the Roman civilisation. It is said that they did so deliberately because they considered truffles to have aphrodisiac properties – hardly an encouragement to chaste living.

During the Renaissance, however, the truffle once again became king of the high table. The Emperor Charles V enjoyed truffles at the dinner prepared in his honour by Bartolomeo Scappi, chef to Cardinal Campeggi, who was entertaining the Emperor. The truffles were stewed in bitter orange juice and also served simply raw in salad. In the eighteenth century, hunting parties were organised to search for *tartufi*. Dogs, rather than pigs, were used in Piedmont, and *tartufi* were found in amazing quantities. It was at that time that all the European royal houses were asking the House of Savoy for experienced men and trained dogs to search for truffles. In 1751 Carlo Emanuele III sent George II two *trifolai* and eight dogs to search for truffles in Windsor Park. Truffles similar to the *tartufi d'Alba* were found in moderate quantities. (In 1986 a sizeable truffle was found in a garden in Dover!)

Black truffles, too, were much more common in the past than they are now. William Whetmore Story, an American who lived in Rome in the 1860s, gives a graphic description of the market in Piazza Navona. There were 'excellent truffles. They grow in great quantities in the country around Rome, and especially at Spoleto, and used to be very cheap before the French bought them up so largely for the Parisian markets.'

I am old enough to have enjoyed truffles in good quantities as a child. Before Mass on Sundays we used to go and buy truffles from the stalls under the arches in the Piazza del Duomo. I was allowed to carry the parcel, and during Mass I held it under my nose, the piquant aroma of truffles mixing deliciously with the heavy scent of the incense. A salad that used to be served in my home at lunch parties was made up as follows: one third of a dish was covered with sliced *ovuli*, the choicest wild mushrooms, another third with Parmesan flakes and the remaining section with sliced *tartufi d'Alba*. The three parts were dressed with olive oil, lemon juice, salt and pepper.

Truffles cannot be cultivated like other fungi. Pliny the Elder wrote *'nascuntur et seri non possunt'* – they grow but cannot be cultivated. And this is still so, despite endless researches into the matter. White truffles grow in symbiosis with poplars, willows, limes, hazel bushes, oaks and hornbeams, in places around 1,000 feet high where rains in August and September keep the soil moist. They are usually found only a few inches below the ground. They are roughly globular in shape and can be as large as 30 centimetres (1 foot) in diameter. These are the real diamonds, since their price per gram increases in direct proportion to their size. There is a closed season for collecting truffles which starts on a certain date in October and ends in December. Truffles are at their best in early November, when they are fully ripe and their flavour is well developed. They keep only for a very short time, but they can be preserved by sterilisation or pounded into a paste and mixed with other ingredients.

I advise anyone who is interested in food to buy a truffle at least once in his lifetime, and handle it and absorb its aroma. To prepare a truffle you must brush it with a soft brush, gently but thoroughly, then rinse it quickly and dry it well. Since truffles are so expensive, they should be served in the best possible way – raw for white truffles, cooked for black ones. White truffles are added to a dish of *tagliatelle* that has been dressed only with butter and Parmesan. They are also added to a creamy *risotto*, to a rich *fonduta piemontese* or to a fresh *Carpaccio*. Black truffles mixed with anchovy fillets and garlic make a divine sauce for spaghetti, *spaghetti alla norcina*. They also change an everyday trout into a *haute cuisine* dish when used to stuff the fish.

The price of truffles has always been exorbitant, but in 1987 there was a shortage and the price jumped to 6,000 lire a gram, three times what it had been the year before. At this price a small fresh truffle weighing an ounce would cost about £80! There are, however, a number of brands of puree on the market, some of which are excellent, containing only truffles and olive oil, while others, less expensive, also contain *porcini*. In London, Fortnum & Mason stock many brands of tinned white and black truffles as well as a purée of truffles and oil scented with truffle. Fratelli Camisa in Charlotte Street sell a purée of white truffles and *porcini* which is satisfactory for cooking.

But it is in Milan, at Via Anfossi 13, that you will find everything that you could want to do with truffles and other fungi. (Whether you can afford it is another question!) The shop La Nuova Casa del Fungo e del Tartufo, belongs to Maurizio Vaglia and Carlo Urbani, who is known as King of the Truffles. There you can buy every kind of *tartufo*, while listening to Maurizio, a Piedmontese, who will extol the merits of the *tartufo bianco piemontese*. His wife, who comes from Norcia in Umbria, will interrupt to tell you that they are nothing compared to the real *tartufo nero* from around *her* home town. A typical example, this, of the Italians' regional chauvinism when it comes to food and cooking. Even if you don't want to buy anything, go there and have a chat with this charming couple; you will witness the almost religious fervour with which Italians discuss matters of gastronomy.

Anna del Conte, *Secrets from an Italian Kitchen*

TURTLE

WE THINK WE HAVE THE HANDLE ON EXOTICS, but here in 1909 we find Lady Clark of Tillypronie, doyenne of a remote estate on Deeside, giving advice on the storing and killing of a turtle, indispensable of course for the turtle soup so beloved of Edwardian dinner tables. Her great book, Elizabeth David's favourite, is full of excellent and sure recipes all collected from her Scottish Highland home. Today on Deeside one is hard put to enhance the beauty with a really good dinner, but then today's royals do not have the gourmet tastes of the Queen's great-grandfather.

NOTES ABOUT USING FRESH TURTLE FOR SOUP, &c.
THE turtle must be put in straw in the cellar and given water every 2 or 3 hours.

It should be beheaded at night, and left hanging neck downwards.

Mrs. Thomas used mushrooms, ham, knuckle of veal, and some wine, and made, with these and the turtle, thick and clear soup, cutlets in Cardinal sauce, and a dish of the fins dressed like calf's head.

The clear soup was best.

Charlotte Clark, *The Cookery Book of Lady Clark of Tillypronie*

UBIQUITOUS

I HAVE LONG felt that the only marriages made in heaven are those in the culinary world. In fact recipes are very like marriages, come to that – some are ill-chosen assortments of ingredients so incompatible that one simply anticipates the divorce, some have a controlling dominant party that overshadows the whole dish and reduces its partner to a nullity, some hum along together rather drearily in a commonplace way – and some just sing, in a manner I have yet to see among folk. The great Arabella Boxer, who together with Tessa Traeger revolutionised magazine food writing in the 1960s, says it better than me.

Pairs of foods that complement each other perfectly make an interesting study. Each country has its own classic combinations, and each individual his own variations. In *My Gastronomy*, Nico Ladenis lists twenty-six of his preferred combinations, which he calls 'marriages made in heaven'. Some seven or eight overlap with my own, while others are perhaps inevitably outside my range of experience, like *foie gras* with Sauternes. I have chosen to stick to more modest ingredients, but the problem here is that many simple foods make such good foils for other foods that it is hard to choose their opposite number. What goes best with lentils, for instance? Game, or duck, or hard-boiled eggs? And what is the ideal vehicle for mayonnaise? Cold lobster is Nico's choice, but even better to my mind is a fairly solid white fish like bass, poached or baked in foil, and served at room temperature. Yet new potatoes, freshly cooked in their skins and served when still warm, are also utterly delicious with mayonnaise, as are hard-boiled eggs. And who's to say what goes best with bread? A wedge of unpasteurised brie, or a ripe tomato, or a slice of raw ham, or homemade greengage jam, or just butter alone?

Many of the best combinations do not even need cooking, like the radishes and butter that are the prelude to so many good meals in simple French country restaurants, or the Marie biscuits and

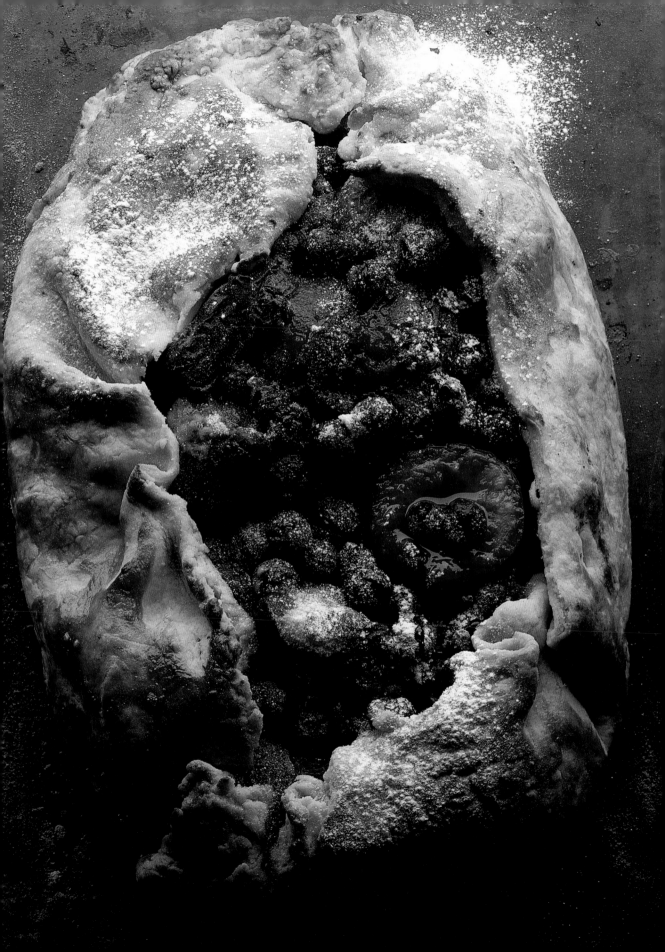

bitter chocolate that Elizabeth David cites in *Summer Cooking* as a good conclusion for a picnic; advice that I have followed many times. Other food combinations are the by-products of cooking that seem to occur naturally, as a bonus for the cook. One such is a hot boiled potato, cut in slices and eaten with wedges of cold butter straight from the fridge. I eat this while making a potato purée, just before pushing the hot potatoes through the food mill. Other delicious conjunctions of taste occur naturally, on the plate, like a lettuce salad immediately after a roast chicken, on the same plate, with the remains of the gravy. (The same principle applies to other roast meats, and even to a beef stew.)

Trying to analyse what makes a perfect combination, I come to the conclusion that it's usually to do with contrast, either of taste, texture or temperature. The bland mozzarella paired with the acidity of the tomato; the peppery bite of the radish with the cool smoothness of butter; and the crisp juicy sweetness of melon with the dry salty flavour of Parma ham. Sometimes however, the pairings transcend such limitations. Eggs, for instance, that go well with assertive foods like bacon and ham are also well matched with the bland potato. Some of my favourite dishes fall into this category: fried eggs with hashed brown potatoes, poached eggs on potato purée, and that old favourite, egg and chips.

Some foods go so well together that it seems hardly worth eating one without the other. The prospect of eating gooseberry pie without cream, for instance, or plum pudding without brandy butter, is hardly worth considering. Everyone must remember a picnic where the vital ingredient has been forgotten, so that one is left with gulls' eggs but no salt, or sausages but no mustard.

Many of our feelings for complementary foods are based on national or even regional features, others on childhood associations. For this reason it is not always easy to appreciate foreign food combinations that lie outside our own experience. Some, like the Scandinavian use of horseradish with fish, or dill with potatoes, have an instant appeal, while others, like the Dutch Christmas dish of cold poached liver eaten on slices of fruit bread, seem merely bizarre. Even the most sophisticated foreigners' tastes seem surprising at times, like the late Baron Philippe de Rothschild, who liked to eat poached haddock with marmalade for luncheon at the Savoy, on his visits to London.

As for childhood tastes, my own seem to have been based almost entirely on sugar, and white sugar at that. White bread and butter spread with sugar, lettuce leaves springled with sugar, and an orange with a sugar lump forced into a hole cut in the top. Later, at boarding school, I came to love eating fried bread spread with marmalade, sometimes with a thin layer of Marmite in between.

My tastes changed, thank goodness. The last food combination that really pleased me was one I happened to chance upon a year ago, returning from a trip to Paris with three jars of flower jelly from Hediard: orange blossom, rose petal, and jasmine. Remembering a dish I used to eat many years ago in New York, of guava jelly with cream cheese and water biscuits, I tried eating them with *fromage blanc* and small Carr's Table Water Biscuits, and found myself hooked. Served at the end of a meal, instead of cheese or dessert, the three disparate elements seem to blend together in a harmonious whole: a combination of flavour and fragrance.

Arabella Boxer, *A Visual Feast*

UNEMPLOYED

WHAT A STRANGE MAN GEORGE ORWELL WAS: Old Etonian, a very red socialist – and now we are told a member of MI5! I love this piece on comfort food and the poor: it sums up the truths the *soi-disant* nutritionists ignore – and note the reference to brown bread.

WHEN I was a small boy at school a lecturer used to come once a term and deliver excellent lectures on famous battles of the past, such as Blenheim, Austerlitz etc. He was fond of quoting Napoleon's maxim 'An army marches on its stomach,' and at the end of his lecture he would suddenly turn to us and demand, 'What's the most important thing in the world?' We were expected to shout 'Food!' and if we did not do so he was disappointed.

Obviously he was right in a way. A human being is primarily a bag for putting food into; the other functions and faculties may be more godlike, but in point of time they come afterwards. A man dies and is buried, and all his words and actions are forgotten, but the food he has eaten lives after him in the sound or rotten bones of his children. I think it could be plausibly argued that changes of diet are more important than changes of dynasty or even of religion. The Great War, for instance, could never have happened if tinned food had not been invented. And the history of the past four hundred years in England would have been immensely different if it had not been for the introduction of root-crops and other vegetables at the end of the Middle Ages, and a little later the introduction of non-alcoholic drinks (tea, coffee, cocoa) and also of distilled liquors to which the beer-drinking English were not accustomed. Yet it is curious how seldom the all-importance of food is recognised. You see statues everywhere to politicians, poets, bishops, but none to cooks or bacon-curers or market-gardeners. The Emperor Charles V is said to have erected a statue to the inventor of bloaters, but that is the only case I can think of at the moment.

So perhaps the really important thing about the unemployed, the really basic thing if you look to the future, is the diet they are living on. . . . I have here a budget which was made out for me by an unemployed miner and his wife. . . . This man's allowance was thirty-two shillings a week, and besides his wife he had two children, one aged two years and five months and the other ten months.

The miner's family spend only tenpence a week on green vegetables and tenpence halfpenny on milk . . . and nothing on fruit; but they spend one and nine on sugar (about eight pounds of sugar, that is) and a shilling on tea. The half crown spent on meat might represent a small joint and the materials for a stew; probably as often as not it would represent four or five tins of bully beef. The basis of their diet, therefore, is white bread-and-margarine, corned beef, sugared tea and potatoes – an appalling diet. Would it not be better if they spent more money on wholesome things like oranges and wholemeal bread or if they even . . . saved on fuel and ate their carrots raw? Yes, it would, but the point is that no ordinary human being is ever going to do such a thing. The ordinary human being would sooner starve than live on brown bread and raw carrots. And the peculiar evil is this, that the less money you have, the less inclined you feel to spend it on wholesome food. A millionaire may enjoy breakfasting off orange juice and Ryvita biscuits, an unemployed man doesn't. . . . When you are unemployed, which is to say when you are underfed, harassed, bored and miserable, you don't want to eat dull wholesome food. . . . You want something a little bit 'tasty'. There is always some cheaply pleasant thing to tempt you. Let's have three pennorth of chips! Run out and buy us a twopenny ice-cream! Put the kettle on and we'll all have a nice cup of tea! . . . White bread and marg and sugared tea don't nourish you to any extent, but they are nicer (at least most people think so) than brown bread-and-dripping and cold water. Unemployment is an endless misery that has got to be constantly palliated, and especially with tea, the Englishman's opium. A cup of tea or even an aspirin is much better as a temporary stimulant than a crust of brown bread.

George Orwell, *The Road to Wigan Pier*

UTOPIA

THE LATE JEREMY ROUND was to me the main contender to carry on the torch of food writing that Elizabeth had lit and Jane Grigson carried forward. Sadly he died all too young, from a heart attack following a gourmet banquet in Hong Kong, leaving too little finished work behind him. I love this poem, inspired 'à la Chesterton' by a particularly pompous pronouncement of Paul Levy's. It makes me grieve what we have missed.

'. . . tea . . . contrary to the belief of the vulgar . . . is seldom drunk with food in China'

Paul Levy, *Observer*, 16 January 1983

JUST once to get it all right!
To wake having had enough sleep, alert
To spring at a day of sufficient exercise,
Balanced diet, faultless personal hygiene,
And satisfying creative endeavour.

To use without exploiting, intelligence,
Skill, fine judgement, compassion, wit, and
Profound understanding. To arrive at evening
Physically tired, at peace, and looking forward
To a sexually and emotionally challenging few hours
Of complete mutual fulfillment.

To always have pens and paper
And stamps and envelopes and current addresses
In the house at the same time. To remember that *mer*
Is feminine, and not to say 'who' in sentences such as,

'Patricia will sit between Mandy and whom?'
Or wash mushrooms that should be wiped with a cloth,
Or use knives anywhere near lettuce.

Never to yield to the thrill
Of letting comparative strangers into the scandalous
Details of a friend's involvement with a Catholic
Priest, or say dishonest things for effect like,
'Who can bear Belgium for more than an afternoon?'

Civilizations pull across ages,
And we toil also, forsaking completeness,
That some day just imaginable, either no-one who doesn't
Will be thought vulgar, or everyone *will* know how
Seldom tea is drunk with food in China.

Jeremy Round

VEGETABLES

THERE WAS A TIME WHEN ENGLAND PRIDED ITSELF on its vegetable cookery. In the 17th century one of the grand courtiers of the day, John Evelyn, wrote a book on salad vegetables. 18th-century books had whole chapters on the importance of not overcooking vegetables. Then came the Victorians, and Tom Beaton virtually ruined English vegetable cooking in his wife's name. True, he plagiarised Fanny Farmer's *Boston Cookbook*, but then the Irish never could cook vegetables. Vegetable cooking was further damaged by canning, freezing and imports. Margaret Coster's *Four Seasons Cookbook* started the swing back to good natural cooking of vegetables in the seasons. Here we have a piece on new potatoes which conjured up all the excitement one used to feel when new potatoes were new and in season. In the last few years I have started buying only home-grown vegetables where possible, and only in season. It has transformed my enjoyment of eating. Tesco's tried to persuade farmers to feed sheep hormones so they could produce small lambs all year, and genetic modification threatens vegetables as we know them. But it is still hard to beat the joy of seasonal produce properly grown.

NEW POTATOES

WHEN we have our own new potatoes, freshly dug if we are lucky just before they are cooked, they are so exquisite that I prefer to serve them absolutely plain in all their pastoral simplicity – smooth, round, and shiny with butter, with perhaps just a jaunty, crisp, sweet-smelling, little sprig of mint or a scattering of chopped chives, but otherwise innocent of all adornment. It seems a waste of time and trouble to cook them in any other way.

Later, you may like to start gilding the lily. Serve pommes de terre rissolées, which are usually a better accompaniment to roast and grilled meats anyway. (Even canned new potatoes can look and taste quite acceptable treated like this.) It's best to use clarified butter for this but, at a pinch and in a hurry, unclarified butter will do. But it must be butter – not margarine – with perhaps a very little olive oil added to prevent it burning.

Take a very thick pan wide enough to hold a pound (450 g) of new potatoes in one layer. Melt 2 oz (55 g) butter in it, and when it stops foaming put in the potatoes, as far as possible the same size and arranged in a single layer. Shake for a minute or two till well coated with the butter, then cover and cook over a low heat for about 30 minutes, shaking occasionally, till the potatoes are golden brown and crisp all over on the outside, and tender and soft inside. Watch that they don't catch during the last few minutes of cooking. Drain off the cooked butter and add a little fresh butter just before serving and season with coarse sea salt.

Or parboil them, drop them into a little boiling cream and cook them gently for another 10 minutes. Then serve them well seasoned with coarse sea salt and freshly ground black pepper, and sprinkled with chopped parsley.

Or just colour sliced cooked new potatoes in a little melted butter, add 4 tablespoons (60 ml) cream into which you have stirred 2 tablespoons (30 ml) French mustard and cook them in this for 5 minutes longer. Oh, how good with chicken or with fish!

Margaret Coster, *The Four Seasons Cookbook*

VEGETARIAN

WHEN I WAS YOUNG, vegetarians were unhealthy-looking people, often with sparse facial hair (both sexes), who wore sandals, smelled stale and musty, and ate revolting food. Many are still like that. Annie Bell has long red-gold hair, a beautiful posture, perfect skin and natural elegance, and her food is so good that I ate it every day for lunch for a month before it dawned on me it was vegetarian. I can actually claim responsibility for, as she puts it,

BOVRIL
puts a smile into Vegetables

TAKE A TEASPOONFUL OF BOVRIL AND ST[...]

BOVR[IL]
MANUFACTURE[D]
BOVRIL LTD LON[DON]
ENGLAN[D]

For rich, satisfying goodness in your vegetable dishes, make it a rule to make them with Bovril. Bovril adds enjoyment and helps you to assimilate your other food. Always keep some Bovril in the kitchen. Obtainable in 1 oz., 2 oz., 4 oz. and 8 oz. Bottles.

'goading me to pick up my pen in the first place', and it is an achievement of which I, a dedicated carnivore, am very proud. However, the difference lies in the fact that Annie is not engaged in some crusade of fascistic martyrdom, and in this introduction to her book *Evergreen* she explains far better than I what I detest in most vegetarians.

A THICK, chilled gazpacho, vibrant and red with tomatoes, eaten with warm, fresh white bread, dipped first into olive oil and then into the soup. Or a Thai salad with thin strips of cucumber, char-grilled baby corn and aubergine, hot and sharp with chilli, lemon juice and sesame. A cheese soufflé risen inches above the rim of the dish into a glossy flat surface, crusty on the outside and ethereal and light inside. Button mushrooms infused with the aromatic flavours of a broth, with freshly chopped herbs and diced tomato stirred into them at the last minute. A thin pastry case spread with a sweet purée of onions, and sliced potatoes, covered with crème fraiche piquant with the flavour of finely grated fresh horseradish: I find vegetarian food fresh and sensual, and alive. Interesting and packed with textures and flavours, it is for me a complete celebration in eating. But there is no reason why as a vegetarian you should not also maintain a taste for 'petits pots au chocolat', made with a silky couverture chocolate, or an almond crumble baked over a base of raspberries and Cape gooseberries, smothered with a foamy kirsch sabayon. Likewise crème brûlée with a thin, crisp surface of caramel, and sticky toffee pudding studded with raisins soaked in sweet wine, then drowned in cream.

Becoming a vegetarian is often seen as a move towards a healthier diet, or equated with abstinence. The decision may be linked to moral, religious or political reasons. All these are relevant, but it is important not to confuse issues with food itself. A vegetarian diet can, like any other, range from the inedible to the sublime. Too often the vegetarian pie you buy is also labelled 'healthy pie' or 'cruelty-free pie' with no emphasis on its gastronomic value. I believe that the confusion of food with issues is an unfortunate one. It seems to haunt vegetarian food in a way in which no other cuisine is affected. Being a vegetarian should not automatically mean a denial of pleasurable foods, or an acceptance of unpalatable ones. A campaigner will put recipes in a book to encourage people, and in the past this has backfired miserably, damaging the reputation of vegetarian food in a way it does not deserve.

According to the Weasel, the *Independent Magazine*'s diary columnist, 'Thousands of years of human experience have taught us that only a limited number of different foods and combinations of food are actually any good. Every now and then someone will invent a new dish that catches on, like crème brûlée, but the cook's main job is to seek to perfect the traditional dishes which everybody knows and likes.' The same premise forms the basis of this book. Familiarity often makes people return again and again to the same dishes, which become a custom and are handed down from one person to another, so becoming traditions. But there is a pitfall: sometimes we are content to eat terrible versions of familiar dishes, allowing the comfort found in familiarity to override gastronomic good judgement. In this book I have drawn from as many different cuisines as possible. Every cuisine has some vegetarian traditions, some more than others. I have returned hungry from a weekend in Paris, almost starving after a week in St Petersburg, and in a blissful state, fit to burst, after a stay in

Italy. Some dishes have simply received a quick buff, others a more radical rethink. But I have not forced newness on old favourites for the sake of it; perhaps a new twist here and there, some added detail and a touch of artistic licence.

Annie Bell, Evergreen

WHAT IS INTERESTING ABOUT *Leaves from a Tuscan Kitchen* is that, although it was the first real vegetarian book, it contains in the first edition a recipe for *Bolito Misto*, that most meat-orientated of dishes.

LASCHI says, 'the epoch of Charles V is the greatest of modern times, for the culture of the spirit induced the culture of the body.' But he does not mention vegetables or herbs at all. For them we must go back to the ancients. Bitterly did the Israelites, when wandering in the desert, regret 'the cucumbers and the melons we did eat in Egypt'; though old Gerarde says, 'they yield to the body a cold and moist nourishment, and that very little, and the same not good.' Gerarde is however hard to please, for he says of egg-plants, under the old English name of Raging or Mad Apples, 'doubtless these apples have a mischievous qualitie, the use whereof is utterly to be forsaken.'

Fennel, dedicated to St. John, was believed to make the lean fat and to give the weak strength, while the root pounded with honey was considered a remedy against the bites of mad dogs. If lettuce be eaten after dinner it cures drunkenness; but Pope says:-

If your wish be rest,

Lettuce and cowslip wine, *probatum est.*

Sorrel is under the influence of Venus, and Gerarde declares that also 'the carrot serveth for love matters; and Orpheus, as Pliny writeth, said that the use hereof winneth love.' Flowers of rosemary, rue, sage, marjoram, fennel, and quince preserve youth; worn over the heart they give gaiety. Rosemary is an herb of the sun, while Venus first raised sweet marjoram, therefore young married couples are crowned with it in Greece. While

'He that eats sage in May

Shall live for aye.'

Sweet basil is often worn by the Italian maidens in their bosoms, as it is supposed to engender sympathy, and borage makes men merry and joyful.

For years English friends have begged recipes for cooking vegetables in the Italian fashion, so I have written down many of the following from the dictation of our good Giuseppe Volpi, whose portrait, by Mr. A. H. Hallam Murray, adorns this little book, and who has been known to our friends for over thirty years.

Janet Ross, Leaves from a Tuscan Kitchen

VOGUE

THIS MAGAZINE HAS ALWAYS PLAYED AN IMPORTANT ROLE in food culture. It gave us our first food columnist, our instructions on how to decorate our tables and, in wartime, how to keep our chins and our standards up.

POWER BEHIND THE THRONE

WE learn again how profound is the instinct that can drive a civilised nation into war. Not the base instinct for domination or power, but the urgent claims of individual self-respect and integrity – it is for these things that we are compelled to fight, and for the good name rather than the glory of our country. Yesterday, the conscience of the nation was symbolised in the fulfilment of a pledge to Belgium; to-day, we know how heavily the bubble reputation weighed against all the casuistries that might have left Poland to face her enemies alone. At such a time we find example and encouragement in their Majesties, for they are the keepers of the nation's conscience and an epitome of the sober virtues of our race. In them we see courage, devotion and sanity; and if we can hold to these qualities as they have done, there will indeed be power behind the throne.

Their lives, and those of the whole royal family, are dedicated to duty as these pictures remind us. In war, their peace-time duties deepen immeasurably: and so with us, also. For if the last war's 'business as usual' motto is over-optimistic for modern conditions, yet it is clear that a vast amount of the business of life must be managed, if not as usual, then as near it as can be contrived. We must eat, sleep, dress ourselves and look after our households. People who have had the severe shock of some great catastrophe sometimes cut themselves off from ordinary life and cannot bear to see others going about their ordinary affairs. It seems as if the world should have stopped when the blow fell. Yet when they recover from the first impact of disaster, a return to ordinary routine, the cares, tasks and occupations of everyday life, soon has a steadying and healing effect.

Multiply this effect by the number of individuals in a nation and it will be seen that the supreme shocks of modern warfare can best be met by the most ordinary behaviour. Heroic sacrifices may or may not be of use, but humdrum commonsense will have its value in every hour and situation of war.

Another reason for keeping as closely as possible to our ordinary habits of life is that we shall disrupt as little as may be the economic structure of the nation; demand and supply will not be so violently disturbed and fewer people will suffer the secondary results of war.

All that is one side of the picture. On the other is the plain fact that there will be inevitable and tremendous changes in civil life and to these all our private lives must be reorientated. Another thing; in the settling-down-to-new-conditions process, let us not settle down too far. A readiness to improvise, to adapt oneself to unforeseen demands and new contingencies, is also a part of war mentality to be cultivated. And if no such demands should come for a time, let us keep ourselves on our toes by making some fairly stern calls upon ourselves and our own resources.

For those who are attached to the auxiliary reserves of the fighting forces, the way is clear; they are under military discipline and must obey orders. Those who have been trained for civil defence also have their work plain before them. For the many who have no official post, no fixed duties, no inevitable daily job, the best advice is to find something to do that will daily demand their attention, take up their time and tax their resources. Don't pick and choose too much or wait about for something to do that is really worthy of you – the chances are that you will still be waiting when the war is over. Do whatever you find near you that urgently wants doing – preferably some useful work outside your own interests and necessities – and if greater things are your destiny, greater things will find you out.

For obvious reasons the work you find for yourself had better be as near as possible. If you live in town, hospitals will want all sorts of lay helpers – ask your doctor about this. Also there are centres for such work as rolling bandages and paddling splints. There are children to look after, the sick to be visited. The great thing is to have some place where your presence is expected and appreciated. In the great ordeal only a stupid braggart would pretend otherwise. If, however, your mind is occupied with something sufficiently difficult and refractory, you will be able to side-step some, at least, of the terrors. But give yourself a time-limit to find your job and begin on it – the shorter the better.

Apart from this job of work, see that all the resources you possess are used. If you have a garden, consider how you can cultivate it to the best war-time advantage. Perhaps you should cut down the roses and the prize delphiniums, dig up the velvet lawn and grow something to eat. On the other hand, to grow vegetables demands much space and fairly constant attention, and if your garden is small, your time much taken up with other things and your gardener gone, as he will be, it may be wisest to leave the flower borders as they are and take the flowers, when they bloom, to the nearest hospital, where they will be welcomed.

If you live in the country and already grow fruit and vegetables, you might add to the national food supply by keeping bees, rabbits, hens or goats. Normally, we import a lot of eggs and honey – any extra ones we can produce will save some precious corner of shipping space. Advice on keeping all these things is easily available and you can soon find out whether in your case it is likely to be a success.

Then it may be worth while revising your own accomplishments. Whatever you do and however closely you keep to the ordinary routine of life, there are bound to be gaps, with pleasure and entertainment in the ordinary sense indefinitely postponed, escorts and good companions called away. Yet there must be relaxation, the terrific tension of life under war conditions demands it, and we must depend on ourselves for most of it. Here are some suggestions.

Learn to cook. Professional cooks will soon be wafted away. Cooking can be fun and if we have to do it, how painful it will be all round if we do it badly!

Sew or knit something, preferably not too complicated. This is not to put your dressmaker out of work but to give you something to do with your hands in hours of waiting.

Another idea on the same lines is to take lessons in carpentry, lay in a stock of wood and tools and set to work on a cupboard or chair.

With most domestic help vanishing or gone already, determine to keep your room, flat, or house, immaculate and charming. You want it not only for yourself but for others. Our homes are

FOOD

to be the centres of that comradeship, comforting and wise cheerfulness which is essential.

Do your beauty exercises and keep your hair and complexion in good trim. It would be an added calamity, if war turned us into a nation of frights and slovens.

If you are fond of bridge, darts, or any mild diversion of that kind, get your company together regularly on some evening of the week and play a quiet game.

Learn or re-learn to play some musical instrument, if possible in the company of other amateur musicians. If you haven't a piano and the violin is too difficult, try the recorder, mouth organ or accordion. Music is the finest antidote to the horrors of war, but you must play for yourself – gramophone records and radio concerts are not at all the same thing. Consider the case of Mr. and Mrs. Malines, the British Consul at Madrid and his wife, through the long tragedy of the Spanish civil war. They were in the British Embassy continuously for thirty-three months and during that time went through innumerable air-raids and bombardments in which the Embassy was struck four times by shell-fire, and the annexe in which they lived, twelve times. During all that while music was the only recreation after days of exhausting work, and they had chamber music regularly three nights a week.

When the noise of bombardment permitted, the sound of violins might be heard upon the air and many people could be seen making their way through the shattered streets of Madrid to listen. Bizarre Spanish scene! Shall we, in the days to come, perhaps equal that?

Vogue, September 1939

WE'VE got to face it: the servant shortage is going to be acute. Londoners, even in the first few weeks since the declaration of war, have found it so, and many country dwellers who have relied in the past on daily help have found that their 'treasure' now has children billeted on her and cannot go out to work. But don't despair: whatever your problems, remember that there are millions of others faced with similar ones, and we must all reorganise our lives to cope with existing circumstances. Efficient organisation, that is the thing that is going to help you now to get the wheels running as smoothly as possible in the difficult days ahead.

LABOUR-SAVING METHODS – Study your kitchen with a critical eye, especially with regard to the placing of furniture. Save steps by placing the kitchen cabinet near the stove and sink. Avoid backache by having everything at a comfortable height. Cut out scrubbing by covering the kitchen table and pantry shelves with a decorative washable linoleum. Reduce stair climbing by collecting odds and ends on a tray near the foot and vice versa, so that one journey either way will serve. Set breakfast the night before and cover it with a light cloth to protect it from dust. Cook the bacon in a fireproof dish in the oven or grill it on a platter under the gas. Soak the porridge overnight and cook it in a double saucepan to avoid the constant stirring and supervision; and substitute, occasionally, packet cereal and fruit. Have, if you can, an electric table toaster, a coffee percolator and a hot plate to keep breakfast warm for the stragglers. If a late supper is wanted, prepare and set a trolley meal on the 'help yourself' plan. Train all members of the family to lend a hand in the house. Team work in dish-washing, each one tidying her own bedroom (an easy matter when stripped of the non-essentials) and cleaning her own shoes, all help greatly in reducing the housework to a minimum. Children too must take their share – help in the garden, keep their own room tidy and look after the pets.

LABOUR-SAVING APPLIANCES – Bad tools make bad workmen, so check up on your household equipment. Invest in some up-to-date labour savers, if you can – such as vacuum or hand sweepers and an electric or weighted hand polisher. Fix an automatic lighter to your gas cooker to save matches and incidentally your temper. A glove duster which polishes and yet protects the hand and a short-handled dusting mop to save back bending as well advised. A whistling kettle is useful for the absent-minded and so is an alarm clock, set to warn you when puddings and pies are ready. If your family believe in a fruit breakfast, buy a juice extractor – it's a time and juice saver.

Dish-Washing – Here method is important. Wash up as you go along and don't clutter up your sink with dirty pots and piled dishes. Use plenty of hot water and a reliable soap-powder and the task is almost a pleasure. Clean dishcloths and towels, a dish-mop and steel wool are necessities; and a tea-towel wrung out of whiting and water, then dried, will keep your glass and cutlery bright and sparkling without the ever-repeating weekly cleanings. Plan your meals in relation to washing up and introduce one-dish courses when possible. Cut down the use of unnecessary utensils when cooking – small squares of paper or baker's bags will hold the dry ingredients instead of plates or cups. Prepare the dishes methodically for washing up; scrape and stack them in their respective kinds, dreg the teacups, soak the cutlery and spoons in a jug of water and supply ash trays at table – these preliminaries will simplify the task greatly. If you would avoid 'dishpan' hands, use a small mop and a mild soap powder, and don't forget the little daily grooming that will keep them in condition.

Cooking – Try casserole cooking when possible, as dishes more or less cook themselves, little fuel is required, and the washing up is greatly reduced. A typical casserole meal is Hot Pot, where the meat, vegetables, gravy and potatoes are all cooked in one dish; a creamy rice pudding, with raisins added, can be cooked along with it to give the correct balance of food. A one-pot meal, where two courses consisting of meat, vegetables, potatoes and pudding are steamed in straight jam-jars in a fishkettle, is another practical idea. A fireproof glass frying pan is also handy, as it can come straight from stove to table; and a table cooker solves many problems. Learn to take short cuts with your mincer, using it for vegetable chopping, marmalade making, and other such jobs. Cut out the tedious making of breadcrumbs for meat rolls, rissoles and other made-up dishes. A slice of bread soaked in hot milk or water in a covered basin for half an hour, then whisked vigorously to free it from lumps, serves the purpose equally well. Dice vegetables or meat for soups to save a final sieving, this incidentally being a much better way for children. Try a high tea or a simple supper in place of the usual evening dinner. Plant your kitchen window box with parsley and pot herbs to give that little touch which matters. Cress will grow on a wet sponge or flannel, and root vegetables are on the spot if stored in a wooden box with sand.

Vogue, September 1939

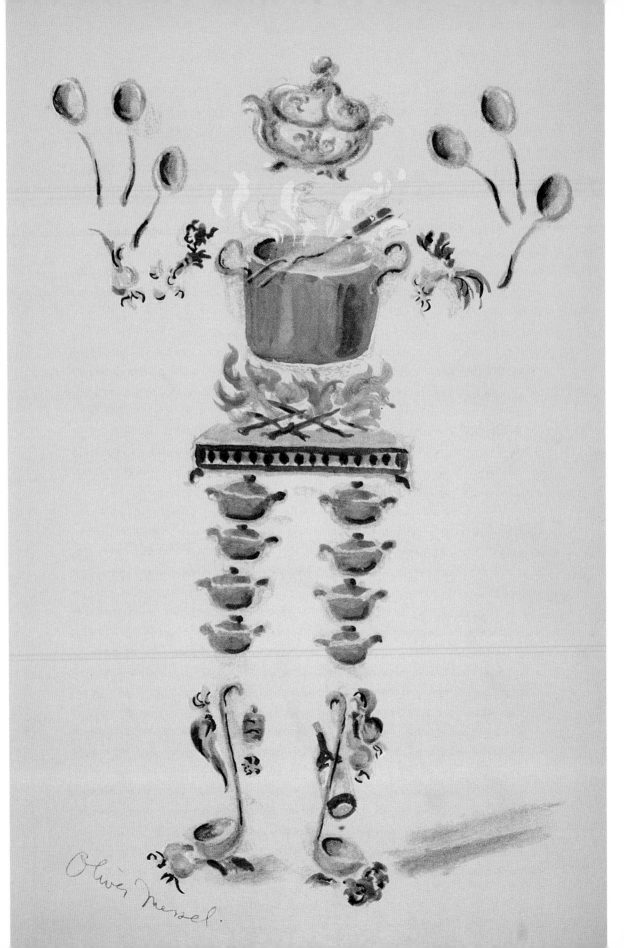

FOOD IS WHAT YOU MAKE IT

TWO-COURSE MEALS. Little meals can be as exciting as huge meals can be dull. Don't blush, be proud, to give your guests a two-course dinner. With a dash of imagination, it will prove as kind to their palates as your purse.

Put banal meat-followed-by-sweet ideas right out of your head. So long as your main dish is substantial your secondary course, whether served before or after, can be as unconventional as you please.

Serve an hors d'oeuvre course or shellfish cocktail, or hot vegetable consommé, followed by a big chicken casserole or fish goulash, piping hot. Serve big bowls of minestrone, followed by cold meats or smoked ham, accompanied by baked potatoes and two mammoth bowls of salad: one seasoned with garlic, the other without, for the inferior few who can't abide it. Or hot hors d'oeuvre (a Persian speciality), followed by cold ham with pickled peaches and potatoes baked in their jackets.

For lunch, a big dish of kedgeree with watercress salad is eternally popular: best with brown wholemeal bread, not white; follow this with all sorts of fresh fruit arranged in separate dishes, and with the cheese and biscuits that men frankly prefer to the most elaborate sweet. If, with foreign cheeses scarce, you can't get a really good cheese, serve delicious cream-cheese snacks instead. A Chinese dish of chicken with rice and pork is another good lunch dish. You'll want something simple and sweetish to follow, such as stewed greengages (fresh or canned) with a dash of sherry added to the dish. Another nice idea for simple lunches is to serve breakfast cups of hot coffee *with* the meal, instead of café noir afterwards.

CANNED FOOD PLUS. Canned foods are sure to play a big part in this winter's menus. It's well worth learning how to doll them up to the best advantage. Most are excellent as they are. But a dash of something fresh, a flavouring of cream, or wine, may turn a pleasant dish into an exciting one.

Canned soups are delicious, but most are now too familiar. It's a shock to recognise at an elegant dinner-table the flavour one has so often turned out of the tin at home. Give your canned soups a cachet of your own. Try mixing them. Cream of mushroom and green pea blend beautifully; so do tomato and green pea or celery; and many others. Add a dash of cream to tomato or asparagus soup – of sherry to consommé. Stir an egg yoke and a little cream into smooth vegetable soup, and serve with grated cheese.

Be imaginative with canned vegetables. Parsley sauce makes broad beans taste fresh from the garden. French beans Lyonnaise have glamour. New potatoes are greatly improved by tossing in melted margarine and garnishing with chopped mint.

When it comes to the sweet, again show your gastronomic sense. Don't slap the pineapples straight from can to dish. Flavour them with kirsch. Flavour greengages with sherry. Pour hot chocolate sauce (two minutes to make) over chilled pears.

There is no end to the more substantial dishes that can be made with canned foods. Several have been already mentioned. Two more good ones are chicken à la king, and lobster Newburg.

GOOD SERVICE. Taste is the least independent of the senses. Your palate is strongly influenced by how a dish looks and how it is served. Deck up your wartime food attractively. Give thought to garnishes. See that each course makes a good entry.

Garnishing food is largely a question of colour sense. A dark parsley garnish, for instance, takes the insipid look off white fish. Good lesser-known garnishes are sliced olives or chilled baby onions for jellied consommé; raisins soaked in wine for fruit salad or stewed fruit; chopped mint and pimento for all egg dishes; little bunches of five or six vegetables for grills.

Nice ways of serving food improve the appetite. Everyone loves individual dishes. A baby casserole apiece costs no more than one large communal one, but seems twice as luxurious. The same goes for the table setting. Give each guest a small toast rack, and an ashtray and matches of his own. For lunch, dishes served in soup plates are unfailingly popular. Everyone likes that traditional German dish (whether it has survived Hitler, we don't know) of boiled chicken and rice and asparagus tips served in soup-plates with lots of broth. Then there's a Yorkshire dish (ideal under rationing) of kidneys and onions served in soup-plates.

A pleasant, companionable way of serving food is to cook it at table in a chafing-dish. Its cheerful sputtering makes conversation flourish. Master the art of making crêpes bar-le-duc yourself: or, simpler, pears flambés.

Vogue, September 1940

COOKING – THE NEW ADVENTURE

EDITOR'S NOTE: Mrs. Lytton Toye's first career was the stage: she still acts in radio plays. An enthusiastic amateur of cooking, she decided ten years ago to take her Cordon Bleu; studied in Paris, Brussels and Vienna. Until war broke out she ran a Cookery School with Marcel Boulestin (her friends now wish that instead of sending their cooks, they had gone themselves).

WE'VE eaten out, perforce, during the war, in restaurants, canteens and what you will. But does this signify that, 'when Peace here does house,' we shall have lost the taste, or urge, to entertain in our own homes? Oh, I hope not. However simple, I would prefer a meal in someone's house or flat to any that I might be offered in a restaurant; for one sees one's friends in their own environment – and if she (or he) has done us the honour and taken the trouble to cook for us, we should be flattered.

Food should be fun; and I mean precisely that. Fun for you to prepare, not a dismal grind; fun for your guests to eat. One's food should be as stimulating as witty conversation, and reflect one's personality much as clothes do.

Deliberate left-overs are a tremendous help to the busy woman. As an illustration I am reminded of a luncheon with an American friend, an exceedingly busy creature, who says 'she can't cook for nuts.'

Our menu was: Beans and bacon (no, not out of a tin, but French beans). Cole Slaw salad. Potted cheese (my contribution). A creme and fruit. Coffee.

When I arrived, some finely chopped onion was murmuring gently in margarine in a flat pan, to which she added chopped bacon; after a minute or so, in went three sliced mushrooms, and seasoning. She covered the pan, leaving it simmering, while she prepared coffee and handed me a cocktail and a breadknife. The runner beans were already cooked, and would go in at the last moment.

'Why not put in a suggestion of nutmeg?' said I. 'Nutmeg?' she replied, blankly. 'Yes, nutmeg. It brings out the flavour of beans; or spinach, or cabbage for that matter. You won't taste it.'

Supping my cocktail, with the bread knife I shredded a half-heart of Savoy cabbage and two sticks of celery as finely as lace and tossed them with a mustardy cream dressing. (Not to interrupt my story, the receipts will come later.)

On an eggless day, use dried eggs and flavour more strongly to drown their definite tang; also work in a nut of butter as you finish cooking.

Did you dislike tapioca since schoolroom days? Pill Pudding, perhaps you called it? I did. And semolina? Odd, one changes: these two are now my standbys. With either, the cream basis works equally well, except that you need a level tablespoonful of either, sprinkled, dry, into the hot milk. Cook rather longer, till tapioca is clear, or semolina thickened.

If chocolate suits your mood, add it or cocoa to the mixture, with a little strong coffee, or essence. With a compote of bottled raspberries you have an elegant sweet; but you will invent variants yourself.

War-time salad dressing, since we lack oil:

Blend a level tablespoonful of dried egg with a tablespoonful of vinegar and one of milk, a coffeespoonful dry mustard, good pinch salt, sugar, a little pepper. Work it smooth, then add enough unsweetened evaporated milk till you have a consistency of thick cream. Few extra drops of vinegar if not sufficiently tart.

This will keep in the refrigerator, so make more than you will use.

Doris Lytton Tate, *Vogue*, February 1945

285

FOOD

WAITING

In Britain waiting is regarded as an amateur occupation, unlike on the Continent where it is a highly respected profession. I have always regarded waiting as an art, but sometimes it acquires the element of slapstick, as this piece from Ludwig Bemelmens' *Hotel Splendide* shows all too clearly.

Our tables – Nos. 81, 82, and 86 – were in a noisy, draughty corner of the balcony. They stood facing the stairs from the dining room and were between two doors. One door led to the pantry and was hung on whining hinges. On wet days it sounded like an angry cat and it was continually kicked by the boots of waiters rushing in and out with trays in their hands. The other door led to a linen closet.

The waiters and bus boys squeezed by our tables, carrying trays. The ones with trays full of food carried them high over their heads; the ones with dirty dishes carried them low, extended in front. They frequently bumped into each other and there would be a crash of silver, glasses, and china, and cream trickling over the edges of the trays in thin streams. Whenever this happened, Monsieur Victor raced to our section, followed by his captains, to direct the cleaning up of the mess and pacify the guests. It was a common sight to see people standing in our section, napkins in hand, complaining and brushing themselves off and waving their arms angrily in the air.

Monsieur Victor used our tables as a kind of penal colony to which he sent guests who were notorious cranks, people who had forgotten to tip him over a long period of time and needed a reminder, undesirables who looked out of place in better sections of the dining room, and guests who were known to linger for hours over an order of hors d'oeuvres and a glass of milk while well-paying guests had to stand at the door waiting for a table.

Mespoulets was the ideal man for Monsieur Victor's purposes. He complemented Monsieur Victor's plan of punishment. He was probably the worst waiter in the world and I had become his commis after I fell down the stairs into the main part of the dining room with eight pheasants à la Souvaroff. When I was sent to him to take up my duties as his assistant, he introduced himself by saying, 'My name is easy to remember. Just think of 'my chickens' – 'mes poulets' – Mespoulets.'

Rarely did any guest who was seated at one of our tables leave the hotel with a desire to come back again. If there was any broken glass around the dining room, it was always in our spinach. The occupants of Tables Nos. 81, 82, and 86 shifted in their chairs, stared at the pantry door, looked around and made signs of distress at other waiters and captains while they waited for their food.

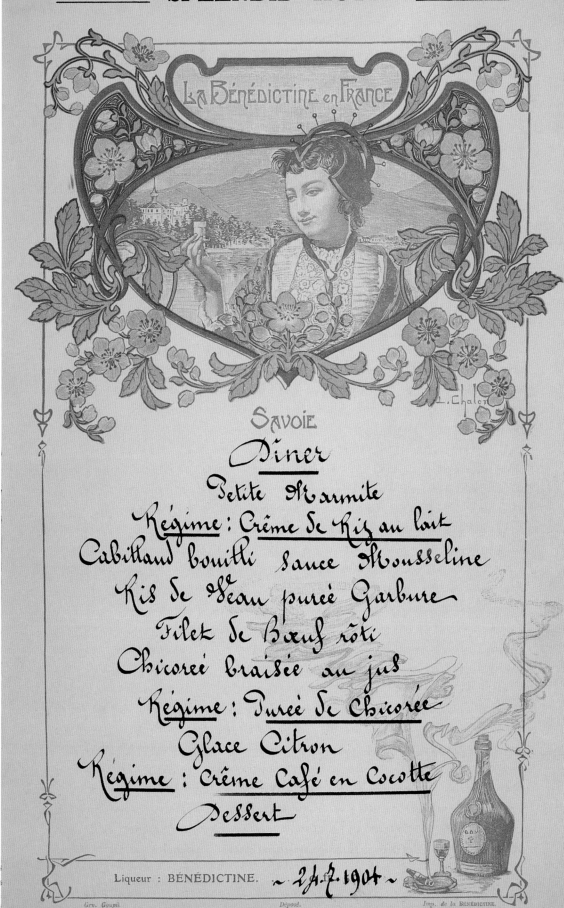

La Bénédictine en France

L. Chalon

Savoie

Dîner

Petite Marmite

Régime : Crème de Riz au lait

Cabillaud bouilli sauce Mousseline

Ris de Veau purée Garbure

Filet de Bœuf rôti

Chicorée braisée au jus

Régime : Purée de Chicorée

Glace Citron

Régime : Crème Café en Cocotte

Dessert

Liqueur : BÉNÉDICTINE.   ~ 24.7.1904 ~

Grav. Goupil.   Déposé.   Imp. de la BÉNÉDICTINE.

When the food finally came, it was cold and was often not what had been ordered. While Mespoulets explained what the un-ordered food was, telling in detail how it was made and what the ingredients were, and offered hollow excuses, he dribbled mayonnaise, soup, or mint sauce over the guests, upset the coffee and sometimes even managed to break a plate or two. I helped him as best I could.

At the end of a meal, Mespoulets usually presented the guest with somebody else's check, or it turned out that he had neglected to adjust the difference in price between what the guest had ordered and what he had got. By then the guest just held out his hand and cried, 'Never mind, never mind, give it to me, just give it to me! I'll pay just to get out of here! Give it to me, for God's sake!' Then the guest would pay and go. He would stop on the way out at the maître d'hôtel's desk and show Monsieur Victor and his captains the spots on his clothes, bang on the desk, and swear he would never come back again. Monsieur Victor and his captains would listen, make faces of compassion, say 'Oh!' and 'Ah!' and look darkly toward us across the room and promise that we would be fired the same day. But the next day we would still be there.

In the hours between meals, while the other waiters were occupied filling salt and pepper shakers, oil and vinegar bottles, and mustard pots, and counting the dirty linen and dusting the chairs, Mespoulets would walk to a table near the entrance, right next to Monsieur Victor's own desk, overlooking the lounge of the hotel. There he adjusted a special reading lamp which he had demanded and obtained from the management, spread a piece of billiard cloth over the table, and arranged on top of this a large blotter and a small one, an inkstand, and half a dozen penholders. Then he drew up a chair and seated himself. He had a large assortment of fine copper pen points of various sizes, and he sharpened them on a piece of sandpaper. He would select the pen point and the holder he wanted and begin to make circles in the air. Then, drawing toward him a gilt-edged place card or a crested one, on which menus were written, he would go to work. When he had finished, he arranged the cards all over the table to let them dry, and sat there at ease, only a step or two from Monsieur Victor's desk, in a sector invaded by other waiters only when they were to be called down or to be discharged, waiters who came with nervous hands and frightened eyes to face Monsieur Victor. Mespoulets's special talent guaranteed him his job and set him apart from the ordinary waiters. He was further distinguished by the fact that he was permitted to wear glasses, a privilege denied all other waiters no matter how nearsighted or astigmatic.

Ludwig Bemelmens, *Hotel Splendide*

AR

My father fought throughout the whole of World War I and would never talk of it. In his declining years I came across his letters home to his mother, and was fascinated to discover how obsessed they were with food. The art of eating on the battle front has always fascinated me, so I was particularly delighted with this Ernest Hemingway piece on eating pasta in the trenches.

The major asked me to have a drink with him and two other officers. We drank rum and it was very friendly. Outside it was getting dark. I asked what time the attack was to be and they said as soon as it was dark. I went back to the drivers. They were sitting in the dugout talking and when I came in they stopped. I gave them each a package of cigarettes, Macedonias, loosely packed cigarettes that spilled tobacco and needed to have the ends twisted before you smoked them. Manera lit his lighter and passed it around. The lighter was shaped like a Fiat radiator. I told them what I had heard.

'Why didn't we see the post when we came down?' Passini asked.

'It was just beyond where we turned off.'

'That road will be a dirty mess,' Manera said.

'They'll shell hell out of us.'

'Probably.'

'What about eating, lieutenant? We won't get a chance to eat after this thing starts.'

'I'll go and see now,' I said.

'You want us to stay here or can we look around?'

. . . It was dark outside and the long light from the searchlights on the front mounted on camions that you passed sometimes on the roads at night, close behind the lines, the camion stopped a little off the road, an officer directing the light and the crew scared. We crossed the brickyard, and stopped at the main dressing-station. 'There was a little shelter of green branches outside over the entrance and in the dark the night wind rustled the leaves dried by the sun. Inside there was a light. The major was at the telephone sitting on a box. One of the medical captains said the attack had been put forward an hour. He offered me a glass of cognac. I looked at the board tables, the instruments shining in the light, the basins and the stoppered bottles. Gordini stood behind me. The major got up from the telephone.

'It starts now,' he said. 'It has been put back again.'

I looked outside, it was dark and the Austrian searchlights were moving on the mountains behind us. It was quiet for a moment still, then from all the guns behind us the bombardment started.

'Savoia,' said the major.

'About the soup, major,' I said. He did not hear me. I repeated it.

'It hasn't come up.'

A big shell came in and burst outside in the brickyard. Another burst and in the noise you could hear the smaller noise of the brick and dirt raining down.

FOOD

'What is there to eat?'

'We have a little pasta asciutta,' the major said.

'I'll take what you can give me.'

The major spoke to an orderly who went out of sight in the back and came back with a metal basin of cold cooked macaroni. I handed it to Gordini.

'Have you any cheese?'

The major spoke grudgingly to the orderly who ducked back into the hole again and came out with a quarter of a white cheese.

'Thank you very much,' I said.

'You'd better not go out.'

Outside something was set down beside the entrance. One of the two men who had carried it looked in.

'Bring him in,' said the major. 'What's the matter with you? Do you want us to come outside and get him?'

The two stretcher-bearers picked up the man under the arms and by the legs and brought him in.

'Slit the tunic,' the major said.

He held a forceps with some gauze in the end. The two captains took off their coats. 'Get out of here,' the major said to the two stretcher-bearers.

'Come on,' I said to Gordini.

'You better wait until the shelling is over,' the major said over his shoulder.

'They want to eat,' I said.

'As you wish.'

Outside we ran across the brickyard. A shell burst short near the river bank. Then there was one that we did not hear coming until the sudden rush. We both went flat and with the flash and bump of the burst and the smell heard the singing off of the fragments and the rattle of falling brick. Gordini got up and ran for the dugout. I was after him, holding the cheese, its smooth surface covered with brick dust. Inside the dugout were the three drivers sitting against the wall, smoking.

'Here, you patriots,' I said.

'How are the cars?' Manera asked.

'All right.'

'Did they scare you, Tenente?'

'You're damned right,' I said.

I took out my knife, opened it, wiped off the blade and pared off the dirty outside surface of the cheese. Gavuzzi handed me the basin of macaroni.

'Start in to eat, Tenente.'

'No,' I said. 'Put it on the floor. We'll all eat.'

'There are no forks.'

'What the hell,' I said in English.

I cut the cheese into pieces and laid them on the macaroni.

'Sit down to it,' I said. They sat down and waited. I put thumb and fingers into the macaroni and lifted. A mass loosened.

'Lift it high, Tenente.'

I lifted it to arm's length and the strands cleared. I lowered it into the mouth, sucked and snapped in the ends, and chewed, then took a bite of cheese, chewed, and then a drink of the wine. It tasted of rusty metal. I handed the canteen back to Passini.

'It's rotten,' he said. 'It's been in there too long. I had it in the car.'

They were all eating, holding their chins close over the basin, tipping their heads back, sucking in the ends. I took another mouthful and some cheese and a rinse of wine. Something landed outside that shook the earth.

'Four hundred twenty or minnenwerfer,' Gavuzzi said.

'There aren't any four hundred twenties in the mountains,' I said.

'They have big Skoda guns. I've seen the holes.'

'Three hundred fives.'

We went on eating. There was a cough, a noise like a railway engine starting and then an explosion that shook the earth again.

'This isn't a deep dugout,' Passini said.

'That was a big trench mortar.'

'Yes, sir.'

I ate the end of my piece of cheese and took a swallow of wine. Through the other noise I heard a cough, then came the chuh-chuh-chuh-chuh – then there was a flash, as when a blast-furnace door is swung open, and a roar that started white and went red and on and on in a rushing wind. I tried to breathe but my breath would not come and I felt myself rush bodily out of myself and out and out and out and out and all the time bodily in the wind. I went out swiftly, all of myself, and I knew I was dead and that it had all been a mistake to think you just died. Then I floated, and instead of going on I felt myself slide back. I breathed and I was back. The ground was torn up and in front of my head there was a splintered beam of wood. In the jolt of my head I heard somebody crying. I thought somebody was screaming. I tried to move but I could not move. I heard the machine-guns and rifles firing across the river and all along the river. There was a great splashing and I saw the star-shells go up and burst and float whitely and rockets going up and heard the bombs, all this in a moment, and then I heard close to me some one saying 'Mama Mia! Oh, mama Mia!' I pulled and twisted and got my legs loose finally and turned around and touched him. It was Passini and when I touched him he screamed. His legs were toward me and I saw in the dark and the light that they were both smashed above the knee. One leg was gone and the other was held by tendons and part of the trouser and the stump twitched and jerked as though it were not connected. He bit his arm and moaned, 'Oh mama mia, mama Mia,' then, 'Dio te salve, Maria. Dio te salve, Maria. Oh Jesus shoot me Christ shoot me mama mia mama Mia oh purest lovely Mary shoot me. Stop it. Stop it. Stop it. Oh Jesus lovely Mary stop it. Oh oh oh oh,' then choking, 'Mama mama mia.' Then he was quiet, biting his arm, the stump of his leg twitching.

Ernest Hemingway, *A Farewell to Arms*

WARTIME BRINGS NOT ONLY FOOD BUT FUEL RATIONING AS WELL, and the need to look for economical methods of cooking. I can remember hay-box cooking. I was young in the years immediately following the war, and we still used to cook things in a hay box. To me it was magic. I could not understand how something with no visible means of heat could be so effective, and it taught me that food can be cooked in many unorthodox ways. I once cooked some brown trout straight from the freezer in a sink full of hot water – and there is always the dishwasher. I wonder if anyone now has or uses a hay box. Among the so-called green fraternity it should be as mandatory as it is indeed effective.

JAM-JAR AND HAY-BOX

1. JAM-JAR COOKING

ADVERSITY may find Jam-Jar cooking an unexpected boon: it is simple and economical for those who have been blitzed either structurally or financially, or both! All you need is a large saucepan, with 2 or 3 jam-jars, and the heat from a gas-ring, or its equivalent. A stew of meat, vegetables and a steamed pudding can all be cooked at once in this way, and you will easily be able to devise your meals so that you can make use of this simple form of cooking. Let me suggest, for example, this very simple meal: Beef Olives, Potatoes and Cabbage, and Steamed Pudding.

Everyone knows how to make Beef Olives, I expect, but here is a brief recipe. Cut some stewing steak into pieces $\frac{1}{4}$ in. thick, beat them out and cut them into small oblongs. On each of these put either a little forcemeat or a bit of sausage meat, roll each up, and tie with a bit of thread or cotton. Stew them in stock in a jam-jar just large enough to hold them, for about an hour-and-a-half.

Any ordinary recipe for steamed pudding can be used, and put this into another jam-jar (this time a straight-sided one, so that the pudding can be turned out), and put both these into your large saucepan after covering them with greased paper, well tied down. The beef and the pudding will take about the same time, but you must have room in your saucepan for two more jars, one for the steamed potatoes and one for the cabbage, and these should be put in towards the end of the cooking allowing the usual time for steaming vegetables, which is about a third as long as when they are boiled. These two jars must also of course be well tied down like the others. If you like the flavour, a little sliced apple may be cooked with the cabbage, the latter being finely shredded.

The saucepan must be closely covered, and the water (which should come about a third of the way up the jam-jars) must be kept well boiling all the time, but naturally only very little heat is required for this.

Note – If space demands it, vegetables such as potatoes, carrots, turnips, etc., can be cooked in the liquid round the jars.

2. HAY-BOX COOKING

THIS little book would not be complete without a short note about hay-box cooking, and here are a few words about the business of using one. The chief principle to observe in hay-box cooking is

FOOD

to *cook the dish first* on the stove or in the oven for a third of the usual time it would take if it were to be cooked entirely by the stove. It must then be transferred quickly to the hay-box, where it must cook for *twice the whole of the usual time given in the recipe*. This is the minimum length of time; there will be no harm in allowing longer, if you can. It will be obviously more convenient to use jars or casseroles without handles than saucepans. Earthenware and fireproof glass utensils have been found to be best, and care should be taken to see that they have really close-fitting lids. If you are using a casserole the lid of which does not fit as well as it might, you can improve matters by sticking the lid on with a paste of flour and water. If suet puddings are cooked in the hay-box, they should be encased in a basin with a patent airtight cover, and put into a pan of boiling water in the hay-box.

It is most important to see that there is *no loss of heat*, or as little as possible, when the jars are transferred to the hay-box from the stove. Meat or fish dishes can, of course, be cooked in the same dish in which they will be served, but in case food has to be transferred from one pan to another on its way to the hay-box, the second pan should be first heated so that the contents do not cool. Be careful to fill each utensil as full as possible, and wrap each up in a piece of blanket or flannel, and put the cushions and the lid down as quickly as possible. You may find it necessary to heat up certain food after it has cooked in the hay-box, in particular in the case of porridge for breakfast, which can be started off with 5 minutes' boiling on the stove last thing at night, and then left to cook all night in the hay-box.

The following brief table for reference has been issued by the Ministry of Food:

	STOVE	HAY-BOX
Vegetable Soups (Dried Peas, etc.)	45 minutes	4 hours
Potato or Root Vegetable Soups	15	1¼
Plain Meat Stew	30	3½
Meat Pudding	45	3
Oatmeal Porridge	5 minutes (boiling)	6 hours (or overnight)
Stewed Rice	2-3	2½
Stewed Dried Fruit	2-3	3½
Stewed Fresh Fruit (Apples etc.)	2-3	1½
Suet Pudding	30	2½

Ambrose Heath, *The Kitchen Front Library*

WEALTH

THE RICH STILL INDULGE IN SUCH EXTRAVAGANZAS TODAY, but they do it privately on their estates, where no one but *Hello* magazine can see them. I think this is a pity, but maybe I am an Edwardian *manqué*.

THE 'Gondola dinner party' given in 1905 at the Savoy Hotel by the Millionaire George A. Kessler in honour of the birthday of King Edward VII.

The most spectacular dinner party to be held at the Savoy took place on 30 June 1905 when George A. Kessler, the champagne millionaire at the head of Moët et Chandon in Europe and America, celebrated King Edward VII's birthday. The forecourt to the east entrance was enclosed and filled with water four feet deep and dyed blue, and was encircled by scenery depicting St Mark's, the Doge's Palace and its surroundings, lit by some 400 Venetian lamps. Into the water had been released salmon, trout and whitebait, whilst on it floated swans, ducks, and a white, silk-lined gondola adorned with 31,000 carnations, roses and 5,000 yards of smilax. In the air above fluttered a hundred white doves.

Waiters costumed as gondoliers served twelve courses to twice that number of diners seated on gold chairs, who included Mme Réjane from Paris and the 'Belle of New York', Edna May. The *maître chef*, Thoraud, surpassed himself in the visual appeal and gastronomic excellence of the fare provided. Three impressive lions carved out of ice bore trays of peaches and glacé fruits; and at the finish a baby elephant carried a foot-tall, candle-lit birthday cake over a bridge from *terra firma* to the gondola. It was followed by a bevy of Gaiety girls drinking the health of the monarch in Moët et Chandon champagne.

Throughout the banquet an orchestra stationed in a smaller gondola played music. Then came a *coup de théâtre*. The lights dimmed as a melon-like moon, suspended overhead, was turned on and Caruso emerged through brocade curtains at the raised end of the gondola to sing – for a *douceur* of £450.

Charles Neilson Gattey, *Foie Gras and Trumpets*

FOOD

WEDDING

CONTEMPORARY LITERATURE IS A GREAT RESOURCE for describing how things were at the time. Automatically the author describes it as it is, without any forced effort at re-creation. We can see this clearly in the following description of a wedding from *Cold Comfort Farm*.

MIDSUMMER day dawned with a thick grey haze in the air and a heavy dew on the meadows and trees.

Down among the little gardens of the still-sleeping cottages of Howling an idyllic procession might have been observed making its way from flower-bed to flower-bed, like ravaging bees. It was none other than the three members of Mrs Beetle's embryo jazz-band, shepherded by the patriarchal form of Agony Beetle himself.

They had been commissioned to pick the bunches of flowers which were to decorate the church and the refreshment-tables up at the farm. A lorry load of pink and white rose-peonies, from Covent Garden, had already been discharged at the gates of the farm; and, even now, Mrs Beetle and Flora were crossing and re-crossing the yard with their arms full of sleeping flowers.

Flora noted the heat-haze with joy. It would be a day of heat; brilliant, blue and radiant.

Adam Lambsbreath had been even earlier astir, making wreaths of wallflowers with which to garland the horns of Feckless, Pointless, Graceless and Aimless. It was not until he actually came to affix the decorations that he observed that none of the cows had any horns left, and had been forced to fasten the wreaths round their necks and tails instead. This done, he led them forth to their morning pasture, singing a smutty wedding song he had learnt from the marriage of George I.

As the day emerged from the heat-haze, and the sky grew blue and sunny, the farm buzzed with energy like a hive. Phoebe, Letty, Jane and Susan were whisking syllabubs in the dairy; Micah carried the pails of ice, in which stood the champagne, down into the darkest and coolest corner of the cellar. Caraway and Harkaway were fixing the awning across from the gate of the yard to the door of the kitchen. Ezra was putting his rows of beans under a net to protect them from damage during the festivities. Mark and Luke were arranging the long trestle tables in the kitchen, while Mrs Beetle and Flora unpacked the silver and linen sent down in crates from a London store. Reuben was filling with water the dozens of jars and vases in which the flowers were to be arranged. Mark Dolour's Nancy was superintending the boiling of two dozen eggs for everybody's breakfast. And upstairs on her bed lay Flora's new dress, a wonder of frilled and quilted, ruffled and tucked, pinked and shirred green batiste, and her plain hat of white straw.

At half-past eight everybody sat down to breakfast in the dairy, for the kitchen was being prepared for the reception, and could not be used for meals to-day.

'I'll just take up 'er breakfast,' said Mrs Beetle. 'She'll 'ave to 'ave it cold to-day. There's 'alf an 'am and a jar of pickled onions. I won't be a jiff.'

'Oh, I've just been in to see Aunt Ada,' said Flora, looking up from her breakfast. 'She doesn't want anything for breakfast except a Hell's Angel. Here give me an egg. I'll mix it for her.' She rose, and went over to the newly-stocked store cupboard.

Mrs Beetle stared, while Flora tossed an egg, two ounces of brandy, a teaspoonful of cream and some chips of ice in a jam-jar, and everybody else was very interested, too.

'There,' said Flora, giving Mrs Beetle the foaming jam-jar. 'You run along upstairs with that.'

So Mrs Beetle ran; but was heard to observe that it would take more than a mess like that to keep *her* stomach from rumbling before one o'clock. As for the other Starkadders, they were considerably intrigued by this dramatic change in Aunt Ada's diet.

'Is the old 'un gone off again?' asked Reuben, anxiously. 'Will she come down and upset everything after all, doo 'ee think, Cousin Flora?'

'Not on your sweet life,' said Flora. 'Everything will be all right. Remember, I told you there was going to be a surprise. Well, it's just beginning.'

And the Starkadders were satisfied.

Breakfast over, they all fell to work like demons, for the ceremony was at half-past twelve and there was much to be done.

Agony Beetle and the jazz-band arrived with their arms full of nasturtiums, sweet-william and cherry-pie; and were sent off on a second journey for more.

Reuben, obeying a request from Flora, pulled out from the cupboard in which it was usually kept the large carved chair in which Aunt Ada had sat on the night of the Counting; and Mark and Luke (who were so stupid that they could have been relied upon to lay a mine under the house without commenting upon it) were told to decorate it with wreaths of rose-peonies.

It was half-past ten. The awning was up, looking immediately festive, as awnings always do. And in the kitchen the two long trestle tables were decorated and ready.

Flora had arranged two kinds of food for the two kinds of guests she was expecting. For the Starkadders and such of the local horny peasantry as would attend there were syllabubs, ice-pudding, caviare sandwiches, crab patties, trifle and champagne. For the County there was cider, cold home-cured ham, cheese, home-made bread and salads made from local fruit. The table from which the County were to feed was rich with cottage flowers. The rosy efflorescence of the peonies floated above the table from which the peasantry would eat.

Wreaths of cottage flowers, like chains of little gems, hung from the rafters. Their reds, oranges, blues and pinks glowed against the soft, sooty-black of the ceiling and walls. The air smelled sweet of cherry-pie and fruit salad. Outside the sun flamed in glory; and inside the kitchen there were these sweet smells and cool, delicious-looking food.

Flora took a last look round, and was utterly satisfied.

Stella Gibbons, *Cold Comfort Farm*

WEEDS

WHEN PATIENCE GRAY'S FIRST BOOK *Plat de Jour* was published in the 1950s, everyone predicted that she would be up there with the greats. She then disappeared from the food scene and we did not discover why until the late 1980s, when her splendid second book

Honey from a Weed was published. We then learned that it was love that had taken her away. She had married a sculptor, and this book records the culinary side of their travels searching for the perfect stone to work with.

EDIBLE WEEDS

EDWARDIAN Englishmen laughed at French governesses for picking wild chervil, dandelions and sorrel in spring for salads, for cutting nettle-heads for soup. The governesses ridiculed the Englishmen for their addiction to stewed rhubarb. Each person, through instinct, habit or prejudice, likes to pursue his or her own way to health.

I became interested in weeds on Naxos: everyone in Apollona, but more especially women and children, wandered about in February and March, before the spring declared itself, in search of weeds, picked before their flower-heads appeared. They called them by the portmanteau name *radíkia*, meaning plants with beneficial roots and leaves, but also specifically dandelions.

Many of these weeds belonged to the daisy and dandelion family. The most beneficent in this group are dandelions, *Taraxacum officinale*, and wild chicory, *Cichorium intybus*, but it includes yellow and purple goat's beard, the latter being wild salsify; wild endive, *Cichorium endivia*; hawkweed, hawksbeard and hawkbit; a daisy, *Bellis silvestris*, larger than the common one; the ox-eye daisy or marguerite; various kinds of sowthistle and a plant called *Urospermum picroides* resembling them (*picroides* meaning bitter, *picra* in Greek). The more bitter the weeds, the better, as far as the Naxians were concerned. Milk thistles were also gathered, as was the blessed thistle. The field marigold, *Calendula arvensis*, was gathered whole when it first appeared, as was the corn marigold, *Chrysanthemum segetum*, and little plants of chamomile.

Their baskets also contained four umbelliferous plants – wild carrot, wild parsnip, wild fennel and wild chervil – and several crucifers – wild mustard, *Sinapis alba*, and allied white rocket, *Diplotaxis erucoides*, growing in cultivated fields, and also yellow rocket, *Eruca sativa*, growing in the wild. In the collection several mints appeared, particularly pennyroyal, *Menta pulegium*, as well as wild thymes and mountain savory, *Satureja montana*.

Most of these plants were gathered by cutting a section of the root, thus preserving the plant entire. Washed at the fountain, they were boiled and served with oil and lemon juice, the lemons picked from neighbouring groves. During the Lenten fast they were eaten in quantity like vegetable *spaghettini*, but without the olive oil.

Filling my water jar at the spring, I had a daily opportunity to examine these weeds and ask advice, and began to gather them myself, but at first always offering

them for inspection. At the time I was reading the landscape and its flora with as much attention as one gives to an absorbing book.

Mediterranean people value 'bitterness' in weeds, as once did all European peoples. On Naxos, on a restricted winter diet, everyone suffered from appalling pains in the liver region, deriving not only from monotonous diet but also from impure water and the terrible north wind. The Sculptor and I soon discovered the benefits conferred by weeds.

Chi vo far 'na bona zena
i magn'un erb' d'tut la mena

Who wants to eat a good supper
should eat a weed of every kind

This old Carrarese saying puts the matter in a nutshell, diversity being as important in weeds as it is in human beings.

Patience Gray, *Honey from a Weed*

Weighty

DIETING IS A THING OF THE CENTURY, and people have become more and more obsessed about weight. My mother was not fat, and rode and gardened for exercise, but she was a great one for diets. I remember one which required she eat oranges and peanuts, and she would solemnly sit down and devour an orange and a saucerful of peanuts before each meal, quite missing the point that they were all she was supposed to eat. When this was pointed out to her she replied indignantly: 'Don't be silly, darling, no one would expect that.' She was quite delighted, therefore, when she discovered Tessie O'Shea's *Slimming Book*, full of delicious recipes with very little sign of banting. I was glad to be reunited with this book after many years.

MEDICAL tests have proved that eating over-sugared, starchy foods is bad for you! So, begin the first month of your diet by eating *nothing* that has flour in it. All you have to do is to say to yourself . . . 'Does this have any flour in it?' If it does – AVOID IT LIKE THE PLAGUE – just say to yourself, 'I shall be very ill if I eat anything with flour in it.' It's a kind of self-hypnosis. Instead, if you feel you *must* have a sandwich or you'll pass out or something, then get yourself a lettuce leaf, spread it with mayonnaise and then pile on any kind of cold meats you want, or cheese, or both. Roll them all inside the lettuce leaf and eat it like you would a sandwich. It tastes just as good, and it helps you enormously to stay off the bread. As I have just said (you may find that I repeat myself a few times . . . I have done this on purpose! I hope you will understand that I *must* get it home to you, what I'm

The Saturday Evening

POST

January 3, 1953 · 15¢

NEW ZEALAND TO BOSTON
IN A 45-FOOT SAILBOAT:

We Made the Impossible Voyage

By LYDIA DAVIS

HOW TO
DIET

Norman
Rockwell

trying to say!) for the first month you must not eat *anything* that has flour in it . . . that means bread, cakes, biscuits, and all those slimming crispbreads and slimming breads and slimming what-have-you's! *But*, you can eat cream, mayonnaise, cheese (all kinds), all meats and all fish. And you can have olive oil, butter, margarine, salt, pepper, all kinds of herbs . . . (doesn't this sound good!). How about it fellas . . . you can have whisky, gin, vodka, dry wine . . . in moderation, of course. Another thing is, if you feel hungry at the beginning of the diet . . . just take another cup of coffee or tea or chew some sugarless gum . . . you can have as much liquid as you want! Although some nuts are low in carbohydrates I advise you to wait until you are sometimes treating yourself to the 'Advanced Diet' dishes before eating them – except when they are used as a dressing with vegetables. Incidentally, a man can always take 10 carbs a day more than a woman . . . if he's six feet tall! *Not* if he's short and stubby. My Dad was a short and stubby man . . . so I know!

ROLLED OLIVE-ANCHOVY IN VEAL

(To serve cold with salad or as a hot vegetable)

Ingredients

3 lb piece of boned breast of veal	1 teaspoon lemon juice
1 teaspoon caraway seeds	sprinkle of garlic salt
22 stuffed olives	sprinkle of pepper
6 slices anchovy	1 tablespoon flour

Method

Wash and pat dry the flat breast of veal. Chop olives in half and place them all over the piece of veal. Then sprinkle the caraway seeds over the olives. Sprinkle lemon juice, and place the anchovies over all. Roll the veal like a sausage, and sew up the ends to keep it from opening. (I like sewing with a darning needle and white cotton.)

Mix garlic salt, flour and pepper together and rub it on to the outside of the meat. I like to rub some bacon fat on to it also, but that's optional.

Place the meat in a roasting bag, make a few holes in it to let the steam out . . . put it into a roasting tin in a hot oven (Mark 7, 425°F.) for 10 minutes, then turn down to low heat (approximately Mark 4, 355°F.) for 2 hours.

Note 1: Remove from oven and place to one side to cool down. Then take the meat out of the bag and place it on a large sheet of aluminium foil . . . turn the sides of the foil up, 'cos I want you to pour all the juices from the bag all over the meat, and not lose any of them. It creates a lovely jelly all around the meat when cold. Close the foil around the meat and place in the fridge. When ready to serve, slice the meat with the set jelly around it and serve with an oil and vinegar dressing on a green salad. It is also good with hot green beans or cauliflower.

It is a lovely meal, with practically NO carbohydrates per serving!

Note 2: Any fat on top of the jelly should be scraped away before cutting.

Tessie O'Shea, *Tessie O'Shea's Slimming Book*

WEST INDIES

FROM THE *VIRAGO BOOK OF WICKED VERSE* comes this humdinger of a wicked poem in the Caribbean manner. I have spent a lot of time in the West Indies, and this verse brings a deal of euphoric recall.

GRANNY IN DE MARKET PLACE

YUH fish fresh?

Woman, why yuh holdin' meh fish up tuh yuh nose?
De fish fresh. Ah say it fresh. Ah ehn go say it any mo'

Hmmm, well if dis fish fresh den is I who dead an' gone
De ting smell like it take a bath in a lavatory in town
It here so long it happy. Look how de mout' laughin' at we
De eye turn up to heaven like it want tuh know 'e fate
Dey say it does take a good week before dey reach dat state

Yuh mango ripe?

Gran'ma, stop feelin' and squeezin' up meh fruit!
Yuh ehn playin' in no ban'. Meh mango eh no concertina

Ah tell yuh dis mango hard just like yuh face
One bite an' ah sure tuh break both ah meh plate
If yuh cahn tell de difference between green an' rosy red
dohn clim' jus' wait until dey fall down from de tree
Yuh go know dey ripe when de lizard an dem start tuh feed
but dohn bring yuh force-ripe fruit tuh try an' sell here
it ehn burglars is crooks like yuh poor people have to fear

De yam good?

Old lady, get yuh nails outta meh yam!
Ah mad tuh make yuh buy it now yuh damage it so bad

Dis yam look like de one dat did come off ah de ark
She brother in de Botanical Gardens up dey by Queens Park
Tourists with dey camera comin' from all over de worl'
takin' pictures dey never hear any yam could be dat ole
Ah have a crutch an' a rocking-chair someone give meh fuh free

FOOD

If ah did now ah would ah bring dem an' leave dem here fuh she

De bush clean?

Well. I never hear more! Old woman, is watch yuh watching meh
young young dasheen leaf wit' de dew still shinin' on dem!

It seem tuh me like dey does like tuh lie out in de sun
jus' tuh make sure dat dey get dey edges nice an' brown
an' maybe is weight dey liftin' tuh made dem look so tough
Dey wan' build up dey strength fuh when tings start gettin' rough
Is callaloo ah makin' but ah 'fraid things get too hot
Yuh bush go want tuh fight an' meh crab go jump outta de pot

How much a poun' yuh fig?

Ah have a big sign tellin' yuh how much it cos'
Yuh either blin' yuh dotish or yuh jus' cahn read at all

Well, ah wearin' meh glasses so ah readin' yuh big big sign
but tuh tell yuh de trut' ah jus' cahn believe meh eye
Ah lookin' ah seein' but no man could be so blased bol'
Yuh mus' tink dis is Fort Knox yuh sellin' fig as if is gol'
Dey should put all ah all yuh somewhere nice an' safe
If dey close Sing-Sing prison dat go be the bestest place

De orange sweet?

Ma, it eh hah orange in dis market as sweet as ah does sell
It like de sun, it taste like sugar an' it juicy as well

Yuh know, boy, what yuh sayin' have a sorta ring
De las' time ah buy yuh tell meh exactly de same ting
When ah suck ah fin' all dem sour as hell
De dentures drop out an' meh two gums start tuh swell
Meh mout' so sore ah cahn even eat ah meal
Yuh sure it ehn lime all yuh wrappin' in orange peel?

De coconut hah water?

Amryl Johnson

XMAS

MY MOTHER WAS AUSTRALIAN, so I knew the bizarreness of eating turkey and Christmas pudding in temperatures of 120 degrees in the shade. Our colonial and imperial heritage has brought strange customs to the far-flung corners of the world, none perhaps so curious as Britons a world away from home sitting down to celebrate the birth of a Jewish prophet who they undoubtedly would not have asked to join them, with a pagan fruit pudding and an American fowl.

AN EMPIRE CHRISTMAS PUDDING

(With accompanying sauces, according to recipes supplied by the King's Chef. Mr. Cedard. with Their Majesties' gracious consent.)

1 lb. of Currants – Australia.

1 lb. of Sultanas – Australia or South Africa.

1 lb. of stoned Raisins – Australia or South Africa.

5 ozs. of Minced Apple – United Kingdom or Canada.

1 lb. of Breadcrumbs – United Kingdom.

1 lb. of Beef Suet – United Kingdom.

6½ ozs. of cut Candied Peel – South Africa.

8 ozs. of Flour – United Kingdom.

8 ozs. of Demerara Sugar – British West Indies or British (

5 eggs – United Kingdom or Irish Free State.

½ oz. Ground Cinnamon – India or Ceylon.

½ oz. Ground Cloves – Zanzibar.

¼ oz. Ground Nutmegs – British West Indies.

¼ teaspoonful Pudding Spice – India or British West Indies.

* ¼ gill Brandy – Australia, South Africa, Cyprus or Palestine.

* ½ gill Rum – Jamaica or British Guiana.

* 1 pint Old Beer – England, Wales, Scotland or Ireland.

* These ingredients may be regarded as optional provided some other liquid such as milk is substituted – in which case, however, the pudding will lose its keeping qualities.

Rose Henniker Heaton, *The Perfect Christmas*

FOOD

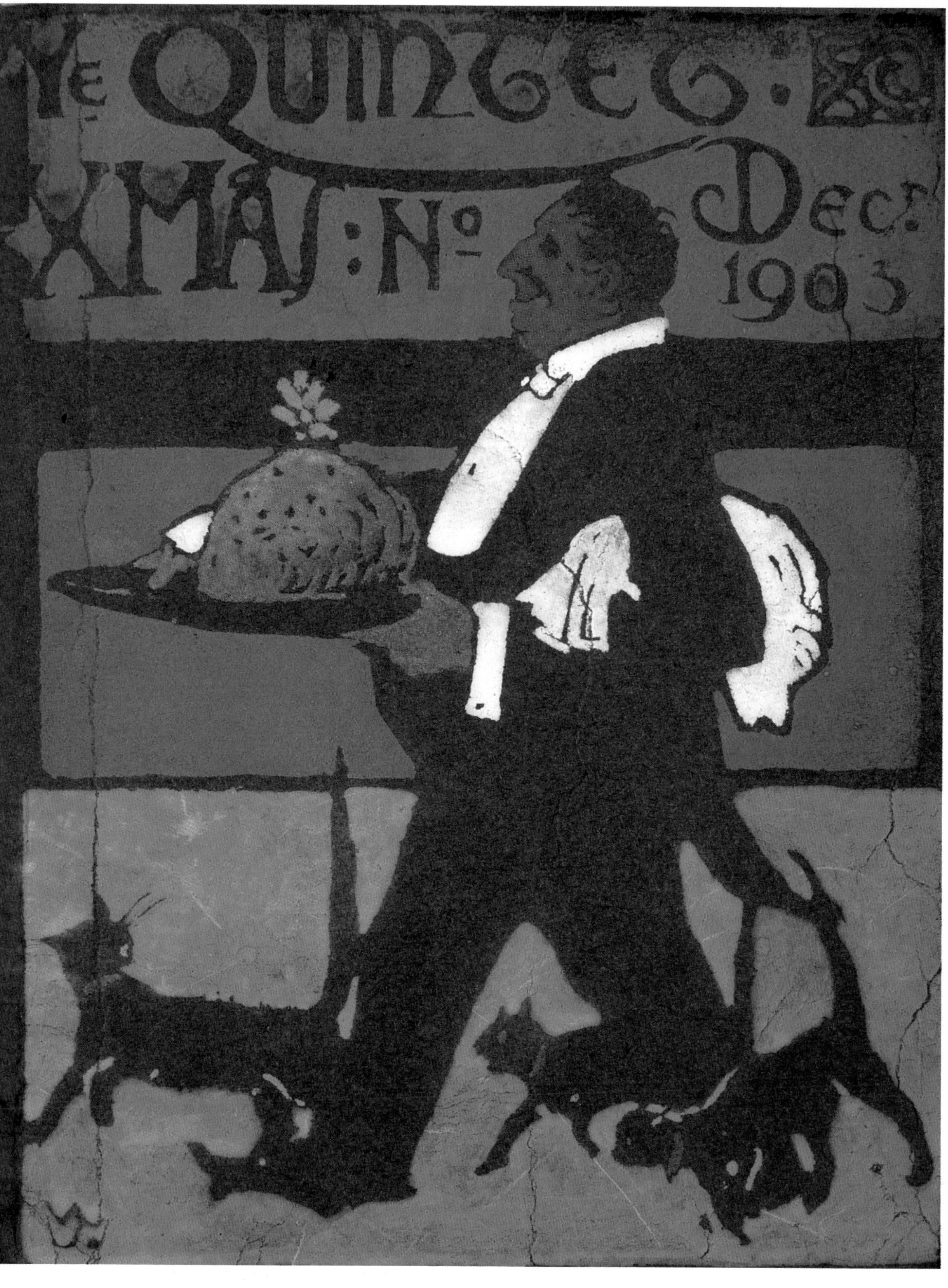
Ye QUINTET
XMAS: No
Decr
1903

XQUISITE

See my comment above on Hunger, and compare what follows with the extract from Massingberd and Watkins' history of the Ritz.

LONDON'S FASHIONABLE HAUNTS

Like Arnold Bennett I hold that hotels and restaurants are superb vantage-points for watching the cavalcade of life. Many people have thought me a trifle odd on account of my habit of lunching or dining alone in some fashionable haunt. I do not think they ever understood my simple explanation – that I liked doing it. Yet that is the truth. I derive great pleasure from an hour or so at a table in a busy restaurant. Not so much from what I eat, but from what I see and hear. Neither am I alone in the enjoyment of this sport. I can also point to Lord Wimborne with his special table at the Ritz, and the Duke of Marlborough, who both sit solitary where others must apparently congregate in numbers.

Because London is indubitably a most shining capital, despite the efforts of its authorities to make it otherwise, I should like to take you on a little tour of the West End, for London can boast of the prettiest women, the smartest men, the best food, and an agreeable atmosphere of cheerfulness. Fashionable London can be a far better tonic than the bluest sky and most golden sun.

It is such a quickly moving, ever-varied panorama, this London, that we must use modern methods to capture its allure. Let us then take a mental talkie camera with us, and let me give you the running commentary? Very well, let's go.

First the Savoy Grill. Perhaps the most cosmopolitan of all the fashionable haunts of London. Sometimes known as a 'certain grill-room in the Strand.' We will go just before luncheon-time. The camera is on a small table in the ante-room, shooting the people taking cocktails. It's a modern-looking room, for the Savoy wears very twentieth-century clothes nowadays.

Scores of people are coming in. Ah! Here's a famous figure. Sir Charles Higham, the greatest advertising man. He is walking with that peculiar staccato gait of his, skinning off his tightly fitting kid gloves. Several smartly dressed ladies, also taking cocktails, greet him.

And here is the slim, good-looking Lord Inverclyde. The dark, striking man with the slight limp is Sir Philip Sassoon.

Behind them comes a tall figure striding with a swing familiar to stage and film fans. He puts up a hand to stroke his lantern jaw. It's Jack Hulbert.

One or two familiar figures are missing. Miss Tallulah Bankhead used to be a regular visitor. She is in Hollywood now. Then we shall not see again the charming sight of Sir Alfred Yarrow, wearing his habitual flowing wide tie and braided jacket, and leading on his arm Lady Yarrow. They were a gallant pair. The veteran shipbuilder died a little while ago.

Here comes another group. Theatre-folk, smartly dressed girls. Following them is their frequent critic, Hannen Swaffer, looking a little like a cross between a Montparnasse artist and a Bloomsbury undertaker. Mr. Swaffer has a long nose, and long noses are said to denote a keen critical faculty. My Fleet Street friends also tell me that in Swaffer's case it denotes one of the best 'noses for news' in the game. The miniature Milky Way of stars sweeps in leaving behind it a trail of sweet perfume. And 'Swaff,' like Nemesis, stalks in the rear.

Now we will take our microphone and lens into the Grill Room itself. As the film people say, the camera 'pans' round the room, picking out celebrities and coming to rest on them for a second. Sir Malcolm Campbell is over there. Now we are looking at a man equally famous in a totally different sphere – Chaliapine, the great Russian opera singer. He is eating spaghetti, his favourite dish.

Pardon me for a moment, he is beckoning me over to his table. With him is an attractive dark girl. Chaliapine introduces me: *'Ma fille.* Meet her while she is still Mademoiselle Chaliapine. Next week she is getting married in Paris.' I offer my congratulations, and say something banal to the great singer about grandfatherhood.

Peter, my favourite waiter, is now telling me that my lunch is served. As I sit I will spot the celebrities for you. There is Lady Dashwood lunching with Lady Bowden. And there is Lady Oxford, looking more like Queen Elizabeth than ever, being entertained by her son Anthony, generally known as Puffin.

I wonder whether there will be any excitement to-day. Twice I have been present in the Savoy Grill when 'incidents' occurred which might have ruffled the mien of Monsieur Manetta.

The first is now history. Like the Ball on the eve of Waterloo, all was gaiety, when suddenly there came a sound. A slap of hand against face. We all stared a second in the temporary hush. A Famous Actress had slapped the face of a Famous Dramatic Critic. She stalked out and he remained quite coolly where he was. We proceeded with our lunches.

The second incident was also pugilistic, though the parties were more in keeping. Two champion boxers, with that retinue of camp followers without which no champion is complete, were at luncheon to discuss the details of their coming boxing match. Disagreement arose. High words followed. Then one of the fighters, remembering what he was, if not where he was, went over to his opponent and tried to start the ring battle there and then. But the retinues intervened and peace was restored. The aforementioned critic, also present, was heard to observe that it was a change for him to be a spectator at such an affair!

Vicomte de Mauduit, *Private Views*

 ARROW

OLD WIVES' LORE AND HERBALISM was in this century set down for all to study, and Mrs Grieve to my mind still does it best. It has now, of course, become a huge industry, another example of people's reluctance to do things for themselves.

YARROW

Achillea millefolium (Linn.)
N.O. Compositae

Synonyms. Milfoil. Old Man's Pepper. Soldier's Woundwort. Knight's Milfoil. Herbe Militaris. Thousand Weed. Nose Bleed. Carpenter's Weed. Bloodwort. Staunchweed. Sanguinary. Devil's Nettle. Devil's Plaything. Bad Man's Plaything. Yarroway.

(*Saxon*) Gearwe

(*Dutch*) Yerw

(*Swedish*) Field Hop

Part Used. Whole herb

Habitat. Yarrow grows everywhere, in the grass, in meadows, pastures, and by the roadside. As it creeps greatly by its roots and multiplies by seeds it becomes a troublesome weed in gardens, into which it is seldom admitted in this country, though it is cultivated in the gardens of Madeira

The name *Yarrow* is a corruption of the Anglo-Saxon name for the plant – *gearwe*; the Dutch, *yerw*.

¶*Description.* The stem is angular and rough, the leaves alternate, 3 to 4 inches long and 1 inch broad, clasping the stem at the base, bipinnatifid, the segments very finely cut, giving the leaves a feathery appearance.

It flowers from June to September, the flowers, white or pale lilac, being like minute daisies, in flattened, terminal, loose heads, or cymes. The whole plant is more or less hairy, with white, silky appressed hairs.

Yarrow was formerly much esteemed as a vulnerary, and its old names of Soldier's Wound Wort and Knight's Milfoil testify to this. The Highlanders still make an ointment from it, which they apply to wounds, and Milfoil tea is held in much repute in the Orkneys for dispelling melancholy. Gerard tells us it is the same plant with which Achilles stanched the bleeding wounds of his soldiers, hence the name of the genus, *Achillea*. Others say that it was discovered by a certain Achilles, Chiron's disciple. It was called by the Ancients, the *Herba Militaris*, the military herb.

Its specific name, *millefolium*, is derived from the many segments of its foliage, hence also its popular name, Milfoil and Thousand Weed. Another popular name for it is Nosebleed, from its property of stanching bleeding of the nose, though another reason given for this name is that the leaf, being rolled up and applied to the nostrils, causes a bleeding from the nose, more or less copious, which will thus afford relief to headache. Parkinson tells us that 'if it be put into the nose, assuredly it will stay the bleeding of it' – so it seems to act either way.

It was one of the herbs dedicated to the Evil One, in earlier days, being sometimes known as Devil's Nettle, Devil's Plaything, Bad Man's Plaything, and was used for divination in spells.

Yarrow, in the eastern counties, is termed *Yarroway*, and there is a curious mode of divination with its serrated leaf, with which the inside of the nose is tickled while the following lines are spoken. If the operation causes the nose to bleed, it is a certain omen of success:

> 'Yarroway, Yarroway, bear a white blow,
> If my love love me, my nose will bleed now.'

An ounce of Yarrow sewed up in flannel and placed under the pillow before going to bed, having repeated the following words, brought a vision of the future husband or wife:

'Thou pretty herb of Venus' tree,

Thy true name it is Yarrow;

Now who my bosom friend must be,

Pray tell thou me to-morrow.'

(Halliwell's *Popular Rhymes*, etc.)

It has been employed as snuff, and is also called Old Man's Pepper, on account of the pungency of its foliage. Both flowers and leaves have a bitterish, astringent, pungent taste.

In the seventeenth century it was an ingredient of salads.

¶*Parts Used*. The whole plant, stems, leaves and flowers, collected in the wild state, in August, when in flower.

¶*Constituents*. A dark green, volatile oil, a peculiar principle, *achillein*, and achilleic acid, which is said to be identical with aconitic acid, also resin, tannin, gum and earthy ash, consisting of nitrates, phosphates and chlorides of potash and lime.

¶*Medicinal Action and Uses*. Diaphoretic, astringent, tonic, stimulant and mild aromatic.

Yarrow Tea is a good remedy for severe colds, being most useful in the commencement of fevers, and in cases of obstructed perspiration. The infusion is made with 1 oz. of dried herb to 1 pint of boiling water, drunk warm, in wineglassful doses. It may be sweetened with sugar, honey or treacle, adding a little Cayenne Pepper, and to each dose, a teaspoonful of Composition Essence. It opens the pores freely and purifies the blood, and is recommended in the early stages of children's colds, and in measles and other eruptive diseases.

A decoction of the whole plant is employed for bleeding piles, and is good for kidney disorders. It has the reputation also of being a preventative of baldness, if the head be washed with it.

¶*Preparations*. Fluid extract, ½ to 1 drachm. An ointment made by the Highlanders of Scotland of the fresh herb is good for piles, and is also considered good against the scab in sheep.

An essential oil has been extracted from the flowers, but is not now used.

Linnaeus recommended the bruised herb, fresh, as an excellent vulnerary and styptic. It is employed in Norway for the cure of rheumatism, and the fresh leaves chewed are said to cure toothache.

In Sweden it is called 'Field Hop' and has been used in the manufacture of beer. Linnaeus considered beer thus brewed more intoxicating than when hops were used.

It is said to have a similar use in Africa.

Culpepper spoke of Yarrow as a profitable herb in cramps, and Parkinson recommends a decoction to be drunk warm for ague.

The medicinal values of the Yarrow and the Sneezewort (*A. millefolium* and *A. ptarmica*), once famous in physic, were discarded officially in 1781.

Woolly Yellow Yarrow (*A. tomentosa*) is very rare, and a doubtful native; its leaves are divided and woolly, the flowers bright yellow.

Mrs M. Grieve, *A Modern Herbal*

FOOD

YOUTH

Roald Dahl with his quirky humour seems to me always to have had the heart of a child. He loved food, and many of his children's books focused on it, *Charlie and the Chocolate Factory* and *James and the Giant Peach* to name but two. Here is an example in his 'Recipe for Making Wonka-Vite'.

RECIPE FOR MAKING WONKA-VITE

Take a block of finest chocolate weighing one ton (or twenty sackfuls of broken chocolate, whichever is the easier). Place chocolate in very large cauldron and melt over red-hot furnace. When melted, lower the heat slightly so as not to burn the chocolate, but keep it boiling. Now add the following, in precisely the order given, stirring well all the time and allowing each item to dissolve before adding the next:

THE HOOF OF A MANTICORE

THE TRUNK (AND THE SUITCASE) OF AN ELEPHANT

THE YOLKS OF THREE EGGS FROM A WHIFFLE-BIRD

A WART FROM A WART-HOG

THE HORN OF A COW (IT MUST BE A LOUD HORN)

THE FRONT TAIL OF A COCKATRICE

SIX OUNCES OF SPRUNGE FROM A YOUNG SLIMESCRAPER

TWO HAIRS (AND ONE RABBIT) FROM THE HEAD OF A HIPPOCAMPUS

THE BEAK OF A RED-BREASTED WILBATROSS

A CORN FROM THE TOE OF A UNICORN

THE FOUR TENTACLES OF A QUADROPUS

THE HIP (AND THE PO AND THE POT) OF A HIPPOPOTAMUS

THE SNOUT OF A PROGHOPPER

A MOLE FROM A MOLE

THE HIDE (AND THE SEEK) OF A SPOTTED WHANGDOODLE

THE WHITES OF TWELVE EGGS FROM A TREE-SQUEAK

THE THREE FEET OF A SNOZZWANGER (IF YOU CAN'T GET THREE FEET, ONE YARD WILL DO)

THE SQUARE-ROOT OF A SOUTH AMERICAN ABACUS

THE FANGS OF A VIPER (IT MUST BE A VINDSCREEN VIPER)

THE CHEST (AND THE DRAWERS) OF A WILD GROUT

When all the above are thoroughly dissolved, boil for a further twenty-seven days but do not stir. At the end of this time, all liquid will have evaporated and there will be left in the bottom of the cauldron only a hard brown lump about the size of a football. Break this open with a hammer and in the very centre of it you will find a small round pill. This pill is WONKA-VITE.

Roald Dahl, *Charlie and the Great Glass Elevator*

CHOC-FULL OF GOODNESS !

ZEALOT

THE NEW WAVE COOKERY REVOLUTION that swept America in the 1980s was spearheaded by five chefs. In the forefront of these was Alice Waters, who also set up farmers to grow her vegetables and inspired the growth of Farmers' Markets. She is a woman I much admire, and this book would not be complete without some reference to her work.

WHEN I cook, I usually stand at my kitchen table. I may pull a bunch of thyme from my pocket and lay it on the table; then I wander about the kitchen gathering up all the wonderfully fresh ingredients I can find. I look at each foodstuff carefully, examining it with a critical eye and concentrating in such a way that I begin to make associations. While this method may appear chaotic to others, I do think best while holding a tomato or a leg of lamb. Sometimes I wander through the garden looking for something appealing, absorbing the bouquet of the earth and the scent of the fresh herbs. Sometimes I butterfly my way through cookbooks, quickly flipping the pages and absorbing a myriad of ideas about a particular food or concept.

You can use these recipes and adapt them to your regional ingredients just as I adapt the recipes of other regions and cooks to the ingredients here in California. I enjoyed a marvelous meal at Frédy Girardet's restaurant just outside Lausanne, Switzerland; the chef had achieved a certain perfection and elegance in his use of regional foodstuffs; I admired and appreciated the meal as a work of art. Back in Berkeley I wanted to re-create a part of it. The first course was fresh foie gras — unobtainable here. So I concentrated on the technique they had used to prepare it: sautéing the goose liver, deglazing the pan with sherry vinegar, adding shallots, parsley, and walnut oil, and pouring the sauce over the liver like a vinaigrette. We prepared the dish at Chez Panisse with duck livers, which are readily available to us at an affordable cost. They do not taste the same as foie gras; but we do not pretend that they do. The dish tastes like duck livers prepared in an interesting way, and that in itself is wonderful. Careful substitutions and adaptations can considerably expand the potential applications of any recipe.

Cooking, preparing food, involves far more than just creating a meal for family or friends: it has to do with keeping yourself intact. Because most people cook and eat three meals a day, this process becomes an integral part of one's daily routine. These eating and cooking habits can either be sensually nourishing, even on an unconscious level, or they can rapidly become redundant. There is a marvelous scene in a film by Les Blank of the morning-coffee ritual of an old Southern lady. We watch her reach into her store of coffee beans for a handful, which she puts in a pan on the stove to roast. When she is satisfied with the degree and depth of roast, she shakes the fragrant beans into a hand-cranked coffee grinder and proceeds to pulverise them into a cloth napkin filter. Then she boils the water and pours it through the coffee-filled filter to produce a cup of coffee for herself – one you know must be wonderful. She sits and drinks her coffee in a totally intimate and relaxed manner, and eventually rises to wash out the napkin and hang it out to dry. This ritual is important because she is making a celebration out of the act of making coffee for herself. For others, this coffee habit can be as alienating as a Styrofoam cup of coffee from a vending machine.

So many people believe that by using a myriad of machines and equipment in their cooking, they're simplifying it and making the whole process easier. Somehow, we have been indoctrinated into believing that by making food preparation easier and less time-consuming, we're gaining valuable free time. No mention is ever made of what we lose by this whittling away at our direct contact with our food or what better thing we might do with the time thus gained. I strongly believe that much of what has gone wrong with American food has been the result of mechanization and alienation that comes with it. The quality of the home food prepared in France has deteriorated, too. It is no longer a simple matter to find hand-kneaded and -shaped bread and homemade aioli. The harsh sounds of the machine have replaced the rhythmic chop of the knife.

I simply don't believe that all the 'gourmet' equipment and utensils are vital. To begin with, the terms 'gourmet' or 'gourmet cooking' have all the wrong associations for me: they somehow seem to imply that one is more interested in the gleaming copper pans and the flashy chrome and plastic of the food processors than in what one is cooking, and certainly more impressed with them than with the food itself. It is far easier to cook with good sharp knives, but you *can* cook without them. Perversely, some of the very best times to cook are those occasions when you are faced with virtually nothing in terms of equipment – you must make do, improvise, and focus primarily on the food itself. So you may gather rosemary branches from the yard and use them to skewer the meat before you put it on the charcoal grill. If you do, you will have learned something fundamental about food, unrestricted and unhampered by equipment. You need to learn to cook first, and then you will learn what equipment is genuinely important to you.

When you use a machine, you never really touch the food, a fact that deprives you of much of the sensual pleasure and sensory experience so important in developing good cooking habits. When learning to make pesto, you *need* to rub the olive oil into the pounded garlic and the basil with your pestle in hand. You *need* to be able to stick your finger into the mixture to feel the transformation of the ingredients. Otherwise the information just does not come through all your senses. The senses of smell, touch, and hearing, in addition to sight and taste, must work together to enable you to judge what is happening to the ingredients. Machines have a place, but only after you have reached a point in your cooking at which you *know* what you are sacrificing in sensory stimulation for the questionable exchange of a slight saving in time and effort.

Every time we make pesto at the restaurant, it's different. If it isn't garlic with a hotter taste or the basil with a bitterness from too much sun, it's the cook pounding it differently – or it may be that the customer who loved it last time isn't in the mood this time. Maybe every six months the waiters are in the right mood, the cooks cook it right, the customers feel like eating that particular dinner, and I feel satisfied with the results; when that happens, I know that it has been worth the effort.

Alice Waters, *Chez Panisse*

'Oh, no! I think Clarissa's got Mad Human Disease.'

ACKNOWLEDGEMENTS

ILLUSTRATIONS

1 Jean Cazals/Quails eggs, *Sunday Independent* Review, 1998; 2 Tessa Traeger/Blue cabbage leaf; 3 Jean Cazals/rhubarb from *Sunday Independent* Review, 1999; 9 Peter Lippmann (Agence Top); 10 Tessa Traeger/Pasta collage of Tuscany; 12 from *A Book of Mediterranean Food* (John Lehmann 1951); 17 from Len Deighton, *Action Cookbook* (Jonathan Cape, first published 1965, Trinity Travel); 20 Norman Rockwell, The Four Freedoms: Freedom From Want, *Saturday Evening Post*, 1943 (Advertising Archives); 24 Manfred Seelow (Agence Top); 27 Kevin Summers/Roasted asparagus with parmesan, *Observer* Life, Nigel Slater's Recipe pages; 32 Jean Cazals/roast beef recipe from Simon Hopkinson, *Independent* magazine, 1996; 37 *Saturday Evening Post*, November 1954 (Advertising Archives); 39 Ferdinando Scianna (Magnum); 41 Willy Ronis (Rapho); 46 Henri Cartier-Bresson (Magnum); 49 Kevin Summers/Cabbage in colander, *Observer* Life, Nigel Slater's Recipe pages; 53 Anthony Blake/The Haeberlin family having lunch, *Great Chefs of France* by Quentin Crewe and Anthony Blake; 57 Margaret Tempest/from *Hare Joins the Home Guard* by Alison Uttley; 60-63 from Simone Beck, Louisette Bertholle and Julia Child, *Mastering the Art of French Cooking* (Alfred A. Knopf 1961); 65 Bert Hardy (Hulton Getty); 68 Canapés d'ecrévisses à la Cardinal, from A. H. Sands, *Ideal Cookery Book* (Mary Evans Picture Library); 71 front cover of *Fine Old Dixie Recipes* (Culinary Arts Press); 74 'Fried Egg' by Claes Oldenburg, 1961/Private Collection (James Goodham Gallery, New York /Bridgeman Art Library); 76 from *Manual of Military Cooking & Dietary* (HMSO 1918) showing methods of collecting fats from washing-up water, cook-houses etc.; 77 hashbrownies from *Alice B. Toklas Cookbook* (Michael Joseph 1954); 79 Mayer/Le Scanff (Garden Picture Library); 87 'Leaning fork with meatball & spaghetti' by Claes Oldenburg, 1994 (AKG Photo); 88 Sundried tomatoes, photographed by Gerrit Buntrock (Anthony Blake Photo Library); 90 from Elizabeth Luard, *The Rich Tradition of European Peasant Cookery* (Transworld 1986). Copyright © Elizabeth Luard, 1986; 93 Tessa Traeger/Parrot fish; 97 Tessa Traeger/Woman in a lumpfish hat dressed in plums and blueberries; 98 from Rosalind Mann and Paul Levy, *The Foodie Handbook*, (Ebury Press 1984). Copyright © Ann Barr & Paul Levy. 102 Kevin Summer/Roasted chickens with bacon, *Observer* Life magazine, Nigel Slater's Recipe pages; 105 Replete diners, 1904, from Abel Faivre in *Le Rire* (Mary Evans Picture Library); 108 'Supermarket Shopper' by Duane Hanson, 1970 (Ludwig Collection, Aachen/Bridgeman Art Library); 110 an old bush cook, from Warren Fahey, *When Mabel Laid the Table* (State Library of New South Wales Press 1992); 112 Tessa Traeger/Cold water crust pie; 119 Advertisement for milk products, 1935 (AKG photo); 125 'Now's the time for Jell-O', advertisement from *Saturday Evening Post*, 1952 (Advertising Archives); 126 Preparing hors d'oeuvre, illustration by B. Baucour (Mary Evans Picture Library); 132 The Jarrow marchers arriving at the Savoy (Hulton Getty Picture Collection); 134 from Caroline Liddell and Robin Weir, *Ices* (Grub Street 1993). Copyright © Caroline Liddell and Robin Weir, 1995; 135 Häagen Dazs advertisement, 1991 (Advertising Archives); 143 Robert Golden (Anthony Blake Photo Library); 151 Hamburger, *You* magazine, photographed by Gerrit Buntrock (Anthony Blake Photo Library); 153 The Kerosene Tin Cooker, from *Miss Williams Cookbook* (Pearson Education 1957); 156 France, 19th century (collection Oberlé-Édimedia); 159 Jean-Loup Charmet; 162 Elizabeth David's kitchen/James Mortimer/Johnny Grey; 166 'We want your kitchen waste', Pig food poster, World War II (Imperial War Museum /Bridgeman Art Library); 171 Moviestore Collection; 175 New Year's menu from Savoy Hotel, from *Hotel Metropole*, a scrapbook of menus collected by Frank Lambeth Chantrain 1888-1914, 1908 (litho) (City of Westminster Archive Centre/Bridgeman Art Library); 176 illustration by Anne Ward and Gerry Thompson from *Astral Sex to Zen Teabags* (Findhorn Press 1994); 178 diagram from E. M. Forster, *The Hill of Devi*, reprinted with permission from the Provost and Scholars of King's College, Cambridge and the Society of Authors as the literary representatives of the E. M. Forster Estate; 181 Tessa Traeger/Tournedos of beef with paupiettes of beef and veal; 186 Postcard 'comme du beurre' (Mary Evans Picture Library); 189 illustration from Alice Laden, *The George Bernard Shaw Cookbook* (Garnstone Press 1972); 195 Shreddred Wheat 'It's All I Want' from the When we Were Young series, 1920s (Advertising Archives); 202 from Eric Weir, *When Madame Cooks* (Philip Allan 1931), illustrations by Réne Bréant; 203 Kevin Summers/Baked onion, *Observer* Life magazine, Nigel Slater's Recipe pages; 209 Robert Doisneau (Rapho); 213 from Vicomte de Mauduit's *They Can't Ration These* (Michael Joseph 1940); 216 Tessa Traeger/Quince in carved wooden bowl; 225 Poster (Imperial War Museum); 231 © The Andy Warhol Foundation for the Visual Arts, Inc./DACS, London 1999. Trademarks licensed by Campbell Soup Company. All rights reserved (Christie's Images); 235 Tessa Traeger/Pacific oyster, *crassostrea gigas*; 244 Jean Cazals/soufflé, Sainsbury's *The Magazine*, 1996; 249 Norman Rockwell, 'Woes of an Army Cook', *Saturday Evening Post*, November 1942 (Advertising Archives); 253 Various dishes from *The Household Encyclopedia*, c. 1939 (Mary Evans Picture Library); 261 Marmite poster by Woolley, reproduced in W. G. Raffe, *Poster Design* (Mary Evans Picture Library); 269 Kevin Summer/Fruits in pastry, *Observer* Life magazine, Nigel Slater's Recipe pages; 275 'Bovril puts a smile into vegetables' advertisement, *Good Housekeeping*, 1945 (Advertising Archives); 282 illustration by Oliver Messell from Marjorie Salter and Adrianne Whitney, *Delightful Food* (Sidgwick & Jackson 1957); 284 Illustrations from *Vogue* by Gordon Davey, September 1940. Copyright © Vogue. The Condé Nast Publications.; 287 Mary Evans Picture Library; 288 illustration from Ludwig Bemelmens, *Hotel Splendide* (Hamish Hamilton 1942); 290 Hulton Getty Picture Collection; 295 Watercolour by Cunningham Bridgman. Copyright © The Savoy Group/The Gondola Dinner at the Savoy, June

1905; 296 Jean Cazals/Christmas cake, *The Christmas Collection* (Hamlyn 1998); 299 from Patience Gray, *Honey from a Weed*, (Prospect Books by special arrangement with Lyons & Burford and The Lyons Press); 301 Norman Rockwell, 'Weighty Matters', *Saturday Evening Post*, January 1953 (AKG photos); 305 Linda Burgess (Garden Picture Library); 306 Illustration by Daphne Jerrold from Rose Henniker Heaton, *The Perfect Christmas* (Eyre & Spottiswoode); 307 Frontispiece by James Wallace for *Le Quintet*, December 1903 © Berwick-upon-Tweed Borough Museum and Art Gallery (Bridgeman Art Library); 313 Mary Evans Picture Library; 316 Mac/*Daily Mail*/Centre for the Study of Cartoons and Caricature, University of Kent, Canterbury – 'Oh no! I think Clarissa's got mad human disease!'

TEXT

11-15 Elizabeth David *A Book of Mediterranean Food* (John Lehmann 1951);. 15-16 Nicholas Freeling *Kitchen Book, The Cook Book* (André Deutsch 1991). Curtis Brown on behalf of Nicolas Freeling, © Nicolas Freeling 1991; 17-18 Len Deighton *Action Cookbook* (Trinity Travel 1965) © 1965 Pluriform Publishing. Permission of Jonathan Clowes Ltd., London, on behalf of Pluriform Publishing; 18 © Lesley Blanch, from *The Wilder Shores of Love* (John Murray 1989); 19-21 © Countess Morphy *Recipes of all Nations* (Herbert Joseph 1935); 21 © Norman Douglas *Venus in the Kitchen* (William Heinemann 1952); 22-3 Diana Kennedy *The Cuisine of Mexico* (Harper & Row 1972); 23-6 Alice Waters *Chez Panisse* (Chatto & Windus Hogarth Press 1984); 26-7 © Nigel Slater *Real Cooking* (Michael Joseph 1977, permission of Penguin Books); 28-31 Reah Tannahill *Food in History* (Penguin 1973). Copyright © Reah Tannahill 1973; 31-3 Clare Macdonald *Scotland* (Little, Brown 1997); 33-5 Sue Lawrence, *Sunday Times*, 1998; 35-6 Lady Jekyl *Kitchen Essays* (reprinted from *The Times*, T. Nelson & Sons 1922); 36-8 Reah Tannahill *Food in History* (Penguin 1973). Copyright © Reah Tannahill 1973; 38-9 Raymond Oliver *The French Table* (Michael Joseph). Translated from French by Claude Durrell, for the Wine and Food Society, 1967; 40-42 A. P. Herbert *Mild & Bitter* (Methuen 1936); 43-4 John Steinbeck 'The Breakfast.' Copyright © 1936 John Steinbeck, permission of McIntosh & Otis; 47 George Moule and Steven Appleby *No, Honestly It Was Simply Delicious But I Couldn't Eat Another Mouthful* (Pan 1984). Copyright © Limbo Books George Moule and Steven Appleby 1984; 48-50 Florence White *Good Things in England* (Jonathan Cape 1932); 50-51 Evelyn Waugh *Black Mischief* (Chapman & Hall 1932). Permission of Peters Fraser and Dunlop Group on behalf of © Evelyn Waugh 1932; 52-3 Quentin Crewe and Anthony Blake *Great Chefs of France* (Gallery Press, a division of W.H. Smith Pub/Mitchell Beazley Marketing 1978). Copyright © Marshall Editions; 54-5 Permission of Scribner, a Division of Simon & Schuster, Inc. from *On Food and Cooking* by Harold McGee. Copyright © Harold McGee 1984; 55-6 extract from Henrietta Green, *Food Lovers' Guide to Britain*, permission of BBC Worldwide Ltd. Copyright © Henrietta Green 1993; 57 Alison Uttley *Hare Joins the Home Guard* (Collins 1941); 58 extract from Kenneth Grahame, *The Wind in the Willows*, copyright the University Chest, Oxford, permission of Curtis Brown; 59 Mrs Martineau *Cabbages and Canteloupe* (Cobden-Sanderson 1929); 60 Kenneth Lo *Peking Cooking* (Faber & Faber 1971). Copyright © estate of Kenneth Lo, permission of Peters Fraser and Dunlop Group; 60-63 from *Mastering the Art of French Cooking* by Julia Child, Simone Beck, Louisette Bertholle. Copyright © 1961 by Alfred A. Knopf Inc.; 63-4 Fanny Craddock *Daily Telegraph Sociable Cooks Book by a Bon Viveur*. Copyright © Daily Telegraph 1967; 64-8 Joseph Wechsberg *Sweet & Sour*, (Michael Joseph 1949); 68-9 Nancy Mitford *The Pursuit of Love* (Hamish Hamilton 1945). Permission of Peters Fraser and Dunlop Group on behalf of the estate of Nancy Mitford © 1945; 70-3 Fine Old Dixie Recipes (Culinary Arts Press, USA 1935); 73-6 *Manual of Military Cooking & Dietary* (H.M. Stationary Office 1918); 76-7 *Alice B. Toklas Cookbook* (Michael Joseph 1954); 77-8 Ann Willan *Reader's Digest Complete Guide to Cookery* (Dorling Kindersley); 78-80 Simon Hopkinson *Roast Chicken and Other Stories* (Ebury Press 1994); 80-81 *Madame Prunier's Fish Cookery Book* (Hurst & Blackett 1938); 81-3 Marcel Boulestin in *Vogue*. The Condé Nast Publications; 83 Maggie Black *The Medieval Cookbook* (Acorn Press, 1986, British Museum Press, 1992); 85-6 Marinetti *The Futurist Cookbook* (Trefoil with Bedford Arts 1989). Translated by and English translation copyright © Suzanne Brill; 89 'Sun Dried Tomatoes' from Lynda Brown *The Modern Cook's Manual* (Michael Joseph 1995), copyright © Lynda Brown 1995. Permission of Penguin Books; 89-92 Elizabeth Luard *The Rich Tradition of European Peasant Cookery* (Transworld 1986). Copyright © Elizabeth Luard 1986; 92 George Lassalle *The Adventurous Fish Cook* (Macmillan 1976). Copyright © George Lassalle 1976; 94 Hilaire Belloc *Food for Thought*. Permission of Peters Fraser and Dunlop Group on behalf of the estate of Hilaire Belloc ©; 95-8 Rosalind Mann and Paul Levy *The Foodie Handbook* (Ebury Press 1984). Copyright © Ann Barr & Paul Levy; 98-100 Victoria Wood 'The Trolly', from *Barmy* (Methuen 1987); 100-101 Philip Harben *Imperial Frying with Philip Harben* (Bodley Head 1960); 103 Julia Drysdale *The Game Cookery Book* (Collins 1975, Macmillan 1983); 103-4 Grace Gardiner and Flora Annie Steel *The Complete Indian Housekeeper & Cook* (William Heinemann 1890); 104-7 Robin McDouall, *Clubland Cookery* (Phaidon Press 1974); 107-9 Anonymous French Conoisseur *Clarisse or The Old Cook* (Methuen 1922); 109-11 extract from *When Mabel Laid the Table* by Warren Fahey (Banksiaman Press 1999); 111-13 Michael Smith *Fine English Cookery* (Faber 1973); 113-14 Florence Marian MacNeill *The Scots Kitchen* (Blackie & Son 1929); 114–16 Raphaela Lewis *Everyday Life in the Ottoman Empire* (B.T. Batsford); 116-17 Georges Auguste Escoffier *Guide to Modern Cookery* (William Heinemann 1907); 117-21 Lady Evelyn Balfour *The Living Soil* (Faber & Faber 1943); 122-3 Sir Harry Luke *The Tenth Muse* (Putnam Press 1954); 124 Ann Ziety 'One day he's gonna cook me a meal' (*Virago Book of Wicked Verse*, ed. Jill Dawson (Virago 1995); 127-8 Irma Rombauer *The Joy of Cooking* (Bobbs Merrill, J.M. Dent 1931); 128-31 Gerald Durrell *Birds, Beasts and Relatives*. Permission of Curtis Brown on behalf of the estate of Gerald Durrell. Copyright © Gerald Durrell, 1969; 131-2 Hugh Montgomery-Massingberd and David Watkins *The London Ritz* (Aurum 1980); 133-6 Caroline Liddell and Robin Weir *Ices* (Hodder & Stoughton 1993, Grub Street 1995). Copyright © Caroline Liddell and Robin Weir 1995; 136-7 Osbert Sitwell *Sing High Sing Low* (Macmillan 1944); 137-9 Freya Stark *Valley of the Assassins* (John Murray 1934); 139 Professor F.S. Bodenheimer *Insects As Human Food* (1951). Copyright © Dr W. Junk 1951; 139-41 Mrs J. Bartley *Indian Cookery 'General' for Young Housekeepers by an Anglo-Indian* (Army & Navy Co-Operative Society, Bombay); 141-2 E. O'E. Somerville and Martin Ross *Some Experiences of an Irish RM* (Longmans, Green 1910). Permission of Curtis Brown, on behalf of Sir Toby Coghill, Bt. Copyright E.O'E. Somerville and Martin Ross; 142-4 Hon Lady Winifred Fortescue *Perfume from Provence* (1935, Black Swan, 1992). Copyright © William Blackwood & Sons 1935; 144-5 Calvin W. Schwabe *Unmentionable Cuisine* (University Press of Virginia 1979). Copyright © Rector and Visitors of University of Virginia 1979; 145-7 from *The Book of Jewish Food* by Claudia Roden. Copyright © Claudia Roden 1996. Reprinted by permission of Alfred A.Knopf Inc. and David Higham Associates; 147-9 Florence Greenberg, *Jewish Cookery Book* (Jewish Chronicle Publications 1947); 149-50 from *American Fried* by Calvin Trillon. Copyright © 1974 by Calvin Trillon. This usage granted by permission; 150-3 Arthur Ransome *The Big Six* (Jonathan Cape 1940); 153 *Miss Williams Cookbook* (Pearson

FOOD

INDEX OF AUTHORS

Adkins, Thomas F. 191
Appleby, Steven 47
Archer, Jeffrey 172

Balfour, Lady Evelyn 118
Bareham, Lindsey 201
Bart, Lionel 198
Bartley, Mrs J. 139
Beard, James 238
Beck, Simone 60
Bell, Annie 276
Belloc, Hilaire 94
Bemelmens, Ludwig 286
Bertholle, Louisette 60
Betjeman, John 206
Black, Maggie 83
Blanch, Leslie 18
Bodenheimer, F.S. 139
Bolcom, William 242
Boulestin, Marcel 81
Boxer, Arabella 268
Brennan, Jennifer 183
Brown, Catherine 208
Brown, Linda 89

Campbell, Joan 249
Carrier, Robert 245
Chatwin, Bruce 227
Child, Julia 60
Chrystos 163
Clancy, Jeremy 254
Clark, Lady 267
Cooper, Susan 239
Coster, Margaret 274
Craddock, Fanny 64
Crewe, Quentin 52
Croft-Brooke, Rupert 158

Dahl, Roald 312
David, Elizabeth 11, 259
Davidson, Alan 205
Deighton, Len 17
del Conte, Anna 265
Douglas, Norman 21
Drummond, J.C. 224
Durrell, Gerald 128
Drysdale, Julia 103

Escoffier, G.A. 116

Fahey, Warren 110
Fisher, M.F.K. 133, 196
Forster, Ian 177
Fortescue, Lady 142
Fothergill, John 230
Freeling, Nicholas 15

Gattey, Charles Nielson 295

Gardiner, Grace 220
Gibbons, Stella 297
Grahame, Kenneth 58
Gray, Patience 299
Green, Henrietta 55
Greenberg, Florence 147
Grieve, Mrs M. 310
Grigson, Jane 232

Harben, Philip 101
Hartley, Dorothy 263
Heath, Ambrose 81, 293
Heaton, Rose Henniker 306
Heiney, Paul 165
Hemingway, Ernest 289
Herbert, A.P. 40
Hindehede, Dr M. 226
Hope, Annette 251
Hopkinson, Simon 80

Jekyll, Lady 29
Johnson, Amryl 303

Kennedy, Diana 22

Laden, Alice 189
Lassalle, George 92
Lawrence, Sue 33
Lee, Laurie 154
Leoni, Peppino 218
Levy, Paul 95, 272
Lewinsky, Ruth 248
Lewis, C.C. 182
Lewis, Rafaella 182
Leyel, Mrs 194
Liddell, Caroline 133
Lloyd George, David 165
Lo, Kenneth 60
Luard, Elizabeth 90
Luke, Sir Harry 122

Macdonald, Claire 31
McDouall, Robin 104
McGee, Harold 54
MacNeill, F.M. 113
Mann, Rosalind 95
Marinetti, F. 85
Martineau, Harriette 58
Massingberd, Hugh 131
Mauduit, Vicomte de 213, 308
Maugham, Somerset 168
Mitchell, M. 190
Mitford, Nancy 68
Morphy, Countess 19
Moule, George 47

Oliver, Raymond 38

Orwell, George 271
O'Shea, Tessie 300
Owen, Sri 199

Patten, Marguerite 221
Piercy, Marge 239
Porter, Cole 243
Pullar, Philippa 212
Python, Monty 247

Ranhofer, Charles 45
Ransome, Arthur 152
Reis, Rebecca 207
Roden, Claudia 145
Rombauer, Irma 127
Root, Waverly 214
Ross, Janet 276
Round, Jeremy 272

Saloman, Rena 193
Schwabe, Calvin W. 144
Simon, André 173
Sitwell, Osbert 136
Slater, Nigel 26
Smith, Joan 179
Smith, Michael 111
Somerville & Ross 141
Spry, Constance 256
Stark, Freya 137
Steel, Flora Annie 220
Steinbeck, John 43

Tannahill, Reay 28, 36
Tate, Doris Lytton 284
Thompson, Flora 263
Thompson, Gerry 176
Toklas, Alice B. 77
Trillon, Calvin 149
Tschumi, Gabriel 157

Uttley, Alison 57

Visser, Margaret 185

Waters, Alice 23, 314
Watkins, David 131
Waugh, Evelyn 50
Wechsberg, Joseph 64
Weir, Eric 202
White, Florence 48
Wilbraham, Anne 224
Willan, Ann 78
Williams, Miss 153
Wood, Victoria 99
Woolf, Virginia 204

Zeldin, Theodore 234
Ziety, Ann 124